# ADMINISTRATIVE TRIBUNALS

*Other RIPA Publications*

COMPUTERS IN THE PUBLIC SERVICE
by G. M. Lamb

STAFF RELATIONS IN THE CIVIL SERVICE: 50 YEARS OF WHITLEYISM
by H. Parris

THE NATIONALIZED INDUSTRIES SINCE 1960:
A BOOK OF READINGS
Edited by Leonard Tivey

COST-BENEFIT ANALYSIS IN ADMINISTRATION
by Trevor Newton

MANAGEMENT IN GOVERNMENT
by C. D. E. Keeling

STYLE IN ADMINISTRATION
Readings in British Public Administration
Edited by R. A. Chapman and A. Dunsire

PUBLIC INQUIRIES AS AN INSTRUMENT OF GOVERNMENT
by R. E. Wraith and G. B. Lamb

ORGANIZATION OF BRITISH CENTRAL GOVERNMENT
1914–1964
Edited by D. N. Chester, Written by F. M. G. Wilson
2nd edition by F. M. G. Wilson

CENTRAL DEPARTMENTS AND LOCAL AUTHORITIES
by J. A. G. Griffith

THE GOVERNMENT EXPLAINS
by Marjorie Ogilvy-Webb

BUILDING BY LOCAL AUTHORITIES
by Elizabeth Layton

BUDGETING IN PUBLIC AUTHORITIES
by RIPA Study Group

NEW SOURCES OF LOCAL REVENUES
by RIPA Study Group

ADMINISTRATORS IN ACTION
Volume I by F. M. G. Wilson
Volume II by Gerald Rhodes

PARLIAMENT AND ADMINISTRATION: THE ESTIMATES
COMMITTEE 1945–1965
by Nevil Johnson

MANAGERIAL AND PROFESSIONAL STAFF GRADING
by Joan Doulton and David Hay

STAFF REPORTING AND STAFF DEVELOPMENT
by Edgar Anstey

THE TOWN CLERK IN ENGLISH LOCAL GOVERNMENT
by T. E. Headrick

BRITISH GOVERNMENT SINCE 1918
Edited by D. N. Chester

# *Administrative Tribunals*

BY

R. E. WRAITH C.B.E.

AND

P. G. HUTCHESSON

*Consultant*

ALISTAIR MACDONALD

*Secretary to the Council on Tribunals 1958–70*

*for the*

ROYAL INSTITUTE OF PUBLIC ADMINISTRATION

LONDON . GEORGE ALLEN & UNWIN LTD

RUSKIN HOUSE MUSEUM STREET

First published in 1973



ISBN 0 04 347002 5 Hardback

Printed in Great Britain
in 10 pt Plantin type
by Alden & Mowbray Ltd
at the Alden Press, Oxford

# PREFACE

In 1950 the Institute of Public Administration, as it then was, sponsored a symposium on the subject of Administrative Tribunals, which resulted in the publication of a short book edited by R. S. W. Pollard.[1] After an interval of more than twenty years the Royal Institute of Public Administration returns to the subject with this full length study. During these years the tribunal scene has been greatly altered by the increase in the number of tribunals and the scope of their jurisdiction, trends which show every sign of continuing. It is hoped that this book will make a contribution to discussion of their future, a subject which is of concern to many lawyers and administrators.

This volume follows a comparable one on Public Inquiries, published in 1971, and precedes a study on the Parliamentary Commissioner for Administration, which may be published next year. Thus, during a period of five years, the Institute will have examined three important institutions designed to resolve difficulties that arise between the citizen and the state, and sometimes between citizen and citizen.

The book is the fifteenth in the Institute's series of major research projects, and the Institute wishes to express its thanks to the Social Science Research Council, whose financial support made the project possible.

The Institute was fortunate to be able to engage the service of R. E. Wraith as the principal research officer on this project. He had already established a high reputation in the Institute for his earlier work on Public Inquiries, and this, the Executive Council believe, will be enhanced by the present volume. The Institute also expresses its appreciation of the valuable service rendered by P. G. Hutchesson, a New Zealand lawyer, who served as associate research officer.

A particularly important contribution to the success of the enterprise was made by Alistair Macdonald who served in the capacity of consultant. Mr Macdonald was Secretary to the Council on Tribunals for the first ten years of its existence, and he brought not only much experience

[1] *Administrative Tribunals*, a Symposium, ed. R. S. W. Pollard (Stevens & Sons, 1950).

to the study but a great deal of wisdom based on a profound and abiding interest in the subject. The Institute is indebted to the Lord Chancellor's Department for allowing Mr Macdonald to assist the Institute in this way.

As is the Institute's usual practice, a steering committee was invited to advise the research team and to keep the project under review. Its members were:

*Chairman* Sir Charles Cunningham, KCB, KBE, CVO, formerly Permanent Under Secretary of State for the Home Department,

Mrs Kathleen Bell, Professor of Social Administration in the University of Newcastle-upon-Tyne; Member, Council on Tribunals,

Sir Diarmaid Conroy, CMG, OBE, TD, QC, President, Industrial Tribunals,

Mrs Chloe Davis, Member, Council on Tribunals, formerly Senior Information Officer, National Citizens Advice Bureaux Council,

J. F. Garner, LLD, Professor of Public Law, University of Nottingham,

I. G. Gilbert, Assistant Secretary, Department of Health and Social Security,

T. D. Kingdom, CB, formerly Controller, Government Social Survey Department; Chairman, RIPA Research Board,

R. A. Lawrie, Assistant Solicitor, Solicitor's Office for the Scottish Departments,

G. Marshall, Praelector in Politics, Queen's College, Oxford,

Terence Parry, General Secretary, Fire Brigades Union; Member, Council on Tribunals,

R. H. Widdows, Assistant Secretary, Lord Chancellor's Office.

The Institute is greatly indebted to them for giving so freely of their time and the fruits of their thought and experience.

The Institute's decision to undertake this project came at a time when the Council on Tribunals was conscious of the need to bring its own detailed information on tribunals up to date. The Council accordingly set in train a full-scale investigation by questionnaire to departments into the facts about the tribunals with which they were concerned. This was of a kind that had not been attempted since the Franks Committee sought evidence in the 1950s. It was possible for the Institute to be associated with this investigation and the results were of great benefit to the study.

As will be apparent, the Institute is much indebted to the Lord Chancellor's Department and the Council on Tribunals for their goodwill and practical assistance. It also received much unstinting help from a large number of civil servants and of tribunal chairmen, members and staff. Departments not already represented on the steering committee were kind enough to read the draft, as were the President of the Pensions Appeal Tribunals and the Registrar of the Lands Tribunal. The Institute is grateful to them for the correction of factual errors and for suggestions for improved drafting, but none of those who checked information or contributed comment or advice – including the members of the steering committee – are committed to any opinions which the authors may express.

The Institute's thanks are also due to A. W. Bradley, Professor of Constitutional Law in the University of Edinburgh, who contributed the historical background to the development of tribunals in Scotland in the first chapter; and to the Institute of Judicial Administration at the University of Birmingham and the National Citizens Advice Bureaux Council, both of which collaborated helpfully with the research staff at various stages of the project.

*Note of general application*

Please disregard inconsistencies between Pensions Appeals Tribunals and Pensions Appeal Tribunal.

The former is the correct name and is used wherever possible, but it is sometimes necessary to put it in the singular to make sense vis-à-vis other tribunals.

This book was written before the abolition of Selective Employment Tax. References to SET should accordingly be read in the past tense.

CONTENTS

# INTRODUCTION

*The Scope of the Study*

This book is about an institution which stands on the frontiers between law and administration. There is no lack of literature on the subject, which forms an important part of every text-book on administrative law and about which numerous books, pamphlets, articles and official reports have been written – some of the most important of which are given in the bibliography. There has not, however, been a comprehensive study of tribunals as a subject in their own right since the last edition, in 1951, of Professor William A. Robson's *Justice and Administrative Law*. It is to be regretted that the author, although pressed to do so, has not been able to find time to undertake a further revision.

The sub-title of Professor Robson's book is *A Study of the British Constitution*, which is indicative of its depth and scope; and much other writing goes deeper than does the present volume into matters of legal philosophy. Indeed, this book is written more from the administrator's than the lawyer's point of view, and its emphasis is on the ways in which tribunals are organized and staffed, and how they work in practice, rather than how they fit into a scheme of jurisprudence.

Most people know something about tribunals, but probably few realize how protean they are and how pervasive they have become. In 1970 some 135,000 citizens were heard by tribunals composed of three of their fellow citizens when they were in dispute with an official, a landlord or an employer about statutory benefits, rents, rates or redundancy payments. These are the areas in which the welfare state has to provide some means whereby its operations may be tidied up at the edges, where the one case in fifty or a hundred which is not clear may be clarified. This is what a tribunal is likely to mean to the average man; though almost as many, whose ideas about their tax liability do not coincide with those of the Inland Revenue, are heard by the General Commissioners of Income Tax.

Apart from the ordinary citizen, for whom any of these circumstances may arise, there are some special categories, whose claim is not to a benefit, or to a reduction in their rent, rates or income tax, but to a more fundamental human right – those whose liberty has been removed, or may be restricted, in mental hospitals, and those immigrants who seek to enter the country, or having entered it to remain.

People of a very different kind, fewer in number but remarkable in their variety, may appear before tribunals of another kind – farmers whose ditches need draining or whose dairies are thought to be unhygienic, bookmakers whose levy to their profession is in dispute, proprietors of independent schools whose standards are in question, pop groups the copyright of whose discs is in doubt, rose growers whose claim to an exclusive bloom is being challenged, the owners of coaches or lorries who wish to ply for hire, or to extend their service.

Apart from individual people, there are cases where firms, public corporations or local authorities seek a fair deal from tribunals rather than justice from the courts – from the Civil Aviation Authority, Industrial Tribunals in one or other of their various jurisdictions, the Lands Tribunal, the 'Tribunal' which controls Patents and Trademarks, the Traffic Commissioners, the Special Commissioners of Income Tax or the local valuation courts – for these last consider not only whether the rateable value of Mr Jones' house shall be reduced by £5 but whether an industrial plant shall be rated at half a million.

The adjudicators in such matters, all of whom constitute statutory tribunals, merge imperceptibly into others who do not – those who determine compensation for criminal injuries, for example, or whether an invalid is entitled to an attendance allowance – and so on into the 'domestic' tribunals which control discipline and professional standards in the major professions.

To the general observer tribunals thus open a window on a fascinating panorama of human activity. To the student of institutions they are pragmatic, illogical and exasperating; for they challenge his instinct to classify them, but leave him chastened in the knowledge that they can only be described; he wants to rationalize them but finds that the most he can do is to rearrange them in a different order.

This feeling of frustration is, however, characteristic of many aspects of administrative law, especially to the layman who tries to see the subject through lawyers' spectacles. He hopes to discover its meaning, scope and manifestations, but finds that these are still matters of debate, and that as a branch of law it is undeveloped and very largely unrecognized. For this if for no other reason the book tries to keep its feet on the ground, and to discuss tribunals in terms of public administration rather than of legal concepts. It is almost wholly devoted to the group of tribunals which are statutorily defined as such by the Tribunals and Inquiries Acts, though some of these have less affinity with one another than they have with other adjudicatory bodies outside the definition. Sufficient reference is however made to these extraneous bodies to make clear that 'tribunal' is an unusually fluid expression. There are, for instance, 'tribunals' which draw their jurisdiction from statute but which are none the less not statutorily defined as tribunals.

As so often with British institutions they have been created to solve problems as they occurred – in this case on the fringes of social legislation – and they have never been centrally planned. In 1932 the Donoughmore Committee on Ministers' Powers discussed them in a general, conceptual way. In 1956 the Franks Committee on Administrative Tribunals and Enquiries dealt with them more specifically, made suggestions for their improvement and proposed a Council on Tribunals to oversee them. This Committee's main proposals were accepted and embodied in the Tribunals and Inquiries Act 1958, but some were rejected or have hung fire for fifteen years, during which time tribunals themselves have continued to grow, both in number and in the kind of issues with which they deal. As to number, the Annual Report of the Council for 1960 lists forty-three; for 1970 fifty-nine; as to the type of issue, the mental health review tribunals, and in Scotland the children's hearings, have taken the 'tribunal system' into areas which neither Donoughmore nor Franks were contemplating.

Accordingly the time seems opportune to look once more at the ground they occupy between government departments and the courts of law. This book is essentially a conspectus and accordingly does not treat any particular tribunal in detail. Others, in universities, have recently engaged in the opposite kind of research, that is into such matters as the details of membership of certain tribunals, or the reactions of the applicants and appellants who appear before them. The two kinds of research in no way conflict.

The aim has been to avoid duplicating the work which is to be found in the standard text-books, so that such practical questions as procedural rules and channels of appeal, or such philosophical questions as justiciability, are only dealt with to the extent necessary to sustain the idea of a general conspectus. There is, however, one exception to this. A draft chapter on Review by the Courts, which would otherwise have been condensed to accord with the book's general purpose, has been left as it was and printed as an appendix, since it appeared that this was an aspect of the subject which had not hitherto been discussed *with specific reference to tribunals.*

Books on government and administration which purport to be written in terms of Great Britain, especially if written in London, are apt to do less than justice to the position in Scotland. This is true of the present work, in the sense that no attempt has been made to be fully accurate in Scottish matters. Thus, references to the Lord Chancellor are not accompanied (as they ought to be) by complementary references to the Lord President of the Court of Session or the Secretary of State; nor references to statutes or statutory instruments by the corresponding references for Scotland. These deficiencies have been accepted in the interests of readability and in order to avoid the kind of repetition that must become tedious. On the other hand it is hoped that due account has been given of substantial differences between English and Scottish practice. The most important of these are that land and valuation matters are differently treated; that there are a few tribunals that are unique to Scotland; that there is a separate Scottish Committee of the Council on Tribunals; and that there are substantial divergencies in the remedies available in administrative law. Moreover, as was noted in the Preface, some account is given of the history of tribunals in Scotland.

CHAPTER I

# ORIGINS AND DEVELOPMENT

## EARLY HISTORY

*The Tradition of Extra-Judicial Remedies*

Most of the administrative tribunals with which we are familiar today are a by-product of the welfare state, and trace their ancestry no further than 1911. Some, of a different kind, derive from the industrial revolution, and especially from the growth of railways, whose affairs required frequent adjudication of a kind which the courts were unable to give. Only the General Commissioners of Income Tax are of any great antiquity.

But although administrative tribunals as we now know them are of recent origin, the administrative tribunal as a judicial phenomenon has exercised the minds of lawyers for many centuries. And since towards the end of this book we must try to see it in this light, we must study, at the book's beginning, why events of the reign of the Tudors and Stuarts still cast shadows over the contemporary scene.

The British constitution tries to keep law and politics apart, and on the whole succeeds, but administrative tribunals inhabit a twilight world where the two intermingle; they are in a sense the orphaned child of both. To the politician they are part of the judicial system in that they enable the ordinary man to obtain a cheap, fair and impartial hearing when he is affected by administrative action; to the lawyer they are not fully within the legal fold since they are, in certain aspects, an appendage of bureaucracy.

Britain has a long history of extra-judicial remedies for the grievances of the ordinary citizen, whether those grievances be against the state or a fellow citizen. The established judicial system (the common law) has never been fully comprehensive in the provision of remedies for all possible types of wrongs and injustices. The result has been the evolution of overtly political remedies,[1] or the establishment of private

[1] E.g. complaints to MPs, Parliamentary Questions, Adjournment Debates, etc.

methods of settling disputes,[2] or the provision by the state of remedies outside the existing judicial system. Also, it has been a long established habit both to clothe judicial actions in administrative forms and to employ judicial officers to perform administrative tasks. Elements of all these except the political remedy may be found in present day administrative tribunals. It is partly this mixture of antecedents and partly the variety of political motives leading to their establishment that has led to the absence of either principle or pattern. They are essentially *ad hoc* and pragmatic.

The history of Britain since the Norman conquest is rich in examples of the developments described above. The evolution of the Lord Chancellor's functions shows how extra-judicial remedies (exercised by an administrator) gradually crystallized into judicial form through the use of judicial methods. In the fourteenth century, when a litigant could not obtain redress in the ordinary common law courts it was open to him to petition the King personally. These petitions were passed over to the Lord Chancellor, as the 'keeper of the King's conscience' to investigate, which initially he did himself in the manner of a mediaeval 'ombudsman'. Later, presumably because of the increase in the number of such petitions, a whole department, in fact a court, was set up to consider them. This was the Court of Chancery, and it is now such an integral part of the English legal system, together with the system of equity which it propounded, that it is easy to overlook the fact that it started life for much the same reason as many later tribunals, namely to provide more convenient and often better alternatives to the existing courts of law, and that it brought a fresh approach to the problem of dispensing justice, untrammelled by adherence to strict rules of procedure and precedents; to that extent it provides a parallel to the establishment of many modern tribunals. It is equally true that in the course of time equity and the Court of Chancery became just as legalistic and formalized in outlook as the common law – a daunting reminder to the tribunals of our own day.

The converse method of employing judicial officials to perform administrative tasks is seen in the office of justices of the peace, originally established (some time before 1200) to exercise a criminal jurisdiction, a function which they still retain. But from at least 1361 they were called upon to exercise administrative functions as well as their criminal jurisdiction, and in the first great period of social control in England, the reigns of the Tudors, they were the chief instrument by which the whole Tudor system of regulation was put into operation.

The list of administrative functions exercised by the Justices of the

[2] E.g. private rules for arbitration.

Peace during the Tudor period is quite bewildering[3] (and shows incidentally that social regulation is no new phenomenon). By the time of Elizabeth I's death they had become the administrative factotum of the State – subject to the remote supervision of the central government the administration of the counties had been virtually handed over to them. They became the general administrators of the land, although in form they continued to exercise these administrative functions according to their accustomed judicial procedure. Today of course their administrative functions are residual, and relate only to certain licensing and matrimonial matters.

The phenomena of special jurisdictions and private methods of settling disputes is also of interest because it foreshadows some contemporary tribunals. Professor Jackson has pointed out:

> 'A "court" was a place for doing business of a public nature, judicial and otherwise, and wherever we find places with any peculiar standing (Royal Forests, Staple Towns, Cinque Ports) or certain industries (lead mining in the Mendips, tin mining in Devon and Cornwall) or classes of men differentiated from the general population (merchants, soldiers, ecclesiastics) we find historically a special body of law with special courts.'[4]

In time most of these mediaeval jurisdictions became absorbed in the common law system but the commercial community has consistently provided alternative machinery to the ordinary courts for the settlement of disputes. An Elizabethan example is a statute setting up a special tribunal for marine insurance because of the 'great charges and delays' caused by the commencement of suits in 'Her Majesty's courts'. The tribunal was required to settle disputes 'in a brief and summary course ... without formalities of pleadings or proceedings'.[5] Lloyd's, the London Corn Trade Association, the London Metal Exchange and the Baltic Mercantile and Shipping Exchange continue to provide private systems of adjudication. More specifically from our point of view, similar arrangements have been established by statute and, as such, now fall within the tribunal field. Examples are the adjudicatory functions of the Comptroller-General of Patents contained in the Patents and Designs Act 1883 which replaced the powers of the Law Officers to

[3] Among other things the Justices were empowered to fix prices, maintain bridges and highways, settle disputes between merchants, license inns, conscript labour for the harvest, deal with weights and measures, and (in 1572) to strike the first compulsory rate for poor relief.

[4] R. M. Jackson, *The Machinery of Justice in England* (Cambridge University Press, 1967), p. 351.

[5] Sir Cecil Carr, *Concerning English Administrative Law*, p. 95.

grant patents and the courts to decide patent disputes with a statutory procedure for the hearing of disputes by a civil servant; the Performing Right Tribunal established in 1956; and the Plant Variety Rights Tribunal established in 1964.

*The Tudor Administrative Courts*

Very little now survives of the Tudor system of administrative courts but they are worth some study because of the lessons to be learnt from this first attempt to implant a system of administrative tribunals in the none too fertile soil of British law and politics. Equally they show that the notion of administrative tribunals is not altogether foreign to the British system of government, a fact often overlooked by commentators.

The Tudor tribunals were set up for much the same reasons as our contemporary ones and fulfilled part of the same function – that is of providing remedies where the courts would not; although in a less principled age it was almost inevitable that they should come to be used as extensions of the government of the day. The King's Council, a heterogeneous group of forty or fifty peers, knights, bishops, lawyers and others, exercised a residuary jurisdiction in offences which endangered the peace of the realm, such as riots and rebellions, which caused it to be used to suppress 'overmighty subjects' who flouted the ordinary law courts. It is an interesting historical example of administrators exercising judicial powers because of the shortcomings of the ordinary courts. The Council continued (in truncated form) after the Revolution of 1688 and was eventually reorganized into the present Privy Council, which to this day carries out functions which are both judicial and administrative (although the membership is separate in each instance).

The Star Chamber provides a closer parallel with modern administrative tribunals. Initially it was just another name for the Council exercising its judicial functions in a Chamber which had a ceiling ornamented with stars, but more and more it delegated these functions to a Committee consisting of four of the King's chief administrators, a peer, a bishop and two judges, who exercised a jurisdiction which Holdsworth described as being 'both large and vague' because of the large number of cases with which the common law could not deal effectively, e.g. cases outside the common courts' jurisdiction, cases in which the King's interests were affected, cases in which the law itself was at fault.[6]

The method by which this 'large and vague' jurisdiction was exercised

[6] *History of English Law*, Vol. 1, p. 478.

was essentially discretionary. The writs beloved of common lawyers were largely dispensed with, and an inquisitorial technique was established by which the parties were called before the court and examined in person (the origin of the modern writ of subpoena), in contrast to the cumbrous system of pleadings and jury trial practised by the common law courts.[7] Moreover, the Star Chamber, through its close connection with that powerful respository of the Royal Prerogative, the King's Council, was able to offer swifter and more effective remedies than the ordinary courts, since it was less prone to be influenced and overborne by 'overmighty subjects'. The most significant aspect of this discretionary procedure, however, was that the Star Chamber was free to decide according to reasons of policy if it was felt that this was required.

Although the Star Chamber may have been instituted as a political means of maintaining the power of the Tudor monarchy its efficiency quickly made it a popular alternative to the ordinary courts – and for the same reasons that are generally cited in justification of administrative tribunals today, namely 'cheapness, accessibility, freedom from technicality, expedition . . .'.[8] The procedures of the common law courts were expensive, complex and time-consuming. They were also increasingly out of touch with the social requirements of the day, having developed at a time when the main purpose of the legal system was to relieve the burdens and protect the privileges of the land-owning interest. They were certainly ill-suited to the interests of the new merchant class which was developing under the Tudors.

Apart from the Star Chamber there were a number of courts, almost wholly administrative in function, set up for special purposes, such as the Courts of Augmentation, First Fruits and Tenths, Wards and Surveyors: these were all financial courts administering various aspects of the royal revenues. The most interesting of these special courts from our point of view is the Court of Requests which was a Committee of the King's Council set up by Henry VIII to hear poor men's causes – a need which arose from the fact that Chancery procedure had already ossified into a system of rules (the 'maxims of equity') just as complicated and technical as the rules of common law. It was controlled by the Lord Privy Seal, then an administrative official, and employed a very informal procedure similar to that of the earlier Chancery court.

[7] The Common law at this time did not allow the parties to testify personally and this seriously hindered complainants.

[8] The advantages of administrative tribunals cited by the Franks Committee (Report p. 9). The only advantage cited which the Tudor tribunals could not claim was 'expert knowledge of their particular subject.'

*Parliament and the Courts*

These early examples of administrative tribunals did not survive the quarrel between the Stuarts and Parliament mainly because they came to be a device to cloak the use of arbitrary power in the mantle of legality – in Maitland's words 'a court of politicians enforcing a policy and not a court of judges administering the law'.

That the victory of Parliament and the ordinary courts over the Crown and the prerogative courts was beneficial for the development of justice in Britain there can be no doubt, but this alliance between Parliament and the courts, and its consequences, has had a profound effect on public law in England. The constitutional principles fashioned in the late seventeenth century still govern the relationship and interplay between the law and politics and still therefore provide the constitutional perspective for any analysis of the place tribunals occupy vis-à-vis the administration and the courts.

One effect of the Parliamentary victory was that the common law courts were left supreme in the judicial field. This, combined with the anathema felt for special tribunals, which had become instruments of persecution, ensured that for a great many years they were not considered an acceptable form of adjudication.

Another effect was that the courts' supremacy in the judicial field was bought at the cost of subservience to Parliament: the judges became 'lions under the mace rather than under the throne'.[9] The opportunity was not taken (as it was later in the United States) to put the courts on an equal footing with the legislature by giving the courts the power to review legislation and actions which offend constitutional rights. A result of this has been a much greater development of private law than public law by the courts. It can fairly be claimed that for many years the judges did not develop even the few methods of control over official actions which they could legitimately claim to exercise, with the result that extra-judicial remedies had to be set up as the need arose.

Finally, by virtue of the Bill of Rights of 1689 and the Act of Settlement of 1701, Parliament rather than the courts became the protector of the Constitution and of civil liberties. In the short run Parliament appeared to be more ardent in asserting its new found sovereignty by protecting and strengthening the rights of its members than in attempting to hammer out fundamental rights for the people. As a consequence the Parliamentary protection of civil liberties was, and still is, largely a matter of accident, a situation which has given rise to what Professor H. W. R. Wade described in his evidence to the Franks Committee as

[9] B. Abel-Smith and R. Stevens, *Lawyers and the Courts* (Heinemann, 1970), p. 8.

'the tangled picture of special tribunals and quasi-judicial procedures (which) is largely the result of the unsystematic attempts of Parliament to fill what is really a lacuna in the judicial system'. He went on to point out that:

> 'it has become very clear that ministerial responsibility, well as it works for the control of general policy, does not meet the need for some method of controlling the innumerable minor acts of government which, often for the very reason that they are only of local importance, are the acts which matter most to the individuals whom they affect. The courts of law cannot control such acts (unless of course they are illegal) because of their complete separation from politics. The dilemmas of administrative justice are, in a sense, the price of this most precious of our constitutional safeguards.'[10]

In other words, Parliament, having pre-empted the field of protecting civil liberties, has from time to time been forced to adopt various *ad hoc* expedients for this purpose.

The difficulty has been that in this country Parliament has never formulated a coherent set of principles on civil liberties, but has relied on *ad hoc* expediences, which have varied not only according to the nature of the circumstances but even according to cycles of legislative fashion. The student who tries to discover how civil liberties are safeguarded must find his way among a maze of remedies – administrative procedures, special tribunals, public inquiries – and now the Parliamentary Commissioner for Administration, whose role may shortly be extended into new areas of government.

A further effect of the Revolution of 1688 and the abdication of the courts from the field of public law (combined with the disinclination of Parliament to fill the gap) has been that this country has not developed a consistent body of administrative law on the continental model. Where the Parliamentarians and the lawyers rationalized their anathema of a protected administration as being inconsistent with the supremacy of Parliament and the accountability of officials, Napoleon a hundred years later perceived that the protection of his officials was a desirable, if not in fact a necessary, element in establishing authority and order after the period of anarchy which followed the Revolution, and developed the *droit administratif* as a special form of administrative law for this purpose.

*Nineteenth Century Developments*

Today in this country more than fifty tribunals are recognized, in the

[10] Franks Committee, Minutes of Evidence, p. 544.

sense that the Council on Tribunals oversees them. Thus administrative tribunals have found their way back into the judicial system from which they were excluded by the aftermath of the 1688 Revolution. The causes of their return are to be found in the industrial revolution of the nineteenth century and the changes and movements of political and philosophical ideas that accompanied it, though it was not until the first decade of the twentieth century that they took firm root, or until after the second world war that they proliferated to the point when their jurisdiction came to exceed that of the ordinary courts in terms of cases considered.

Before discussing these developments a word must be said about a 'tribunal' which has spanned the centuries, undergone many metamorphoses and survived into the twentieth century – the only one to have roots so deep.

*The General and Special Commissioners of Income Tax*

The use of unpaid local dignitaries to oversee the collection of taxes for the state stretches back at least to the fourteenth century and it was this machinery which Pitt employed for the collection of the first income tax under the Income Tax Act of 1799 (introduced to finance the Napoleonic War). The administration of income tax was entrusted to the existing Land Tax Commissioners, who were retitled the Commissioners for the General Purposes of Income Tax, these being local gentry (with considerable property qualifications). Both taxpayers and surveyors[11] could object to the assessments, these objections being heard and determined by a tribunal of Commissioners of Appeal, of whom there were three for each county. In 1803 the Commissioners of Appeal were abolished and the General Commissioners became the sole appellate body.

The Special Commissioners were introduced by Pitt in 1805 in an endeavour to lighten the load of the General Commissioners, and took over the granting of charitable exemptions and the assessment of income from government securities, and in 1842 certain taxpayers (mainly traders and professional people) were given the option of appealing to either set of Commissioners. The General Commissioners, characterized by their local and amateur basis and jealous of their independence of authority, remained in control of the administration of taxation until the end of the nineteenth century. The only inroad on their independence was the right given to both the Crown and taxpayers in 1874 to require the Commissioners to state a case for the determination of the

[11] Exchequer officials who were the forerunners of the present day Inspectors of Taxes.

High Court on the grounds that their decision was erroneous in point of law.

In 1915 the Surveyor was for the first time given power to assess and collect a tax (in the case of weekly wage-earners) and thereafter the administrative duties of the General Commissioners were taken over by officers of the Crown, a change which was endorsed by the Royal Commission on Income Tax in 1920. However 'assessors' were not finally abolished until 1946 and it was not until 1964[12] that the General and Special Commissioners became in law an independent appeal tribunal and nothing else. No longer are they also an adjunct of the local magistracy. At the time of the Franks Committee, the General Commissioners were appointed in England and Wales by the Land Tax Commissioners (who were mostly magistrates) primarily from among their own number and the Special Commissioners by the Treasury. The General Commissioners are now appointed by the Lord Chancellor.

*The Board of Railway Commissioners*

The only other contemporary tribunal with roots in the nineteenth century is the Transport Tribunal, as it is now called, which can trace its ancestry to the Board of Railway Commissioners of 1846. In the century which has intervened between the two there have been so many metamorphoses that the Tribunal of today, itself attenuated by recent legislation, is unrecognizable from the ancestral body, but the story none the less warrants a brief account in this survey.

The Board must be seen in the context of the many boards for special purposes that proliferated throughout the century, and which resulted from the fact that although Parliament could legislate the Government could not administer. The few departments of state were concerned with the budget, law and order, foreign affairs, the colonies, defence, trade and comparable matters, but none was concerned with social policies or their implementation. Outside the boroughs, which were concerned with local trade rather than with municipal administration, and which were in any case largely corrupt, local government was represented by the Justices of the Peace, who understood little and sympathized less with the new and overwhelming problems of urban poverty and sanitation, or the advance of the new technology from which sprang the canals, the railways and all the other manifestations of the new industrial age. Accordingly the social legislation which Parliament was compelled by circumstances to enact came to be implemented by a complex of national and local boards, largely overlapping at the local

12 Income Tax Management Act 1964.

level but with separate purposes, separate franchises and the power to levy separate rates.

These boards were primarily executive and administrative in character; charged with implementing a particular policy they were usually given sweeping, almost arbitrary powers, among them the power to decide certain disputes. To that extent they might be thought to be tribunals, but such disputes usually arose from the active implementation of its own policy by a board. The more static type of tribunal, deciding disputes arising out of a policy implemented by others (usually the Government or a department of state), is a later development, as we shall see. In political terms the most significant aspect of these boards is the fact that they were allowed to make and implement their own policy, a state of affairs which continued until in the latter half of the nineteenth century they were either superseded by civil service departments or merged into the new local authorities.

The Board of Railway Commissioners was distinguished from the rest because its antecedents had given it greater adjudicatory powers, for while its main purpose was to regulate proliferation and cut-throat competition it could in the process settle disputes between opposing private interests. Within a very few years, however, the need had changed to one of protecting the public from the effects of monopoly, brought about by amalgamations, and the Board was abolished in 1851. The Canal and Railway Traffic Regulation Act of 1854 then attempted to prohibit discrimination and to establish openness and equality for the railways' users.

At first the Government looked to the courts to ensure this. Where a person or company felt that the illegal preference or unfair charges provisions of the 1854 Act were being flouted he could bring his complaint before the Court of Common Pleas, which was empowered to make all such inquiries as may be deemed necessary 'assisted by such engineers, and other persons' as the court required. It might be thought that this enabled the court to co-opt experts as assessors to assist the court in reaching a decision, but in fact this interpretation was not adopted and experts were expected to 'assist' the court by being witnesses on behalf of one of the parties to the case, as in other litigation.

This first attempt to bring the courts into the arena of specialized disputes was not entirely happy either for the judges or for those seeking their services. Lord Campbell, Lord Chief Justice at this time, complained that Parliament was trying to turn his judges into railway directors[13] while a Select Committee Report in 1872 remarked that:

'questions of undue preference are often so technical, so dependent on

[13] Jackson, *Machinery of Justice in England*, p. 293.

> special circumstances of railway management, and so closely connected with questions of 'due facilities' as to lead your committee to the conclusion that even this part of the Act has not been as much brought into play as it would have been if speedy and summary reference could have been made to a tribunal having practical knowledge of the subject.'[14]

The issues raised in litigation between traders and railway companies were too technical for the ordinary courts and altogether so foreign to their ordinary functions that, following the recommendation of the Select Committee, the Regulations of Railways Act 1873 set up a new commission known as the Railway and Canal Commission. This consisted of three Commissioners, one of whom was a lawyer and another a person acquainted with railway management. They were required to adopt a procedure 'as simple and inexpensive as possible' and to investigate complaints of unfair preference between companies or traders; to see that proper facilities were given for the interchange and forwarding of traffic; and to settle various types of disputes arising between railway companies and their users.

In the event this tribunal did not prove satisfactory and it was reconstituted with wider powers by the Railway and Canal Traffic Act 1888. The new Commission consisted of a High Court judge and two other members, one of whom was required to have had experience in railway management. Among a number of innovations the most important was the allowing of bodies such as local authorities, Justices in Quarter Sessions and chambers of commerce, to make complaints to the Commission or to be represented at hearings even though they themselves had not suffered from the actions of a railway company.

This is by no means the end of the story of the development of the Railway Commission into the present Transport Tribunal, but in the development of tribunals generally the Railway and Canal Commission of 1873 and 1888 became something of a prototype for future tribunals in the membership pattern (three members, with a lawyer chairman and another member with expert qualifications), in there being no appeal on findings of fact, in adopting a procedure which was adversarial but less formal than a court of law and less rigid on matters such as locus standi, and in deciding questions (e.g. fairness of charges) which were matters of administrative policy rather than questions of law.

With the decline of canals, and the major railway amalgamations of 1921, the Commission reappeared as the Railway Rates Tribunal, with

[14] Report of Joint Select Committee on Railway Companies Amalgamat ion Parliamentary Papers, 1872, Vol. 13, Reports from Committees, p. 67.

a wide jurisdiction primarily in relation to railway charges, but its powers were variously amended until it was finally renamed the Transport Tribunal by the Transport Act 1947.

*The County Courts*

By a coincidence the year 1846 saw not only the appointment of the Railway Commissioners but the introduction of the County Courts Act. Its interest for our subject lies in what it set out to achieve, viz.

> 'a system of local civic tribunals adapted to the needs of the great masses of the population and the maximum convenience of forum, simplicity of procedure, suitors being able to obtain relief and defend themselves . . . with summary determination and moderation of expenses'.

Thus did the cycle of events which we noted in the Tudor and Stuart ages project itself into the Victorian age. Over a hundred years later the Franks Committee were to commend what by then were called administrative tribunals for their greater:

> 'cheapness, accessibility, freedom from technicality, expedition, and expert knowledge of a particular subject'.

The institution with which the Committee was making this favourable comparison was – *inter alia* – the County Court.

*Workmen's Compensation*

Before leaving the nineteenth century we may note one development which took place at the century's close, namely the Workmen's Compensation Act of 1897, which aimed at providing a right to compensation of injuries 'arising out of and in the course of employment'. It had been hoped that disputes arising out of compensation claims could be settled inexpensively by arbitration, but in practice a great many cases ended up before County Court judges, and indeed the phrase 'arising out of and in the course of' was soon reverberating round the Court of Appeal and the House of Lords. It remained an eminently litigious subject until workmen's compensation was incorporated in the wider national insurance scheme in 1947 under the name 'industrial injury', when disputes came to be resolved by national insurance tribunals.

## ADMINISTRATIVE TRIBUNALS IN SCOTLAND

The history of administrative tribunals in Scotland has yet to be written.

It must be emphasized that the separate and distinctive features of the Scottish system of justice render many of the foregoing pages, based on the history of the English legal system, inapplicable to Scotland. Not only the system of courts but also the structure of domestic government within Scotland has shown many differences from the English counterpart. Of course, the two systems share many common features and in Scotland as in England, legal history furnishes antecedents of today's administrative tribunals. Despite their separate origins, the two systems have from time to time come close together as a result of political union and administrative centralization. The Union of the Crowns in 1603 and the Union of the Parliaments in 1707 each strengthened links between the systems of justice and government. More recently, economic, social and technological development has given rise to many problems which need and have received common legislative attention. The great bulk of the welfare and regulatory legislation which tribunals administer today is common to both jurisdictions. The fact that both systems share the same final court of appeal in civil matters makes possible a common approach to the main principles of judicial review.

Scottish legal history points to a much closer relationship between the administration of justice and the conduct of government than a superficial understanding of the separation of powers doctrine would admit. As in England, there was a period before the modern differentiation of legislative, executive and judicial institutions and functions had developed. Distinct judicial institutions appeared later in Scotland than in England, and the separation of functions occurred later still; indeed the differentiation of functions was probably never complete so long as Scotland was an independent kingdom.[15] Three or four centuries ago, both at national and local levels, the same governmental organs exercised administrative, legislative and judicial functions. The growth of separate arrangements for judicial work during the sixteenth century was as much for reasons of practical convenience as for reasons of principle. The College of Justice was formally constituted in 1532 to give a firm and continuing basis to the Court of Session[16] and the High Court of Justiciary with criminal jurisdiction was established in 1672. Yet the King's Council continued to exercise both civil and criminal jurisdiction and today it is difficult to see why certain cases came to the Council rather than to the Court of Session or the High Court of Justiciary.[17]

[15] G. Donaldson, *Scotland, James V to James VII* (Oliver & Boyd, 1965), p. 289.

[16] R. K. Hannay, *The College of Justice* (1933).

[17] Donaldson, *Scotland*, p. 288.

Since its inception, the Court of Session had been able to exercise some control over the jurisdiction of subordinate and inferior courts,[18] a task which during the sixteenth and seventeenth centuries was itself subject to intervention from the Council. After the Union of 1707, the abolition of the separate Privy Council for Scotland had repercussions for the role of the central civil court similar to those arising from the disappearance of conciliar jurisdiction in England: it was thereafter the duty of the Court of Session to provide redress for citizens' grievances which formerly had gone properly to the Privy Council.[19] By comparison with the common law courts in England, the supervisory control of the Court of Session was marked by a greater flexibility that must in part have been due to the fact that no separate court of equity developed in Scotland. Through the exercise of the 'nobile officium', the Court of Session had an ultimate right to provide an extraordinary equitable remedy in a situation in which the strict law provided none.[20] The eighteenth-century Scottish law reports provide numerous examples of an extensive supervisory jurisdiction being exercised by the Court of Session over inferior courts and tribunals, and this jurisdiction was not ignored in legal scholarship.[21]

For certain purposes, the Court of Session itself could take on a different form to exercise a specialized jurisdiction. By what the late Lord President Cooper called 'a remarkable anticipation of the modern *ad hoc* tribunal'[22] the multifarious ecclesiastical business arising after the reformation and associated with parish churches, manses, stipends and teinds (or tithes) was vested first in statutory commissions and then transferred to the Court of Session itself, sitting as the 'Commission for the Plantation of Kirks and the Valuation of Teinds'. In this capacity between 1707 and 1925, the Court of Session performed a wide variety of administrative and judicial functions for the church, during a period when the church itself had major public responsibilities in the government of Scotland, for example in the poor law and in education. (Since 1925, what remains of this jurisdiction is undertaken by a judge sitting as Lord Ordinary on Teinds.) In a similar way today, senators of the College of Justice may sit to exercise a specialized statutory jurisdiction as the Lands Valuation Appeal Court, hearing appeals

[18] *Introduction to Scottish Legal History* (1958) (Stair Society, Volume 20), Chap. III by J. I. Smith at p. 27.

[19] Lord Kames, *Historical Law Tracts*, 4th ed. (1817), p. 228.

[20] *Introduction to Scottish Legal History*, Chap. XXIV by Lord Cooper, p. 345, and for a recent example see *Ferguson et al.* 1965 S.C. 16.

[21] See in particular *Baron Hume's Lectures*, Vol. 5 (1967) (Stair Society, Vol. 20), ed. G. C. H. Paton, pp. 270–5.

[22] *Introduction to Scottish Legal History*, p. 348.

against rating assessments made by local Valuation Appeal Committees, and, less frequently, as the Registration of Voters Appeal Court and the Election Petition Court. In 1708, a Court of Exchequer for Scotland was re-constituted and equipped with procedures similar to those in the English Court of Exchequer but in 1856 its jurisdiction was transferred to the Court of Session, which still deals with revenue cases by procedures derived from English revenue practice.[23]

At a more local level, the sheriff and his court from medieval times to the present day have exercised both important judicial functions (civil and criminal) and also administrative duties. The sheriff in origin was a royal official wielding delegated royal power and responsible to the King in administrative, financial, military and judicial matters. He was concerned generally with the state of the locality and the preservation of the King's peace. Today, although the judicial functions of the Sheriff court are the most prominent, the Sheriff Principal retains very many administrative functions, especially in local government matters where appeal may lie to the sheriff from decisions of a local council or licensing authority or where his approval may be needed before certain action is taken by a local council.[24] Other local courts with a medieval origin included the burgh courts which afford another example of a jurisdiction combining both judicial and administrative functions in one body.[25] Their work included minor criminal matters and many matters of mercantile regulation (for example the control of markets, weights and measures and the assizes of bread and ale); unlike the sheriff court, the burgh courts have declined in importance as their functions were lost to other judicial and administrative institutions. In origin, the Dean of Guild Courts were closely related to the burgh courts; they exercised an aedilic jurisdiction, mainly concerned with the maintenance of certain minimum standards within the urban environment, or 'nychtburheid' (neighbourhood), for example the prevention of fire hazards and nuisances, and control over the building and repair of urban property in so far as neighbouring owners and occupiers were affected. Today a statutory jurisdiction has survived and it is through the Dean of Guild Court today in towns and cities that permission is

[23] A concise account is given in D. M. Walker, *The Scottish Legal System: An Introduction to the Study of Scots Law* (3rd ed., W. Green, 1969), pp. 223–5.

[24] See the Report on the Sheriff Court, 1967, HMSO, Cmnd. 3248, Chap. VIII and Appendixes VIII and IX.

[25] *Introduction to Scottish Legal History*, Chap. XXIX, by G. S. Pryde, at p. 386, and same author, 'Burghal Administration' in *A Source Book of Administrative Law in Scotland* (ed. M. R. McLarty. London, Hodge, 1956), pp. 1–11.

given under public health legislation for new buildings, improvements, repairs and demolitions.[26]

The office of justice of the peace was introduced into Scotland by James VI in 1609. The Scottish justice was never to acquire as important or as wide a range of functions as his English counterpart, although various statutory responsibilities in local government matters were discharged by him before the modern local government system was created. The justices still exercise certain licensing functions and may sit as a court for the recovery of small debts but their criminal jurisdiction is strictly limited. Many other inferior courts and tribunals, often exercising administrative functions, have existed in Scotland. The heritable jurisdictions arising from the feudal system were not abolished until 1747. The Commissioners of Supply were established by statute in 1667, with the original functions of levying and collecting the land tax; consisting mainly of land-owners nominated by the Crown, they came to be the most important organs of local government in the counties until county councils were created in 1889. Their fiscal duties are now exercised by the General Commissioners of Income Tax. Before 1847 the administration of the poor law was primarily in the hands of the parish kirk session acting in conjunction with the heritors, or freeholders, of the parish.

Outside the main stream of central and local government, various instances of specialized jurisdictions may be found. An Act of 1592 created what seems to have been a mining jurisdiction, possibly comparable with that of the Stannary courts in England; this jurisdiction was vested in an official known as Master of the Metals and had the express aim of avoiding 'the langsum course and great expenssis of the ordinar justice'. No records survive of this jurisdiction and when colliers and salters were freed from servitude before 1800 they were brought like other servants and workmen within the 'labour jurisdiction' of the justices of the peace.[27] Anticipating the creation of county courts in England, the Small Debt (Scotland) Act 1837 vested jurisdiction over small debts in a number of local courts.

During the nineteenth century many specialized organs of central and local government were established, often with power to settle disputes arising out of the exercise of their administrative functions. These have now been superseded by the government departments and local authorities of today. It will be seen from later chapters in this book that a number of important differences in the use made of administrative tribunals still exist between England and Scotland. Thus,

[26] J. McKechnie, in *A Source Book of Administrative Law*, pp. 95–104.

[27] W. Croft Dickinson, in *Introduction to Scottish Legal History*, p. 405.

some special jurisdictions exist in Scotland which have no counterpart in England (for example the Scottish Land Court and the Crofters Commission) and some important English tribunals are not found in Scotland (for example, the Mental Health Review Tribunals).[28] Moreover, Scottish legislation has shown a greater preference than in England for the statutory arbitration, for example in agricultural law and in land valuation, but today the majority of administrative tribunals are common to both England and Scotland. It is significant that the Tribunals and Inquiries Act 1958 established a Scottish Committee of the Council on Tribunals rather than a separate Scottish Council as recommended in the Franks Report. No distinctively Scottish contribution has been made to discussions in this century regarding the constitutional status and use of administrative tribunals[29] and it may be concluded that, while their history has been different, the role of tribunals in the Scottish system of law and government today is broadly the same as in England.[30]

## THE ADVENT OF THE MODERN TRIBUNAL SYSTEM

The origins of the modern lay tribunal, far removed from the courts in constitution and method, lay in the National Insurance Act of 1911. In an earlier measure – the Old Age Pensions Act of 1908 – the Liberal Government had learnt from the discouraging experience of workmen's compensation and had avoided the courts, placing the administration of the scheme in the hands of 'pensions committees' of the major local authorities. An appeal against their decisions lay first to the committees themselves and thence to the Local Government Board.[31]

However, disenchantment with the courts was not the only reason for the search for alternative methods of settling disputes. The attractions of the German system of social benefits also had a good deal of influence on the two main architects of the social policies of the Liberals at this time, namely Lloyd George and Churchill. Churchill wanted to 'thrust a big slice of Bismarckianism over the whole underside of our industrial system'[32] and Lloyd George had made a visit to Germany in 1908 with the express purpose of inspecting the German social insurance system at first hand.

[28] Below, pp. 53–4.

[29] See e.g. Lord Cooper's papers on administrative justice, printed in *Selected Papers 1922–1954* (1957) at pp. 26–38 and 266–75.

[30] See also J. D. B. Mitchell, *Constitutional Law* (2nd ed. 1968), Chap. 16.

[31] Abel-Smith and Stevens, *Lawyers*, pp. 116–17.

[32] See B. Gilbert, *The Evolution of National Insurance in Great Britain* (M. Joseph, 1966), p. 253.

The outcome was a scheme set out in Part II of the National Insurance Act 1911 for unemployment insurance whereby employers, employees and the State contributed to a fund out of which workmen were to be paid 7s a week during unemployment. The scheme followed the German system in most details, even down to the method of registering contributions by sticking stamps in an 'unemployment book' kept by the employer.[33] More important from our point of view, the German method of settling disputes was also adopted. The scheme was administered by the Board of Trade which appointed 'insurance officers' to whom application for unemployment benefit had to be made in the first instance. All questions in connection with such claims were determined by the insurance officer, and a workman who was dissatisfied with his decision could require the insurance officer to refer the case to a 'court of referees'. These 'courts' consisted of a chairman appointed by the Board of Trade, one member drawn from an 'employers' panel' and one member drawn from a 'workmen's panel' representing the trade of the applicant. The Board of Trade appointed the employers' panels while members of the workmen's panels were elected by ballot by the workmen in the trades concerned. A further and final right of appeal was provided from a decision of a court of referees to an 'umpire' who was a national appellate authority appointed by the Crown.

Political pressures prevented the extension of this system to national health insurance (which was set out in Part I of the National Insurance Act 1911). Because of the then entrenched position of the friendly societies and commercial insurance companies it was politically necessary to incorporate both these in the administration of the scheme. Payment of health benefits was normally made through an 'approved society', and in the case of dispute between a claimant and his society the matter was to be settled according to rules of the society. In other words, on a local level the approved society took the place of the court of referees in the case of national health insurance. In certain cases, provision was made for a right of appeal to a body known as the 'Insurance Commissioners'. There were four Insurance Commissions, each being primarily an administrative body for a particular part of the country but they did have the incidental task of determining such questions as the rate of contributions to be paid and whether the type of employment came within the scope of the scheme, there being a general right of appeal in such cases to the county court with a further right of appeal on a question of law to the High Court. In other cases the Insurance Commissioners acted as a final appeal in disputes between

[33] M. Bruce, *The Coming of the Welfare State* (4th ed., Batsford, 1968), p. 198.

claimants and approved societies or an insurance committee (where the claimant was not a member of an approved society), or between one approved society and another. In carrying out these adjudicatory functions the Insurance Commissioners were empowered to appoint referees to hear and determine appeals and disputes on their behalf or to hear and determine cases themselves either summarily or after a hearing.

Thus four different methods of settling disputes were conceived within a decade. Workmen's compensation became the province of County Court judges, old-age pensions were handed over to local authorities for administration, unemployment insurance fostered a new set of tribunals, and national health insurance was largely administered through existing friendly societies or industrial insurance firms.

Of these four, by far the most interesting from our point of view is the establishment of the courts of referees and the umpire for the unemployment insurance scheme. These 'courts' introduced a concept new to British administration, namely the local tribunal, non-legal in character and having representatives from the same class as those most likely to be affected by the decision. As Abel-Smith and Stevens observe:

> 'What had been drafted as one possible procedure under the workmen's compensation became the only legitimate procedure under National Insurance . . . The courts had been deliberately bypassed. As a result the insured person needed to incur no costs in using the procedure under the Act. The tribunals were providing a free service to their users and in front of them legal representation was unnecessary.'[34]

This was to provide the model for the future, and the use of special tribunals was extended to other fields. In 1919 the large number of claims for war pensions arising from the First World War generated the first pensions tribunal, designed to deal with claims as informally and inexpensively as possible, and consisting of a lawyer, a medical practitioner and a service member, i.e. a disabled officer or soldier of equivalent rank to the claimant. Where the appeal related to the amount of the assessment another doctor replaced the lawyer.

In the same year the Industrial Court introduced a special tribunal – though its function was arbitration rather than adjudication – into the field of industrial relations. The Court had a wide jurisdiction to deal with nearly all types of industrial disputes between employers and employees, but the parties could not approach the Court directly; they had instead to report to the Minister of Labour, who could refer

[34] Abel-Smith and Stevens, *Lawyers*, p. 117.

the case to the Court provided both parties agreed. The proceedings were usually held in camera and kept as informal as possible; thus legal representation was only permitted with the Court's consent, and it was not always granted. The flavour of the proceedings reflected contemporary trade union antagonism towards the ordinary courts. Ten years earlier Trade Boards, to be succeeded by the Wages Councils of our own day, had introduced a lay adjudicatory element into determining fair wages in small and unorganized trades, where unionism was weak.

Another interesting development in Scotland in 1919 was the establishment of a rent tribunal to settle disputes between the Scottish Health Department and local authorities in public housing schemes; it was to Scotland that the Ridley Committee looked in 1945 when seeking a solution to the problem of controlling rents for furnished accommodation.

In 1925 the 'referee' system was extended to claims for widows', orphans' and old age contributory pensions, although not in precisely the same form as for unemployment insurance. The referees for widows', orphans' and old-age pensions were in fact lawyers appointed by the Minister of Health on the nomination of the Attorney General, and they sat individually to hear appeals against the rejection of claims by the Minister. Of some interest is the unofficial division that was made between senior and junior referees. Of the sixteen referees, two were usually described as the 'senior referees', their function being not to act as a court of appeal from the junior referees, but to deal with cases involving important points of principle, it being thought that in order to preserve uniformity it would be of value to have two referees whose opinions were recognized by the remainder as carrying special weight.

Contemporaneously with the establishment of these special tribunals, some of the statutory boards and commissions began belatedly to acquire adjudicatory functions, mostly short-lived because the era of administration by *ad hoc* boards and commissions was drawing to a close. We have already noted that the Local Government Board became the appellate body in respect of non-contributory old age pensions. In 1909 the Board had also replaced Quarter Sessions as the appellate body in the case of an order made by a local authority to 'close' a dwelling house on the grounds that it was unfit for human habitation[35] and in 1902 the Board of Education had likewise been given power to decide disputes between local education authorities and the managers of denominational schools.[36] When given this type of adjudicatory function

[35] *Local Government Board* v. *Arlidge*, [1915] A.C. 120 concerned the Board's procedure in deciding such an appeal.

[36] *Board of Education* v. *Rice*, [1911] A.C. 179 concerned just such a dispute.

the Boards tended, however, to use the public inquiry procedure, rather than act as a special tribunal and this carried over when their duties were taken over by government departments.

*The Donoughmore Report*
All this illustrates a flight from the courts, whose potential jurisdiction was being further diminished by the tendency during this period for Parliament to grant specific legislative and judicial powers to Ministers as part of the general growth of administration in such fields as public health, welfare, slum clearance, and education. In 1929 the then Lord Chief Justice, Lord Hewart, became so alarmed at the general trend that he launched his well-known assault on 'the new despotism'. This was a scathing attack on the ousting of the courts and the growth of arbitrary power in the hands of the bureaucracy: 'it is they (civil servants) who seek it; it is they who ask for it, and it is they who contrive it'.[37]

Lord Hewart was saying, albeit intemperately, what other judges and academic lawyers had been saying in more measured terms, and the Government could not ignore the views of the holder of such high judicial office. In the same year they appointed the Committee on Minister's Powers (the Donoughmore Committee).

The Report of the Donoughmore Committee[38] might have been a landmark in the development of administrative law, but in relation to administrative tribunals it is now of little more than historical interest. Given terms of reference which were a legal strait-jacket, it produced very few concrete recommendations and was an academic dissertation rather than a basis for action. The Committee was asked to consider the powers exercised by or under the direction of Ministers by way of delegated legislation and 'judicial or quasi-judicial decision and to report what safeguards are desirable or necessary to secure the constitutional principles of the sovereignty of Parliament and the supremacy of the Law'. The Committee had rather more to say on the subject of delegated legislation, upon which it made some important recommendations, than on the subject of tribunals, of which it reported that the fears expressed by Lord Hewart and others were groundless. 'Our conclusion on the whole matter is that there is nothing radically wrong about the existing practice of Parliament in permitting the exercise of judicial and quasi-judicial powers by Ministers and of judicial power by Ministerial Tribunals . . .'[39] Among the main recommendations the

[37] *The New Despotism*, pp. 157–8.
[38] Cmd. 4060, April 1932 (Reprint 1966).
[39] Report, pp. 115–16.

Committee made were that 'judicial' as distinct from 'quasi-judicial' decisions should normally be entrusted only to the ordinary courts; that in those exceptional cases where this was not possible the decision should be entrusted to a tribunal rather than a Minister personally; that such tribunals should be independent although appointed by the Minister in consultation with the Lord Chancellor; and that 'quasi-judicial' decisions should be left to a Minister unless his department had an interest in the decision going one way rather than another (in which case the decision should be remitted to a tribunal). The Committee went on to make certain recommendations regarding the rights of the parties (e.g. right to be heard, reasons to be given for decisions, right of appeal to the High Court on points of law, etc.).

The Donoughmore Report was criticized for its unduly legalistic approach (as in the distinction between 'judicial', 'quasi-judicial' and 'administrative' acts and the copious citation of case-law), its emphasis on 'the time-honoured shibboleths about the separation of powers and the rule of law',[40] its assumption of the existence of legal impartiality and the objective interpretation of statutes, and because the opportunity was not taken to work out a new and more logical theory of administrative law and a rational system of administrative tribunals.

### *The Second World War and After*

With the blessing of Donoughmore behind them, tribunals took firmer root during and after the Second World War. Compulsory national service generated appeals for exemption on grounds of hardship, occupation and conscience, and claims arose for compensation and war damage. All these were dealt with by tribunals, most of which continue to have a legal existence today, although they are dormant.

Agriculture, so vital to Britain's war economy, was subjected to rigorous controls which generated a whole new machinery of lay adjudication, exemplified by the War Agricultural Executive Committees established in 1940. These were committees of local farmers, acting as agents of the Minister and with extensive powers to give directions regarding the use of land, or to take possession or terminate the tenancy of poorly farmed land. Another aspect of this wartime regulation of agriculture may be seen in the establishment of the Milk and Dairies tribunal in 1944. In 1947 it was decided that there should be a right of appeal against the decisions of Executive Committees and the Agricultural Land Tribunals were established. With the decline in the official

[40] Abel-Smith and Stevens, *Lawyers*, p. 120. The authors comment that the Report 'did more to emphasize the primitive state of political science in England than to solve any constitutional problems.'

powers of the Committees, the jurisdiction of the agricultural land tribunals has now developed into a statutory form of arbitration for the settlement of landlord and tenant disputes: the emphasis on good husbandry and efficient management remain, as a hangover from the origins of the jurisdiction.

The Pensions Appeal Tribunals of 1943 supplemented, and largely replaced, that of 1919.

In the field of post-war domestic policy tribunals other than the ordinary courts continued to proliferate, and they fell into two main groups – those, dubbed by Lord Reading 'the camp-followers of the Welfare State',[41] which arose from the social security programme of the post-war Government, and those which arose from policies of increasing regulation.

The former were set out in four principal statutes – the National Insurance Act 1946 (which created the National Insurance Commissioner and national insurance local tribunals – these superseded the unemployment insurance tribunals, which had themselves replaced the 'courts of referees' in 1936 while retaining the principle of a three-man lay tribunal with one member to represent 'work-people'); the National Health Service Act 1946 (which established the various national health service tribunals to deal with the difficulties of incorporating medical practitioners into the national health service); the National Insurance (Industrial Injuries) Act 1946 (which replaced the old system of workmen's compensation – in the form of an adversarial contest between employer and employee – by incorporating industrial injuries into the national insurance scheme and establishing medical appeal tribunals to adjudicate on the medical aspects of claims); and the National Assistance Act 1948 (which modified the then existing unemployment assistance tribunals). These national assistance tribunals also replaced local authorities as the appeal body in respect of the now obsolescent non-contributory old-age pensions (see p. 33). To bring the history of this line of tribunals up-to-date, they were replaced by the supplementary benefit appeal tribunals in 1966 on the introduction of the present social security scheme.

The regulatory type of tribunal, established in the 1840s for the railways and in the 1930s for road and air traffic,[42] was extended into new fields, notably into the supervision of independent schools and children's voluntary homes and the control of furnished rents.

An important tribunal which does not fall into either of our two

[41] 206 H.L. Deb. col. 1.

[42] The Traffic Commissioners 1933 and the Air Transport Licensing Board 1938.

categories was the Lands Tribunal, established in 1949 to bring together under one expert jurisdiction a miscellany of arbitral arrangements concerning the valuation of land and property.

*The 1960s*

The 1960s brought three important developments. First, the control of furnished rents at a 'reasonable' level as an emergency measure in the post-war housing crisis was extended to an objectively 'fair' rent for private unfurnished property (to be extended in the early 1970s to the public sector). Second, the unprecedented growth from 1965 onwards of the industrial tribunals, first established for one relatively narrow purpose but rapidly extending into multi-purpose 'labour courts'. And third, the extension of tribunals into two areas of human liberty – appeals against restriction on grounds of mental health and against refusal of permission to enter or to remain in the country on grounds of nationality.

In general the 1960s were characterized by a trend in British government towards a more open kind of administration, exemplified variously by the appointment of the Parliamentary Commissioner for Administration, the renewed emphasis on natural justice demanded by the courts, the restriction of Crown privilege and the giving of reasons by tribunals and Ministers as required by the Tribunals and Inquiries Act 1958. In the area of tribunals the trend is exemplified by the two we have just mentioned – those concerned with mental health and immigration – since these are matters which until recently were dealt with administratively. But perhaps the most important manifestation of the trend – possibly its genesis – was the appointment of the Franks Committee and its Report.[43]

*The Report of the Franks Committee*

The appointment of the Franks Committee in 1955 had something in common with that of the Donoughmore Committee in 1929, in that each owed its existence to an underlying unease which was 'sparked off' by an accidental happening, the one by Lord Hewart's book and the other by the Crichel Down Inquiry.[44] This inquiry earned an unexpected niche in history, both from the principles and from the publicity that flowed from a relatively trivial happening, and it came to represent a watershed between an older paternalism and what Franks came to call 'openness'. To change the metaphor, it was a pebble which started a

[43] Report of the Committee on Administrative Tribunals and Inquiries, Cmnd. 218, July 1957.

[44] Cmd. 9176 June 1954, Reprinted 1964.

landslide, for the wide-ranging investigations of the Franks Committee bore no relation to an indiscretion over a decision to acquire some land. The Committee's terms of reference were:

To consider and make recommendations on:

(a) The constitution and working of tribunals other than the ordinary courts of law, constituted under any Act of Parliament by a Minister of the Crown or for the purposes of a Minister's functions.

(b) The working of such administrative procedures as include the holding of an inquiry or hearing by or on behalf of a Minister on an appeal or as the result of objections or representations, and in particular the procedure for the compulsory purchase of land.

After hearing a vast amount of evidence from every possible source[45] the Committee produced a concise and forthright Report. It began by enunciating the three principles of 'openness, fairness and impartiality' which, it believed, ought to characterize tribunal proceedings. It then sought to cut the umbilical cord between tribunals and departments:

'We consider that tribunals should properly be regarded as machinery provided by Parliament for adjudication rather than as part of the machinery of administration.'

Having thus defined its position, the Committee made a number of recommendations, both in general terms and in regard to particular tribunals. Many of these remain the starting point for discussion of the various aspects of tribunals which this book will discuss, and it will therefore be more appropriate to introduce them in later chapters and in relation to particular topics. An 'over-arching' recommendation concerned the supervision of tribunals, which the Committee proposed should be placed in the hands of an executive body to be known as the Council on Tribunals. An account of this body, which was not to be established in the manner recommended but which has nevertheless been an important element in the situation since 1959, is given in Chapter 8.

The Report was both an achievement and a disappointment. Its main achievement was to identify more clearly a new phenomenon which had appeared unobtrusively on the borderline between the Administration and the Judiciary, and to give tribunals a status higher than that which they had previously enjoyed. In contrast with Donoughmore, which had confined itself to general constitutional principles

[45] This published evidence remains a most valuable source of reference for the student of public administration in this country.

and sought to re-establish the legal imperatives of the Rule of Law, the Franks Committee distilled out of its examination of the workings of particular tribunals the social (as opposed to the legal) requirements of natural justice, and in doing so shifted the viewpoint from the powers of the executive to the right of the citizen.

The disappointing aspects of the Report are doubtless more evident today, with the advantage of fifteen years' hindsight, than they were at the time. They lie chiefly in the fact that the Committee were not able to consider matters which were not, but could well be, amenable to decision by tribunal,[46] that the Report did not attempt to discuss or enunciate any principles for the setting up of tribunals or to discuss the criteria which made an issue justiciable, and that certain matters were considered but somewhat cursorily dismissed – for example the rationalization of procedures and the amalgamation of jurisdictions that have much in common. The Committee apparently saw itself as merely initiating a review of tribunals, of beginning a task which would be continued by the proposed Council.

Nevertheless the Report represents a watershed between a recent past when tribunals were regarded as unavoidable expedients and a future when they are coming to be accepted for what they really are – an important part of the judicial system of the country.

[46] A point made at the time by J. A. G. Griffith, (1959) 22 M.L.R. 125.

CHAPTER 2

# A SURVEY OF EXISTING TRIBUNALS

It ought to be reasonably simple to make a list of those tribunals whose writ runs in Great Britain today, but the attempt to do so is constantly thwarted by difficulties of definition. It is far from simple to say what a tribunal *is*.

The word itself is imprecise, being used rhetorically to describe the House of Lords or the power of public opinion, or specifically to describe a small body of adjudicators using their knowledge of the law, or of some subject outside the law, or merely their common sense, in order to adjudicate in a dispute. The Civil Aviation *Authority* is a tribunal, but so is the National Insurance *Commissioner*, the Immigration *Adjudicators*, the Agricultural *Arbitrators*, the national health service *Executive Councils*, the Local Valuation *Courts* and the *Comptroller-General* of Patents. The very phrase 'Administrative Tribunals' which is the title of this book is, as we argue on p. 223, an unfortunate and even misleading one. In short, the nomenclature of the subject is chaotic.

In the main the book is based on a study of those tribunals which are defined as such in the schedules to the Tribunals and Inquiries Act 1971 and which accordingly come under the general oversight of the Council on Tribunals, and we begin with a description of these. Later we shall discuss the wide miscellany of other bodies which have attributes normally associated with tribunals, or which make judicial decisions outside the ordinary courts of law, but which are not brought within the scope of the Act or the oversight of the Council.

An alphabetical list of the tribunals which fall within the narrower definition is published each year in the Annual Report of the Council on Tribunals, together with the statutory authority of each and the number of cases dealt with annually. In order to see this strange assortment in perspective, however, it will be helpful to rearrange the list according to some system. Unfortunately tribunals are resistant to neat classification. Their origins are pragmatic in that they result from decisions by Parliament or by ministers to assign particular responsibilities in particular ways. It follows that one cannot say that there are certain predetermined kinds of tribunal in the sense that there are well-defined principles governing the type of issue which ought or ought not to be delegated to a tribunal, or conversely the type of tribunal which ought to determine a particular type of issue.

Equally there are no satisfactory ways in which tribunals can be classified. Any classification must necessarily be *ex post facto*; moreover some tribunals fit appropriately into more than one classification while others would have to be 'bent' to fit into any classification at all. To attempt to classify them in terms of subject matter, for example, may be helpful in showing the vast range of human activity on which they impinge, but it is unhelpful in that it serves to emphasize the diversity of tribunals and to conceal their common features; moreover it classifies under one heading tribunals of widely different types. For example, the Plant Varieties Tribunal could be called 'agricultural' because it is about plant breeding or 'commercial' because it is about copyright. Rent tribunals have one foot in 'social welfare', in that they deal with security of tenure and personal hardship, and the other in the economics of housing. The industrial tribunals deal with both employment and taxation. Moreover the correlation between the subject matter of a tribunal and the department administratively responsible for it is by no means complete; for example, adjudication in tax matters is divided between tribunals whose 'parent' departments are the Lord Chancellor's Office, the Inland Revenue Department, the Department of Employment and the Ministry of Agriculture, and, since the introduction of Value Added tax, the Board of Customs and Excise.

Again, a classification by function might well start, for example, from the hypothesis that one should try to distinguish the judicial, the administrative and the licensing function; this would prove to be valid up to a point, but the exceptions would rapidly make the generalizations meaningless. The same would apply to any attempted classification of structure, either in terms of national, regional and local organization or in terms of the multifarious procedures for appeal.

Nevertheless, it may be useful to attempt a broad survey (failing a strict classification) of the subjects with which tribunals have to deal, if only as a convenient method of straightforward description. Two provisos must be accepted. The first is that others would prefer to arrange them in a different order;[1] the second, that any arrangement will produce anomalies, which could only be corrected by a rearrangement which would produce other anomalies. No classification by subject matter could be logical or watertight.

[1] Comprehensive analyses by subject matter have been made by Sir Carleton Allen, QC, in his article 'Administrative Jurisdiction' (1956) Public Law 13, and by Professor J. F. Garner in *Administrative Law*.

## Survey by Subject Matter

The broad headings adopted here are *Social Administration*, *Economic Matters* and matters relating to *Revenue*.

(Note: The figures in parentheses give the number of cases disposed of by particular tribunals in England and Wales in 1971.)

### SOCIAL ADMINISTRATION

Under this heading we group tribunals which deal with personal welfare, service pensions, education, employment, the national health service and immigration:

1. *Personal Welfare*. These are the tribunals with which the average citizen is most likely to come into contact, as they deal with the benefits available under national insurance and social welfare legislation, and with specific aspects of personal welfare:

(a) *Supplementary Benefit Appeal Tribunals*, which hear appeals against decisions of the local officer of the Supplementary Benefits Commission, affecting in the main supplementary pensions and allowances (27,852), but recently extended to cover payments under the Family Income Supplements Act (1,753). They also hear appeals in respect of certain Selective Employment Tax refunds (15) – see under *Revenue*.

(b) (i) *National Insurance Local Tribunals*, which hear appeals from decisions of insurance officers (or references by them) (National Insurance 24,673, viz. unemployment benefit 19,694, sickness benefit 6,545, maternity benefit 428, widow's benefit 217, guardian's allowance 15, retirement pension 632, death grant 78, child's special allowance 1; industrial injuries 4,661; family allowance 825).

(ii) *The National Insurance Commissioner*, who hears appeals from local tribunals (1,564 national insurance, 624 industrial injuries, 49 family allowances).

(c) *Medical Appeal Tribunals*, which hear appeals from departmental medical boards about industrial injuries (17,614).

(d) *Mental Health Review Tribunals*, which assess fitness for discharge from a mental hospital (1,021).

(e) *Children's Hearings*,* a Scottish tribunal difficult to categorize, which broadly speaking has replaced the juvenile courts for children under 16 (5,243).

(f) *Children's Voluntary Homes Appeal Tribunal*, which determines appeals against ministerial requirements to close down or remedy some defect in voluntary children's homes (nil).

(g) *Rent Tribunals*,[4] in respect of security of tenure for occupants of furnished premises (10,913).

2. *Service Pensions*

(a) *Pensions Appeal Tribunals*, which determine appeals from decisions of the Minister on entitlement or assessment of war pensions and certain other types of military service pension (3,463).

(b) *Police Pensions Appeal Tribunal and Firemen's Pensions Appeal Tribunal*, which determine disputes about the pensions payable to police officers or firemen who have served overseas (nil).

3. *Education*

(a) *Nurses' Training Institution Appeal Tribunal*, which may hear appeals against refusal of recognition by the General Medical Council (nil).

(b) *Independent Schools Tribunal*, which determines appeals against ministerial requirements to close down or remedy some defect in an independent school (i.e. a school financed and supported independently of a local education authority) (4).

4. *Employment*[5]

(a) *National Service Tribunals*, which although legally still in operation are now dormant and inoperative. Thus the Military Service (Hardship) Committees, the Referees under section 23(3) of the National Service Act 1948, and the Conscientious Objectors' Local and Appellate Tribunals have not heard any cases since 1960. However, occasional cases may still be heard by the Local Reinstatement Committees, which hear disputes about the rights of servicemen to be reinstated in their former civilian employment; or to be compensated for a failure to reinstate and the Appellate Tribunal, the Umpire under section 41(1) of the National Service Act 1948.

(b) *Industrial Tribunals*. These have been the most rapidly growing tribunals, and the most flexible, since they have continuously undertaken new jurisdictions. They were originally established in 1964 to determine appeals by employers against the assessment of the industrial training levy, but between 1964 and 1971 their jurisdiction was expan-

[4] Also classified under Economic Policy (Housing).

[5] This does not of course include *un*employment benefit, which was listed under 'Personal Welfare' above.

ded to include appeals from the Minister's refusal of refunds of Selective Employment Tax,[6] disputes over redundancy payments (8,651), contracts of employment (68), compensation for loss of office under various statutes (11) and the definition of 'dock work' under the Docks and Harbours Act 1966 (6). The Industrial Relations Act 1971 further extended their jurisdiction to embrace various kinds of alleged 'unfair industrial practice', breach of rules by employers' organizations or trade unions or breach of duty by employers and within a year or two the implementation of the Equal Pay Act 1970 will diversify it still further.

5. *National Health Service*

Tribunals dealing with national health service matters could be regarded as a specialized branch of 'employment' tribunals, in that their purpose is to regulate the relationship between the medical profession and the service. Their task is simply to determine complaints on matters of discipline within the national health service, but the various intertwined threads of appeal by which this simple aim is achieved are so complicated as to defy brief description.

Placing brevity before accuracy, however, we may say that *Executive Councils* in each local health authority area appoint *service committees* for the main branches of the profession, which may hear complaints from patients, and which dealt with 826 cases in 1971. If an Executive Council finds a complaint justified it may take disciplinary action, but either complainant or doctor has a right of appeal to the *Secretary of State*, who is in turn advised by medical and dental *advisory committees*. In more serious cases, such as might warrant a doctor being crossed off the list of practitioners, yet another 'tribunal' is available, the *National Health Service Tribunal*.

To add to this accumulation of bodies there are also the *Medical Practices Committees* which determine questions relating to the inclusion of a practitioner's name on an Executive Council's list when the number of applications to be included in the list exceeds the number of vacancies, and *local medical committees* which investigate technical matters such as excessive prescribing and failure to keep adequate patients' records, referred by the Minister. And even this is not a complete list of the adjudicatory procedures in this sphere, for the general appellate functions of the Minister have not been fully detailed and the disciplinary powers of professional associations such as the BMA have scarcely been touched on. Moreover, any patient who considers that a prac-

[6] Industrial tribunals are listed under *Revenue* below in relation to the industrial training levy and SET.

titioner has been negligent in his advice or treatment may have a remedy in damages at common law.

These labyrinthine arrangements were necessary to achieve a working relationship satisfactory to the medical profession and to the Minister and are, fortunately, *sui generis.*

6. *Immigration*

Probably no tribunals operate in a more sensitive area at the time of writing than those concerned with immigration and we are justified in dealing with them at slightly greater length. Before 1969 the Home Secretary had a complete discretion to admit or refuse to admit an alien into the United Kingdom, or having admitted him to decide that he should no longer be permitted to stay in this country. Similarly under the Commonwealth Immigrants Acts of 1962 and 1968 immigration officers were given a wide discretion to admit or refuse Commonwealth citizens seeking entry to this country, although there were rather more exemptions from the exercise of this discretion than in the case of aliens. In 1969, however, it was decided that both these discretionary powers should be subject to a right of appeal, together with the Home Secretary's discretion in regard to the deportation of both aliens and Commonwealth immigrants. The Immigration Appeals Act 1969 therefore established a two-tier tribunal to deal with such appeals. Under the provisions of this Act and the corresponding provisions of the Aliens (Appeal) Order 1970, an appeal lay against the refusal overseas of an entry certificate or visa; against a refusal by the Home Secretary to extend the stay of a person already admitted to the country for a limited period; against deportation, except on the recommendation of a court; and against certain other decisions taken in the administration of immigration control. There are also extra-statutory arrangements under which the Home Office concedes an appeal to passengers who are refused entry on arrival in this country although they hold entry certificates, vouchers, visas or work permits. Appeal lies to an *adjudicator* in the first instance, and there is a further right of appeal by either party to an *Immigration Appeal Tribunal,* whose decision is final.[7]

In cases where 'it appears to the Secretary of State that the decision or action was taken in the interests of national security' – or, in the case of an alien, on grounds of a political nature – there was under the 1969 Act a special procedure. The case was heard, not by an adjudicator or by the ordinary Appeal Tribunal, but by a special panel of that Tribunal, nominated by the Lord Chancellor and the Home Secretary jointly. At

[7] In some deportation cases the appeal lies direct to the Appeal Tribunal.

the hearing, if the Home Secretary had so certified, matters the disclosure of which he considered would be contrary to the interests of national security could not be disclosed to the appellant.

The Immigration Act 1971, however, which came into operation on 1 January 1973, and under which all appeals must now be brought, confers no right of appeal against refusal of entry if the reason for refusal was that it would not be conducive to the public good (s.13(5)), or against curtailment of stay or refusal to extend it (s. 14(3)) or deportation (s. 15(3)) if the decision is based on security or political grounds.

In 1971 the adjudicators heard 1,944 cases and the Appeal Tribunal 118.

## ECONOMIC MATTERS

Under this heading we have grouped those tribunals dealing with agriculture and the use of land, commerce, transport and housing, because in each case there is a commercial element in the matters which the tribunal is requred to determine.

### 7. *Agriculture*

This embraces a number of tribunals loosely connected with agriculture or the use of agricultural land, viz.

(a) *Agricultural Land Tribunals*, the main purpose of which is to settle disputes between landlord and tenant in respect of notice to quit, bad husbandry and drainage; they also settle responsibilities between one landowner and another, e.g. for drainage and clearing ditches (102).

(b) *Arbitrators under the Agricultural Holdings Act 1948*, to whom landlords and tenants may be required compulsorily to submit certain disputes over agricultural tenancies (260).

(c) *The Crofters Commission.** This tribunal, peculiar to Scotland, performs a similar function to Agricultural Land Tribunals in England and Wales, namely settlement of disputes between landlords and crofters over such matters as the termination of tenancies, etc., but it has, additionally, a strong policy purpose, namely the maintenance and encouragement of crofting as a system of farming (111).

(d) *The Commons Commissioners.* This is one of the most recent tribunals to be set up and is designed to do the 'once-for-all' job of determining disputed claims in respect of the use of common land. Hearings began in 1972.

(e) *Forestry Committees* which hear appeals from restrictions or requirements imposed by the Forestry Commission. The Commission has very wide discretionary powers including restricting the felling of trees (by the refusal to grant the necessary licence) or directing that certain trees must be felled. Any person aggrieved by such a direction or the refusal to grant a licence may appeal to a three-man committee appointed by the Minister (nil).

(f) *Plant Variety Rights Tribunal* (one), and the Controller of Plant Variety Rights.

(g) *The Milk and Dairies Tribunal*, which holds hearings in connection with decisions given by a Minister, either originally or on appeal, with regard to the registration of dairy farms and the issue of milk producers' and dairies' licences.

8. *Commerce.*

It could be argued that a number of tribunals which have already been discussed under other headings (e.g. the Plant Variety Rights Tribunal or possibly the Independent Schools Tribunal) are connected with 'commerce' in its widest sense, but for convenience we have restricted our survey to three tribunals which are wholly commercial in character:

(a) *The Controller of Patents* (in his adjudicatory role in respect of patents, registered designs, and trade marks) (7,208).

(b) *The Performing Rights Tribunal* which determines disputes about the performance or broadcasting of copyright works (one).

(c) *The 'Tribunal of Enquiry' under the Prevention of Fraud (Investments) Act 1958* which is an example of the regulation of a particular type of trading activity. Under the 1958 Act a licence is required for dealing in securities (unless the dealer is a member of the Stock Exchange or comes within certain other exemptions). If the Department of Trade and Industry refuses to issue the appropriate licence there is a right of appeal to a tribunal which is a rather peculiar hybrid. This has no specific title but is simply referred to in the legislation as a 'tribunal of inquiry', which is not strictly accurate either, because although the tribunal reports to the Minister, a finding in favour of the applicant must be accepted by the Minister (nil).

9. *Transport*

This includes four main tribunals.

(a) *The Traffic Commissioners* which are in effect three-man tribunals dealing with the licensing, and conditions attaching to the licensing, of public service (passenger) vehicles (17,212).

(b) *The Licensing Authority for goods vehicles*, which in practice is the chairman of the local Traffic Commissioners sitting alone, and under another name, to hear and determine applications for licences for goods vehicles (5,992).

(c) *The Transport Tribunal*, which as we shall see has undergone a considerable metamorphosis in its time, having once had a very powerful and wide-ranging jurisdiction which has now diminished to almost residual proportions. Its main function now is to hear appeals from the determinations of licensing authorities for goods vehicles, but curiously not from determinations of the Traffic Commissioners in regard to the licensing of public service vehicles, where appeal lies to the Secretary of State (17). It is also left with the rather odd first-instance jurisdiction of settling disputes over charges made for the carriage of mail, the armed services and the police by rail, but in practice this has become a dead letter.

(d) *The Civil Aviation Authority*, an administrative body with a judicial (i.e. licensing) function in respect of air services, air travel organizers, and operating staff (4,284).[8]

10. *Housing*

(a) *Rent Tribunals*,[9] which adjudicate when there is a dispute, or reference, as between landlord and tenant in regard to the rent or security of tenure of furnished dwelling accommodation (approx. 8,000).

(b) *Rent Assessment Committees*, which assess a fair rent for regulated unfurnished tenancies on appeal from the decision of a rent officer (3,908).

REVENUE

11. *Taxation*

(a) Income and capital tax appeals are dealt with by the *General Commissioners* and the *Special Commissioners*, whose jurisdiction overlaps to a large extent as appeals against tax assessments can in most cases be made to either body, the choice being in the hands of the taxpayer. The two tribunals have a different composition and serve different functions. The General Commissioners are rather like 'local lay magistrates', whereas the Special Commissioners are an expert tribunal composed of people with either legal or taxation expertise appointed by the Treasury, and a hearing before the Special Commissioners is often preferred where technical points of law are involved. Whilst the Special Commissioners are full-time civil servants they naturally act independently of the Board of Inland Revenue. Both sets of Commissioners do however have exclusive jurisdiction over some matters, e.g. General Commissioners hear all appeals in Great Britain

[8] This figure relates to the Authority's predecessor, the Air Transport Licensing Board. The new Authority operated from 1 April 1972.

[9] Also listed under 'Social Welfare' in relation to security of tenure. The total number of cases heard was in fact 15,793.

in respect of personal allowances whilst all appeals in regard to surtax are heard by the Special Commissioners.[10] In addition to the General and Special Commissioners there are two other tribunals which have responsibility for Inland Revenue taxes. First there is an appeal *tribunal set up under section 463, Income and Corporation Taxes Act 1970* which hears appeals in regard to 'dividend-stripping', 'bond-washing' and other similar tax avoidance devices (23). Secondly there is the Board of Referees (5), but this is now largely obsolescent. Originally set up in 1915 in connection with the Excess Profits Duty the Board was later given jurisdiction on special matters such as allowances for expenditure on machinery or plant, but nowadays this five-man tribunal is mostly concerned with hearing a trickle of outstanding appeals on surtax to be paid on the undistributed income of a company.

(b) Selective employment tax appeals are for the most part determined by the *Industrial Tribunals* (203). This apparently anomalous incursion of these tribunals into the field of taxation is explained by the fact that when SET legislation was introduced only the then Ministry of Labour had the necessary information and machinery to implement it – to make, for example, the necessary distinction between manufacturing and service industries. It may also seem odd to find the *Supplementary Benefit Appeal Tribunals* (20) in the same fiscal context. They come into the SET picture because, together with the Supplementary Benefits Commission, they are concerned with special refunds to certain households employing nurses or domestic servants.

(c) Appeals against assessments to VAT are determined by the new Value Added Tax Tribunals.

12. *Tribunals Concerned with Statutory Levies*

There are two tribunals which hear appeals in respect of the statutory assessment of a levy, not in the form of a tax or benefit for the state, but to carry out a compulsory form of self-improvement within a particular trade or industry.

(a) *Industrial Tribunals* consider appeals in respect of the assessment of industrial training levy, this being the earliest of their jurisdictions (223).

(b) *The Betting Levy Appeal Tribunal* hears appeals in respect of the assessment of a levy on bookmakers which the Horserace Betting Levy Board is empowered to make for the improvement of the horse-racing industry (101).

[10] In 1969 the General Commissioners heard 908,174 cases of simple adjournment or delay and 2,450 'contentious appeals'. The Special Commissioners heard 3,832 cases.

13. *Property Valuation and Rating*

(a) *Local Valuation Courts*[11] which hear appeals from determinations made by the local valuation officers of Inland Revenue in respect of the rateable value of properties (24,515).

(b) *Lands Tribunal*, which has a wide and disparate jurisdiction. It acts as the national appellate authority for a number of separate jurisdictions, for example appeals from local valuation courts, determinations as to value by the Inland Revenue, or the Minister or local planning authority under the Town and Country Planning Acts, or when the compensation for compulsorily acquired land is being disputed. But it is the tribunal of first instance in about half the cases brought to it, and it has some important jurisdictions of a different kind – power to modify or discharge restrictions affecting land under section 84 of the Law of Property Act 1925,[12] and powers under the Rights of Light Act 1959 (1,108).

(c) *The Iron and Steel Arbitration Tribunal* which was set up to determine the compensation payable by the Iron and Steel Board to individual firms in consequence of the nationalization of the steel industry (nil).

## THE POSITION IN SCOTLAND

There is a large area of common ground between tribunals in England (and Wales) and Scotland, or of ground where the difference is not substantial, but simply flows from statutes comparable in purpose but different in nomenclature and detail. Thus the arrangements for national insurance and supplementary benefit are common throughout Great Britain; for the national health service they are similar but derive from the National Health Service (Scotland) Act 1947 instead of from the National Health Service Act 1946; for industrial tribunals they derive from the same statutes but operate under separate English and Scottish regulations. It would not be particularly instructive to pursue such differences in detail,[13] but mention must be made of two areas – rating and land – where the difference is substantial, and of two tribunals which are unique to Scotland.

The actual work of the Scottish *valuation appeal committees* (407) does not differ greatly from that of the English local valuation courts,

[11] 'Valuation Appeal Committees' in Scotland.

[12] Some of these applications, which number some thirty or forty a year, relate to large building schemes and are of considerable social significance.

[13] The broad picture can conveniently be visualized by comparing the lists of tribunals under the surveillance of the Council on Tribunals and of its Scottish Committee at the end of any of the Council's Annual Reports.

the differences being more in the method of their appointment (discussed in Chapter 4) and in the relatively small number of hearings which allow them to be serviced by part-time solicitors in private practice. The Scottish *Lands Tribunal* (100) on the other hand, is a very different kind of body from its English counterpart. Provision for a Lands Tribunal for Scotland, to operate from an appointed day, was made in section 10(2) of the Lands Tribunal Act 1949, but the appointed day was delayed until 1 March 1971 because of an insufficient prospective workload, and even so it does not determine the appeals from valuation committees which, as we have just seen, form a major part of the work of the Lands Tribunal for England and Wales. Between 1949 and 1971 the work intended for the Tribunal continued to be dealt with by official arbiters, and the Tribunal was really opened to deal with the feudal reform provisions of the Conveyancing and Feudal Reform (Scotland) Act 1970, and to handle the heavy volume of land valuation cases following previous planning legislation, together with an increasing number of appeals against valuation of land for compensation following compulsory purchase, and for taxation purposes.

The two Scottish tribunals which have no counterpart in England and Wales are the *Crofters Commission* and the *Children's Hearings.* Their function was briefly summarized in the foregoing list (marked with an asterisk), but each has a peculiar constitutional interest when considering administrative tribunals as a whole, and we shall return to them in other contexts.

It has to be remembered that in terms of population, and consequently in the volume of work, Scotland is equivalent to a region. The point becomes relevant when we come to discuss such matters as the structure, membership and staff of tribunals, when it is important to avoid false comparisons between the two countries. The following are examples of comparative figures:

| | *England and Wales* | *Scotland* |
|---|---|---|
| Redundancy payments | 8,651 | 832 |
| Pensions | 3,463 | 297 |
| Rent assessment | 3,908 | 392 |

The classification which we have attempted has included almost all the tribunals currently under the supervision of the Council on Tribunals. Only three small and esoteric tribunals have slipped through the net, and fortunately one of these has never been constituted and the other two have never met. Our survey has therefore been reasonably complete. It calls, however, for a number of comments.

*First*, tribunals are often only one aspect (sometimes a relatively insignificant one) of the system of administration in their particular field. For example, in 1970 insurance officers determined 17½ million claims for national insurance, industrial injuries and family allowance benefits, but only 36,000 went to a tribunal on appeal. The converse of this is provided by the Civil Aviation Authority, which is dominant in air transport administration in that it is a tribunal of first resort, i.e. one cannot begin to operate a commercial airline without first applying to it.

*Second*, the classification also conceals the *metamorphosis* which is characteristic of some tribunals and which largely explains their present jurisdiction. The example of the gradual enlargement of the industrial tribunals was mentioned on p. 46, but the classic example is perhaps the Transport Tribunal. Early attempts to use the judges as railway commissioners and the subsequent establishment of the Railway and Canal Commission have already been described (Chapter 1). In 1921 the powers of the Commission in respect of rates and charges were transferred to a Railway Rates Tribunal, a three-man tribunal consisting of a lawyer, a person experienced in commerce, and a person experienced in the operation of railways, while the Commission became more concerned with the operation and management of railways.

With the nationalization of the transport industry in 1947, control of public transport passed to a new body, the Transport Commission, which replaced the Railway and Canal Commission. The jurisdiction of the Railway Rates Tribunal was also transferred to a new body, the Transport Tribunal. This Tribunal was given jurisdiction to hear applications for increased rail fares throughout Britain but in 1962 this jurisdiction was confined to the 'London Passenger Transport Area'. In practice this meant that London Transport and British Rail (the only two authorities which operate rail services in this area) had to apply whenever they wished to increase London rail fares. Outside the London area, British Rail became free to fix such charges, terms and conditions as they think fit for passenger fares. The Tribunal had a similar jurisdiction in regard to road passenger fares in the 'London special area', but in 1969 the jurisdiction over London fares was withdrawn, leaving the Tribunal with the peculiar first instance jurisdiction already described of settling disputes over charges made for the carriage of mail, the armed forces and the police by rail.

*Third*, this classification tends to conceal underlying *affinities* between tribunals in different fields. For example, the Plant Variety

Rights Tribunal, the Performing Rights Tribunal, and the adjudicatory functions of the Controller of Patents are all primarily concerned with settling disputes between citizen and citizen in different commercial fields, but all involving the use of copyright material. Again, mental health tribunals and immigration tribunals are both concerned with the liberty of the subject, while another group, the industrial tribunals, the Police and Firemen's Pensions Tribunals and the national health service tribunals, are all concerned with working relationships and the terms and conditions of employment or service.

One apparent 'affinity' that we shall discuss more fully in the final chapter, when discussing rationalization, arises from rents and rates. It seems on the face of it surprising that these related matters should require three separate tribunals for the resolution of disputes – the rent tribunals, rent assessment committees and local valuation courts. On closer examination the matter is not so simple, as very different criteria must be employed in reaching decisions (though this need not necessarily mean that different tribunals are required to employ them). Perhaps what is really illustrated is a human characteristic of tribunals, namely that having been created to perform a very specific task they find it difficult to adapt to other tasks.

*Fourth*, the classification conceals the extent to which some tribunals are used not only to adjudicate but to further social policies. The main purpose of agricultural land tribunals, for example, is ostensibly to settle disputes between landlord and tenant by protecting tenancies, compensating tenants for improvements and allowing tenants to ignore covenants which impede the proper use of agricultural land, while on the other hand allowing landlords to terminate tenancies in the interests of good husbandry; but in so doing they promote the social policy of efficient agricultural production. In Scotland, as we shall see, one of the main purposes of the Crofters Commission is to encourage croft farming as a policy.

Again, rent tribunals and rent assessment committees, although they appear to be concerned with the settlement of disputes between private citizens, in fact perform the regulatory function of keeping rents at a 'reasonable' or 'fair' level, and thus prevent the exploitation by landlords of an acute housing shortage. Significantly, once a tribunal has started to consider an application for a fair rent for an unfinished property it *cannot* be withdrawn.[14] In this regard rent tribunals and rent assessment committees are in fact an indirect means of controlling 'monopolistic'

[14] Rent Act 1968 s. 73(1). A tribunal enters upon consideration of a reference when its members have considered the papers. *R.* v. *Tottenham Rent Tribunal ex. p. Fryer Bros (Properties) Ltd*, [1971] 3 All E.R. 563.

situations, particularly, in the case of the former, in regard to security of tenure (as are the agricultural land tribunals). Other tribunals which have an underlying social aim of preventing the exploitation of monopolies are the Plant Variety Rights Tribunal, the Performing Rights Tribunal, and (in relation to compulsory licensing) the Comptroller General of Patents and the Patent Appeal Tribunal.

Another form of social policy is evident in the trade levy tribunals. For example, it was thought desirable that those making profits out of industry and horse-racing ought to be compelled to plough some of those profits back into improvement. And redundancy payments had two basic objectives: one economic, the other social. The economic purpose was to ensure the efficient use of manpower by redeployment; the social purpose was to compensate for loss of office, a right or privilege long recognized for higher management and now extended to all workers.[15]

Of a different order is the social policy underlying a large group of tribunals concerned with either licensing, registration, regulation or setting of standards, which have been established as an aid to interventionist policies which have sought to regulate particular activities (mostly of a trading or commercial nature) in the public interest. Examples are the tribunals dealing with independent schools, children's voluntary homes, milk and dairies, wireless telegraphy, nurses' training, public service and goods vehicles, air operators' and travel organizers' certificates, and licences to deal in securities. In each case the issue before the tribunal is whether the applicant has reached the particular standard required to permit him to be given (or retain) a licence.

Sometimes the tribunal is only one cog in a bigger administrative machine dealing with licensing or registration, and where this is so the administrative and judicial elements in their decisions will vary with circumstances. Thus if the Traffic Commissioners are considering an unopposed application for a licence to operate a public service vehicle they are making a largely administrative decision, though in the course of making it they have to consider judicially whether the applicant's financial standing or his maintenance facilities satisfy a required standard. Admittedly, since they are the final arbiters on whether the required standards are reached there is a large judicial element in their decision, but it does not compare with the situation where they are considering an opposed application to run a bus service. In this case there is a clear *lis inter partes*; another bus operator may maintain that

[15] Cp. the Minister in moving the Second Reading of the Bill, 711 H.C. Deb. col. 33 *et seq.*

the route was already sufficiently well served and the tribunal will have to judge on the evidence which of the two is right.

*Redundant or Little-used Tribunals*

We may conclude this discussion of the tribunals under the Council's aegis by remarking that a number of them, including some which might have been expected to play a useful part in administration or social policy, appear not to have done so. In fact a few, although provided for by statute, have never even been constituted, for example those concerned with mines and quarries and air safety. Others have heard so few cases that it may be wondered whether their existence is justified. Only five cases of fraud prevention have ever been heard, the first in 1944, a negligible number concerning performing rights or plant varieties and only two or three a year by an independent schools tribunal. In some cases (independent schools being an example) the potential occasions are obviously few; in others, for instance those dealing with various forms of copyright, occasions for dispute must be more frequent and it is arguable, though not susceptible of proof, that the mere existence of the tribunal as a potential channel of appeal encourages negotiation.

On the other hand, the fact that a tribunal may meet rarely and deal with very few cases is not necessarily a true indication of its importance or influence. To take an extreme example, the *Nurses' Training Institution Appeal Tribunal* has only met once, in 1963, since provision was first made for it in the Nurses Act 1957. The appeal which it considered, however, against withdrawal of recognition, disclosed serious weaknesses in the system of inspection by the General Nursing Council from which the withdrawal of recognition had resulted. The GNC later accepted that this was so, and the deficiencies in the system were rectified, thus bringing about a nation-wide improvement in this particular matter.[16]

Parliament, then, has defined over fifty adjudicatory bodies as tribunals by scheduling them to the Act. The criteria which it has employed in including some and excluding others are reasonably apparent, but they are not exact, and in such an amorphous subject exactitude is perhaps impossible. For example, they include one, the Milk and Dairies Tribunal, which is advisory and not adjudicatory, and others, for example the Traffic Commissioners and the National Health Service Executive Councils, whose adjudicatory functions are small in comparison with their administrative ones, and which are in

[16] The case is referred to in the Annual Report of the Council on Tribunals 1963 (para. 91).

any case concerned with the somewhat specialized adjudications of licensing or professional discipline. They include also the Transport Tribunal, which is described in its parent statute as a 'Court of Record', as well as the Lands Tribunal, which has most of the attributes of a court of law.

The number of bodies which could be added to this fifty must, of course, turn on the definition that one chooses to adopt. The following is a useful one, in that it distinguishes a tribunal from an inquiry:

> '(Tribunals) have a regular or permanent existence, a defined area of jurisdiction, and the function of deciding or adjudicating in disputes'

in contrast to public inquiries which are constituted *ad hoc* to inquire into particular matters, and are for the most part only concerned to establish acts and to make recommendations.[17] Read in context, the definition assumes that the applicant or appellant is given the opportunity of a personal hearing.

Within the definition, but outside the jurisdiction of the Council on Tribunals, there is a remarkable range of institutions.

## TRIBUNALS OUTSIDE THE ORTHODOX DEFINITION

First there is a group which has affinities with those that we have described but which for various reasons fall outside the definition. It is difficult to say precisely how many of these there may be, since there is no official register and it seems to be nobody's business to keep track of them. The last time the attempt was made to hold a 'census' was when information was sought from departments by the Franks Committee in 1956, and in the published Memoranda several exotic specimens may be located, varying from a group of referees appointed by the Minister of Agriculture to hear appeals against refusal to license bulls, boars, rams and stallions to a Shipping Claims Tribunal appointed by the Lord Chancellor, which had received one claim, in 1940; this was, however, still pending in 1956 for presumption of death and letters of administration.

We comment briefly on six of the better known, five of which incidentally post-date the Franks Committee, in order to indicate the range of possibilities:

Criminal Injuries Compensation Board
Foreign Compensation Commission

[17] J. F. Garner, *Administrative Law*, pp. 184–5. The Milk and Dairies Tribunal falls under the definition of an inquiry, except that it is a permanent body and is not constituted *ad hoc*. In other words it is neither one thing nor the other.

Gaming Board
Law Societies Legal Aid Committees
Parole Board
Attendance Allowance Board.

*The Criminal Injuries Compensation Board*

This is not an orthodox tribunal in that it has no statutory basis, having been established administratively in 1964 to consider claims for *ex gratia* compensation to the victims of crimes of violence. The reason for this arrangement was that the scheme was thought to be highly experimental. The idea of a non-statutory tribunal to deal with unusually speculative matters is of some general interest, and it is perhaps worth quoting the Home Secretary at the time:

> 'It is because of the doubt about the extent to which the scheme will be needed, and because of the difficulty of ensuring that in a pioneer scheme the public money is not wasted on undeserving or fraudulent claims, that the Government think the sensible thing to do is to start on an experimental basis which can be modified later if necessary. We propose that compensation should be paid *ex gratia* because we do not think that the State can be held liable for injuries caused to people by the acts of others.'[18]

The Board comprises a Chairman and eight members (all legally qualified) and applications are dealt with, on the papers, by a single member. The applicant may however ask for a rehearing, in which case he will be heard by three members of the Board (excluding the one who made the first determination), or alternatively the single member may refer an application to such a hearing.

There is no appeal from the decision of the three members, but it has been decided in a leading case that, contrary to the original belief, the courts have jurisdiction to correct a decision that was wrong in law.[19]

The experimental days of the scheme may be said to be over, since the Board have solved a number of early problems and have settled down to a regular volume of work. This is borne out by the fact that although at the time of writing there is no change in its non-statutory basis the Government have gone on record as saying that they hoped 'soon to begin a review of the scheme with a view to appropriate legislation'.[20]

[18] 694 H.C. Deb. col. 1127.

[19] *R.* v. *Criminal Injuries Compensation Board, ex p. Lain*, [1967] 2 All E.R. 770.

[20] 838 H.C. Deb. col. 371. The number of applications resolved during each of the three financial years to 31 March 1971 was 5,985, 6,817 and 5,893 respectively (about 90 per cent by single members) and the sums disbursed £1,672,958, £1,996,584 and £2,114,189.

*Foreign Compensation Commission*

This is described in the Commission's Annual Reports as a judicial tribunal which has also administrative functions. Its purpose is to register, and to adjudicate upon, claims submitted by British subjects as a result of nationalization or sequestration in foreign countries – claims which are met, or met in part, from moneys paid to the U.K. Government by foreign governments under treaty, or provided additionally by Parliament.

The original statute dealt with the position in Yugoslavia and Czechoslovakia, but the Commission's operations were to be extended by Order in Council to meet new situations, and Orders have in fact been made in relation to Egypt (1962 and 1971), Hungary (1963) and the USSR (1969).

There are three Commissioners in addition to the Chairman, before whom anyone may appear personally or by counsel or solicitor. In spite of what might appear to be the unpredictable and *ad hoc* nature of its work the Commission has in fact been occupied as a regular tribunal since its inception.

It falls outside the orthodox definition, however, and was expressly excepted by section 11(3) of the Tribunals and Inquiries Act 1958 from the supervision of the High Court.[21] The reason lies in the nature of its jurisdiction. The 'end product' of the Commission's work is the distribution of a lump sum. This is a fully discretionary matter, unsuited to procedural rules or to appeal, and the Commission was indeed likened by the Lord Chancellor when he spoke to the Act in Parliament to 'a Sovereign dispensing justice to his subjects'.

*The Gaming Board for Great Britain*

The Board was established by the Gaming Act 1968, and was to be the chief instrument by which the Act's intentions would be implemented. It comprises a full-time chairman and three part-time members – a former Deputy Commissioner of Metropolitan Police, the Chairman (an actuary) of a famous insurance company, a race-horse owner and a solicitor.

The distinctive feature of the Board, considered as a 'tribunal', is its unfettered power. The Act was designed to put an end to a scandalous

[21] It is not, however, so excepted in the Tribunals and Inquiries Act 1971, the position having been modified by s. 3 of the Foreign Compensation Act 1969. This followed the case of *Anisminic Ltd* v. *Foreign Compensation Commission*, in which the House of Lords intervened not in regard to a valid determination by the Commission, which was exempt from review under s. 4(4) of the Foreign Compensation Act 1950 and under s. 11(3) of the Tribunals and Inquiries Act 1958, but in regard to its jurisdiction, holding that it had acted *ultra vires*, [1969] 2 A.C. 147.

situation in which the police were finding it impossible to enforce the law, especially in the face of certain court decisions, with the result that England was becoming a 'gamblers' paradise'. Neither Government nor Opposition wished to limit the Board's powers, and indeed the Opposition spokesman, the then Mr Quintin Hogg, Q.C., would have given the Board 'as complete authority over the gaming business as the Jockey Club and the National Hunt Committee have over racing'; he several times referred to it as 'a kind of statutory Jockey Club'.[22] The Board was to keep the 'extent and character' of gaming in this country under continuous review, and it was hoped that its Annual Reports would bear comparison with those of H.M. Inspector of Constabulary relating to police and crime. Apart from this general function the Board advises the Home Secretary on regulations and the licensing authorities (i.e. the magistrates) on a wide variety of matters; it has also the three specific executive functions of granting 'certificates of consent' (a necessary preliminary to any application to magistrates for a licence), certificates for the supply and maintenance of gaming machines, and certificates for the staffs of gaming establishments. It appoints and supervises a body of inspectors.

In exercising these powers the Board may regulate its own procedure, and is merely required to *reach an opinion* about the suitability of applicants for certificates, which may not be questioned and against which there is no appeal; on the other hand the Board never refuses an application without offering a personal hearing. The Board is required to 'act fairly'[23] but it need not reveal the source of any information it may have received about applicants and it need not give reasons for its decisions.[24]

What this amounts to is that the Board's primary function is to exercise a constant supervision over gaming for profit, and to ensure that those engaged in it are capable in all respects of complying with the requirements of the law. A consequential function, though an onerous one, is adjudication; in which, however, owing to the character of its work, the Board enjoys procedural privileges.

[22] H.C. Report of Standing Committee B, 1967–8, Vol. III, Cols. 157–60.

[23] The leading case is *R.* v. *The Gaming Board for Great Britain, ex p. Benaim and Khaida* (the Crockford's case), [1970] 2 All E.R. 528, in which the Master of the Rolls, Lord Denning, defined the exact nature of 'natural justice' in relation to the Board's decisions.

[24] The House of Lords case of *Rogers* v. *The Home Secretary* and the *Gaming Board for Great Britain* v. *Rogers* [1972] 3 W.L.R. 279 established that the public interest requires that all information received by the Gaming Board for Great Britain about an applicant for the Board's certificate consenting to his applying for a licence under the Gaming Act shall be immune from disclosure by the Board and its officers. Thus the Tribunal enjoys Crown privilege.

*The Legal Aid Committees of the Law Society*

The Legal Aid and Advice Act 1949 conferred powers on the Law Society to make a scheme for the administration of the Legal Aid Fund.[25] Under the scheme a network of 'Local Committees' (forty-eight in number in England and Wales)[26] receive applications for legal aid, and, if they approve, issue legal aid certificates. These local committees fit into a framework of fourteen 'Areas', based on the administrative counties and the London Boroughs, with headquarters in the major cities. These are administered by 'Area Committees', among whose functions are those of considering appeals against the refusal of legal aid by local committees, or against the terms and conditions imposed, there being no further appeal if a local committee's decision is confirmed. Area committees also consider original applications for certificates of legal aid in the appellate courts. Both local and area committees are accordingly tribunals in terms of the broader definition.

For 'tribunal' purposes area committees are in effect panels of between sixteen and fifty-two members, comprising solicitors and barristers in the proportion of three to one, though normally a hearing would be conducted by three members. Local committees comprise such number of solicitors and barristers (not being less than five) as area committees may determine.

Appellants or applicants may appear before area committees, and may be represented, and the proceedings resemble those of a normal tribunal. The majority of cases relate to divorce and other matrimonial matters, a minority to such questions as landlord and tenant disputes, debt or claims arising out of accidents.

The administrative machinery of the scheme, in terms of premises and staff, is on a very large scale. In 1970–1, 204,297 applications were received by local committees, 159,507 civil aid certificates issued and 22,557 refused. Area committees received 2,332 applications, granted 1,290 certificates and refused 754.[27]

*The Parole Board*

The Parole Board has somewhat less affinity with orthodox tribunals than those which we have been describing, partly because in its favour-

[25] Legal Aid and Advice Scheme 1967 (published by the Law Society). Amended 1970 and 1971; the 1970 amendment brought the Lands Tribunal within the scope of legal aid. Now the Legal Aid Scheme 1973.

[26] There is a comparable, though not identical, Scheme for Scotland under the provisions of the Legal Aid and Solicitors (Scotland) Acts 1949 and 1960.

[27] Twenty-First Annual Report of the Law Society (1970–1) on Legal Aid and Advice, published by HMSO in collaboration with the Lord Chancellor's Office.

able determinations it is only advisory to the Home Secretary, and partly because it does not hold hearings but reaches its decisions on the papers. Nevertheless it occupies an independent position between the executive and the judiciary, and release on parole is subject to a two-stage adjudicatory process of great importance to prisoners. The possibility of parole applies to those serving sentences of over eighteen months, each of whom will in due course reach a 'parole eligibility date'; comparable, though not identical, arrangements exist for life prisoners. Some time before the eligibility date the first adjudication is made at the prison by a 'Local Review Committee', comprising representatives of the prison's Board of Visitors, probation officers and independent people, sitting with the Governor or his representative. Before his case is considered the prisoner may, if he wishes, have a personal interview with one member of the Committee.

The Committee's recommendations go to the Home Secretary, who may refuse parole but cannot grant it unless he is given a favourable recommendation by the Parole Board. In practice all cases which have received a favourable recommendation (about 35 per cent of the cases reviewed locally in 1971), together with some others not so recommended but which have special features meriting further consideration (about 10 per cent) are referred to the Board. Unfavourable recommendations by the Board in these cases virtually amount to decisions, as the Home Secretary has no option but to refuse parole. In 1971 the Board did not recommend parole in 22·5 per cent of the cases referred to it as having been considered suitable for parole by local review committees, and in over 70 per cent of the cases referred to it notwithstanding an unfavourable local recommendation.

The Board consists of a Chairman and thirty-one members drawn from the legal, medical, educational, academic and other professions, together with a number of lay members. It is a single national body, i.e. it is not regionalized, though for convenience its members now meet in Birmingham and Manchester as well as in London.

There is a separate Parole Board for Scotland.

*The Attendance Allowance Board*

This Board, established by the National Insurance (Old persons' and widows' pensions and attendance allowance) Act 1970, is an interesting example of a statutory body which combines administrative, advisory and judicial functions. It consists of experienced medical practioners and a member from outside the medical profession, all of whom have a specialized concern with the needs of the disabled, and their ultimate purpose is to determine claims by disabled people for the statutory allowance for help with the domestic mechanics of life. They are responsible for the general oversight of the scheme, and section 5(1) (b) of the Act gives them the specific task of *advising* the Secretary of State on how it is working.

Their judicial function is one which they must in the nature of things very largely delegate, and the Act allows them to refer individual cases for investigation, or to delegate their own powers of decision, to one or more medical practitioners, who operate from the Department's regional centres. Delegated powers are also given to medical officers at the Department's Central Office at Blackpool both as to initial claims and to applications for review (i.e. appeals). But in spite of this general delegation the Board themselves scrutinize a sample of decisions made by delegates with a view to ensuring uniformity and consistency of standards, review applications where their delegates are unable to reach conclusions, and may themselves make initial decisions.

There is a right of appeal on a question of law to the National Insurance Commissioner against decisions given on review applications.

The Board is not a designated tribunal, and since its normal outward manifestation consists in a doctor visiting the home of someone who is bed-ridden or house-bound this is perhaps understandable. But it exemplifies the making of decisions which cross the borderline between being administrative and being judicial.

## DOMESTIC TRIBUNALS

There is then a large group of voluntary associations, indeterminate in number, which in one aspect of their activities may be considered as tribunals, in that they have the power to inflict penalties on their members affecting their 'property' (in the widest sense) or their reputations. Professional associations, trade unions and clubs are obvious examples.

As to the professions, Parliament has from time to time thought fit to intervene in the public interest by establishing a register of practitioners of particular professions, and by providing a legislative framework within which their governing bodies shall take disciplinary action against members guilty of criminal offences or professional misconduct. This was first done in the Medical Act 1858 and most recently in the Medical Ancillaries Act 1960, which embraced certain professions 'supplementary to medicine', namely chiropodists, dieticians, therapists, remedial gymnasts and radiographers. In the century between these dates other legislation had also brought dentists, pharmacists, veterinary surgeons, nurses, midwives and opticians within the statutory fold, as well as solicitors and architects. Parliament does not purport to say how discipline shall be exercised, this being left to such bodies as the General Medical Council and the Council of the Law Society, but in this small, well-defined group of professions it has accepted ultimate responsibility, through legislation, for protecting the public.

Outside the group, the numbers of voluntary organizations which can impose penalties on their members in more or less serious degrees is almost unlimited. Trade unions are an obvious example, and in these days when certain forms of sport are 'big business' such bodies as the Football Association and the Jockey Club can fine, suspend or even take away a man's livelihood; and this power to penalize continues with diminishing seriousness through the whole gamut of clubs and social organizations. It is the responsibility of these associations to manage their affairs as they think best, and generally speaking the courts will only intervene if it can be shown that they have failed to comply with their own rules, or have acted in breach of contract or without regard to natural justice.[28] But they are tribunals by definition.

## THE MAGISTRATES' COURTS

The Franks Report refers to 'tribunals other than the ordinary courts of law'. Generally speaking magistrates' courts are ordinary courts of law, though they have also licensing and matrimonial functions, but what is of particular interest in this context is that over a very wide range of statutes they are given what amounts to the function of an appellate tribunal against the decisions or orders of local authorities. The point is possibly of academic rather than practical importance, since they very rarely exercise these powers and many experienced magistrates would probably not even know that they existed. Nevertheless the laws governing highways, public works and public health are rich in such provisions.

For example the Highways Act 1959 contains no fewer than fifteen sections which allow an appeal to the justices against the decisions of local authorities in such matters as street works, building construction, powers of entry, traffic signs, overhanging trees, advertising, overflowing water, fencing and many other matters. A few such cases do in fact come before the magistrates from time to time, especially in relation to private roads, but for the most part these are planning matters, and

[28] The subject has been thoroughly discussed in the literature of administrative law, and is only mentioned here for completeness. See especially W. A. Robson, *Justice and Administrative Law*, Ch. 4, and J. F. Garner, *Administrative Law*, pp. 250–6.

virtually indistinguishable appeals go to the Minister under planning legislation, to be heard by an inspector.

In public health there is an occasional appeal to the magistrates under the Food and Drugs Act 1955, concerning food declared by the local health inspector to be unfit for human consumption, but similar provisions of which most magistrates would be unaware relate to local authority decisions in such varied matters as caravans, nurseries, nursing agencies, slaughter-houses, fire precautions, pet shops and the hospitalization of the chronic sick. A pedlar may appeal to the magistrates if refused a licence by a Chief Constable.

There is a certain logic in these provisions, in that persons aggrieved by the way in which a local authority exercises statutory power are given the right to appeal to a local court. Perhaps it is as well that they are not more widely used. If they were they could become an intolerable burden to the local bench.

One or two other provisions seem to have no rationale. For example, under the Road Traffic Act 1972 (sections 85(3) and 90) there is an appeal to the magistrates against the licensing authority on the ground that a driving test was not properly conducted or that a licence was unreasonably refused on grounds of disability.

Even more mysteriously, the Industrial Assurance Act 1923 (section 32), provides that a dispute between a collecting society or industrial assurance society and the member assessed or any other aggrieved person may be referred to a county court or, if the amount does not exceed £25, to a magistrates' court for settlement in accordance with the Friendly Societies Act 1896.

## THE HIGHER COURTS

What is an 'ordinary court of law'? We have already seen that the Transport Tribunal is a Court of Record[29] and academic lawyers have frequently said that there is no clear distinction between a court and a tribunal. Perhaps the 'tribunal' side of an ill-defined watershed is characterized by expertise in the subject matter and flexibility in organization and procedure. If this is accepted there are two or three bodies in the hinterland between the Lands Tribunal, the most court-like of the tribunals proper, and the High Court itself – the Restrictive Practices Court, the National Industrial Relations Court and the Patents Appeal Tribunal. All are presided over by High Court Judges

[29] A Court of Record may be defined as a Queen's Court whose acts and judicial proceedings are permanently recorded and which may (though not necessarily must) have the power to fine and imprison.

and are Courts of Record of equivalent status to the High Court, but all are assisted by persons chosen for non-legal expertise, who could perhaps be called assessors.

The Restrictive Practices Court, which must determine whether restrictive agreements exist in various fields of manufacture and commerce, and whether it is in the public interest that they should be controlled, is assisted by a panel of not more than ten persons which currently includes academic economists, company directors and trade unionists; while the National Industrial Relations Court is assisted in the wide jurisdictions conferred upon it by the 1971 Industrial Relations Act by 'other persons with special knowledge of industrial relations'.

Scotland provides, in the Scottish Land Court, a striking example of a body which it would be difficult to categorize as 'court' or 'tribunal'. It is a court in that its Chairman, who must be an advocate of the Scottish Bar of not less than ten years' standing, has the same rank and tenure of office as a Judge of the Court of Session, and in that it adopts the Court of Session's procedures and rules (including the rules of evidence). It may be thought of as a tribunal partly because its members, other than the Chairman, are chosen on account of their expert and practical knowledge of agriculture, and partly because the Court makes extensive use of delegation, whereby the expert members sit with legal assessors in various parts of Scotland, thus bringing adjudication to the doorsteps of litigants. It is concerned with those questions which in England are determined by agricultural land tribunals, but its jurisdiction is much wider and takes in almost every aspect of the regulation of relationships between landlord and tenant. Historically it has also had much to do with the regulation of crofting, in the northern crofting counties as elsewhere, but since the Crofters Commission was re-established by the Crofters (Scotland) Act 1955 its jurisdiction has diminished in these counties; however, it discharges similar responsibilities throughout the rest of rural, agricultural Scotland. It is a court whose writ runs in a wide variety of matters concerning tenancy, succession, good use, capital improvements, compensation and other matters in respect of farming land; a court which, however, resembles a tribunal in the expertise of its membership, in the subject matter of its adjudications and in the way in which it does its work.[30]

There is no particular point in trying to delineate the watershed

[30] Comparatively little has been written about the Scottish Land Court. The above facts are drawn largely from an essay by G. R. Lamb in a short collection published as *The Scottish Legal System* (C. J. Cousland & Sons, Edinburgh, sponsored by the Edinburgh and East Scotland Branch of the Royal Institute of Public Administration).

between courts and tribunals more clearly, but it is of interest that in a recent speech the Lord Chancellor adumbrated the possibility of bringing the courts and tribunals closer together. In a presidential address to the Holdsworth Club[31] he asked the question 'May it not be that a judge sitting alone has his limitations?', and went on to draw attention to the 'distinguishing mark of *ad hoc* tribunals that have so vastly proliferated' – the presence of a lawyer-chairman supported by two lay members who can overrule him.

## TRIBUNALS OF INQUIRY

For the sake of completion, and because of their name, we must conclude with some reference to the 'Tribunals of Inquiry' established by the Tribunals of Inquiry (Evidence) Act 1921, though in the common use of the words they are neither tribunals nor inquiries. They are in fact inquisitions, not concerned with law, policy or administration but for the most part with some suspected impropriety or negligence in public life.

The Act has rarely been invoked, for there have only been seventeen Tribunals since 1921, and of these five were concerned with subjects which would now be dealt with by an inquiry power of the Police Act 1964. The others have reflected the original purpose of Parliament in passing the Act, which they did hurriedly in 1921 to provide powers to deal with allegations by a Member of Parliament of misconduct by Ministry of Munitions officials. Most of the Tribunals since have mostly been concerned with alleged negligence, misconduct or corruption in a public authority, though two – into subsidence in the Doncaster Area in 1928 and into the loss of the submarine *Thetis* in 1939 – were mainly technical, and the Aberfan Tribunal was also much concerned with technical matters.

Disquiet about the working of the Act, especially in regard to the 'Radcliffe Tribunal' in 1962, and dissatisfaction with the alternative procedure of the notorious Denning inquiry into the Profumo affair, led the Government to appoint a Royal Commission in 1965 to review the workings of the Act and to consider whether Tribunals of Inquiry should be retained or replaced by some other procedure. The Commission reported in 1966,[32] but the Government have so far taken no action on its recommendations.

[31] 3 March 1972. The speech is referred to again in Chapter 10, on p. 250.

[32] Report of the Royal Commission on Tribunals of Inquiry, Cmnd. 3121, 1966.

Two pieces of evidence submitted to the Commission sum up the real purpose of Tribunals of Inquiry, and distinguish them clearly from the tribunals which are the subject of this book:

> 'An objective of paramount importance is the restoration of public confidence.
>
> The primary purpose of a Tribunal of Inquiry is to satisfy the public that a proper investigation has been made into a matter about which there is a great deal of public disquiet'.[33]

[33] Mr Justice Milmo, Documentary Evidence p. 41 and Mr W. L. Heywood, Oral Evidence, p. 154.

CHAPTER 3

# STRUCTURE

The purpose of this chapter is to describe how tribunals are organized, and to discuss whether their structures differ as much as they do because of the nature of their jurisdiction, the number of cases with which they deal, or merely because of accidents of history. The word 'structure' is used to embrace two sets of circumstances which are to some extent inter-related; first, whether they are organized on a national, regional or purely local basis; second, whether there is a hierarchical system in which a national or regional president exercises authority or whether there is simply a network of tribunals acting in isolation from each other.

A first glance may suggest that tribunals are indeed either nationally, regionally or locally based, but as so often happens convenient simplifications have soon to be abandoned, since exceptions become so frequent that what emerges is not so much a three-fold division as a spectrum embracing almost as many tribunals as there are shades of colour. Nevertheless the national, regional and local classification is at least useful as a starting point.

## 'NATIONALLY-BASED TRIBUNALS'

These are the single tribunals, with a jurisdiction extending to the whole of Great Britain but whose sole headquarters are in London, where they normally meet. They fall into three rather different groups:

*Firstly*, there are two which are distinct by virtue of being solely or predominantly 'courts of appeal' from lower tribunals – the National Insurance Commissioners and the Immigration Appeal Tribunal.[1]

The National Insurance Commissioners are the final authority for determining appeals from decisions of some 200 national insurance local tribunals or, on points of law, from 13 medical appeal tribunals

[1] The Immigration Appeal Tribunal has an original jurisdiction in the rare cases of appeal under s. 15(7) of the Immigration Act 1971 (only three hearings up to June 1972), which are concerned with deportation. The Lands Tribunal exercises original and appellate jurisdictions in more equal proportions.

sitting in 22 different centres, and their headquarters are at 6 Grosvenor Gardens, SW1. Straightway a partial exception has to be noted, since although this is a single tribunal for Great Britain two Commissioners work, for convenience and in recognition of national susceptibilities, in Edinburgh and Cardiff, and appellants living in the north or west of England may go to one or the other.

The Immigration Appeal Tribunal (Thanet House, Strand, WC2) hears appeals against the decisions of adjudicators stationed in various parts of the country.

*Secondly*, there are four tribunals with national jurisdictions which do not operate outside London – the Civil Aviation Authority, the Betting Levy Appeal Tribunal, the Transport Tribunal and the Comptroller General of Patents, Designs and Trade Marks. The last named, although it lies within the ambit of this survey, is exceptional in that the 'tribunal' is a civil servant acting judicially at a public hearing, from whose decision appeal lies to a High Court judge sitting alone; the Comptroller delegates his function to Assistant Comptrollers and 'superintending examiners', or, in the case of hearings about design, to established civil servants of normal grades. These various officials are in fairly continuous session at the Patent Office in Chancery Lane, and between them they hear nearly 7,000 cases a year, mostly about trade marks.

The Civil Aviation Authority is an administrative – and within a broad framework set out in the Act a policy-making – body, so that its adjudicatory functions, which relate to licensing, are incidental to considerably wider purposes. It does not, however, like its predecessor the Air Transport Licensing Board, receive representations or complaints. As a tribunal it hears contested applications from air service operators (a quorum of one with an appeal to the Minister). It also deals with written submissions from appellants against the refusal of various kinds of individual licence (e.g. pilots or maintenance engineers).

The Betting Levy Appeal Tribunal (17 Southampton Row, WC2) has the simple function of hearing appeals by bookmakers against assessments made upon them by the Horserace Betting Levy Board – work analagous in a restricted field to that of the General Commissioners of Income Tax. It comprises a chairman and two members, all part-time, and although it heard 101 appeals in 1970 it held few sittings and the scale of its work is not of an order to raise problems of organization.

Lastly in this group there is the Transport Tribunal (York Buildings, WC2). As we have already noted, it was established as the Railway Rates Tribunal in 1921 with wide jurisdiction, but the jurisdiction of what is now its Railway Rates Division has contracted to two matters – the carriage of mail and the transport of the armed forces and police; the Road Haulage Division, established by the Transport Act 1962, exercises appellate jurisdiction in appeals against the decisions of the Licensing Authorities of the eleven Traffic Areas relating to the carriage of goods by road. Legislation has completely eroded its railway functions, and the Transport Act 1968 has at least temporarily reduced the number of road haulage appeals to a very small number, partly because sections 71–84 of the Act (which would greatly have increased the number of opposed applications for licences) have not been activated. Accordingly the Tribunal is currently working well below its potential capacity. Although this is a single tribunal for Great Britain there is, for convenience, a special panel of members for Scotland, and Scottish cases are heard in Edinburgh, and to that extent the Tribunal does operate outside London.

*Thirdly*, there are three tribunals which are London-based, but which go 'on circuit', the Lands Tribunal, the Special Commissioners of Income Tax and the Pensions Appeal Tribunals.

The Lands Tribunal (3 Hanover Square, W1) resembles a specialized court of law, though rather less than half the cases of which it disposes come to a formal hearing (in 1970, for example, 679 out of 1,511). It was established on 1 January 1950 to replace various panels of arbitrators, referees and others by a permanent judicial body composed partly of lawyers and partly of valuers, and it exercises the very wide jurisdiction in matters relating to land that was described on p. 53. The Tribunal's jurisdiction covers England and Wales[2] and arrangements are made for members to go on circuit where it seems appropriate to hold hearings away from London. In an average year they hear 200–250 cases in provincial towns. Various circumstances determine the planning of provincial tours by members, but in principle they will go to any town, of whatever size, which is near the land in question, provided suitable accommodation can be arranged.

The Special Commissioners of Income Tax (Turnstile House, Holborn, WC1) have a long history of changing functions, which have in the past included assessment and executive work, but since 1964 they have simply been an appeal tribunal, partly on certain specific aspects of taxation, including surtax, and partly as an alternative – available to all appellants – to the General Commissioners (see p. 80 below). There are eight full-time Commissioners, drawn from the legal profession and the civil service, of whom the 'Presiding Special Commissioner' is *primus inter pares* rather than president. The Commissioners' jurisdic-

[2] As was stated on p. 54 a Lands Tribunal for Scotland, with somewhat different purposes, was created on 1 April 1972.

tion is over the United Kingdom, but for historical reasons they exercise the functions of the General Commissioners in Northern Ireland, where in a recent year their sittings totalled 55 days. Otherwise they were on circuit in Scotland for 8 days and in various towns in England for 33, disposing of some 2,500 cases.

Finally there are the Pensions Appeal Tribunals (Staffordshire House, Store Street, Tottenham Court Road, WI) which exercise two distinct kinds of jurisdiction – 'entitlement' and 'assessment'. The former deals with appeals from decisions of the Department of Health and Social Security that disability is not attributable to military or civil defence service, and the latter with appeals from the Department against the degree of disablement which is held to have arisen from such service. The nature of these jurisdictions involves a somewhat elaborate system of panels (see p. 84 below). Constitutionally the Tribunals' jurisdiction covers England and Wales, but because appellants are normally suffering from some degree of illness or disability tribunals meet regularly in nine provincial centres; moreover members of the panels live in all parts of the country and normally sit in the centre nearest to where they live. Accordingly the Tribunal has the appearance of being regionally based, but there are no regional offices or staff and in fact it is a national tribunal, with its administration concentrated in London.

## 'REGIONALLY'-BASED TRIBUNALS

The versatile word 'region' is widely used in Great Britain, but it has no precise meaning. The administrative regions used by most government departments roughly coincide, but because of the disparate nature of their functions they do not do so exactly, with the result that there are, for example, eight regions of the Ministry of Agriculture, Fisheries and Food but twelve of the Department of Health and Social Security; eleven Traffic Areas but fifteen Regional Hospital Boards. Even the regional 'capitals' may be in different towns for different purposes. Birmingham is a natural centre for the West Midlands and almost every government department has its regional office in that city – indeed in one particular quarter of the city.[3] On the other hand the Eastern Counties of England have always presented an administrative problem, so that some government regional offices are in Cambridge and others in Nottingham; while certain *tribunals* have decided that neither meets their need, so that the Rent Assessment Panel is administered from Ipswich and the Industrial Tribunal from Bury St Edmunds. In saying that certain tribunals are organized 'regionally', therefore, we simply

[3] Though the MAFF regional office is in the country west of Wolverhampton.

mean that they are based on a limited number of provincial centres, in each of which there is a local staff.

The most interesting in the context of this chapter, by virtue of the 'presidential' system which is built into their structure, are the industrial tribunals and the rent assessment committees, and we shall revert to them at the conclusion of this general review; the others are the Traffic Commissioners, the industrial injuries medical appeal tribunals, the mental health tribunals and the agricultural land tribunals.

The industrial tribunals work in a constantly changing *milieu* and their structure is currently subject to radical alterations designed to deal with their expanding frontiers. The unusual number of separate jurisdictions which they had already acquired (p. 46) were increased by the Industrial Relations Act 1971, and at the time of writing the seven provincial centres in which they were originally established are in the process of being increased to more than twice that number.

Chairmen presiding in the provincial centres are not regional presidents in the formal sense, though in fact they enjoy a great deal of autonomy and are wholly responsible for the conduct of tribunals in their regions and for the administration of their regional offices. There is, however, a national President, who sits as a chairman himself and advises his colleagues; he lays down the general lines of national policy and ensures uniformity of practice and procedure. The rapid growth of the Tribunal makes it difficult to give accurate figures, but at the time of writing there were five chairmen in London, other than the President, and twenty in the regions; there were also about sixty part-time chairmen.

Rent assessment committees have the duty of determining a 'fair' rent in terms of the Rent Act 1968 for regulated tenancies of unfurnished dwellings below £400 rateable value in London and £200 elsewhere, in cases where there has been an objection to a rent officer's determination. Their structural organization is based on sixteen 'Panel Areas', though in regional capitals their accommodation is always separate from that of the Department of the Environment, and they hold their hearings at a number of different towns within the panel areas. The pattern departs from the standard regional pattern mainly because of the greater subdivision of south-east England, where there are separate panel offices at Luton, Reading, Maidstone, Brighton and Southampton.

There is a presidential system at 'regional' level, though there are relatively few full-time appointments.[4] The aim is to have a president

[4] The first full-time appointment was that of the legally qualified Vice-President of the London Area, the President himself doing a 'most-time' rather than a part-time job; but at the time of writing there is a growing number of full-time appointments.

and one, two or three vice-presidents in each panel area, with sufficient chairmen and members to spread the work in accordance with the availability of each individual, an organization which has been found appropriate to the 3,000 or more cases which the committees hear each year. Administration is provided by departmental civil servants, seconded to panel offices, but the president is able to give guidance and advice to his panel members and to ensure uniformity of procedure and consistency of policy.

There is no national president, but by convention the London President acts in this capacity, and indeed convenes and chairs six-monthly meetings of area presidents as well as being in frequent touch with them individually. Broadly speaking, therefore, the rent assessment panels and committees exemplify a complete (i.e. national and regional) presidential system.

At this point one may properly include the rent tribunals, on the ground that although there are forty-two of them, and thus they can hardly be called 'regional', they are nevertheless organized so as to fall within the sixteen areas of the rent assessment panels, from whose membership they are now appointed by the regional president. Outside London (where the work of tribunals and committees alike is greater than that for the rest of the country) the two are virtually integrated, and future legislation arising from the Report of the Francis Committee[5] may make the integration complete.

It is also worth adding at this point (though the matter is discussed more fully at p. 245) that rent assessment panels also provide the membership of rent scrutiny boards to scrutinize fair rent assessments for council houses; but these boards, which have an audit rather than a judicial function, are not included in the Schedules to the Tribunals and Inquiries Act 1971.

The Traffic Commissioners, established by the Road Transport Act 1930, superseded local authorities as the body for licensing and regulating public service vehicles, and their organization is determined by the terms of the Act, which divided England and Wales into eleven 'Traffic Areas'. The Commissioners are a tribunal, in the stricter judicial sense, in that they determine opposed applications for (passenger) road service vehicles. They also make decisions granting unopposed licences, or varying and revoking licences, which some would call 'administrative', but which have to be announced at a public hearing, and reasons for which have to be given in cases of refusal. The Commissioners are further responsible, in conjunction with the technical officers of the Department of the Environment, for a constant volume

[5] Report of the Committee on the Rent Acts, Cmnd. 4609.

of routine work concerned with safety and the inspection and maintenance of vehicles. They are in fact an administrative body exercising judicial functions, and in this they bear some resemblance to the nationally based Civil Aviation Authority. There is however no national president, the eleven chairmen being full-time servants of the Crown, who in addition to their public hearings decide certain applications of a minor kind, where no right of objection has been exercised, in chambers. They have full administrative responsibility in their respective regions, but none is *primus inter pares*, and the fact of being servants of the Crown places them outside the presidential system, which normally implies that presidents have an overtly independent status. The Commissioners hold quarterly conferences to discuss new legislation and problems of mutual interest, under a rotating chairmanship.

The chairmen also hold the personal appointment of 'licensing authority' for goods traffic by road, thus constituting a separate jurisdiction over the licences both of commercial operators and of 'heavy goods vehicle' drivers; in which capacity they have part-time deputies.

Of the four remaining tribunals which are regionally based, the medical appeal tribunals accord geographically with the twelve regions of the Department of Health and Social Security (though they actually meet in twenty-two different centres), the mental health review tribunals with the fifteen Regional Hospital Board Areas and the agricultural land tribunals with the eight regions of the Ministry of Agriculture.

Medical appeal tribunals determine over 20,000 appeals a year, and chairmen may well sit daily in heavily populated areas, though elsewhere weekly or fortnightly sittings would be normal. There are, however, no full-time appointments, and administrative arrangements are in the hands of the staff of Regional Controllers of the DHSS.

Mental health review tribunals exist as a safeguard for patients suffering from mental disorders and compulsorily detained in mental nursing homes and hospitals, including Broadmoor or Rampton Hospitals. They consider applications for review from patients or their relatives against continued detention, and also advise the Secretary of State on any cases he may refer to them. Over a thousand such applications and references were dealt with in 1971. There are no full-time appointments. A Regional Chairman is in administrative charge of the tribunal in each region, but he is not deeply involved in routine administration, which is provided by the staff of the Regional Hospital Boards. He has, however, the duty of selecting panels appropriate to particular hearings. The legal members who preside at the hearings are customarily known as 'presidents'.

The agricultural land tribunals were originally appeal tribunals from the 'War Ags.' of the Second World War and their successors the County Agricultural Executive Committees. They now exercise a wide jurisdiction under the various Agriculture and Agricultural Holdings Acts, but in practice most of their hundred or so cases during an average year are concerned with notices to tenant farmers to quit or with directions to carry out drainage works under a later statute, the Land Drainage Act 1961. The eight regional chairmen, who are legally qualified, are all part-time and their hearing duties are not heavy, though they have advisory duties and deal with interlocutory applications. For the most part, however, ordinary administration is a function of the Ministry's Regional Offices.

## SPECIAL AREAS

It is possible that a tribunal, being a body with 'special' adjudicatory powers, may have to go wherever the 'special' circumstances exist. Thus the immigration adjudicators, a tribunal hearing appeals against decisions of the immigration control authorities, were originally stationed full-time at two airports, three seaports, and two industrial areas as well as in central London. The Immigration Act 1971 diminished jurisdiction at the port of entry (adjudicators being retained only at Dover and Southampton), and at the time of writing the Chief Adjudicator is embarking on an embryo regional organization, in terms broadly of south, midlands and north.[6] There are twenty full-time adjudicators elsewhere, each of whom is a 'tribunal'. Since between them they currently dispose of well over 2,000 cases a year, the scale of the organization is not inconsiderable, and the Chief Adjudicator is in practice also the chief administrator. The tribunal exemplifies flexibility in the structure of adjudication, and is also an illustration of the presidential system, although the term is not used.

Another example of a special area is provided by the Crofters Commission in Scotland, which is confined geographically to the seven northern counties. It is primarily an administrative body, established to further a particular agricultural policy in these crofting areas, but it has important judicial functions relating to such matters as the ownership, letting, sub-division and efficient use of crofts. It has a full-time chairman and six part-time members, and exercises its tribunal functions either at its regular monthly meeting at a central place or by delegation to two of its members in prescribed areas within the counties concerned.

[6] The Immigration *Appeal Tribunal* is of course a single national body, in London.

## 'LOCALLY'-BASED TRIBUNALS

There remain a number of tribunals which either derive from the areas of local authorities, or are based on some smaller *ad hoc* area designed to meet the requirements of their work.

Among the first group are the local valuation courts, the National Health Service Executive Councils and service committees and a new Scottish tribunal, the 'Children's Hearings'.

The structure of the local valuation courts, which in recent years have been dealing with between 25,000 and 35,000 appeals annually, is unusual, and derives from the fact that they inherited their functions from local government. Until the Local Government Act 1948 valuations for rating were made by the rating authorities themselves, and appeals lay to assessment committees, whose areas normally included several rating authorities (there being a further right of appeal to Quarter Sessions). The 1948 Act transferred the function of valuing to the Inland Revenue, the District Valuer being an official of that Department, and local valuation courts replaced assessment committees as the appellate body, with a further appeal to the Lands Tribunal. The whole process was divorced from the local authorities, but local government influence remains strong, both in the fact that a high proportion of councillors continue to serve in the new courts and that the geographical areas are based on those of the old assessment committees.[7]

There are in fact ninety-five panel areas in England and Wales, and one of their unusual features is that subject to the final approval of the Secretary of State for the Environment the panels draw up their own internal constitutions. With few exceptions these are joint schemes between county and county borough councils. Each court exists independently of any other, and there is no national or regional direction, though in practice occasional conferences are held by chairmen and clerks on a 'regional' basis, the word in this context meaning little more than north, west and south.

The NHS Executive Councils are based straightforwardly on 132 local health authorities. There are accordingly 528 service committees, since each Council has a medical, a dental, a pharmaceutical and an ophthalmic committee which investigates allegations, by members of the public or otherwise, that doctors and others have failed to comply with the terms of service of their contracts with the Executive Council. There is a chairman, vice-chairman and thirty members on each Council and a chairman and six members on each committee, but there is no organiza-

[7] But see p. 296 et seq.

tion linking the 132 Councils together and no hierarchical system. 826 allegations were investigated through this system in 1971.

Children's Hearings were authorized by Part III of the Social Work (Scotland) Act 1968 and became operative on 15 April 1971. They consider the circumstances of children referred to them by an official known as a 'reporter' as being in need of compulsory measures of care. They comprise fifty-two 'children's panels' which have jurisdiction within the geographical areas of local authorities, which also appoint the reporter and are responsible for general administrative arrangements. This is a tribunal of considerable importance which heard nearly 6000 cases in its first year.

The other tribunals which are locally based but are unconnected with local authorities are those which carry the heaviest case-loads of all, namely the social security tribunals and the General Commissioners of Income Tax.

Of the former, the national insurance local tribunals, which hear nearly 30,000 insurance and over 6,000 industrial injury cases in an average year, are not in fact isolated from the Department's regional organization, since they are sited for general convenience near their local offices,[8] and Assistant Regional Controllers are responsible for their organization. But they are 'local' in the sense that they are numerous, that there is no national or regional president and that they accordingly exist in isolation from each other. There are 120 supplementary benefit tribunals[9] dealing with a steadily rising volume of work (recently increased by the provision for family income supplementation) of the order of 15,000 hearings in 1968 but approaching 30,000 in 1971.

Finally, the General Commissioners of Income Tax are, as we have seen (pp. 24 and 51) a unique judicial institution. Today they are an appeal tribunal against assessments and certain other decisions of the Inspector. The great bulk of their work is, however, concerned with routine 'delay cases', where the taxpayer has given notice of appeal but for one reason or another has failed to follow it up. The Commissioners have power to award penalties for various tax offences. Their appointment was transferred from the Land Tax Commissioners to the Lord Chancellor on the recommendation of the Franks Committee. Their organization reflects their history, as their 'divisions' are usually groups of parishes, sometimes bearing the name of an ancient local church

[8] Frequently in the same building as the local offices. This is deprecated by the Department but is forced on them by the difficulty of finding alternative accommodation.

[9] Reduced from 151 on 1 July 1971 in order to eliminate delays caused by the accumulation of cases in little-used hearing centres, and to accelerate the flow of work.

rather than the populous industrial or commercial area which they serve. There were until recently 652 such divisions in England and Wales, but a programme of amalgamation is in hand which had reduced them to 460 at the time of writing and will eventually reduce them to about 400. There is of course no regional or presidential system. Like the local valuation courts the General Commissioners appoint their own Clerk – normally a solicitor with experience of tax work – and they are not served by the staff of the Board of Inland Revenue.

## INFLUENCES ON STRUCTURE

Since tribunals were created at widely different times and for widely differing purposes, and usually with narrow jurisdictions, it is not to be expected that their organization would follow any uniform plan. A few generalizations may be made about the influences which have helped to fashion the present structure; in a later chapter we will explore the question whether a more coherent one would be possible or advantageous.

The first and most obvious influence on structure is the *case-load*, in terms of the number of applications or appeals received and the average time required to deal with each; the proportion withdrawn or simply abandoned is also relevant, since the time involved in the processing of such cases is little less than that of those which actually come to a hearing.

There is first the group whose average annual hearings run regularly into five figures (15–30,000), and who get through their work by meeting in a great many places as well as (in populous areas) having frequent sessions and large panels on which to draw in order to spread the load. These are the tribunals dealing with national insurance, supplementary benefit, rates and furnished rents.[10] Somewhat surprisingly, the national insurance medical appeal tribunals also deal with something of the order of 20,000 – surprisingly, because they meet in only twenty-two centres where facilities for medical examination are available and medical consultants within reach.

Most of these tribunals can, without detriment, get through their cases quickly, though the complaint has been made that medical appeal tribunals, under pressure for a quick decision, may sometimes

[10] Official statistics also show the Traffic Commissioners as dealing with upwards of 17,000 cases in a year, but this figure is misleading. The vast majority of these are unopposed applications, and it merely happens that the regulations require details to be read out at a hearing of the Commissioners. The number of opposed cases, requiring adjudication after a hearing, is probably no more than a tenth of the larger figure.

sacrifice thoroughness to speed. Sometimes this criticism is justified; sometimes it is ill-informed, as claimants often seem to expect a medical examination when it is not necessary. For the rest the occasional case, especially if an appellant is legally represented, may take an hour, but some only a few minutes, and it is possible to deal with six or eight in a half day. By contrast the industrial tribunals can only manage a statistical average of less than three a day in redundancy cases, though these tribunals have a high proportion of late withdrawals, which reduces the average of hearings. As we have said, these withdrawn cases may fairly be included in the case load since an equal amount of preparation has gone into them; moreover it is often the fact of seeing the terms of a dispute officially set out, with the prospect of having to make or defend a case in public, that is the cause of withdrawal by the claimant, though late settlements by employers are generally attributable to late agreement by the Department of Employment to accept responsibility for rebate. Some tribunals, on the other hand, may only hear one case at any given session; this could apply to such diverse tribunals as agricultural land, mental health review or the Special Commissioners of Income Tax, while an industrial tribunal needs to set aside several days for a reference under the Docks and Harbours Act.

A second influence is the *nature of the jurisdiction.* At one extreme, the Comptroller of Patents, the Civil Aviation Authority or the Lands Tribunal are generally hearing applications or appeals from people or firms of good financial standing, in matters involving large sums of money and professional representation, and it is not inappropriate that they should come to a central tribunal in the capital.[11] In the middle, so to speak, applicants for licences to run a bus service, or farmers concerned with a notice to quit or a drainage problem, can reasonably be expected to travel to a regional centre, though the Traffic Commissioners do in fact go on circuit; while at the other extreme supplementary benefit appeal tribunals are dealing with the poorest and least mobile, and it is appropriate that the tribunals should as far as possible go to the appellant, that is to say they should meet in as many places as possible.

This, however, raises a problem of some difficulty, which particularly affects supplementary benefit and national insurance local tribunals, which have it in common that a high proportion of appellants – as many as 50 per cent overall – simply fail to appear and offer no explana-

[11] The reason why the Lands Tribunal so frequently goes 'on circuit' is as much to enable it to inspect the land involved as to save appellants a journey to London. Incidentally, the 'small man' does often apply to this Tribunal, which is the only one for which legal aid is available.

tion. The reasons for this are not yet thoroughly understood,[12] but a contributory factor seems to be distance. In rural or semi-rural areas the proportion of absentees is very high indeed, and there is evidence that the journey by train or bus is a deterrent. Travelling expenses can be claimed, and if ready cash is not available a travelling warrant can be drawn, but not surprisingly people already disheartened by financial difficulties are easily discouraged by a barrier of this kind. It is reasonable to suppose that the more places in which a tribunal met the more appellants there would be;[13] but there is obviously a limit to what can be done, and, as we have seen, the supplementary benefit tribunals have recently been reduced in number from 150 to 120 because some of the outlying ones were not only extravagant in terms of overhead cost[14] but were not able to provide members of panels with a sufficient volume of regular work to justify their appointments and to give them adequate experience of adjudication.

A closely allied problem is that of publicity. For example, there is evidence that when a social security or rent tribunal has been the subject of a television programme there is a sudden increase in appeals. Although this soon dies away it is evident that if tribunals were to set out to attract business, so to speak, by increasing the number of tribunal points and by advertising their wares, they could vastly increase their 'intake'. It is a somewhat delicate matter of judgment how far there is an obligation (of a statutory-cum-moral kind) to *encourage* appeals, as distinct from dealing with those which arise from a reasonable service of information – what in fact is reasonable encouragement or a reasonable amount of information?

Finally, one cannot avoid the influence of *historical background*, or more specifically of when a tribunal in its present or some previous form was inaugurated. Leaving aside the General Commissioners of Income Tax, the oldest tribunals today are those dealing with supplementary benefit, national insurance and local rates; one common feature of all three is that there is no hierarchical structure, while in the case of the first two administrative arrangements for hearings are

[12] It is hoped that current research at the University of Newcastle-upon-Tyne will throw light on what is probably a fairly complex matter. Another reason is undoubtedly that it costs nothing to appeal, and that many appeals are made on impulse.

[13] Cp. Annual Report of the Council on Tribunals 1960 (para. 61) on the subject of rent tribunals – 'There are indications that in some areas amalgamation of tribunals has led to the closing down of local offices and this in turn has led to a marked falling off in applications from the areas affected'.

[14] The alternatives were either keep appellants waiting a long time for their cases to be heard, which is impossible in cases of urgent need, or to convene a tribunal at some considerable cost to hear an individual case.

made by officers in the parent department, and in that of the third there is a very close relationship with local government. The more modern tribunals, on the other hand, such as rent assessment committees, industrial tribunals and the immigration adjudicators and Immigration Appeal Tribunal, are more ostensibly independent of a parent department and their organization stems from a national president. It is tempting to postulate progression from one type of tribunal to another, from a lower to a higher form of evolution, so to speak. But it would be difficult to sustain such a hypothesis, and the mundane truth is that tribunals have continued as they happen to have begun, and that the later tribunals are regional, presidential and more manifestly independent simply because they were created at relatively recent dates, when the general concept of a tribunal had become more mature and sophisticated, and when the influences of the Franks Report and of the Council on Tribunals had begun to make themselves felt.

## THE PRESIDENTIAL SYSTEM

Certainly the most interesting development from the structural point of view has been the recent application of the presidential idea to tribunals which meet locally in a great many different places. The earlier presidential tribunals were those which were nationally based, such as the Chief Insurance Commissioner or the Lands and Pensions Appeal Tribunals. The first of these holds hearings in Edinburgh and Cardiff and the others meet in many parts of the country on circuit, but they have no provincial offices or staff, and are London-based.

The position of the Chief Insurance Commissioner (there are nine other commissioners) is somewhat less than that of 'president' as the word is now used, but considerably more than *primus inter pares*. Thus in matters of adjudication his position is equal to that of any other Commissioner, and he has no power to overrule their decisions. On the other hand in matters of administration his role, though not precisely differentiated from theirs by statute, is in practice substantial, and he has a few statutory powers which they have not, e.g. that of directing that an appeal be dealt with not by one commissioner but by a tribunal of three. In practice also he speaks for the whole body of Commissioners both in their external relations and in matters of internal administration.

The President of the Lands Tribunal is responsible for the selection of appropriate members for particular cases – some of his seven colleagues being lawyers and others valuers and surveyors – and for himself hearing cases which involve novel or substantial points of law.

In conjunction with the Tribunal's Registrar he is also responsible for general administration.

The President of the Pensions Appeal Tribunals is responsible nationally for the administration and proper functioning of the tribunals, and he also sits as one of the legal chairmen at entitlement appeals. The post is nominally part-time but in practice has been virtually full-time, as can be conjectured from the fact that between them the tribunals handle about 3,500 cases a year. He plays a supervisory and co-ordinating role by visiting the provincial centres from time to time, and thus keeping in personal touch with his chairmen. The actual selection of panels is more than usually complicated, since the medical members, including chairmen in the case of assessment panels, are senior medical men of consultant status; it may be necessary to arrange for particular specialists to hear particular cases and all the medical members, unless retired, are liable to be exceptionally busy men. Accordingly invitations to sit have to be arranged by a 'clerk of the lists' and issued by the Secretary, but this is done in consultation with the President.

It was, however, a new departure in the mid-1960s when industrial tribunals and rent assessment committees, whose first requirement is to be established permanently in all parts of the country, should have been based on a presidential system manifestly separated from departmental administration, instead of following the precedents of the social security and rent tribunals and being serviced by their parent departments. The circumstances in which it happened are instructive.

The two tribunals reached a similar destination by very different routes. Rent assessment committees had to be established immediately in all the main centres of population, and were launched by regional presidents, among whom the London President, by invitation of the Minister, became *primus inter pares*. The industrial tribunals more resembled the grain of mustard seed. They grew, with surprising speed, from a Tribunal originally provided for by section 12 of the Industrial Training Act 1964, the organization of which was to be controlled from London to multi-purpose tribunals with a statutory regional structure bearing the generic title 'industrial tribunals', an expression which had first appeared in the Industrial Tribunal (England and Wales) Regulations 1965, to which the Industrial Training Act had given rise.

*Industrial Tribunals*

In 1963 the Council on Tribunals was consulted by the Ministry of Labour on proposals to provide for 'industrial levy appeal tribunals' in the Industrial Training Bill which became law in 1964. The Ministry were proposing that these should be appointed locally and *ad hoc*, through the machinery of their regional offices, as was the case with the 'compensation appeal tribunals', which then existed to determine compensation for loss of office in the nationalized industries and local government. The Council thought it would be better if standing tribunals were set up for each region.[15] This would have two advantages; members would be available to serve at short notice, there being a large element of guess-work in estimating how many appeals might be forthcoming; and if the work proved onerous, or if the jurisdiction of the proposed tribunals should ever be extended, there would be the basis of a country-wide organization.

The Ministry responded to these representations by proposing that the new Tribunal should take as its model the Pensions Appeal Tribunal, the relevant point being that the Lord Chancellor should be invited to appoint a President for England and Wales, and that 'such number of tribunals should be established as the President may determine'. It will be recalled that the Pensions Appeal Tribunal is not strictly speaking a regionally-based tribunal, since it has no staff outside London; it does however meet in the principal provincial centres, and its adoption as a model did not preclude the later establishment of standing councils in each region.

The Ministry did not, however, merely take the point of the Council's criticism – they went further and adduced arguments in support of their own new proposal which could well apply to any future scheme to establish country-wide tribunals in furtherance of new social policies. These were firstly that the presidential system offered flexibility, thus countering the initial difficulty of estimating 'demand' and any later difficulty caused by fluctuation in demand (they noted, for example, that pensions appeals had themselves fluctuated very considerably from one year to another); second, that the same flexibility enabled justice to be reasonably accessible to the appellant; and third, that it was likely to promote consistency in methods and decisions, an opinion for which they drew support from the Franks Committee.[16]

In the following year, in preparation for the Redundancy Payments Act, the Ministry themselves proposed 'all-purpose' tribunals which would incorporate the training levy appeals and the new redundancy payment appeals in the same jurisdiction, and would also take over disputes on compensation arising under various statutes and under

[15] Annual Report 1963 para. 9.

[16] Report, para. 220 – 'We understand that the appointment of a President for the [Pensions Appeal] Tribunals has greatly assisted in their administration and has led to a high degree of consistency in their methods and decisions.'

section 4 of the Contracts of Employment Act 1963. The Council on Tribunals welcomed this 'concentration of jurisdiction in fewer and stronger tribunals'.[17] There was a school of thought at the time which demurred, on the ground that it was misguided to give 'special' tribunals a wide and general jurisdiction, for example to ask the same people to hear appeals against assessment of liability (training levies) as against assessment of entitlement (redundancy payments). The considerations which prevailed, however, were the great economy in administration, the opportunity to attract people of higher calibre to serve as chairmen and members, and the fact that even though the nature of the jurisdictions differed they had it in common that right decisions could well rest on an understanding of industrial conditions.

As we have seen, the frontiers of these tribunals have been extended by further legislation, and at the time of writing the regional organization is being rapidly developed to meet the anticipated demands of the Industrial Relations Act.

The possibility of extension appears to have been foreseen, for in speaking to the Bill in Parliament the Minister of Labour had this to say:

> 'I would not rule out the possibility that as the tribunals become established and gain experience, further functions relating to industrial relations might be given to them. I believe they will constitute a valuable experiment in our industrial relations system and I hope we can keep an open mind on the development of their role in the future.'[18]

This speech coincided with the appointment of the Donovan Commission, who were invited in evidence by the Ministry of Labour 'to consider whether the jurisdiction of the existing tribunals should be enlarged so as to comprise "all disputes between the individual worker and his employer" '. The Commission concluded that in principle this ought to be done,[19] and the Industrial Relations Act 1971 has fulfilled their expectations by still further enlarging the scope of their jurisdiction to include alleged 'unfair industrial practice', breach of rules or breach of duty.

*Rent Assessment Committees*

We shall be describing on p. 292 why in 1965 no tribunal in the

[17] Annual Report 1965, para. 17.

[18] 711 H.C. Deb. 26 April 1965, cols. 45–6.

[19] Royal Commission on Trade Unions and Employers' Associations. Chapter X of their Report (Cmnd. 3623, June 1968) develops their proposal to extend the jurisdiction of the industrial tribunals under the new name of 'Labour Tribunals'.

general field of valuation was thought appropriate to determine 'fair rents'. There was however an additional and more fortuitous reason why no attempt was made to consolidate the existing Rent Acts and to integrate the furnished and unfurnished jurisdictions – namely the overriding need for speed. The Milner Holland Report had disclosed the seriousness and extent of London's housing problem and the Rachman case had publicized its more scandalous aspects. It was politically necessary to give the public confidence that the problem of rents was being tackled vigorously and impartially (and incidentally to make harassment a criminal offence without further delay). The rent tribunals as they then existed did not measure up to the need. Their organization was inflexible, one tribunal being tied by statute to one locality; they had been left alone with little guidance or direction for nearly twenty years, and worked in isolation from each other; and not unnaturally they had got into a rut.

These statements are borne out by those who were closely associated with the legislation of 1965, by the experience of the Council on Tribunals and earlier by the evidence before the Franks Committee. Both the Franks Report and the Council's Annual Reports show that there were considerable divergencies both in procedural practice and in criteria of judgment between one rent tribunal and another; they show moreover that there were more complaints from the public about rent tribunals than about any other.[20] Dissatisfaction is also reflected in the number of certiorari applications in the 1950s and early 1960s, a number of which are noted in Appendix 1. Evidence of a more anecdotal kind is that when in the early 1950s members of the Council made special efforts to visit rent tribunals they tended to be received with gratified surprise that someone should show an interest in them. Until then each tribunal had ploughed a lonely furrow.

The Minister believed that the Rent Act's success would depend firstly on rent officers of high personal quality, in whom the attributes of conciliator and social worker would count for more than expertise in valuation; and secondly on an appeal machinery which would be flexible and would allow independent presidents to exercise personal leadership and initiative:

'We have decided that once we have selected the right men and women

[20] Franks Report, para. 161. See especially Annual Reports of the Council for 1959 (paras. 87–8), 1960 (para. 59) and 1961 (paras. 40–52). It will be noted that the Council pressed for the amalgamation of the two tribunals. Because of the urgency of the Government's timetable they were unable to press their point, but they were instrumental in securing a new clause on Report Stage which brought tribunals and assessment committees into an interim association, with the possibility of eventual integration (Annual Report 1965 para. 21).

for the job the best thing to do is not to smother them in detailed legal and statutory instructions, but to define their job and then rely on their power of judgment'.[21]

What the Minister appeared to have principally in mind was that there should be a flexible organization, which would allow presidents to select committees to sit wherever they were most needed; that decisions should nevertheless be consistent; and that the public should feel confidence in what was being done. His arguments were in fact close to those of the Ministry of Labour two years earlier in relation to industrial tribunals.

There was, however, an additional reason which caused the organization to be based straightway on regional presidents. All tribunals are called upon to make decisions in which on the one hand they must apply the law to the facts, but on the other hand must apply their special knowledge and experience to particular situations. The degrees in which these two different kinds of judgments will prevail must vary from one kind of tribunal to another. Industrial tribunals, for example, are largely concerned in redundancy payment cases with applying the law to the facts, though their knowledge of industrial conditions allows them to appreciate the facts more thoroughly than might an ordinary court. The Rent Act, on the other hand, requires assessment committees to take account of '. . . *all* circumstances (other than personal circumstances) and in particular the age, character and locality . . .' of a dwelling in determining what would ordinarily (ignoring the scarcity factor) be a 'fair rent'. Members of a committee would be fully justified – indeed the courts later held that they might in certain circumstances be bound[22] – to make decisions in the light of their own knowledge and experience. Accordingly in determining the structure of adjudication the Minister had to look for a body of people with comprehensive local knowledge in an area large enough to be economically administered. This circumstance, together with the others we have mentioned, pointed towards regional panels, with presidents who combined local experience and knowledge with standing in the local community.

### *Later Presidential Tribunals*

When the Immigration Appeals Act 1969 established adjudicators at strategic points in the country, with a central Appeal Tribunal in London, the scale of the arrangements was too modest to equate with

[21] 710 H.C. Deb. cols. 47–8.

[22] *Crofton Investment Trust* v. *Greater London Rent Assessment Committee*, [1967] 2 Q.B. 955. See p. 273.

those of the ubiquitous rent assessment panels and industrial tribunals as a 'presidential system'. Nevertheless it contained the essential element of manifest independence from the Home Office, and when after the 1971 Immigration Act the emphasis of the work shifted from ports of entry to the main centres of immigrant population, an embryo regional system began to be developed, with the Chief Adjudicator in London corresponding to a national President.[23]

Four years later, and in a wholly different sphere, the value added tax tribunals broke away from the traditional patterns of the Inland Revenue commissioners, general and special, and established a national and regional presidential system.

*The Advantages of the Presidential System*

Since the presidential system is finding favour as the type of organization best suited to tribunals which operate throughout the country, and which cannot be administered directly from London, and since it has been welcomed by the Council on Tribunals, we conclude by summarizing the advantages that are claimed for it. We mention them briefly, as it will be necessary to return to them from time to time in other contexts.

There is *first* the question of manifest independence from a parent department, emphasized by the fact that presidential tribunals have their own independent premises, on whose notice-boards and stationery the name of a government department does not appear. There is no evidence that tribunals which are served by departmental staff, or even held on departmental premises, are less impartial or independent than others, but their public appearance is obviously open to criticism. One might in theory suppose that it was more urgent to have a presidential system for tribunals where the issue was between citizen and state rather than between citizen and citizen, but neither rent assessment panels nor (in much of their jurisdiction) industrial tribunals quite bear this out. Manifest independence is important whatever the nature of the issue.

*Second*, there is a group of considerations which could be brought together under the general head of 'communication'. One aspect of this is communication between a department and a tribunal, which ought occasionally to take place but which is open to the criticism of interference with independent adjudication if a department communicates directly with, say, a local tribunal chairman. If there is a national or regional president who stands above the battle such communication

[23] I.e. in relation to adjudicators throughout the country. There is of course a President of the Appeal Tribunal.

is eased. Similarly there are matters on which it is easier for the Council on Tribunals to communicate with a president than with either a department or a local tribunal chairman.[24]

Another aspect of communication is the passing, up and down the line, of information and ideas. For example, the bi-annual meetings of rent assessment panel presidents under the aegis of the London President have served the dual purpose of advising the Department and of keeping their own panels in touch with current legislation, recent court decisions and the practice of panels in other parts of the country. Some presidents have devised check lists of points to be accounted for at hearings, of basic questions to which answers must always be sought, or of criteria which should be applied in particular situations, and have circulated these as *aides-mémoire* to tribunal members. Visits by a national President to the regions, by regional presidents to local tribunals, or occasional conferences of them all foster team spirit and a sense of purpose which is none the less important for being somewhat elusive to define. In the light of hindsight it is evident, for example, that the rent tribunals' deficiencies in the 1950s and early 1960s need not have developed if they had been supported by such a system.

*Third*, presidents, and particularly regional presidents, play an important part in public relations. The public becomes aware not of an amorphous department but of a prominent local figure, inevitably known for other public activities. This has a specific as well as a nebulous advantage, for the presidents' professional contacts in many fields have not only established the tribunals' reputation but have brought presidents into contact with potential new members, the recommending of whom to the national President, or to the Lord Chancellor or the Minister, can be an important responsibility.

*Fourth*, although primarily the head of a team of adjudicators a president is also head of an office administered by a seconded civil servant, whom he is able to advise and support more easily and appropriately than could the Department.

*Fifth*, and less visible on the surface, national presidents exercise a considerable influence over the development of tribunal case law through their function of selecting cases to be reported.

*Sixth*, the presidential system promotes consistency, not only of practice and procedure but of decisions, the converse of which was to be seen in the rent tribunals of the 1950s.

The advantage of flexibility which is claimed for the presidential

[24] See Annual Report 1969–70 para. 50. 'Where tribunals are organized under a President with some administrative responsibility for their working, we find that our task of keeping a general oversight . . . is very much less difficult.'

system is perhaps over-stated, for government departments can be equally flexible. For example officials of the DHSS are quick to adjust supply to demand by asking tribunal members to cross their normal frontiers should occasion arise, by establishing tribunals in new places or closing them down should they become redundant. On the other hand, presidents can stimulate, inform or broaden the experience of members, and ascertain that all are carrying a fair share of duty, more effectively than a regional office of the Department.

National insurance and supplementary benefit appeal tribunals, together with local valuation courts, are in fact the most important tribunals now remaining outside the presidential system, and the question whether they should be brought within it is one of topical importance.

CHAPTER 4

# MEMBERSHIP

We turn to the various ways in which tribunals are constituted, how their members are appointed, and what are their qualifications and terms and conditions of service.

## THE COMPOSITION OF TRIBUNALS

There are four distinguishable patterns – first, where the tribunal is an individual sitting alone; second, where all members are entitled to be present, with provision for a quorum; third, where there is a single panel from which are normally selected a chairman and one or two other members; and fourth, where there is a chairman sitting with members of 'representative' panels.

### *An Individual Sitting Alone*

The National Insurance Commissioners, of whom there are ten, sit singly to hear appeals,[1] as do the road haulage licensing authorities in traffic areas and immigration adjudicators at ports of entry or in urban centres. Representatives of the Comptroller of Patents may sit alone or with technical assessors, but they are individually responsible for decisions. The eight members of the Lands Tribunal frequently sit alone, though it may be decided that two shall sit together if a case is unusually burdensome or presents novel or difficult points of law. The eight Special Commissioners of Income Tax, on the other hand, may sit singly or may require a quorum of two according to the nature of a case.

### *A Fixed Membership and a Quorum*

There is then a group which has a fixed membership of a chairman, deputy chairman and four, five or six other members, all of whom are entitled to be present at any hearing, but where the procedural rules

[1] Though section 70(3) of the National Insurance Act 1965 provides for a tribunal of three Commissioners to hear cases involving 'a question of law of special difficulty'.

provide for a quorum. The Transport Tribunal, the Civil Aviation Authority, the national health service committees and the Performing Rights and Betting Levy Appeal Tribunals come into this category. So too may the General Commissioners of Income Tax, where the number of Commissioners appointed for a Division is small[2] though they are not statutorily required to have a chairman but merely choose one of their own number for convenience.

*The 'Single Panel' System*

In this pattern the quorum will be a chairman and one or two other members, but these are drawn from large panels instead of from a small fixed membership. The largest are those of the local valuation courts, the average size of which is about thirty, including a chairman and two deputy chairmen, members being invited by the Clerk to serve in ordinary rotation.

Medical appeal tribunals usually have two chairmen available, and members (medical practitioners of consultant status) are drawn from panels of about twenty. An unusual feature of these tribunals is that their members may serve *ex officio* in areas other than their own, and though in the nature of things this is rare it is not unknown.

Finally, the Immigration Appeal Tribunal uses the single panel system, and the General Commissioners of Income Tax may be said to do so in the larger Divisions.

*The 'Representative Panel' System*

It would be reasonable to suppose that a general panel has been preferred to a fixed membership where the volume of work is such that it has to be widely spread but where it is not necessary to distinguish between members representing different interests. On the whole the facts support this supposition. In most of the other tribunals, however, members are drawn from more than one panel, in order that interests which might be considered to be in conflict, or alternatively whose views ought to be heard, may have equal representation, with an independent chairman, normally a lawyer, to hold the balance. Although these members may be statutorily described as 'representative' the words need to be treated with reserve, as they are not there to oppose one another but to act judicially, and in practice most decisions by 'three-man' tribunals are unanimous. They are perhaps better described as 'balanced' tribunals.

[2] It is difficult to categorize the General Commissioners, since they may number as few as five in any one Division or as many (in one instance) as twenty-seven.

Among typical interests to be balanced in this way are those of employers and employed (national insurance), landowners and farmers (agricultural land),[3] consumers, producers and retailers (milk and dairies) and psychiatrists and laymen (mental health review). The pensions appeal tribunals are somewhat more elaborate, owing to the varied status of their clients; there is on the one hand a medical panel (though this in practice needs to be broken down into differing specialisms); on the other are three panels which are drawn upon according to whether the appellant is a service man, a civil defence worker or a civilian; the Schedule to the Act goes even further and provides that the lay members of a tribunal assessing disability must be of the same sex and rank during service as the claimant. The supplementary benefit appeal tribunals are also drawn from two panels, one of which could be called representative in that it consists of people 'appearing to the Minister to represent workpeople', commonly called the 'trades council representatives'; the other members are too diverse to be called representative, except in so far as they represent the local community at large.

*Industrial Tribunals – A Compromise*

Industrial tribunals, which used to be within the representative system of 'employers and employed persons', have had for political reasons to move to what is in the strict sense a single panel, but one in which the concept of balance is maintained. As a result of the TUC campaign against the Industrial Relations Act, those members of the 'employed persons' panel who were officials of trade unions were instructed by the TUC to resign, and a number did so. Accordingly the Secretary of State decided to amend the Regulations so as to abolish the two panels and to set up one panel 'of persons appearing to the Secretary of State to have knowledge or experience of employment in industry or commerce appointed by the Secretary of State after consultation with such organizations or associations of organizations representative of employers or employed persons as the Secretary of State considers to be appropriate'.[4] The intention was that there should be one panel from which the President or regional chairmen would select balanced tribunals for dealing with different types of case; it would have some resemblance to the panel of Justices of the Peace for a magistrates' court.

This arrangement has its advantages, since it underlines the point

[3] In this case there is also a smaller panel of drainage experts, to be called upon in appropriate cases.

[4] Industrial Tribunals (England & Wales) (Amendment) Regulations 1971 (S.I. 1971 No. 1660).

made above that members sitting on a tribunal ought not to regard themselves as 'representatives' of opposing interests but as judicial officers charged with the function of deciding a case upon the facts and the law. In the early days of industrial tribunals the Lord Chancellor of the day, Lord Gardiner, spoke of them in the following terms:

> 'The two members are chosen from panels appointed by the Minister of Labour after discussing with both sides of industry. One sometimes hears the members erroneously referred to as "the employer's representative" or the "employee's representative". They are not. They represent no-one, except the interests of justice. Each is an entirely independent judicial officer, who decides a case upon its merits, upon the evidence and law applicable. They are no more representative of each side of industry than a Justice of the Peace is representative of the stratum of society from which he comes.'

*Rent Assessment Panels – A Hybrid*

It would be remarkable if there were not at least one important tribunal which refused to fit into a category, and in this particular context the tribunals constituted from rent assessment panels are difficult to classify. In theory the panel is a general one, from which any two members may be invited to serve with a chairman on a rent assessment committee; in practice the panel is representative of lawyers, surveyors and laymen, and almost invariably the committee is composed of one of each, the chairman being usually the lawyer, occasionally the surveyor, and rarely the layman. In theory a rent tribunal is a fixed body of three, all of whose members sit on all occasions, save that the President of the assessment panel may replace unavoidable absentees from the panel list; in practice the difference (except in London) becomes blurred, so that it is possible for the same three panel members to doff an assessment committee hat and don a tribunal one when it is convenient to deal with furnished and unfurnished rents in the same neighbourhood on the same day.

## THE APPOINTMENT OF CHAIRMEN AND MEMBERS

The Franks Committee found that most chairmen and members of tribunals were being appointed by the Minister whose Department dealt with their subject matter. They believed this to be wrong in principle, although they were careful to say that they had received no significant evidence that any influence was exerted by departments on tribunals, and they recommended that in future all chairmen should be appointed by the Lord Chancellor. They resisted strong representations that other members should be appointed in the same way, believing this to be impracticable, or at best a transparent formality, but equally they were satisfied that appointments 'should not rest with the Minister concerned with the subject matter of the adjudications'. In order to enhance the independence of tribunals, both in appearance and in fact, members ought in their view to be appointed by the Council on Tribunals.[5]

Fifteen years later some progress has been made towards complying with their recommendations about chairmen, but not about members. Approximately two-thirds of all statutory tribunals now have chairmen who are either appointed directly by the Lord Chancellor or whose appointment, in accordance with section 7 of the Tribunals and Inquiries Act 1971, is indirect, i.e. the actual selection for a particular area or session is made by a Minister or President but from a Lord Chancellor's panel.[6] Of the remaining third most can be accounted for by exceptional circumstances. For example, the Civil Aviation Authority, the Traffic Commissioners and the Road Traffic Licensing Authorities are, as we have seen, primarily administrative or advisory bodies which also exercise the judicial function of licensing. The Special Commissioners of Income Tax and the representatives of the Comptroller General of Patents are civil servants. In these cases it is understandable that the Minister should continue to appoint. The National Health Service Executive Councils and committees are to a large extent professional disciplinary bodies, though with lay representation, and they elect their own chairmen. The General Commissioners of Income Tax for England and Wales, all of whom are appointed by the Lord Chancellor, have, as we have already noticed, no statutory need for chairmen.

There remain two unexpected exceptions, where the Minister still appoints. One is the Chief Immigration Adjudicator, and of course his fellow adjudicators, among whom he is *primus inter pares*. This follows the recommendation of the Wilson Committee on Immigration Appeals,[7] which proposed that these appointments should remain in the hands of the Home Secretary and quoted in support the views of the Franks Committee (Report paragraphs 47 and 48) that

'...there are objections to extending the Lord Chancellor's responsibility for appointments to tribunals beyond the range within

[5] Report para. 45–58.

[6] These include the national insurance local and medical appeal tribunals, rent assessment committees and tribunals, supplementary benefit appeal tribunals and various unused national service tribunals.

[7] Cmnd. 3387, para. 153.

which he and his Department can give proper consideration to each appointment and obtain information about candidates' qualifications.'

While this may appear unexceptionable, it ignores two facts – first that the Lord Chancellor appoints much larger panels of chairmen for other tribunals (for example, for over a hundred supplementary benefit appeal tribunals and nearly two hundred national insurance local tribunals);[8] and second, that the exceptionally sensitive nature of this particular jurisdiction makes the prestige and manifest independence of a Lord Chancellor's appointment, which is how the Franks Committee seemed to think of it in other contexts, more than usually desirable.

Finally chairmen of Milk and Dairies Tribunals continue to be appointed by the Minister of Agriculture (even though panels of *members* of agricultural land tribunals are appointed by the Lord Chancellor). The reason for this is that what is now called a tribunal was originally intended, in war time, to be a purely administrative control, without any appeal machinery. Provision for appeal was introduced at the Committee stage as a result of pressure from the farming interest in Parliament, but even so the 'tribunal' remains an advisory and not a judicial body, the word tribunal being something of a misnomer.[9]

*Members Other Than Chairmen*

With regard to members, the Franks Committee's recommendation that the Council on Tribunals should appoint has come to nothing, and the general rule is that the Minister appoints,[10] and is accountable to Parliament for the appointments he makes.

In certain cases, however, the Lord Chancellor does so. For example, the National Insurance Commissioners and the Immigration Appeals Tribunal are both appellate, and in the former all Commissioners are equal so far as jurisdiction is concerned; members of the Lands Tribunal are also on an equal juridical footing with the President, and in any case the Lord Chancellor has long been associated with the Lands Tribunal, as also with the Pensions Appeal Tribunals and the General Commissioners of Income Tax. In all these cases, therefore, there is good reason for the appointments to be made by the Lord Chancellor.[11]

[8] There are 19 full-time and 10 part-time immigration adjudicators.

[9] See footnote to p. 59.

[10] The appointment of members of supplementary benefit appeal tribunals is made by officers of the DHSS in Regional Offices on behalf of the Secretary of State, under an instrument delegating this authority signed in June 1971.

[11] The National Insurance Commissioners are in fact appointed by the Crown on the recommendation of the Lord Chancellor.

Less explicably, as we have noted, members of agricultural lands tribunals share this honour. A chapter of accidents brought this about. Under the Agriculture Act 1947 (9th Schedule) the Lord Chancellor appointed chairmen and the Minister selected members from panels nominated by persons appearing to him to represent the interests of farmers and landowners (in practice the National Farmers' Union and the Country Landowners' Association). In 1951 the High Court held that a certain tribunal had been improperly constituted and was a nullity, on the ground that an acting-secretary had invited two representative members to serve, after consulting his chairman, and had signed the letters of invitation in his own name as Secretary; he neither wrote on behalf of the Minister, nor had the Minister in any case delegated authority which would have enabled him to do so.[12] Although this decision was reversed by the Court of Appeal[13] the constitution of agricultural land tribunals was understandably a sensitive subject, and was made more so by the realization that a Minister could, as an owner of land, be a party to a case before the tribunal. Accordingly the law was changed by the Agriculture (Miscellaneous Provisions) Act 1954 (section 4 and Schedule 1), whereby chairmen of tribunals appoint the representative members from panels drawn up by the Lord Chancellor – an onerous matter for him, incidentally, since over 550 representative members are currently involved.

There is another curious exception where an historical accident has been perpetuated – members of an independent schools tribunal are appointed by the Lord President of the Council. During the preparation of the 1944 Education Act the First Parliamentary Counsel thought that appeals against closure orders ought to be dealt with by an administrative tribunal rather than a court of summary jurisdiction, but wished to avoid the possibility that Ministers might be accused of being judge in a cause which they were prosecuting. The final form of the arrangement is attributable to Sir John Anderson, who was then Lord President.

There are two other exceptions to the general rule of appointment by Lord Chancellor or Minister – one in England and Wales and one in Scotland – where chairmen and members alike are appointed by local authorities, or by a body closely associated with them.

The English case is that of the local valuation courts, whose members are appointed by county and county borough councils in their capacity as 'scheme-making bodies' under section 88 of the General Rate Act, 1967. For the most part counties have combined with county boroughs

12 *Woollett* v. *The Minister of Agriculture*, [1954] 2 All E.R. 776.

13 [1954] 3 All E.R. 529.

within their borders, or sometimes with each other, so that the total number of local valuation areas is ninety-five. The schemes themselves are subject to the approval of the Secretary of State, but his direct interest goes no further than this and the actual appointment of members is a local matter for the 'Appointing Authorities'. It is remarkable that this should be so for one of the major tribunals under the surveillance of the Council on Tribunals.

To complicate this somewhat involved narrative still further, appointment to these courts, under their local name of valuation appeal committees, is made in Scotland in a totally different way. Although the history of the transfer of rating appeals from local authority committees to independent tribunals followed much the same course as in England, members of the Scottish valuation appeal committees are appointed by the Sheriff, acting in his administrative capacity, a procedure for which there is of course no parallel in England and which is unusual in this particular context even in Scotland.

A striking difference in practice is that it is customary for all members of a valuation appeal committee (who may number anything from fifteen to thirty) to sit at, or at least to be summoned to, every sitting, instead of sitting three at a time in rotation from a panel roster.

It would, however, be misleading to compare the English and Scottish institutions, because of the very great discrepancy in the volume of appeals they hear. Each of the 95 English panels hears on an average something of the order of 250 appeals in a year; the 35 Scottish areas average fewer than 20. This makes it possible for the committees to be served by part-time secretaries who are for the most part solicitors in private practice, and who incidentally are also appointed by the Sheriff. This is in fact a tribunal which is very much within the Sheriff's province, i.e. within the province of a judge.

By way of contrast, and somewhat surprisingly, the General Commissioners of Income Tax in Scotland are appointed directly by local authorities. Even in England the Lord Chancellor appoints on the recommendation of advisory committees representing the counties, the larger towns and the grouped London Boroughs. But in Scotland they are not even nominally appointed by the Lord President of the Court of Session, as might be expected – though he must approve their dismissal – but by the county councils and the city councils of Edinburgh, Glasgow, Dundee and Aberdeen. There are 38 such appointing authorities and commissioners sit in 57 divisions. In addition to the Commissioners appointed by local authorities a Sheriff-Principal is *ex officio* a General Commissioner for any division wholly or partly within his sheriffdom and a salaried sheriff substitute is *ex officio* a Commissioner for any division wholly or partly within his district. In a recent year there were 491 ordinary Commissioners, 16 of them women, and 32 sheriffs.

On the other hand members of the two purely Scottish tribunals – the Crofters Commission and the Children's Panels – which both for different reasons have to have close links with local government in their day-to-day work, are appointed by the Secretary of State, though a Children's Panel Advisory Committee in each local authority advises him on suitable candidates for appointment.

One may sum up by saying that as in so many aspects of tribunals there is an historical explanation for a good deal of what appears to be irrational, but that Franks would – understandably – have preferred this particular aspect to be tidier than it is.

## QUALIFICATIONS AND SELECTION

Since the rationale of special tribunals is very largely that their members have qualifications or experience relevant to the subject matter of the adjudication it is manifestly impossible to make comprehensive generalizations about them; one would merely find oneself making a catalogue. Perhaps the most interesting questions to examine are these: to what extent are chairmen required to be legally qualified? What experience is looked for among members of single general panels? What kind of people serve on the representative panels? What is the definition of the 'layman', whose presence is required on a number?

### *Chairmen*

It is only in a minority of cases that the requirement of a legal qualification is absolute, that is to say that the chairman shall, in the customary phrase, or some variation of it, be a 'barrister or solicitor of not less than seven (or ten) years' standing'. This applies, as is to be expected, to the principal appellate tribunals – e.g. the National Insurance Commissioners, the Lands and Immigration Appeal Tribunals, and to those where the expertise of the other members is medical, e.g. the pensions appeal and national insurance medical appeal tribunals. It applies also to the industrial tribunals, where there is already a considerable body of case law, and to a few others which meet infrequently, such as the Agricultural Land, Betting Levy Appeal and Performing Rights Tribunals. An interesting variation is supplied by the Independent Schools Tribunal, whose chairman must be a practising member of the Bar, and in practice the Lord Chancellor invariably selects one who is also a 'family man'.

Then there are a few where a legal qualification is not a statutory requirement but where it is considered advantageous, the two most important being the national insurance local tribunals and the immigration adjudicators. In practice none of the former are now without legal training, the last 'non-legal' incumbent having retired in 1971. This is as it should be since a high proportion of cases involve applying complicated statutory provisions to the circumstances of individuals, and it is often necessary to be familiar with previous decisions of the National Insurance Commissioners.

The principal tribunals for which a legal qualification is not specified at all are the rent tribunals and rent assessment committees, local valuation courts and supplementary benefit appeal tribunals, though in practice, as we have said, the first are usually chosen from the legally qualified members of the rent assessment panel.

The Franks Report recommended that 'chairmen of tribunals should ordinarily have legal qualifications' since 'objectivity in the treatment of cases and the proper sifting of facts are often best secured by having a legally qualified chairman'. These qualities are often to be found in men not trained for the law, and stronger arguments for legal training may well be that it is often necessary to apply statute law or case law to complex situations; to control proceedings at a hearing in a 'court-like' manner, even if not according to court rules; and to see, as far as possible, that unrepresented appellants are not at a disadvantage. A further reason is the right of appeal on questions of law provided by the Tribunals and Inquiries Act 1958.

On the other hand, there are certain arguments *against* the appointment of legal chairmen which the Franks Committee did not take into account. It might, for example, be thought that since the Rent Acts are by no means simple the appointment of legal chairmen of rent assessment committees could well be a statutory requirement. But the presidents of some rent assessment panels attach importance to their ability, in a case involving an especially difficult point of law, to put a valuer or layman in the chair specifically in order that the lawyer member may be free to concentrate on the legal issues. Again, the status of chairman is manifestly higher than that of his colleagues (even his fee being somewhat larger), and to give the lawyer members of panels a monopoly of this status would run counter to the Minister's intention that professional valuers should have a key function and a standing in the operation of the Act equal to that of anyone else. It would also impede the promotion of valuers or laymen to presidential or vice-presidential posts. It would be possible to extend the same line of reasoning to any tribunal whose determinations depend heavily on any non-legal expertise.

Chairmen of supplementary benefit appeal tribunals are selected more for their knowledge and understanding of social problems and they have less statute law to apply. Their tribunals often have more of the character of social case-work conferences. The Acts and regulations which concern them tend to contain quite specific provisions, like scales of entitlement, yet at the same time allow discretion – unlimited in quantum and not governed by case law – in regard to exceptional needs and situations. Much of the tribunals' business is accordingly to establish facts about personal circumstances. A legal qualification is not, therefore, expected of the chairmen and most of them are in fact laymen. In this respect they are not differentiated from members and some began their tribunal service as members. What is looked for is 'a person of standing with administrative experience in central or local government, in the running of important voluntary organizations, or substantial businesses, or in the professions or with experience as a Justice of the Peace'.

Among tribunals at the 'administrative' end of the spectrum, the Chairman of the Civil Aviation Authority is chosen for his political experience and it is civil servants who adjudicate in patents and trade marks. Chairmen of Traffic Commissioners are appointed by the normal process of competition or selection board, the possession of a legal qualification is in fact held to be an advantage, but it is the invariable practice of the Secretary of State to appoint a barrister or solicitor to the part-time post of Deputy Chairman. Chairmen and their deputies may either be promoted or transferred from within a government department or recruited from outside the Civil Service.

*Members*

The qualifications for ordinary membership naturally reflect the fact that tribunals are 'specialized courts' – hence the general qualification is professional knowledge or practical experience of the subject matter of the adjudication or the situation of the appellant. Having said this it is hardly necessary to say more, since the kind of people whose participation is sought could almost be deduced. Thus a number, such as those dealing with pensions entitlement and industrial injuries, are composed of doctors, with a legal chairman; some, such as the Betting Levy Appeal and Performing Rights Tribunals, need business accountants, though the latter also need someone acquainted with music and the arts; while the Civil Aviation Authority seeks representation from economics, law, business and administration. It is interesting that two important tribunals whose members may sit alone recruit from alternative professions; thus members of the Lands Tribunal may be either lawyers or valuers, and there are in fact more of the latter, while the Special Commissioners of Income Tax may recruit from among barristers or civil servants with Inland Revenue experience (the last-named, however, not to exceed half the total). The General Commissioners, on the other hand, are simply people of standing who are local, either by residence or occupation, and are required to be knowledgeable about local trade and business. Names of persons for appointment are recommended to the Lord Chancellor by ninety-six Advisory Committees based on major local authorities. The net for immigration adjudicators is thrown unusually wide, and the Home Secretary in appointing them may take account of a variety of attributes – judicial experience, the administration of complex legislation, a strong interest in the subject, experience of immigrants or of people who may have difficulty in understanding and asserting their rights.

Tribunals whose members are drawn from panels of specialists naturally have the help of professional bodies in suggesting the names of candidates; indeed such consultation is sometimes mandatory.[14] Thus doctors may be proposed by the Royal Colleges in London, or the medical faculties of universities, hospital authorities or NHS Executive Councils in the provinces. Surveyors and valuers are commonly sought through the agency of the Royal Institute of Chartered Surveyors. A pattern common to a number of tribunals is employer-employee representation, with a legal chairman. With national insurance local tribunals arrangements are somewhat more elaborate, invitations to nominate being given to local employers' associations, local authorities (as large employers of labour), individual local employers and Chambers of Commerce or Trade. By agreement between the Department and the TUC names of employed persons representatives are canvassed from local branches of trade unions covering the principal local industries. The whole emphasis is on locality. The DHSS receive nominations for membership of supplementary benefit appeal tribunals from local trades councils.

Of perhaps greater interest is the way in which the less easily definable 'layman' is sought for the small group of tribunals on which he is represented. The NHS Executive Councils have fifteen professional and

[14] For example, s. 2(2) of the Lands Tribunal Act 1949 *requires* consultation with the President of the Royal Institute of Chartered Surveyors. As an historical curiosity the London Building Acts Tribunal of Appeal, which was first established by s. 28 of the London County Council (General Powers) Act 1890 and has held one hearing in the last three years, consists of six persons, four of whom are *nominated* by the Royal Institute of British Architects, the Chartered Surveyors' Institution, the Institution of Structural Engineers and the London Master Builders' Association.

fifteen lay members, eight of the latter being appointed by the local health authority. The remaining seven appointments are in the hands of the Secretary of State, who takes considerable trouble to ensure that the result is a balanced one; from the resulting membership three doctors and three laymen are appointed to the specialized committees. The Secretary of State attempts to ensure that:

> 'a Council includes a solicitor; a married woman with children; a woman connected with local women's organizations; representatives of agricultural or industrial workers and other persons who are generally representative of those using the National Health Service. He looks to organizations such as the Federation of Trades Councils, Women's Institutes and Women's Royal Voluntary Service for nominations.'

For rent assessment panels soundings are taken through Clerks of local authorities, trade unions, Members of Parliament, social welfare organizations and citizens' advice bureaux, and a somewhat similar net is cast by the Department of Health and Social Security for the tribunals concerned with benefits.

The metaphor of casting a net is possibly apt, for there is an element of chance and hope about the resulting catch. Arrangements for identifying prospective *chairmen* are more formalized. The Lord Chancellor's Office maintains a list of people suitable and available for appointment to public office of all kinds, including tribunals, and as we have seen there is a Lord Chancellor's panel for particular tribunals from which chairmen may be selected by a Minister for particular areas. The Inns of Court are also able to put forward names of their members. The compilation of lists recommended to the Lord Chancellor is the subject of careful prior investigation by departments. For example, the names of potentially suitable chairmen of national insurance local tribunals, normally barristers or solicitors, are obtained from Registrars of County Courts, town clerks and clerks of local magistrates; nominations are also sought from the CBI and TUC.

The manner of recruiting *members* other than chairmen, however, is a large subject which will repay more thorough research than is possible in this study.[15] We refer to it again in general terms at the end of this section, but meanwhile we revert to some account of the terms and conditions of service which govern tribunal appointments.

## TERMS AND CONDITIONS OF SERVICE

Few things reveal the diverse nature of tribunals so clearly as a glance

[15] Such research is in fact being undertaken. See footnote at p. 113 below.

at the terms and conditions of service of their presidents, chairmen and members, for they vary from permanent pensionable appointments to part-time voluntary service.

There are some fifty or sixty permanent, salaried and pensionable appointments whose terms can be likened to those of the judiciary or the civil service. They are the President and Vice-President of the Immigration Appeal Tribunal, the Chief Immigration Adjudicator and his permanent colleagues, the President and permanent chairmen of the Industrial Tribunal, the President and members of the Lands Tribunal, the National Insurance Commissioners and the President of the Transport Tribunal.[16] To these may be added the Chairman and Deputy Chairman of the Civil Aviation Authority in so far as their function is judicial.

Where legal qualifications are required the appointments are 'banded', in terms of salary and status, by the Lord Chancellor broadly in accordance with professional standing, and although there is no exact equivalence with the courts these leading tribunal appointments variously approximate to those of Queen's Bench Masters, County Court judges and above.

The Chief Immigration Adjudicator and his permanent colleagues, on the other hand, are specifically equated with Assistant Secretary and Principal respectively in the Civil Service, which appears somewhat anomalous.

There are then eight Special Commissioners of Income Tax who are civil servants in fact (though with a measure of independence from normal regulations appropriate to their judicial function); and two Assistant Comptrollers and eight Superintending Examiners in the Patent Office who give varying proportions of their time to 'tribunal' work. The eleven Chairmen of Traffic Commissioners are servants of the Crown, appointed by the Secretary of State, but entirely independent of him in the discharge of their judicial duties.

These seventy or eighty people, by virtue of their work and status, represent the permanent 'judiciary' of the tribunal world.

Next there is a large category of chairmen and members who either serve on panels, in the case of tribunals which meet regularly, or may be appointed *ad hoc* when they meet rarely, who are paid a fee for each day or sitting. These fees are modest by the standard of professional fees today, and in the case of doctors, barristers, solicitors, valuers and others would scarcely compensate for loss of earnings. They may on the other hand be financially attractive to people who have had a substantial

[16] This was written before very much was known about the value added tax tribunals.

drop in income on retirement. It seems possible, however, that the matter may not be of overriding importance, since most people would continue to serve whether they were paid a fee or not;[17] those who have retired are content to do the work both for its interest and remuneration and those in professional practice may well regard it as public service.

There are curious variations in the amount of the fees payable, which lead one to speculate why one department values the services of tribunal members a few pounds, or even a few pence, higher or lower than another. A figure which recurs for chairmen is of the order of £22, though the chairmen of national insurance and supplementary benefit appeal tribunals receive somewhat less, £20.50 and £18.90 respectively.[18] The fees of members other than chairmen range between £12 and £21, and include a nice distinction between a part-time immigration adjudicator (£17.85) and a doctor on a medical appeal tribunal (£17.25). Rent assessment panels value the services of their chairmen at £20.50, their professional members at £17 and their lay members at £13.65.

These discrepancies arise partly from the ways in which fees are negotiated. In general they are determined by the Civil Service Department and the Lord Chancellor's Office in collaboration, but for doctors they are negotiated by the Civil Service Department and the British Medical Association.

There remains a considerable sector where there is no remuneration, and where members and sometimes chairmen share with magistrates and (at the time of writing) local councillors the distinction of working for nothing at all. This is so of local valuation courts, the General Commissioners of Income Tax and members of the National Health Service Executive Councils and committees. It is true also of members (other than chairmen) of national insurance (local) and supplementary benefit appeal tribunals, who may only claim the sum, agreed between the Prime Minister and the TUC, of £4.75 for loss of earnings. In the pastoral world, agricultural land and milk and dairies tribunals representative members are also unpaid.

[17] Some interesting facts are given in *Public Administration*, Summer 1971, p. 218, in an article by W. E. Cavenagh and D. Newton, part of the study referred to in the footnote to p. 113 below. Between 70 per cent and 90 per cent of members of three tribunals stated that they would do the work without payment, but practising lawyers to a considerably less degree than other categories.

[18] Normally, however, only half those particular fees would be paid for what usually amounts to a half-day session. The actual sums will have been raised by the time this book appears, but the same discrepancies remain.

*Frequency of Sittings*

To see these facts in perspective it is necessary to remember that the services of many fee-paid, part-time members – and even chairmen – are called upon very infrequently. Average figures are meaningless owing to the great discrepancies not only between one tribunal and another but between London, the big cities and the rural areas, but in the tribunals which sit regularly and rely wholly or partly on part-time chairmen and members under-work is as great a problem as over-work. This has been especially true of mental health review and supplementary benefit tribunals and of some national health service committees, where it has been thought necessary to have members available for particular areas but where long periods of time have gone by without an opportunity to call upon them.

On the other hand it is possible for some tribunals to call upon their members fairly often. In the group which deals with social security, rent and rates, the medical appeal tribunals are perhaps the most consistently occupied; occasionally chairmen may be asked to meet daily, and weekly meetings are normal, though the aim is to employ panel members not more than once a fortnight, unless they are retired. Rent tribunals (though not assessment committees) may meet three or four times a week in London and Birmingham and once or twice elsewhere. The same may apply to chairmen of national insurance local tribunals, though the aim is to employ panel members only about once a month in rotation. Members of local valuation courts might at the most be called upon once a week immediately after a revaluation, scaling down to once a month. Figures of this kind clearly mean very little, but are perhaps sufficient to substantiate the statement that fee-paid members do not on the whole receive a great many fees.[19]

Outside this group there are some part-time tribunals (e.g. agricultural land) which may only hold six or ten meetings in a normal year, others (e.g. the Independent Schools Tribunal) only one or two. The General Commissioners of Income Tax may meet three or four times a year in some Divisions but up to sixty times in the City of London. Among the 'business-type' tribunals which use part-time members the Civil Aviation Authority is by far the most heavily pressed, meeting regularly on two or three days a week.

*Length of Appointment, Age and Disqualification*

Here again we encounter variations and discrepancies which are not

[19] Except in the occasional cases where an individual is a member, and may indeed be chairman, of more than one tribunal. The point is mentioned again on p. 114 below.

important in themselves but are a further illustration of diversity and its resulting vagaries.

Part-time appointment is most commonly for three years with the possibility of renewal. The main departures from this are in immigration, where full-time adjudicators are appointed for ten years and part-timers for only one; while at the appeal tribunal level the President is appointed for five years and 'lay' members for three. Local valuation courts follow the aldermanic pattern of six years, half the members retiring at the end of three; while appointments as General Commissioners of Income Tax are during the pleasure of the Lord Chancellor, subject to a retiring age of 75.

There are some fairly predictable disqualifications from service, other than the improbable ones of bankruptcy or criminal activity; they fall into two main groups – political activity or an interest in the subject matter of adjudication.

It is fairly usual to disqualify Members of Parliament,[20] candidates for election (unless and until they fail to secure election) and political agents, to which are occasionally added persons notably active in national or local party politics. Such restrictions prevail in the fields of social security, supplementary benefits, rents and immigration. Civil servants and local government employees are also excluded from rent assessment panels, as they are from the Independent Schools Tribunal. Disqualification on account of interest in the subject matter takes various forms. The Civil Aviation Authority requires a declaration of interest, whether as a shareholder or otherwise, in the business of an operator; General Commissioners who may be solicitors, accountants or bank managers may not hear appeals involving their clients; and panel members of the Traffic Commissioners, must declare an interest if they are members of a local authority's transport committee, an employee of a passenger transport undertaking or a member of a Transport Users' Consultative Committee. In such cases, however, they would not normally be selected.

A different kind of difficulty may arise when a man is a member of a tribunal but may in his professional capacity represent the interests of those who could be claimants; for example, a land agent member of an agricultural land tribunal or a trade union member of an industrial tribunal may be called upon to represent the interests of farmers or dismissed employees, or a surveyor one of the parties at a rent assessment

[20] For the most part the statutory disqualification of MPs now takes the converse form – a debarment of members of tribunals from Parliament, through the House of Commons Disqualification Act 1957 (schedule 1). Other disqualifications may be set out in letters of appointment.

committee. These contingencies have in fact been considered by the Council on Tribunals and the principle is accepted that it is not improper for a man to act in both capacities as long as he is representing his client's interests at a tribunal other than the one on which he actually serves. Similarly a barrister who is chairman of a national insurance local tribunal may be briefed to appear for an appellant to the National Insurance Commissioners as long as the appeal is from the decision of a tribunal other than his own. Nor, of course, should a solicitor hear an appeal in which his firm has been retained as legal adviser to the appellant.

In some cases there are no negative disqualifications but only positive qualifications, such as being a member of the medical profession or of the Bar;[21] this is so for the permanent salaried appointments and for a few others, e.g. the medical appeal, industrial and Betting Levy Appeal tribunals.

The age of compulsory retirement has its own particular vagaries. It may be 65 with a possible extension to 70, or 72 (now the most usual) or 72 with a possible extension to 75 (pensions appeal and rents), or occasionally there may be no limit at all. The point was referred by the Lord Chancellor to the Council on Tribunals in its first year of office in respect of agricultural land tribunals, for which there was then no age limit, and their recommendation has probably influenced later practice. They distinguished between chairmen (72 with very exceptional extension to 75) and members (an absolute age limit of 70). Their suggestion that by the age of 70 members might be getting out of touch with modern methods of farming would perhaps seem something of an understatement to their sons, but the Council did also advocate a larger proportion of much younger men.[22]

## SOME STATISTICS OF MEMBERSHIP, INCLUDING PROPORTION OF WOMEN MEMBERS

Finally it may be of interest to indicate the numbers serving on certain tribunals in England and Wales, in particular those which work on a system of panels, and to note the areas in which the services of women are most used or neglected. For convenience we start with the eight tribunals in which there is a Lord Chancellor's Panel of chairmen, recalling that in three of these there is a statutory requirement that the chairman shall be legally qualified (Q), in three it is usual in practice (q)

[21] In accordance with the normal principle a doctor may not be a member of a medical appeal tribunal considering an appeal made by one of his patients.

[22] Annual Report 1959, p. 22.

and that only in supplementary benefit appeal tribunals are chairmanships open to a wide range of experience. The facts are most conveniently expressed in tabular form, the membership of women being given in parentheses.

| *Tribunal* | *Chairmen's Panels or Chairman/Deputy Chairmen* | *Members' Panels* |
|---|---|---|
| Industrial[a] | 9 (0) full-time (Q) | 397 (7) |
| | 35 (0) part-time (Q) | |
| Medical Appeal (Ind. Inj.) | 27 (0) (Q) | 256 (2) |
| Mental Health Review | 103 (5) (Q) | 313 (9) medical |
| | | 272 (101) lay |
| National Insurance | 275 (6) (q) | 5,465 (1,515) |
| Pensions Appeal | 16 (0) (Q) | 34 (6) |
| Rent (unfurnished) | 207 (14) (q) | 416 (71) |
| Rent (furnished) | 42 (3) (q) | 84 (19) |
| Supplementary Benefit | 240 (37) | 1,361 (297) |

[a] The rapid growth of these tribunals is shown by the fact that this figure, relating to the beginning of 1971, had by the end of 1972 risen to 29 full-time chairmen, while efforts were being made to recruit another four or five hundred panel members.

The cases in which women's appointments exceed 10 per cent are the chairmanships of supplementary benefit appeal tribunals (18·4 per cent) and membership of panels in national insurance (27·7 per cent), supplementary benefit (21·8 per cent), rent assessment (17 per cent), rent tribunals (22·6 per cent) and the laymen's panel of the mental health review tribunals (40·8 per cent). The figure for national insurance reflects a statutory requirement that 'where the claimant is a woman, one of the members of the tribunal, if practicable, shall be a woman'.

One of the largest of all panel membership lists is that of local valuation courts, there being 95 chairmen (one for each panel area in England and Wales), 230 deputy chairmen and approximately 2,475 other members. These include about 300 women.

As a matter of curiosity the largest panels (excluding chairmen) are

| | |
|---|---|
| National Insurance | 5,465 |
| General Commissioners | 4,889 |
| Local Valuation | 2,475 |
| Supplementary Benefit | 1,361 |

The next largest is then rent assessment (416).

The foregoing tribunals meet regularly. One or two others which are less significant in that they only meet occasionally, but nevertheless maintain standing panels, are:

Agricultural Land: One chairman and 2 deputy chairmen for each of the 8 regions
299 farmers
252 landowners (4 women)
42 land drainage experts

Milk and Dairies: One chairman for each of the 8 regions with panels of
92 consumers' representatives (28 women)
91 producers' representatives
28 producer/retailers' representatives.

On the Independent Schools Tribunal there are two legal chairmen and 21 members of the 'educational panel' of whom eight are women.

No woman has yet been appointed a National Insurance Commissioner, a member of the Lands Tribunal, a Special Commissioner of Income Tax, to the Civil Aviation Authority or, perhaps predictably, to the Betting Levy Appeal Tribunal. On the other hand the General Commissioners of Income Tax, all of whom are appointed by the Lord Chancellor, include 103 women among their membership of 4,889.

Statistics of this kind are not kept up-to-date from year to year in any one place, and the ones we have quoted relate to approximately January 1971, being taken from a questionnaire to departments. The Council on Tribunals (Annual Report 1969–70) have quoted a global figure given by the Lord Chancellor's Office relating to mid-1969, which includes the National Health Service Councils and committees, as well as a number of smaller tribunals which we have not mentioned, though it excludes the General Commissioners of Income Tax. The figure was 21,007 Presidents, Vice-Presidents, chairmen, deputy chairmen and members, of whom 2,281 were appointed, nominated or recommended by the Lord Chancellor.

## SOME GENERAL CONSIDERATIONS

The facts that we have given leave unanswered some of the most interesting questions, answers to which could only be obtained from fuller research than is possible in a general conspectus of the kind which this book attempts. We know, for example, what channels are used by departments or by the Lord Chancellor's Office in seeking suitable candidates for appointment. But how far in their turn do these agencies cast their net? Are there yet unexplored 'fishing-grounds'? What kind of people emerge from the selection process, in terms of their occupation, social class, age or political allegiance? To what extent are they a 'stage army' of pluralists, who serve not only on other tribunals but on local councils and magistrates' courts? Are we in any danger of running short of candidates, either for chairmanships or panel membership? The answers to questions of this kind could only be elicited by intensive field-work in selected areas and for selected tribunals. Research of this kind has never been done, but fortunately it is now in progress.[23] Meanwhile we may conclude this section with some general impressions gained during the course of the study, supported at certain points by the research results so far published.

It is a matter of common observation, and not infrequently of complaint, that the average age of tribunal members is high and that tribunals have become too much the province of the retired. There is nothing remarkable in this, for the problem is common to local councils, benches of magistrates and virtually all forms of public service, it being a simple fact of life that most people have not the necessary freedom from their ordinary employment until they are middle-aged or elderly. Moreover there is nothing wrong in people using a life-time's experience to help resolve the kind of issues with which tribunals deal, provided they have also the right qualities of impartiality and judgment. It is, however, an aspect of tribunal membership which is strongly criticized by those who believe that young appellants would feel more at ease with their near contemporaries, and indeed that people of more nearly comparable age and circumstances would have a better understanding of appellants' problems. The Claimants' Unions, an energetic pressure group, are especially critical of the supplementary benefit

[23] In the Universities of Birmingham and Newcastle-upon-Tyne.

In the former Professor Winifred Cavenagh is conducting a long-term research project into the precise questions we have posed. The first stage is limited to the West Midlands Region and is concerned with the Rent Assessment Panel (with special reference to assessment committees), the Mental Health Review Tribunal and the industrial tribunals. Later it is possible that the project will be extended to other tribunals and other parts of the country. Meanwhile some preliminary findings have been published in two articles in *Public Administration*, Winter 1970 and Summer 1971. Acknowledgment is made to these two articles in support of views expressed in the remainder of this section.

In Newcastle-upon-Tyne research sponsored by the DHSS is proceeding under the direction of Professor Kathleen Bell, a member of the Council on Tribunals. It is to be a comprehensive study of social security tribunals in the Northern Region and in Scotland. It will include research into the subject matter of this chapter, though as part of a wider plan which will also assess the attitude of appellants, and of those who do not appeal, towards the tribunals.

appeal tribunals in this regard, believing that their elderly and prosperous members, as they regard them, are less fitted to determine the claims of the under-privileged than the under-privileged themselves, and that minority groups such as the coloured immigrant community should have some kind of representation.

Concerning age, it does in fact appear from comparative statistics published in the Birmingham study that rent assessment panels compare unfavourably, if that is the way to regard it, with local councils, a quarter of their members being over 65 and another 40 per cent between 55 and 64. (Mental health review tribunals are a good deal younger.) Again, the Newcastle research shows that 39 per cent of national insurance local tribunal chairmen fall in the 50–59 age bracket and 67 per cent in the 50–64 bracket. The statistical information is as yet too slender to allow firm statements, but it certainly seems that greater attention ought to be paid by the recommending and recruiting agencies to ways of attracting younger men and women.

These figures about age are mentioned since age is an attribute of tribunal membership which cannot help but strike the more casual visitor to their hearings. Other criteria used in the Birmingham study are less apparent to him, e.g. social class, education, income and political orientation. There is however one other circumstance which even a brief acquaintance with a wide range of tribunals brings to light, namely that a great many people are members, and may be chairmen, of more than one tribunal. Instances include one person, a woman incidentally, who was actually chairman of three, another was chairman of one and a member of two others, as well as holding other kinds of judicial office. Nor are the activities of pluralists confined to a particular group, such as social welfare. Lawyers especially move easily from rent assessment to milk and dairies, agricultural land to national insurance, redundancy payments to mental health. So strong is the outward impression of 'pluralities' that it is interesting to see the impression confirmed in the Birmingham study, notably in relation to rent assessment committees, where 79 per cent of the chairmen and 59 per cent of all members had other judicial or 'semi-judicial' experience, a third as members of other tribunals and a quarter as magistrates. Only one person in the particular Birmingham sample belonged concurrently to more than two tribunals, but others were either General Commissioners of Income Tax, agricultural or industrial arbitrators, deputy (i.e. reserve) Traffic Commissioners or members of national insurance local tribunals or local valuation courts in addition.

There is no reason to draw an unfavourable conclusion from this. On the contrary those who argue for more rational arrangements, with fewer and larger tribunals and greater inter-changeability of personnel, should approve it. It suggests that those who advise the Lord Chancellor or the departments have been able to identify a considerable number of people who possess the 'judicial mind' and are able to apply it to a wide variety of situations; though it would be interesting to know how many of the pluralists are lawyers[24] (so many of the chairmanships being restricted to them), and how many laymen, valuers or specialists of other kinds. But although one need not necessarily deplore such pluralism it does suggest that public service of a judicial kind may not be as widespread as the figures superficially suggest, and that people who have the time, and are accordingly likely to be over retiring age, are establishing themselves as a recognizable part-time judiciary. It may even suggest, though this is speculation, that it is becoming hard to find enough people.

This last point may well become important, and it provides an appropriate note on which to end. In the course of this study it has been examined and discussed, but it must be confessed that with one exception there is little evidence of any actual scarcity of potential chairmen or members. It appears that it is often difficult to find a particular kind of expert (on drainage) to sit on agricultural land tribunals, while in urban and industrial areas it is not always easy to maintain the medical membership of tribunals, as doctors with the necessary qualifications almost invariably have other heavy commitments. But apart from these it is only in the industrial tribunals that a warning note has been sounded.

Here the circumstances are admittedly exceptional. These tribunals are currently called upon not only to expand physically but to undertake a new and difficult jurisdiction over cases of unfair dismissal under the Industrial Relations Act 1971, in which 'there will be sharp disputes over questions of fact as well as an abundance of difficult questions of law'. This was foreseen early in 1970, when the legislation was first adumbrated, and the problem was brought to the Lord Chancellor's attention by the Council on Tribunals in a letter dated March, 1970, from which the foregoing phrase was quoted.[25] The main burden of the

[24] It is known, though not in terms of a precise figure, that some barristers prefer to hold a number of part-time tribunal chairmanships to continuing private practice in the courts, finding the work more interesting and satisfying.

[25] The letter is reprinted as Appendix A to the Annual Report of the Council for 1969–70. In practice, the President of the Industrial Tribunal has found it easier to recruit full-time chairmen (including some who were previously part-time) than new part-time ones. Availability for fifty days in the year is considered a minimum requirement, and few people with adequate court experience are able to offer this.

letter was that the qualifications of chairmen might have to be lowered. Although formally these require a 'barrister or solicitor of not less than seven years' standing' the chairmen have hitherto been of very high calibre, including judges from H.M. Overseas Service and experienced barristers. Such men would not be available to preside over tribunals which might have to be envisaged in 'every sizeable country town' and they would need to be supplemented by local solicitors with limited experience of court work, and none at all in matters as contentious as the Industrial Relations Act is likely to produce. The proposals to which this letter led lie somewhat outside the scope of this chapter, though we shall return to them elsewhere. For the moment it is sufficient to say that it may be easier for Parliament to decide that there shall be tribunals to adjudicate in the disputes generated by new social policies than to discover where the men and women to constitute them are to be found.

## CHAPTER 5

# STAFF

Studying these different aspects of tribunals – structure, membership, staff and so on – is very like looking into a child's kaleidoscope; with each turn of the fingers the same familiar pieces keep falling into new and unfamiliar patterns. This chapter deals with the status and duties of the principal officers who serve tribunals. In order to avoid comparing like with unlike, which is a constant pitfall of this study, we will work towards isolating those tribunals which are staffed by civil servants on secondment or 'loan' from government departments and which meet regularly in all parts of the country.

We start accordingly with those which fall *outside* this definition, either because their staff are *not* civil servants, or because tribunal work is only incidental to other work, or because they have no staff outside their London bases.

As with some other areas of British administration, there is a tiresome confusion caused by the indiscriminate use of the words 'secretary' and 'clerk', with or without capital letters, as titles of senior or junior posts. A 'Secretary' may be a fairly senior administrative officer who would appoint more junior 'clerks' to attend tribunal hearings; a 'Clerk' may be a senior administrator, or a man who services a tribunal, or indeed both. It is impossible to use the words consistently, and they must simply be taken as they come, in the hope that the context will suggest the function.

*Tribunal Staffs with no Civil Service Connection*

In this category there are two which are separated from departmental administration to an exceptional degree, largely because their roots are in local rather than central government.

Local valuation courts are served by a 'Clerk' appointed by the area panel in their full discretion. The appointment does not require the approval of the Secretary of State, who however must approve his salary, which is paid from central funds. He is neither a civil servant nor truly a local government officer, though his conditions of service are based on those of the National Joint Council for Local Authorities' Administrative, Professional, Technical and Clerical Services. In the local government tradition his salary is based on a panel classification determined by population, or to be more accurate in this instance the number of rateable hereditaments or, alternatively, the net annual value of certain classes of hereditament. Most Clerks today are appointed from among Deputy or Assistant Clerks, but the original appointees came mainly from the pre-1948 area assessment committees or local government.

National Health Service Executive Councils likewise appoint their own Clerks, but in this case the Secretary of State's approval is required. Again the Clerk has no definable status in civil service or local government terms, but his conditions of service are prescribed by regulation[1] and are agreed with the Administrative and Clerical Staffs' Whitley Council, an inheritance from the old Insurance Committees. His remuneration also depends on population.

The occasional national health service 'Tribunal', on the other hand (i.e. the disciplinary tribunal constituted under section 42 of the National Health Service Act, which sat on two occasions in 1970), is serviced by a practising solicitor with the comprehensive title of 'Clerk/Secretary'.

In a different tradition are the General Commissioners of Income Tax, who are left entirely free by the Lord Chancellor's Office to appoint their own Clerks, and if necessary Assistant Clerks, though the Lord Chancellor has the reserve power, after consulting the commissioners, of dismissal. The typical Clerk is a solicitor in private practice employed part-time and conducting the Commissioners' business from his own office, but occasionally a retired Inspector of Taxes has been appointed, and there are a few full-time appointments, two in London, one in Birmingham and one serving a group of divisions in Bedfordshire and Hertfordshire. A Clerk's remuneration is determined by the Board of Inland Revenue, with the consent of the Minister for the Civil Service, and for part-time Clerks is based on the amount of work in the three years preceding the appointment (or date of salary review). The remuneration of full-time Clerks is related to that of civil servants.

The Betting Levy Appeal Tribunal, which is also concerned with determining a financial obligation, has followed a similar course in being served by a fee-paid solicitor in private practice.

Two other rarely summoned revenue tribunals are serviced by a barrister who carries the title of 'Registrar' – the Board of Referees for Capital Allowances and a tribunal which may be appointed under the Income and Corporation Taxes Act 1970.[2]

[1] Regulation 14(3) of the Executive Council Regulations 1969.

[2] S. 26 of the Capital Allowances Act 1968 and S. 463 of the Income and Corporation Taxes Act 1970.

*Tribunal Work Incidental to Other Work*

This is a large category, with many sub-divisions.

First, there are the Civil Aviation Authority (formerly the Air Transport Licensing Board) and the Traffic Commissioners, whose work is administrative and advisory more than judicial. The administration of the former is entrusted to an Assistant Secretary of the Department of Trade and Industry, and of the latter to a Principal or Senior Executive Officer (according to the size of the Traffic Area) of the Department of the Environment. Both bodies are in a sense adjuncts of the administration in that they are responsible for standards, qualifications (e.g. of aircrew or drivers), safety and maintenance, as well as the granting of unopposed applications for licences; their judicial work, which consists of hearing opposed applications for licences, is a relatively small part of their total function.

In a somewhat similar category are the important hearings into the registration of Patents, Designs and Trade Marks, where secretarial duties are performed by departmental staff operating under the instructions of an office head who is himself the 'tribunal'.[3]

The staffing of mental health review tribunals has no consistent pattern, as the incidence of work varies greatly from one region to another, but in general it is part of the regional administration of the Department of Health and Social Security. Final responsibility would rest with a Principal in a regional office, but day-to-day administration would be done by an officer of the executive grades; in some regions, notably those containing Broadmoor and Rampton Hospitals, a good deal of the time of a Higher Executive Officer would be occupied; elsewhere only perhaps half the time of an Executive Officer.

At the other end of this particular spectrum are a number of tribunals which are called upon to meet so rarely that appropriate departmental staff are able to make arrangements for them *ad hoc*. Agricultural land tribunals are a partial exception in that they meet often enough to have a Higher Executive Officer in each regional office specializing in their management, and there is a tribunal office which can be identified by the public; but the work is not full-time and it is simply necessary to arrange that the officer's other day-to-day work is of such a nature as not to conflict with tribunal duties when they occur. But the tribunals which deal, for example, with independent schools,[4] forestry, milk and

3 The Plant Varieties Rights Tribunal, though at the time of writing it has only met once, is similarly served.

4 By an interesting historical quirk the Secretary of the Pensions Appeal Tribunal serves as secretary to the Independent Schools Tribunal on the rare occasion that it meets.

dairies, performing rights and other matters merely require the occasional attention of departmental staff.

*Tribunal Staff concentrated in London*

These are the full-time staffs of the Special Commissioners of Income Tax, the Lands Tribunal and the Pensions Appeal Tribunals. All three, however, go on circuit to provincial centres and are within what one might call the general tribunal network in that they commonly meet, outside London, in the premises of some other tribunal, such as a rent assessment panel or an industrial tribunal. The staff of the National Insurance Commissioners are also concentrated in London so far as England is concerned, though as we have seen there are offices with small permanent staffs in Edinburgh and Cardiff, while the London-based Transport Tribunal also hears Scottish cases in Edinburgh.

The principal officers of all these tribunals are civil servants of grades ranging from Higher Executive Officer to Principal, and with one exception their duties are purely administrative. The exception is the 'Registrar' of the Lands Tribunal, ranking some way above a Principal, who has two jurisdictional responsibilities in addition to his administrative ones, namely the making of interlocutory orders on application by parties, after hearing counsel, solicitors or the parties themselves, and the taxation of *inter partes* costs and legal aid costs.

*The 'Stock' Tribunals*

There remain the tribunals which continually recur as the 'hard core' of the institution, and which are characterized by more or less continuous adjudication in all parts of the country and by a staff relationship of varying degrees of intimacy with a government department. They are, in alphabetical order:

Immigration Adjudicators
Industrial Tribunals
Mental Health Review Tribunals
National Insurance Local Tribunals
National Insurance Medical Appeal Tribunals
Rent Assessment Committees
Rent Tribunals
Supplementary Benefit Appeal Tribunals.

But although they have in common the attributes we have mentioned their senior staffing arrangements are by no means similar. The principal officer may be a relatively senior administrator who himself appoints others of clerical or secretarial grade to act as clerks at particular hearings; or he may combine general administration in an area or region with himself acting as clerk to the tribunals within it; or there may be no officer other than a tribunal clerk, and even so the clerkship may not be a formal appointment but may be allocated to any local civil servant of appropriate experience.

Thus in immigration the chief officer is known as Secretary of the Appellate Authorities and head of the Appeals 'Secretariat', being a Senior Executive Officer seconded from the Home Office, who among other things would nominate the hearing clerks. The Secretary of the Industrial Tribunals, at their headquarters, is a Chief Executive Officer from the Department of Employment, while the chief officers in the regions are Higher Executive or Executive Officers holding the title of 'Assistant Secretaries'; the Secretary to the National Insurance Commissioners is a Senior Executive Officer seconded from the Department of Health and Social Security for full-time administrative duties; the Rent Assessment Panel Secretaries are mostly Higher Executive Officers (a Principal in London) seconded from the Department of the Environment; and the chief officer for mental health review in each hospital region is a principal in the Department of Health and Social Security. Each would appoint subordinate members of their staffs to act as clerks to hearings of industrial tribunals, rent assessment committees and mental health review tribunals respectively, though rent *tribunals* are normally served by the same Executive Officers acting under the general direction of Panel Secretaries.

National insurance and supplementary benefit appeal tribunals are both serviced directly by the Department of Health and Social Security, but, since they have very different historical origins, in very different ways.

There is at least one full-time clerk to supplementary benefit tribunals in each of the Department's regions, but as few tribunals are busy enough to justify a full-time clerk of their own the clerk is not confined to a particular tribunal, and he will combine general administration with attendance at hearings. Such clerks are deployed from an office at the Department's Regional Headquarters, which also organizes the case lists and hearings. They are Executive Officers on secondment from the Department for not less than two years; on appointment it is made clear in writing that they are servants of the tribunals.

For national insurance local tribunals, on the other hand, routine servicing, e.g. listing cases to be heard and calling members for a tribunal, is in the hands of Managers of local offices of the Department, and the tribunal clerk is a clerical officer who is interchangeable with any other officer with the requisite knowledge. These are not, in other words, formal appointments, and the servicing and support of tribunals is part of ordinary departmental work. The same principle applies to medical appeal tribunals, though since they are regionally and not locally organized routine servicing is undertaken by the Regional Controller and the clerk is an Executive Officer.

It should be said at once that the close departmental connection cannot be detected by the outside observer except when hearings are actually held in local offices of the Department. A hearing held in a town hall, for example, is wholly free from any departmental atmosphere, and the insurance officer (or in appeals to a medical appeal tribunal, the Higher Executive Officer) presenting the Department's case has no discernible advantage over the appellant. Where it is absolutely unavoidable to hold appeal tribunals in the Department's local offices, every effort is made to keep the hearings well apart from the actual working areas of the office.

*Summary of Staffing Arrangements*

To sum up, history has bequeathed a number of different patterns of administration. The General Commissioners of Income Tax inherit an old tradition; local valuation courts assumed the mantle of the old local authority assessment committees when rating valuation was 'nationalized'; adjudication in supplementary benefit and national insurance has developed from patterns established in the earliest legislation; while the mid-1960s brought a new trend towards 'presidential independence' as illustrated by the industrial and immigration tribunals and the rent assessment panels. It is improbable that this variety will ever disappear or that different ways of doing things will coalesce into a uniform system. The staffing arrangements of the General Commissioners, the NHS Executive Councils, the mental health review tribunals or the Traffic Commissioners, for example, will always need to be tailored to their special circumstances. On the other hand the group of tribunals for which presidential administration has been preferred to departmental servicing have some common characteristics and could possibly benefit from common staffing arrangements; while the question whether the social security group of tribunals would find advantage in a presidential system is currently being considered.[5] Again, although post-war legislation has continued the association of local valuation courts with local government the actual nature of their jurisdiction – the valuation of property – is akin to that of the Lands

[5] The difficulty, which we discuss more fully in the concluding chapter (p. 291) is that although national insurance and supplementary benefit are both aspects of social security in its broad sense, the two jurisdictions resemble each other much as do oil and water.

Tribunal and the rent assessment panels. The question whether there is enough common ground among a large enough group of tribunals to contemplate a common staffing service is considered in some detail in the concluding chapter, where we also give some statistics of supporting staff and discuss the possibility of a career structure within the service of tribunals, or of an association with the reformed Court Service.

All that we have said so far relates to the relatively senior staff who act in some cases as Clerks to tribunals (as in those dealing with social security) or as administrative Secretaries or Deputy Secretaries in regional offices (as in the presidential systems where a Clerical Officer would normally act as clerk to an actual hearing).

A chapter which purports to give some account of the staffing of tribunals ought, however, to mention the junior supporting staff. Upwards of 1,200 people,[6] many of them locally recruited – i.e. not seconded – are now employed in the service of the principal tribunals which come within the oversight of the Council on Tribunals, while hundreds of others are employed by the other tribunal-type bodies that we described on pp. 59–70. Of this 1,200 about 600 are in the presidential tribunals and one or two others, about 250 in the local valuation courts and the *equivalent* of about 350 in the social security group, where the work is spread among a larger number as part of more general duties.

Meanwhile, there are three further aspects of the work of the more senior staff which merit discussion – the varying roles played by the officials who act as 'clerks' at hearings; the relationship which exists between staff and the general public; and the degree of independence of staff from departmental influences.

*The Position of the Clerk at a Hearing*

This is matter in which there are important differences of function which cut across the various groupings that we have been discussing. For the 'clerk' sometimes retires with a tribunal as its professional adviser; sometimes he joins them but only to provide information and keep the papers in order; and sometimes he is excluded from the tribunal's discussion altogether.

We select three examples of each, choosing tribunals which are otherwise dissimilar.

[6] A breakdown of this figure is given in the concluding chapter (p. 304). In very broad terms about 400 are Senior Executive, Higher Executive or Executive Officers, 600 Clerical Officers or Clerical Assistants, and the remainder typists, copyists and ancilliary staff.

At the former A.T.L.B. the Clerk used to retire with the tribunal and act as 'clerk to the court', advising the Authority on points of procedure or matters of policy relevant to an application; at local valuation courts he advises on statute law and case law and on precedents relevant to an appeal, and also ensures that the tribunal considers only the relevant evidence produced in court; while at supplementary benefit appeal tribunals he may, on a strict interpretation of the rules, be asked to withdraw but is almost invariably present, and among his duties is to call attention to and advise on the legislation.[7]

These three tribunals have in common that their membership is unlikely to include a lawyer and that they exemplify the strength of the amateur element in adjudication. On the other hand neither are the clerks themselves legally qualified, but are examples of a very common phenomenon in the tribunal world – the administrator who has had to acquire a sound working knowledge of a particular branch of the law. When we come to deal with the representation of appellants we shall encounter a similar phenomenon – the trade unionist who through continually representing his members in a particular context becomes highly competent in the same way. The question of formal legal training for senior tribunal staff is, however, one which deserves consideration, not only because of its obvious advantages but because it is frequently assumed by parties and their solicitors that the tribunal staff with whom they are dealing in the events leading up to a hearing are qualified lawyers.

There are then a number of tribunals where the clerk normally retires with the members (or stays with them in the case of those tribunals where it is the parties who withdraw) but only to play the more restricted role of providing information and producing documents. Examples are the mental health review tribunals, the pensions appeal tribunals and (though practice may vary from one panel to another) rent tribunals and assessment committees.

Finally it is the practice of immigration adjudicators, industrial tribunals and the Special Commissioners of Income Tax *not* to be accompanied by their clerk when they retire to consider their decision.

At a hearing before a National Insurance Commissioner the 'Clerk to the Court', known by that description, performs functions similar to those of a judge's associate, and in addition to taking a note of the arguments and the evidence helps the parties (many claimants being

[7] Supplementary Benefit (Appeal Tribunal) Rules 1971. Rule 11(1) says that the Clerk shall be present at all sittings, but Rule 11(8) says that 'For the purpose of discussing their determination on any matter the Appeal Tribunal may order any person to withdraw'.

unrepresented) in a variety of ways. The question of his retiring with the Commissioner hardly arises, however, since by statute every decision of a Commissioner must be in writing, and is therefore in practice always reserved. Similarly in the Lands Tribunal decisions are almost invariably reserved, to be read at a later date, and neither the Registrar nor the 'Clerk of Court' retire with the members.

It is a matter that is almost entirely regulated by administrative practice, since with four exceptions[8] rules of procedure are silent upon it, and in two of these the reference is very allusive, i.e. it is possible to infer that the clerk is not necessarily *ex*cluded. It is strange that there should have been this neglect, since the Franks Report (para. 61) thought that clerks ought to be debarred from attending unless sent for to advise on a specific point, but went on to say that their duties ought to be regulated on the advice of the Council on Tribunals. The Council's first Annual Report (1959, para. 7) referred to their expectation of being asked to consider the question comprehensively, but since then nothing has been heard of it. It is something that the Council could well study, but in any event it ought in our view to be dealt with, preferably along the lines indicated by Franks, in procedural rules for all tribunals.[9]

The independence of a tribunal is obviously emphasized in the eyes of appellants if it is seen that its members withdraw to make their decision in the absence of an official. It is perhaps more important than in a court of law that this should be made manifest, because a department is so often one of the parties in dispute. The other side of the argument is that expert tribunals with lay clerks merge imperceptibly into lay tribunals with expert clerks, and that it may be difficult for a proper determination to be made in the absence of a key figure.

*Tribunal Staff and the General Public*

In theory tribunal staff are anonymous figures and would not normally be reckoned among those civil servants who deal with the public 'across the counter'. In practice the way in which certain tribunals are organized and conducted may result in the staff playing an important part in public relations.

This is especially true of those tribunals whose presidents or chairmen hold part-time appointments, and where the secretary or clerk is the administrator who supplies the vital element of continuity; even when presidents or chairmen are full-time they may regard their own appoint-

[8] Local valuation courts (Reg. 9, 1956); national insurance and medical appeal tribunals (Rules 9(5) and 19(3), 1967 respectively); and supplementary benefit appeal tribunals (Rule 11(1) 1971).

[9] See next chapter.

ments as judicial rather than administrative. The Senior and Higher Executive Officers who hold the chief administrative posts in some tribunals are therefore in exceptionally responsible positions. Being seconded by their departments to institutions which are by definition independent they themselves have no administrative chief, and it is they rather than the chairman and members who represent the tribunal in the eyes of the public in all the preliminary stages of an application or appeal. The public in this context may mean firms of solicitors or surveyors, commercial or industrial undertakings, trade unions or voluntary organizations, as well as individuals of every kind with deeply held grievances. The Secretary therefore has to deal as helpfully as possible with a very wide range of outside interests and, though he may telephone or correspond with his chairman between sessions, to take a good deal upon himself.

He may well have been transferred to tribunal work from a departmental post in which he was part of a hierarchy with clearly defined responsibilities; on appointment to a headquarters or regional tribunal post he may become the effective head of a considerable organization, responsible only to a chief who has been appointed from outside the Civil Service, and primarily for his judicial experience. In provincial outposts within a region an executive officer's responsibilities may be more modest in scale but he is completely on his own.

Tribunal 'clerks' in the narrower sense, whether their formal role at a hearing is a prominent one or not, also act as a bridge between the tribunal and those who appear before it, and their qualities can be an important element in the atmosphere of the proceedings and the impression which the appellant will take away with him. Because the clerk's contribution to a tribunal's proceedings must be as unobtrusive as possible, his importance is easily overlooked.[10]

### *The Independence of Tribunal Staff*

The recent emergence of presidential systems raises anew questions which were discussed but discounted by the Franks Committee – whether it is proper for tribunal staff to be seconded by departments which have a direct interest in the subject matter of the adjudication or whether there should be, under the Lord Chancellor's Department, 'a central corps of clerks from which a service could be provided for all

[10] The Council on Tribunals have mentioned a few occasions on which a Clerk to a tribunal has 'appeared to play too prominent a role' in the proceedings or has been 'allowed to take too active a part' in them (see the Annual Reports of the Council for 1959 (para. 89) and 1960 (para. 53). What these criticisms seem to imply is weakness or inefficiency on the part of the chairmen rather than any particular fault on the part of the clerk.

tribunals'.[11] We discuss the practicalities of this in some detail in the concluding chapter.

For the moment it is sufficient to draw attention to the fact that although tribunals are in theory as independent as the courts they are, in this particular matter, considerably less so in practice. For example, while presidents and chairmen have increasingly been given an administrative or supervisory, as well as judicial role, they have no power to recruit staff, but must accept whomsoever a department, or its regional officer, may nominate; while the staff themselves are in an ambivalent position, being seconded or 'loaned'[12] from the departments to which they belong, and in which their future promotion and career may generally be assumed to lie; there being, as matters stand, no career prospect in the service of tribunals alone. These arrangements place departments and staff alike in a potentially invidious position.

For example, it would be possible for departments to assign staff to tribunals for irrelevant or unsatisfactory reasons; or to communicate with them on matters in which they have a direct interest; or for the staff themselves, in all good faith, to maintain personal links with their own departments, being put in a position where a clash of loyalties is difficult to avoid.

The Franks Committee inquired into these matters, after hearing representations that tribunals were too dependent upon, or influenced by, 'parent' departments, and they also considered whether the quality of tribunal staffs would be improved by a centralized service. Indeed, they went out of their way to ask the Permanent Secretary to the Lord Chancellor to return to them and give evidence a second time in order to express views on a number of specific points, of which this was one.[13]

Sir George Coldstream (the then Permanent Secretary) thought that the question was inseparable from the larger question of whether tribunal *members* should be appointed by the Lord Chancellor. His view was that they should not, since the patronage of the Lord Chancellor, which was personally and meticulously exercised, would necessarily be replaced by a more impersonal bureaucracy within his Department, which would in consequence acquire some of the attributes of a Ministry of Justice, and would need, for example, to establish a regional organization. The cost would be great and the gain illusory. Matters should be left as they were, and the Lord Chancellor should continue

[11] Report, paras. 59–61.

[12] A number of our informants maintained that 'loaned' was the more accurate expression, since 'secondment' implies a more formal arrangement than in fact exists. The position of some tribunal staff, in relation to their future career, is curiously indefinite.

[13] Minutes of Evidence, Day 24.

to appoint members only to those tribunals for which, for historic reasons, he already had direct responsibility.

If, however, it *were* decided to make the Lord Chancellor responsible for appointing tribunal members there would be no difficulty in assuming also responsibility for a service of tribunal clerks; though it would be expensive and did not appear to him to be necessary.

The Franks Committee (paragraphs 59–61) accepted these views, adding reasons of their own why they thought disadvantages would outweigh advantages.

However, the events of fifteen years have considerably altered the background against which the Permanent Secretary was speaking. First, the number of people employed full-time by tribunals has very greatly increased. The two largest employers of staff – the industrial tribunals and the rent assessment panels – have both been created since 1957, as have the immigration and mental health review tribunals; while the work of others, notably the supplementary benefit appeal tribunals, has increased. Second, the growth of the presidential system has meant that tribunal staffs are identifiable, whereas previously work was spread over large numbers of people who were also performing other duties. Third, the argument that the Lord Chancellor's Department was not designed, and ought not to be designed, to undertake a large administrative task with regional offices (thus approximating to a Ministry of Justice) has been overtaken by events. The Courts Act has brought about just such changes. Accordingly we argue in Chapter 13 that the possibility of a Tribunal Service, standing either on its own or as part of the new Court Service, ought to be re-examined.

CHAPTER 6

# PROCEDURAL RULES AND PROVISIONS FOR APPEAL

The procedural rules discussed in this chapter relate simply to the *conduct* of proceedings; there are other rules which take us beyond conduct and into the realm of principle, e.g. those which relate to the right of representation, the power to exclude the public, the burden of proof and dependence on precedent. These will be discussed in Chapter 10, when we attempt to compare tribunals with the ordinary courts of law.

Even with this limitation it is necessary to be selective, in order to avoid becoming entangled in innumerable small differences between one tribunal and another. The matters which seem to be of some importance are:

Procedure before the hearing
- Knowledge of the right to apply
- Method of lodging application or appeal
- 'Pleadings'
- Knowledge of the case to be met
- Notice of hearing

Procedure at the hearing
- The right to a hearing
- Non-attendance by parties
- Locus standi
- Power to regulate own proceedings
- Order of events
- Adjournment, postponement, removal

Procedure in regard to evidence
- The rules of evidence
- The oath, cross-examination, written representations
- Discretionary power

Decisions

Provisions for appeal

## THE PROCEDURAL DILEMMA

The problem confronting most tribunals is how to combine an orderly procedure with an informal atmosphere. Informality is one of the advantages often claimed for tribunals over the ordinary courts.[1] Informality may be of no particular advantage in, say, the Lands Tribunal, but it can be vital to the ordinary person who finds any kind of public appearance somewhat alarming but who nevertheless has to present himself before a tribunal in order to claim some right or benefit; the prospect can be even more disturbing if to substantiate his claim he has to reveal the details of his financial circumstances or personal or family relationships. He is likely to be reassured by the informal atmosphere of tribunals concerned with rent or social security payments, or of a hearing by the General Commissioners, where for example, he may well be one of a few people apparently having a conversation across a table. At most the formalities of seating, or of 'taking the stand' to give evidence, will be of the slightest. As to actual procedure the chairman will normally say, quite conversationally, that he will ask one party to speak first and then ask the other if he wants to ask any questions, and then do it the other way round.[2] One must not of course under-rate the importance of who speaks first and who speaks second, or how evidence is admitted, but the observer wishing to study procedure at a tribunal will, on the whole, find very little to study. On the other hand there are tribunals (for example the Lands Tribunal, the Special Commissioners for Income Tax, and the Transport Tribunal) which are virtually indistinguishable from the ordinary courts in their formality and procedure.

There is in fact a marked distinction between those tribunals which have borrowed extensively from the courts and those which have deliberately attempted to avoid a quasi-legal procedure. The procedure of the Lands and Transport Tribunals provides for interlocutory proceedings before the Registrar, the consolidation of proceedings, the hearing of preliminary points of law, evidence by affidavit, the parties being limited to the grounds pleaded, discovery of documents, and so on. The Transport Tribunal goes even further – in addition to providing for interrogatories it is provided that 'where not inconsistent with these Rules the general principles of practice or any particular practice of the Superior Court (i.e. the High Court in England and Wales and the Court of Session in Scotland) may be adopted and applied, at the discretion of the court'.[3] By way of contrast the rules

[1] See e.g. Franks Report (para. 64, p. 15).

[2] This kind of preliminary explanation can be quite important, for quite apart from informing the parties it can put them at their ease. Experienced chairmen usually explain that if the parties do not understand the procedure at any point they should not hesitate to ask the tribunal.

[3] Rule 47, Transport Tribunal Rules 1965, S.I. 1687.

of supplementary benefit tribunals provide for none of these procedures.

Given the diversity and range of formal and informal procedures, the dilemma is two-fold: on the one hand procedure should not be so technical and formal as to discourage legitimate applications, and on the other even the most informal of tribunals will need some guidelines if the proceedings are to be fair to both parties. This is a tightrope which not all tribunals have managed to walk successfully.

The point was put with great clarity by Lord Gardiner (then Lord Chancellor) in a speech at the opening of the Central Office of the Industrial Tribunals:

> 'Tribunals try to be free from technicality. A tribunal must have a framework of procedure within which to operate. Experience has shown that informality of atmosphere in hearings before tribunals can be positively inimical to orderly procedure. Within that framework of procedure, it is essential that there should be sufficient informality of atmosphere to put the lay litigant at his ease. Lawyers sometimes forget what an ordeal it is for the ordinary citizen to go to law. 80 per cent of the cases coming before the Industrial Tribunals are claims for redundancy payments. Many of the applicants, and a number of the respondents, are unsophisticated people caught up in a vast machine which they do not understand. They are frightened of what they imagine a court to be, and it is a major part of a tribunal's function to put them at their ease so that they present cases as well as possible. A tribunal must be tolerant and patient with the litigants before it, who are usually unrepresented, are often incapable of expressing themselves adequately, and are nearly always overwhelmed by the occasion. It is therefore essential that the proceedings should be kept as simple and as informal as possible within the framework of the procedure laid down by law.'

## THE NEED FOR PROCEDURAL REQUIREMENTS

Given the fact that the diversity of circumstances in which tribunals operate inhibits the standardization of procedures, are there not some procedural matters which should be common to all or most of them? The common denominator is probably the three characteristics formulated by Franks: openness, fairness and impartiality. Clearly the application of these characteristics to a particular case at a particular tribunal will depend on a number of factors – the attitude of the members of the tribunal, the relationship between the tribunal and the department, the setting in which the hearing takes place, the opportunity of the parties to know the case they have to meet and so on. The most perfect set of procedural rules will not ensure openness, fairness and impartiality, but equally it will be almost impossible to impart these qualities into a hearing if the procedural rules of the tribunal are insensitive to them.

Is it then possible to identify those features of tribunal procedure which contribute to openness, fairness and impartiality? The Franks Report itself spelt out in broad terms what was meant:

> 'In the field of tribunals openness appears to us to require the publicity of proceedings and knowledge of the essential reasoning underlying the decisions; fairness to require the adoption of a clear procedure which enables parties to know their rights, to present their case fully and to know the case which they have to meet; and impartiality to require the freedom of tribunals from the influence, real or apparent, of Departments, concerned with the subject-matter of their decisions.'[4]

The common law also provides some guidelines for good procedure, in the form of the rules of natural justice, which require that no man shall be a judge in his own cause, and no judicial decision shall be made without the parties being given an adequate opportunity to be heard. Tribunals, like the courts, must observe these rules.

As to specific issues of procedure, the Franks Report made some seventeen detailed recommendations on the procedure applicable to tribunals generally[5] and over thirty further recommendations in regard to particular tribunals. These recommendations provide a useful starting point for discussion on many aspects of procedure, as does the division made by the Report into pre-hearing procedure, procedure at the hearing, and procedure after the hearing.

## PROCEDURE BEFORE THE HEARING

### *Accessibility*

Pre-hearing procedures are particularly important because of the need for tribunals to be easily accessible to the ordinary citizen. In this regard the courts provide an interesting comparison: under the present procedures of the courts it is extremely difficult (and most unusual) for a layman to start an action himself. To give some idea of the hurdles facing the layman intrepid enough to dispense with the assistance of

[4] Report, p. 10.
[5] Report, pp. 91–3.

the legal profession, *County Court Practice 1971* contains over 100 pages dealing with the commencement of proceedings, particulars of claim, service, defence and counterclaim, third party procedure, interrogatories, discovery and inspection of documents, the amendment, transfer or consolidation of proceedings – all matters which are likely to arise in a county court action before there is a hearing. In the High Court the prospect is even more daunting. For a simple claim the layman would find that he would, in addition to the formidable discovery and inspection, have to grapple with such things as a writ, statement of claim, statement of defence, counter claim, request for particulars, third party notices, interrogatories, affidavits and the like,[6] all couched in unfamiliar language. Not surprisingly most laymen find it necessary to instruct a solicitor to commence proceedings and settle the pleadings, but clearly the *raison d'être* of many tribunals would be destroyed if this were to be a prerequisite to the obtaining of a hearing. If tribunals are to be easily accessible to the ordinary citizen the pre-hearing procedure should be reduced to the simplest possible form.

*Knowledge of Right to Apply*

The first essential in the cause of accessibility is that a claimant or appellant ought, where possible, to be made fully aware of his right to apply to a tribunal. Obviously, where the application must be made in the *first instance* to the tribunal (as in the case of an application to the Performing Rights Tribunal, an agricultural land tribunal, or a rent tribunal) this must depend on general knowledge aided by official publicity, but where the tribunal acts as an *appellate* authority in regard to the decisions of an official, or an inferior tribunal, the claimant or appellant ought as a general rule to be advised of his right of appeal when notified that his application or claim has been disallowed. The Franks Report attached great importance to this,[7] and in fact where there is a right of appeal, or a further right of appeal, the claimant or appellant is notified of the fact in one way or another. There is, however, no uniform way of letting him know. In some cases it is a statutory obligation (e.g. in national insurance and immigration) but in others claimants or appellants may be dependent on the good offices of a department or an official to learn of their rights of appeal. For instance the Supplementary Benefits Commission is not *obliged* to give notice that there is a right of appeal against its determinations, even though it may do so as a matter of practice. Elsewhere there is considerable variation. The notice

[6] The pleadings in a complex case would be far more involved than those recited here.

[7] Report, para. 67, p. 17.

of decision of a local valuation court simply contains a footnote to the effect that an appeal may be made against the court's decision to the Lands Tribunal 'in the form prescribed by the Lands Tribunal Rules 1963 . . .'. The Department of Education and Science when issuing a notice of complaint about an independent school simply encloses a copy of the Independent Schools Tribunal Rules 1958, leaving it to the prospective appellant to discover how and when an appeal may be made. On the other hand several departments publish notes and pamphlets for the guidance of claimants or appellants setting out the statutory provisions (including the right of appeal) in clear and simple language.[8] More helpfully still, in the case of most decisions or actions taken under the Commonwealth Immigrants Act 1962 or the Aliens Order 1953, notice of the decision or action (to be given in writing to the affected person as soon as practicable) must not only set out the reasons for the decision or action, the right of appeal and how it must be exercised, but also the facilities available for advice and assistance (p. 179).

*Method of Lodging an Application or Appeal*

In keeping with the principle of accessibility the method of lodging an application or appeal ought to be as simple as possible, with a reasonable time limit, and in practice most tribunals conform to these requirements. Sometimes it is obligatory to use a statutory form to lodge an appeal (as with local valuation courts[9] and pensions appeal tribunals[10]). Appeals to national insurance and medical appeal tribunals may be made by notice in writing stating the grounds of appeal sent to any 'local office' of the Department of Health and Social Security; similarly with supplementary benefit appeals, save that the grounds of appeal need not be stated.

There is also a good deal of variation between tribunals as to the time limits within which an appeal must be lodged. The norm is possibly 21 days (national insurance and supplementary benefit) and the minimum 14 days (certain appeals to an immigration adjudicator). Where medical assessment is in issue the limits are more generous; three months is allowed for an appeal to a medical appeal tribunal, and no less than a year for a pension claim to a pensions appeal tribunal.

In the Lands Tribunal, with its great diversity of jurisdictions, there is a corresponding internal diversity of time limits – 30 days for appeals

[8] Examples are *Supplementary Benefits Handbook* and *The Right To Help*; *Agricultural Land*; *Industrial Relations*: other explanatory leaflets are issued by departments in respect of rent tribunals, medical appeal tribunals, mental health review tribunals, pensions appeal tribunals etc. (see p. 178).

[9] Valuation Lists (Proposals for Alterations) Regulations 1963.

[10] Rule 4, Pensions Appeal Tribunals (England and Wales) Rule 1971.

against determinations by local authorities or the Commissioners of Income Tax, or for a reference in respect of arbitration, 28 days for an appeal against a decision of a local valuation court, and 21 days in a number of other cases.

*'Pleadings'*

The lodging of a notice of appeal may be all that is required of an appellant or claimant before the actual hearing, or it may be no more than the first step in a set of formal 'pleadings'. This exemplifies the procedural dilemma – if too much paper-work is required the prehearing steps can become over-complicated, unduly protracted and necessitate the employment of a lawyer, but on the other hand if too little information is given to the tribunal beforehand, the hearing itself may become unduly protracted.

Probably the simplest prehearing procedure for appellants and claimants relates to supplementary benefit appeals where an appellant is required to do no more than state in writing that 'I wish to appeal against . . .'. Again, as we have already noted, an appeal against an immigration officer's decision, may in certain cases,[11] be lodged orally. These two instances are exceptions, inasmuch as most tribunals require at least a short statement of the grounds of appeal, but even this may present problems to some appellants to 'personal welfare' tribunals. In the case of national insurance, mental health and most immigration appeals there is a short printed form available which requires the grounds of appeal to be briefly stated; in practice tribunals are prepared to accept the barest of statements.[12]

The dilemma is this. The form of appeal must clearly be simple if it is to be managed by those who are not good at expressing themselves. But if it is too simple, or if as with some kinds of immigration appeal it is merely by word of mouth, it could result in frivolous, vexatious or hopeless appeals. More typically it seems to result in appeals made on impulse, in the heat of the moment, and not seriously thought out, with the result that when the moment comes the appellant simply stays away. This is thought to be a contributory factor to the very high degree of absenteeism among those who appeal to the social security tribunals.

[11] I.e. appeals against refusal of entry to a Commonwealth citizen by an immigration officer, or against the conditions imposed on entry, or against a refusal of entry to a seaman or prohibition on landing, or against a consequential direction for removal to another country (Rule 5(1) Immigration Appeals (Procedure) Rules 1970).

[12] A point which has emerged clearly in the Newcastle-upon-Tyne research referred to on p. 113.

In all the cases we have mentioned, the lodging of a notice of appeal is all that is required of the appellant before the actual hearing. It is normally the responsibility of the department or officer concerned (the Supplementary Benefits Commission, the immigration officer, the insurance officer, the hospital authority for mental health patients) to inform the tribunal beforehand of the facts of the case, sending a copy of the papers to the appellant.

On the other hand there are those tribunals which may require something rather more than 'I think the insurance officer was wrong', or 'I think I should be released from . . . mental hospital', and who would be much assisted by a system of 'pleadings' but are nevertheless confronted with the problem of appellants incapable of preparing pleadings themselves and who may not be able to afford professional assistance. Two tribunals in particular which have been faced with this problem are the Industrial Tribunals and the Pensions Appeal Tribunals. Each has adopted a different solution but in each case the method adopted suits the needs of the case and may provide a model for other tribunals.

The approach adopted by the industrial tribunals arose out of the unsatisfactory nature of redundancy payment applications. Originally the form of application merely required the applicant to set out the names and addresses of the parties and then to fill in a blank space headed 'Grounds of this application are as follows:——————'. This resulted in many and various forms of pleading, often giving the tribunal and the other side little indication of the case, e.g. 'My trade union knows all about my case'. Even where the grounds were set out reasonably fully there was always the likelihood that certain material facts (such as the hours of work, details of salary or wages or the amount of the redundancy payment offered) would be omitted. Because of these shortcomings, a questionnaire-type form was adopted in 1967 and revised in 1972; by answering its questions the applicant is almost certain to set out the basic facts on which he relies.[13]

The pensions appeal procedure adopts the different approach of requiring the Department to take the initiative in getting the pleadings together. On receipt of a notice of appeal, the Minister (but in fact the Department of Health and Social Security) is required to prepare a Statement of Case setting out the medical history of the appellant as known to the Department, together with any other relevant facts and the reasons for rejecting the claim.[14] This is then sent in duplicate to the appellant, who is at the same time informed that if he wishes he can

[13] Reproduced as Appendix II.

[14] Rule 5, Pensions Appeal Tribunals (England and Wales) Rules 1971.

submit an Answer (on a form supplied by the Minister) refuting all or any part of the Statement of Case, together with any documents in support of his case. The Minister when he receives the Answer is then entitled to comment in writing on the Answer, although if he does so a copy must be sent to the appellant. Three copies of all the documents (the Statement of Case, appellant's Answer and Minister's comments) are then forwarded by the department to the Pensions Appeal Tribunal. This enables the tribunal to receive a full set of case papers while sparing the appellant the problem of consulting rules of procedure and becoming involved in other legal complexities.

At the other end of the scale there are those tribunals which require proper pleadings in the manner of the High Court and which have provision for interlocutory proceedings to settle the issues raised on the pleadings. The most complicated such procedure is that of the rarely-used Performing Rights Tribunal. Another (and more normal) example would be that of the Lands Tribunal (which approximates to a specialized court). The procedure differs according to the nature of the proceedings, but to give two instances from the Tribunal's appellate jurisdictions, where the appeal is against a determination by a Minister, an acquiring authority or a local planning authority (e.g. of compensation for planning decisions restricting new development), the appellant is required to set out in his notice of appeal (which must be in duplicate), his name and address, the name of the determining authority and the date, reference number and short particulars of the determination, the description of the land involved, the question which the appellant requires to be determined (including 'a statement of the figure representing the amount or value which the appellant requires to be so determined'), the grounds of appeal, whether the appellant intends to call an expert witness, and the appellant's address for service.[15] The Registrar sends the duplicate copy to the determining authority which is then required to forward a copy of the determination to the Registrar. The President of the Tribunal can also request the determining authority to furnish particulars of any determination relevant to the appeal,[16] but apart from this the determining authority is not required to furnish details of its own case prior to the hearing (except for details of the evidence of any expert witness).

However, where the appeal is from a decision of a local valuation court the parties are required if the net annual value of the property exceeds £500 or the appeal is on a point of law, to exchange a Statement of Case and a Reply thereto including the facts to be proved, the points

[15] Rule 3, Land Tribunal Rules 1963.
[16] Rule 8, Land Tribunal Rules 1963.

of law on which the parties intend to rely, valuations and details of comparable properties on which it is intended to rely at the hearing.[17] The conditions precedent to this requirement of further pleadings – concerning the £500 and the point of law – have the result that this requirement does not in fact apply to ordinary domestic hereditaments.

This procedure obviously requires the appellant to make the initial running in the case. Furthermore it would obviously be beyond the capabilities of most appellants to produce these particulars[18] but the exchange of valuations and other information greatly assists the parties in preparing for a hearing and is conducive to the settlement of cases before the hearing takes place.

Before leaving the subject of pleadings or preliminary information, some attention should be paid to practice of what might be termed 'non-statutory' pleadings ('non-statutory' in the sense that there is no provision in the procedural rules for a system of pleadings). Some tribunals, lacking any express power to institute a system of pleadings have found it expedient to resort to the general power of being entitled 'to regulate their own proceedings' to introduce pleadings. The pre-hearing procedure of appeals to the National Insurance Commissioner from decisions of national insurance local tribunals provides a good example. As we shall see there is no automatic right to a hearing on these appeals (the grant of a hearing being at the discretion of the Commissioner) and there is therefore a clear implication in the statutory procedure that appeals may be decided simply on the case-papers. However neither the Act nor the Regulations[19] shed any light on what these papers are and who submits them to the Commissioner. What in fact happens is that at the stage of actually submitting an appeal, the claimant is required to complete a form supplied by the local insurance office on which the grounds of appeal (if different to the grounds submitted to the national insurance local tribunal) must be set out. This form must be sent to a local office of the Department of Health and Social Security and the insurance officer then prepares a submission setting out the issues. The Chief Insurance Officer subsequently sends a letter to the claimant informing him that his appeal has been sent to the Commissioner and enclosing copies of the submission and case

[17] Rule 11, Land Tribunal Rules 1963.

[18] Before being critical of the Lands Tribunal on this account it should be pointed out that, unlike most tribunals, legal aid and advice is now available in respect of its proceedings.

[19] National Insurance Act 1965; National Insurance (Determination of Claims and Questions) (No. 2) Regulations 1967. Reg. 12 empowers the Commissioner to determine the procedure 'in connection with the consideration and determination of any appeal'.

papers sent to the Commissioner. A form is also enclosed on which the claimant can request an oral hearing and submit any evidence or observations in reply to the insurance officer's submission. This non-statutory procedure, it will be noted, is in practice very similar to the statutory procedure of a pensions appeal tribunal.

*Knowledge of the Case to be met*

So far we have discussed pre-hearing procedure in terms of the parties' obligations to provide case papers and information for the tribunal but another and no less important aspect of this procedure is the extent to which it gives the other party, particularly the appellant, an indication of the case to be met at the hearing. To quote Franks:

> 'The second most important requirement before the hearing is that citizens should know in good time the case they will have to meet, whether the issue to be heard by the tribunal is one between citizen and administration or between citizen and citizen.'[20]

The procedures we have described, although varied, all fulfil this requirement. The insurance officer's initial decision, the immigration officer's report, the Departmental submission to a pensions appeal tribunal, the exchange of Statements of Case and Reply thereto prior to Lands Tribunal hearings of certain appeals are all likely to give the appellant some indication of the case he is likely to meet. Even in the case of appeals to the National Insurance Commissioner where there is no statutory provision requiring the respondent to state the grounds on which he relies, the non-statutory practice described above ensures that a claimant is not taken unawares by a new argument advanced on appeal by the insurance officer. Again, in the field of citizen *v.* citizen disputes, the questionnaire-type forms used by the industrial tribunals have the effect of giving both parties an indication of the opposing cases.

There are, however, some exceptions. For example, information may be withheld from appellants at tribunals dealing with immigration, mental health, the national health service, pensions and some forms of traffic licensing; but there are reasons (which we discuss on p. 280) why this is so in these particular cases. There is, however, no provision for the Supplementary Benefits Commission to give reasons for rejecting a claim. Should an appeal be made to a tribunal the observations of the Commission's officer will be circulated with the papers, and from that stage the appellant will be at no disadvantage. It remains that he might have refrained from appealing at all because of not having had a full explanation of why he was refused benefit in the first place. It would

[20] Report, Para. 71, p. 17.

seem logical that the Franks recommendation that tribunals should give reasons for their decision if requested to do so, which is embodied in section 12 of the Tribunals and Inquiries Act, should be made applicable to the 'tribunal' of first instance, i.e. the statutory officer who makes the original decision.

If appellants are usually given an indication of the case they are likely to meet, departments are not always so fortunate, particularly in those cases where the grounds of appeal may be stated in the briefest and most uninformative manner. For instance, an income tax notice of appeal has to state the grounds of appeal but this is of limited value as a statement that 'the assessment is excessive' satisfies this requirement (this is true also of a notice of appeal to a local valuation court). The notice of appeal goes to the Inspector of Taxes who tries to settle the matter by correspondence or interview, and in this way, if the appellant is cooperative, each side will discover the basis of the other's case. If, however, the appellant refuses to participate in these preliminary negotiations, he will very likely be given an indication of the Crown's case but the Crown will be unable to discover the basis of his case.

*Notice of Hearing*

This is the last aspect of pre-hearing procedure which calls for comment. Over the greater range the amount of notice required to be given ranges from 'seven days' (Mental Health Review Tribunal), to 'not less than twenty-eight days' (Independent Schools Tribunal, Betting Levy Appeal Tribunal). The personal welfare tribunals (national insurance, supplementary benefit, medical appeals) require 'reasonable' notice of the time and place of the hearing but the immigration appeals procedure simply requires 'notice' to be given. At the other end of the scale, the Performing Right Tribunal Rules have an unusual procedure of having a hearing (of which the parties get at least fourteen days' notice) to decide the date of hearing. The General Commissioners of Income Tax are obliged only to give 'reasonable' notice, which in general would be thirty days.

## PROCEDURE AT THE HEARING

*The Right to a Hearing*

We are concerned here with the rules dealing with how a hearing is to be conducted, but the initial question to be determined is whether there is a *right* to a hearing at all. At least one tribunal (the National Insurance Commissioner) may dispose of appeals 'on the papers', that is to say without the parties being heard in person at all. Oral hearings before the Commissioner are not as of right: but are granted on request unless, after considering the papers and the reasons put forward in the request, the Commissioner is satisfied that the appeal can properly be determined without a hearing (in practice, over 75 per cent of appeals are disposed of in this way). On the other hand, should the Commissioner consider it desirable, he can order an oral hearing even though not requested by the appellant. Immigration appeals may also be disposed of without a hearing if one has not been requested, or the appellate authority decides on the papers to allow the appeal, or the appellant is outside the United Kingdom, or if in the case of an objection to a removal to a particular country the authority considers a hearing is not warranted. In the case of one or two other tribunals (among them rent tribunals) the parties must give notice that they desire to be heard, but if one party does give notice there must be a hearing.

*Non-attendance by Parties*

On the other hand in many cases where it is mandatory for the tribunal to hold a hearing, one or both parties frequently fail to appear (see p. 82). Different tribunals have different provisions regarding this problem of non-attendance. Rent tribunals are obliged to proceed to determine or dismiss the reference (assuming that by the time it is realized that the parties are not going to appear the tribunal will have 'entered upon consideration of' the case);[21] the National Insurance Commissioner and supplementary benefit appeal tribunals may 'proceed to hear and determine the case or give such directions as they think proper'; agricultural land tribunals and an independent schools tribunal may either adjourn the hearing, dismiss the application or appeal, or proceed to hear and determine it in the absence of a party; while local valuation courts 'may proceed with the hearing on the assumption that he (i.e. the non-attending party) does not desire to be heard'. Some tribunals make specific provision for excuses for non-attendance to be received and taken into account: thus if a reasonable explanation of absence is given to a medical appeal tribunal or a national insurance local tribunal at or before the hearing, the hearing must be adjourned for at least one month and further notice given. The Lands Tribunal on the other hand has a discretion to set aside its determination *following* a hearing, if a sufficient reason for the absence is produced within seven days of the tribunal's determination. The most favourable rules in regard to non-attendance are the Pensions Appeal Tribunals Rules. These make provision for two different sets of circumstances; firstly, if a claimant fails to prosecute his case and also fails to satisfy the Presi-

[21] Rent Act 1968, s. 73(1).

dent that there was sufficient reason for not doing so, instead of being dismissed or proceeded with in his absence, the case is placed on the 'deferred list'[22] and the claimant notified of this. He then has *twelve months* in which to ask that the case be restored to the hearing list: the case will then be restored unless the President is satisfied that the failure to prosecute the appeal was due to wilful default.[23] Secondly, the claimant may wish the case to proceed, but in his absence. The Rules provide that an appeal *cannot* be heard in the claimant's absence unless he so requests, and even then the tribunal may decline to proceed with the case if they consider that his presence is necessary.[24] In the case of a claimant who cannot attend through infirmity, the President may arrange for him to be visited by one or more members of the tribunal to take his evidence.[25]

*Locus Standi*

All that one can say in a small compass about *locus standi*, i.e. who is entitled to appear and to be heard, is that there are wide divergencies arising out of the nature of the jurisdiction. In the generality of tribunals in which an individual is claiming a right or benefit locus is restricted; for example, to the claimant and a departmental representative at a social security tribunal or to the lessee, lessor and local authority at a rent tribunal. On the other hand at a dispute before an industrial tribunal under section 51 of the Docks and Harbours Act any employer or employee in the harbour concerned enjoys locus, and at an agricultural land tribunal anyone at all who cares to lodge an objection.

*Power to regulate own Proceedings*

It is not uncommon for a tribunal to be given a general power to regulate its own proceedings. Indeed, because of the uneven nature of statutory rules of procedure, and of certain gaps in their provisions which may or may not be intentional, it is a power of some importance.

Later in this chapter we discuss how much procedural detail ought to be included in the rules and how much left for the tribunal to determine *ad hoc*. Meanwhile, we have already given one example in relation to the pre-hearing procedure on appeals to the National Insurance Commissioner, where the rules appear to be defective (p. 138). Another concerns the *adjournment, postponement or removal* of hearings, matters in which some tribunals are given wide statutory powers and others

[22] Rule 10, Pensions Appeal Tribunal Rules 1971.
[23] Ibid., Rule 26(3).
[24] Ibid., Rule 20.
[25] Ibid., Rule 21.

more limited ones; in some cases, however, they are not mentioned at all, and the tribunal must rely on its own regulatory powers.

Thus the rules for national insurance local tribunals contain a provision regarding what is to happen if a case has been adjourned because a claimant has been unable to appear, although there is no specific power to adjourn in the first place, the adjournment being covered by the tribunals' power 'to give such directions with a view to the determination of the case as they may think proper . . .'.[26] Similarly the general interlocutory powers of the Lands Tribunal are adequate to allow postponement or removal of hearings in appropriate cases, before the appointed hearing commences.[27] Once the hearing is called the power to adjourn rests with the Tribunal Member.

By contrast, local valuation courts have wide powers to 'postpone or adjourn the hearing of any appeal for such time and to such place and upon such terms, if any, as it thinks fit . . .'.[28]

Another matter in which the power to regulate its own proceedings is important is the *order of events*, in which it is the exception rather than the rule for any order to be specified in the rules.[29] It is usual for it to be determined *ad hoc* at the beginning of a hearing, an arrangement which has its advantages when one contestant may be represented and the other not, or where, at a supplementary benefit appeal tribunal for example, an appellant may have difficulty in expressing himself. The question whether an unrepresented appellant should be required to speak first touches on a more fundamental point than those with which this chapter is concerned, and we revert to it (p. 261) when comparing tribunals with the ordinary courts of law.

Other matters with which it might be thought appropriate to deal under the general head of 'Procedure at the Hearing' are likewise postponed to Chapter 10, namely the right to representation (p. 263), *in camera* hearings (p. 276) and the withholding of evidence from a party (p. 280).

## PROCEDURE IN REGARD TO EVIDENCE

### *The rules of evidence*

We are not concerned with 'rules of evidence' as lawyers understand that

[26] Reg. 8(2) National Insurance (Determination of Claims and Questions) (No. 2) Regulations 1967.

[27] Rule 31, Lands Tribunal Rules 1963.

[28] Reg. 8, Rating Appeals (Local Valuation Courts) Regulations 1956.

[29] E.g. the rules of rent tribunals, supplementary benefit appeal tribunals, national insurance local tribunals, the National Insurance Commissioner, medical appeal tribunals, pensions appeal tribunals and independent schools tribunals do not make any mention of an order of events.

term (e.g. in regard to hearsay or leading questions, etc.), because the applicability of those rules will vary from tribunal to tribunal and even from hearing to hearing. In the same way the nature of the evidence upon which a tribunal will rely to reach its decision and the form in which it is presented will vary widely according to the type of tribunal, the nature of the issues before it, and the type of appellant who appears before it.

Some tribunal rules go so far as to expressly exclude the strict rules of evidence. Thus agricultural land tribunals, pensions appeal tribunals and independent schools tribunals are not bound to reject any evidence 'on the grounds only that such evidence would be inadmissible in a court of law'. In the case of many other tribunals there is no such provision. Obviously the niceties of the evidential rules of the courts have no place in the proceedings of a supplementary benefit appeal tribunal and in this case the tribunal's power to regulate its own procedure can be used to ensure that too much technicality does not intrude into the proceedings. But the position is less clear in the case of national appellate bodies such as the National Insurance Commissioner or the Lands Tribunal. Franks took the view that in the case of the Lands Tribunal and other 'more formal tribunals' there is 'no good reason why the same rules of evidence as in courts of law should not apply',[30] yet there is no indication in the rules of either the Lands Tribunal or the National Insurance Commissioner as to whether the strict rules of evidence apply at the hearings of these bodies.[31] In contrast the Transport Tribunal Rules contain a provision (Rule 47) providing for the adoption and application of the general principles of practice of the High Court (or the Court of Session in Scotland), which would include the application of the strict rules of evidence to hearings.

The Court of Appeal and the Divisional Court have given a number of decisions that tribunals are not normally bound by the technical rules of evidence. In what is generally regarded as the leading case[32] on this point Lord Denning, M.R., said:

[30] Report, p. 22.

[31] In practice, the National Insurance Commissioner does not apply the strict rules of evidence (preferring to keep the procedure as informal as possible) while the Lands Tribunal adheres to the High Court procedure of evidence being given orally, on oath, and subject to the rules of evidence.

[32] *T. A. Miller Ltd* v. *Minister of Housing and Local Government*, [1968] 2 All E.R. 633. In this case the 'tribunal' was a planning inquiry into an appeal against an enforcement notice, and the decision was in fact made by the Minister on the recommendation of his inspector. But a similar judgment, quoted by Lord Denning, had previously been given in a case relating to industrial injury (*R.* v. *Deputy Industrial Injuries Commissioner*, [1965] 1 All E.R. 81).

'Tribunals are entitled to act on any material which is logically probative, even though it is not evidence in a court of law. . . . Hearsay is clearly admissible before a tribunal. No doubt in admitting it the tribunal must observe the rules of natural justice, but this does not mean that it must be tested by cross-examination. It only means . . . that the other side must have a fair opportunity of commenting on it and contradicting it.'

*The Oath, Cross-examination, Written Representations*

Little need be said about these more routine aspects of evidence. There are no tribunals which must always administer the oath, there are some which have a discretion,[33] and a great many which have no express power to do so,[34] although in many cases they may do so under the power to regulate their own proceedings or there may be statutory provision for appropriate regulations to be made. For example, section 75(2) of the National Insurance Act 1965 enables regulations to be made for administering the oath to witnesses. This is usually done as a matter of practice on Ministers' inquiries into contribution matters;[35] there is no comparable provision for a local tribunal or for the Commissioner.

There is now (with one exception) no restriction on the right to cross-examine witnesses, and this is an area in which there has been progress since Franks drew attention to the fact that there were then some tribunals which required the parties to address questions to witnesses through the chairman (Report page 22); this may still be required by a service committee of a National Health Service Executive Council. The rules of the Pensions Appeal Tribunals actually require that the witnesses of unrepresented appellants may be examined by the chairman on their behalf if they so desire.[36]

Most tribunals also accept written representations in lieu of personal attendance by the parties to give oral evidence.[37] Sometimes these must

[33] E.g. the Lands Tribunal, Pensions Appeal Tribunal, agricultural land tribunals, local valuation courts.

[34] E.g. national insurance tribunals, rent tribunals, supplementary benefit appeal tribunals. In national insurance the oath is in fact administered on 'Minister's questions', i.e. inquiries into contribution matters.

[35] Reg. 2(3).

[36] Rule 13(1), Pensions Appeal Tribunals (England and Wales) Rules 1971.

[37] The only tribunal which requires the appellant to attend the hearing personally is the Pensions Appeal Tribunal – unless the appellant is too infirm to do so (in which case the tribunal goes to him) or is resident outside the UK (in which case a medical examination is made in the country of residence). The Lands Tribunal as a matter of practice also requires the personal attendance of the parties and witnesses – a dispensation in favour of affidavit evidence is rarely given.

be in the form of a sworn affidavit (as in the case of the Lands Tribunal, agricultural land tribunals, the Performing Rights Tribunal and an independent schools tribunal), though defendants may be required to attend the hearing personally to be cross-examined.

*Discretionary Powers in regard to Evidence*

We turn now to a tribunal's powers to *obtain* evidence.

The accepted legal convention is that it is for the respective parties to decide what evidence should be presented to a court. The court may assist the parties in obtaining that evidence by the issue of a writ of subpoena to reluctant witnesses or by ordering the discovery of documents, but it is no part of a judge's task to enter the arena and gather evidence himself. This is part of the adversarial philosophy of the courts and it is reflected in those tribunals which adhere most closely to adversarial practice. Thus the Transport Tribunal has powers very similar to those of the High Court to issue summonses for the attendance of witnesses and to order the discovery and production of documents[38] on the application of a party. Similarly, a number of other tribunals[39] use the procedure set out in section 12 Arbitration Act 1950 which requires the parties to apply to the High Court (not the tribunal) for witnesses to be subpoenaed or documents to be produced. In this type of procedure, the tribunal is entirely dependent on the parties for the evidence on which to reach its decision.

This is in marked contrast to those tribunals which are able to obtain evidence for themselves (indeed they may on occasion have to if they are to reach a sensible decision). Thus a tribunal may have power to order a party to furnish documents or other information direct to the tribunal: an example is the Civil Aviation Authority's powers to call upon applicants or objectors to provide any additional information the Board may require to dispose of a case.[40] The implications of a tribunal receiving confidential information in this way are discussed later (see p. 280). Or the tribunal may have power to call for reports from independent experts, or to call witnesses itself. For instance a pensions appeal tribunal 'may summon before it expert or other witnesses'[41] and, where it is of the opinion that a difficult medical or other technical question arises, it may 'take the opinion of a medical specialist or other technical expert in such manner as may appear ... to be convenient'.[42] An interesting variation is the procedure which

[38] Rules 33–37, Transport Tribunal Rules 1965.

[39] E.g. Performing Rights Tribunal, independent schools tribunal, Lands Tribunal, mental health review tribunals.

[40] Reg. 9, Civil Aviation (Licensing) Regulations 1964.

[41] Rule 12(4), Pensions Appeal Tribunals (England and Wales) Rules 1971.

[42] Ibid., Rule 15.

enables insurance officers and national insurance local tribunals to refer questions of fact to two 'local referees' for a report. These referees who must be drawn from the employers' and employees' panels and must reside in the same neighbourhood as the claimant, are required to interview the claimant and then submit a report to the tribunal (or the insurance officer).[43]

Another feature of the inquisitorial approach is the wide power given to some tribunals in regard to inspection and examination. Three tribunals dealing with land or property[44] have power to inspect the land or premises concerned, subject to notice being given to the parties who are entitled to attend the inspection together with their representatives and expert witnesses. Three other tribunals (rent tribunals, independent schools tribunals and local valuation courts) which might also be expected to have specific powers of inspection, do not, although in each case it is common practice for inspections to be made.[45]

Similarly the medical members of those tribunals[46] whose decisions may turn on the medical condition of the claimant or applicant almost always carry out a medical (or psychiatric in the case of mental health review tribunals) examination of the claimant or applicant under their statutory powers to do so.

These powers (of calling for further information, obtaining reports, summoning further witnesses, inspecting property and examining the applicant) are all indicative of an inquisitorial approach to the gathering of evidence. However it must be emphasized that merely because a tribunal has any or all of these powers it will not necessarily use them. The Lands Tribunal for instance has power to require any party to furnish any document or other information which it may require and has wide powers of inspection but remains firmly committed to the adversarial method of obtaining evidence. In the final analysis the approach adopted (adversarial or inquisitorial) will depend as much on the personal preference of the chairman and members of the particular tribunal as on the content of the procedural rules of the tribunal.

## DECISIONS

Tribunals are subject to *common law restrictions* in regard to decisions

43 Reg. 17, National Insurance (Determination of Claims and Questions) (No. 2) Regulations 1967.

44 I.e. Lands Tribunal, agricultural land tribunals and rent assessment committees.

45 Under the power to regulate own proceedings (see above p. 142).

46 Pensions Appeal Tribunal, medical appeal tribunals, mental health review tribunals.

(they must not be 'unreasonable', they must not have an error of law apparent on the face of the record, etc.). Within those limits and subject to any right of appeal most tribunals are free to decide on the issues before them as they think fit. Thus a rent tribunal in assessing a 'reasonable' rent simply has to do just that – in the words of the Rent Act 1968 (section 73) the tribunal 'after making such inquiry as they think fit and giving to each party . . . an opportunity of being heard or . . . of submitting representations in writing . . . (a) shall approve the rent payable under the contract, or (b) shall reduce the rent to such sum as they may, in all the circumstances, think reasonable, or (c) may, if they think fit in all the circumstances, dismiss the reference (or, under section 75 if the rent is already registered) (d) may increase the rent payable.' Thus, in terms of the statute rent tribunals have an unlimited discretion as to the amount that may be assessed as a 'reasonable' rent. There is no formula in the Act requiring the rent to be related to market value, the rating value or any other criteria. On the other hand a tribunal could not adopt some formula of its own that would be 'unreasonable' in the eyes of the High Court. The common law restrictions are designed to persuade lesser tribunals to adopt a 'judicial' cast of mind when deciding cases, even though a tribunal may apparently have a discretion to decide how it chooses.

Many other tribunals have *statutory restrictions* of one form or another placed upon the ambit of their decisions. There may for instance be limitations as to jurisdiction, that is, within the field of a tribunal's operations there may be certain matters specifically excluded from its purview. Examples are the matters reserved to the Secretary of State under the National Insurance Act 1965[47] and the National Insurance (Industrial Injuries) Act 1965.[48] If in a case before it a national insurance local tribunal or the Commissioner forms the opinion that a 'Minister's question' arises (to use its traditional name) the tribunal is required to direct that it be referred to the Minister for determination.[49] Similarly, a rent tribunal has no jurisdiction to assess the rent of a furnished letting if the rateable value of the dwelling exceeds £200 (or £400 in Greater London).[50]

[47] S. 64 (whether the contribution conditions for any benefit are satisfied, in which class of insured persons a claimant falls, who is entitled to an increase in benefit when there are two competing claims for the same increase).

[48] S. 35 (whether a person is employed in insurable employment and any question as to the liability and amount of contributions).

[49] S. 71, National Insurance Act 1965; s. 47 National Insurance (Industrial Injuries) Act 1965.

[50] S. 71, Rent Act 1968: s. 70 specifies certain other exceptions, e.g. holiday homes, hotels, leases from the Crown.

Again, even though a tribunal may have jurisdiction to decide a matter, it may be restricted as to the factors which it can take into account in reaching its decision. To continue with examples in the field of rents, it is not uncommon for tenants of furnished accommodation to advance shortcomings in the services which the landlord has agreed to provide as a reason for reducing the rent, but this is not a matter which a rent tribunal can take into account in assessing a 'reasonable' rent (any shortcomings by either party are a matter for the county court on the grounds of breach of contract). Another example in this same field is the statutory instructions given to rent officers and rent assessment committees for the assessment of a 'fair' rent – in determining a fair rent a committee (or a rent officer) is required to have regard 'to all the circumstances (other than personal circumstances) and in particular to the age, character and locality of the dwelling house and to its state of repair'.[51] Furthermore, the committee is required to assume that the number of houses available for rent in the locality is equal to the number of persons wishing to rent them,[52] i.e. the rent must be assessed without any regard to scarcity value. This represents an attempt to import a measure of objectivity into the assessment of rents, but in the final analysis a tribunal's assessment of the monetary value to be placed on these factors in a particular case is entirely discretionary and subjective.

Or the boundaries within which a tribunal can exercise an element of discretion may be circumscribed by statute. For instance, supplementary benefit appeal tribunals can only 'substitute therefor any determination which the (Supplementary Benefits) Commission could have made', which means in effect that in normal circumstances amounts of benefit are determined not by the tribunals but by a Schedule to the Act.[53] In such cases the tribunal has no discretion at all. But of course what is often at issue is whether the circumstances are normal or not. If the tribunal decides that there are exceptional circumstances it may make such addition 'as may be appropriate to take account of those circumstances' (para. 4 of Schedule 2). Here the 'criteria' are so vague as to give tribunals an open-ended discretion.

A final restriction which should perhaps be mentioned for the sake of completeness is precedent (i.e. the extent to which a tribunal follows its previous decisions); but this is another of the matters which it is more appropriate to discuss in Chapter 10.

The giving of *reasoned* decisions, was strongly advocated by Franks (para. 98):

[51] Ibid., s. 46(1). [52] Ibid., s. 46(2).

[53] Ministry of Social Security Act 1966, s. 18(3) and schedule 2.

'We are convinced that if tribunal proceedings are to be fair to the citizen reasons should be given to the fullest practicable extent. A decision is apt to be better if the reasons for it have to be set out in writing because the reasons are then more likely to have been properly thought out. Further, a reasoned decision is essential in order that, where there is a right of appeal, the applicant can assess whether he has good grounds of appeal and know the case he will have to meet if he decides to appeal.'

This recommendation was accepted in principle when the Tribunals and Inquiries Act was being drafted, with one important reservation. All tribunals under the general supervision of the Council on Tribunals (with the exception of revenue tribunals) are now under a duty to furnish an oral or written statement of the reasons for a decision if requested to do so.[54] The Franks statement gives two arguments in favour of a reasoned decision: it would assist appellants and there would be more likelihood that the tribunal will have brought its collective mind to bear on the issues involved before making its decision. A third argument not mentioned by Franks is that a reasoned decision makes a tribunal more amenable to the supervisory jurisdiction of the High Court in regard to errors on the face of the record, a fact which is reinforced by section 12(5) of the 1971 Act which provides that any statement of reasons shall be taken to form part of the record. It should also be mentioned that, notwithstanding section 12, many tribunals are required by their own procedural rules to give written statements of the reasons for their decisions irrespective of whether any request is made.[55] The National Commissioner, who is not so required, does so none the less, thus providing another example of the inconsistency with which the subject is surrounded.

There are the usual inconsistencies. Thus a pensions appeal tribunal need give only a 'short indication'[56] of its reasons, while a medical appeal tribunal initially gives claimants only a summary of the decision and findings,[57] even though a full copy of the decision (including

[54] S. 12, Tribunals and Inquiries Act 1971. Reasons need not be given or may be restricted if national security is involved or if the request is made by a person not primarily concerned and it would be 'contrary to the interests' of any person primarily concerned to divulge the reasons to the requesting person (s. 12(2)).

[55] Examples are rent assessment committees (but not rent tribunals) independent schools tribunals, supplementary benefit appeal tribunals, agricultural land tribunals, Lands Tribunal, Performing Rights Tribunal, immigration appeals adjudicators and tribunals, national insurance local tribunals, Transport Tribunal.

[56] Rule 18, Pensions Appeal Tribunal Rules 1971.

[57] Reg. 12(2), National Insurance (Industrial Injuries) (Determination of Claims and Questions) (No. 2) Regulations 1967.

reasons and findings) may be obtained on request.[58] Most tribunals are free to decide for themselves the *form* in which decisions are given but medical appeal tribunal decisions must be given on a 'form approved by the Minister';[59] supplementary benefit appeal tribunals also, although not bound to do so, almost invariably set out their decision on a form supplied by the department. Moreover, in both cases the departmental form makes a distinction between findings of fact and reasons, when the two may be inseparable (e.g. a finding of cohabitation is surely the reason for refusing a supplementary benefit appeal); this may well stem from a literal application of the Franks recommendation that 'a tribunal should send to the parties a written notice of decision, which should set out the decision itself, the findings of fact by the tribunal, the reasons for the decision and the rights of appeal against the decision'.[60]

A matter not dealt with in the Franks Report or the Tribunals and Inquiries Act) is the *minority or dissenting opinion*. We have seen that most tribunals consist of more than one person. In only three instances does it appear that the decision of a tribunal *must* be unanimous in such cases: a pensions appeal tribunal,[61] medical boards[62] and local valuation courts (where, if the tribunal consists of two members who fail to agree, the case must be referred to a differently constituted tribunal). In most cases provision is made for the majority opinion to be the decision of the tribunal[63] – in some instances provision is made for the President or chairman to have a second or casting vote in order to ensure that a majority is achieved.[64] Where a tribunal is not unanimous and there is a right of appeal, the minority opinion may be of considerable interest to an unsuccessful party and it might be thought that in such cases the minority opinion ought to be made available to the parties as well as the reasons of the majority. Very few tribunals have any provision at all as to minority opinions: of those that do, rent assessment committees are specifically prohibited from making any reference in a decision to

58 Ibid., Reg. 13.

59 Reg. 12(1), National Insurance (Industrial Injuries) (Determination of Claims and Questions) (No. 2) Regulations 1967.

60 Franks Report, p. 92.

61 As a result of the decision of the High Court in *Minister of Pensions* v. *Horsey*, [1949] 2 K.B. 526.

62 Reg. 5(3) (b), National Insurance (Ind. Inj.) (Determination of Claims and Questions) (No. 2) Regs. 1967. A three-man medical board, however, is unusual, as it is only called when the normal two-man board is unable to reach agreement.

63 E.g. medical appeal tribunals, national insurance local tribunals, agricultural land tribunals, independent schools tribunals.

64 E.g. industrial tribunals, Lands Tribunal, Performing Rights Tribunal, mental health review tribunals, supplementary benefit appeal tribunals.

the fact that it is a majority decision or to any minority opinion, and only national insurance local tribunals and medical boards (but not medical appeal tribunals) are required to record if a decision is not unanimous and the reasons given by the minority member for dissenting. Industrial tribunals are not so required by their Rules, but do so in practice both in justice to the parties and for the assistance of an appellate court.

## PARTICULAR SETS OF RULES

So far we have discussed procedure in terms of individual rules in which there is considerable variation between one tribunal and another. Likewise, when one turns to compare one set of rules with another, variation and diversity are the most obvious impression. A brief look at three separate sets of rules illustrates the point.

Probably the briefest rules are those for rent tribunals, namely the Furnished Houses (Rent Control) Regulations made in 1946.[65] These consist of barely two pages of rules (and a further page of schedules) and omit any provision as to an order of events at the hearing, what happens if a party fails to attend, matters of evidence such as cross-examination, evidence on oath, inspection of premises, and any power to correct errors or slips. Brevity is of course not of itself a vice: the rules made for rent assessment committees in 1971[66] (after some six years of operation with only the bare rules laid down in the Act itself) are only slightly longer than those for rent tribunals but unlike the latter they do provide for non-attendance of the parties, cross-examination, inspection of premises and the correction of accidental errors or omissions.

In general terms the rules of 'informal' tribunals such as those concerned with rents, national insurance and supplementary benefits contain the minimum requirements to bring the parties together and set the stage for an informal inquiry. At the other end of the scale one might consider the rules of the Performing Rights Tribunal[67] which has the most complicated pre-hearing procedure of any tribunal. Proceedings before the tribunal are commenced by an application (on an appropriate form), accompanied by a statement of the case intended to be made out and a list of documents in the applicant's possession. The

[65] Although the present statutory authority of rent tribunals is the 1968 Rent Act, no rules of procedure have been promulgated under that Act, and until they are, by virtue of the savings clause in schedule 16(1) of the 1968 Act the 1946 regulations remain.

[66] Rent Assessment Committees (England and Wales) Regulations 1971.

[67] Performing Rights Tribunal Rules 1965.

application is then advertised and within the time specified in the advertisement (being not less than twenty-one days) any person or organization (an 'intervener') can apply to be joined as a party. After the filing of statements of case and documents by the licensing body against whom the proceedings are brought and interveners there may follow a convoluted procedure for 'objections to originator's credentials' and 'objections to intervener's credentials' which in itself can give rise to a hearing quite separate from the main hearing, and which has its own procedure regarding the lodging of objections, giving notices, etc. There is also provision for statements of case and answers to be amended and then (when it might be thought that the case could at last be heard) the chairman is required to 'appoint a date and place for the attendance of the parties for the purpose of his giving further directions as to the further conduct of the proceedings', which may include the setting of a date for hearing, the conduct of further interlocutory matters, etc.

A party to a hearing before the tribunal may thus be faced with the prospect of a number of hearings, e.g. a hearing to determine credentials, a hearing to set the date of hearing and dispose of interlocutory matters (which may give rise to still further hearings) before his application is finally heard on the merits.

A middle course is pursued by the immigration rules[68] which, if a personal judgment is permitted, come close to the ideal in two ways.[69] First, they contain provision, either in a positive or negative form, for all the particular matters mentioned in this chapter, which must benefit both the tribunals and the parties. Second, the procedure (especially in regard to the immigration officer's report – discussed at p. 270 – the mandatory notice of the facilities available for advice and assistance, and the provision for notice of appeal to be given orally in some cases) has clearly been drafted with great care to meet the particular circumstances in which an appeal is likely to arise.

Not only is there considerable variation between one tribunal and another but also between the procedures imposed on any one tribunal if it enjoys a number of disparate jurisdictions, a complication which could become more widespread if tribunals ever came to be grouped in fewer and larger units. Thus the Industrial Tribunals at one time had five sets of rules of procedure for six jurisdictions. Under the Regulations which followed the 1971 Industrial Relations Act these were reduced to three, one set covering the principal jurisdictions but two others being required for industrial training and selective employ-

[68] Immigration Appeals (Procedure) Rules 1970.

[69] We are here concerned with the drafting of the rules, not with their policy content (see later p. 313).

ment payment appeals. There are material differences between them, e.g. on rights of audience.

### THE DRAFTING OF RULES OF PROCEDURE

There is great variety in drafting, which arises from the absence of a central drafting body, and which makes comparison between different sets of rules difficult except in the most general terms – indeed procedural provisions themselves are sometimes to be found in 'Rules', sometimes in 'Regulations', sometimes in 'Orders' and sometimes in the statute itself, or in a Schedule to the statute.

The rules dealing with the holding of hearings in public provide a good illustration of individuality in drafting, even in straightforward matters. The common provision that the hearing shall be in public with a general discretion to sit in private if this is thought to be warranted is expressed in the following variety of forms: the tribunal shall sit in public[70] 'unless there are exceptional reasons which make it desirable', or 'unless the board shall otherwise decide', or 'unless for any reason the tribunal determines', or 'unless the tribunal determines at the request of a party', or 'unless the court otherwise order on the application of any party to the appeal and upon being satisfied that the interests of one or more parties to the appeal would be prejudicially affected', or 'unless the president determines that in the interests of justice or public policy . . .', or 'except in so far as the chairman of the tribunal may for special reasons otherwise direct', or 'because of exceptional circumstances', or 'provided that, if all parties consent' etc., etc., the hearing may be held in private.[71] One might also consider the wording used to express this same provision in regard to rent tribunals:

> '. . . and the Tribunal may if they think fit, and at the request of either party shall unless for some special reason they consider it undesirable, allow the hearing to be held in public.'[72]

[70] Agricultural land tribunals; or 'the hearing shall be held in public' (air operators' certificates tribunal), or 'the hearing of an appeal shall be in public' (children's voluntary homes tribunal), or the 'tribunal shall hold a hearing which shall be in public' (medical appeal tribunals) and so on. Even on this small point there is no uniformity. The statutory references are given below.

[71] Examples taken from the Independent Schools Tribunal Rules 1958, Civil Aviation (Licensing) Regs. 1964, Children Act (Appeal Tribunal) Rules 1949, Industrial Tribunals (Redundancy Payments) Regs. 1967, General Rate Act 1967 (s. 76(2)), Wireless Telegraphy Appeal Tribunal Rules 1953, Nat. Ins. (Ind. Inj.) (Determination of Claims and Questions) (No. 2) Regs. 1967, Air Operators' Certificates Regs. 1966, Iron and Steel Arbitration Tribunal Rules 1968.

[72] Reg. 8(1), Furnished Houses (Rent Control) Regs. 1946.

## IMPROVING TRIBUNAL PROCEDURES

The most striking features of this survey of procedures are the variation in the quality of their drafting and the lack of guidance on a number of important points to tribunal members or to those appearing before them.[73] A general power for a tribunal to regulate its own proceedings can make good such deficiencies, but equally it can add to variety and inconsistency, since an experienced chairman may use it to ensure a judicious blend of order and informality while in the hands of another it may become what one witness before the Franks Committee described as 'proceedings so informal that it is virtually a family party of some kind'.[74] As the Chairman of the Committee pointed out:

> 'On the one hand informality can be taken to mean simplicity of conduct of proceedings, the absence of some of the more formalised procedures normally required in courts of law. If you like, from that point of view, informality is a matter of atmosphere, the way in which things are done. On the other hand informality can mean just an absence of any regular procedure . . .'[75]

As our survey shows, procedural rules are still characterized today by divergencies and shortcomings. A solution proposed to the Franks Committee by legal witnesses was the idea of a standard code[76] or set of codes[77] of procedure for tribunals. At first sight this is an attractive idea but it was rejected by the Committee on the grounds that 'the detailed procedure for each tribunal should be designed to meet its particular circumstances'.[78] With this one must agree – the uniformity of a standard code would create more problems than it would solve. But what is required is not uniformity as such, but greater consistency, which Franks thought would best be achieved by a central drafting body.

For the Franks Report did in fact envisage a central drafting authority (the Council on Tribunals).[79] Moreover in 1932 the Donoughmore Committee had expressed considerable disquiet about the practice of regulations being drafted by departments: '. . . the work is uneven – some is good and some is bad',[80] and had gone on to suggest the possi-

73 See p. 314.
74 Sir George Coldstream, Minutes of Evidence, p. 642 para. 3488.
75 Ibid., para. 3489.
76 E.g. by the Law Society, ibid., p. 339.
77 Professor F. H. Lawson.
78 Report, p. 15.
79 Franks Report, p. 91, para. 8 of main recommendations.
80 Report of the Committee on Ministers' Powers, p. 49. In evidence to the

bility of 'a central supervising drafting department which would tend to secure uniformity of practice'. Other suggestions made with the same intention to the Franks Committee were that the rules of procedure for all tribunals ought to be drafted by the Lord Chancellor,[81] or made by a new Administrative Court in the same way as the Rules of the Supreme Court.[82]

The idea of a central drafting body has not come to fruition – the Council on Tribunals was not given this power as suggested by Franks, as the Government believed that such a body would not be equipped to exercise it; it is instead limited to commenting on the product of departmental drafting. Given the limitations of its consultative role the Council has made numerous suggestions for the improvement of particular rules, many of which have been accepted by the departments concerned, but the fact remains that the Council is often consulted too late and must perforce confine itself to commenting within the framework proposed by the department (but see p. 210).

It also seems to us reasonable that the procedural rules of all tribunals should cover the heads and sub-heads listed at the beginning of this chapter, together with the following which we shall be discussing at a later stage:

Representation
Burden of Proof
Evidence
Public and Private Hearings
Withholding of evidence and exclusion of parties.

It may be said that such rules would be unnecessarily full, and that they could impair the informality of tribunals. But even the most informal tribunals cannot ignore these matters when they arise in the course of a hearing, and it is in fact the content of these rules rather than their format which will decide whether a tribunal is formal or informal. The immigration adjudicators work according to rules covering virtually all these points and there is no evidence that this has impaired their informality or efficiency.

The Franks Committee did not feel able to go very far in such matters, but conclusions that were valid in 1956 may well need to be re-examined

Franks Committee the Permanent Secretary to the Lord Chancellor explained that regulations for tribunals are 'normally drafted by the legal adviser to the Department' (Minutes of Evidence, p. 209, para. 1706). We understand that there has been no change in this practice.

[81] A proposal put forward by the Law Society. Minutes of Evidence, p. 617. The Permanent Secretary to the Lord Chancellor thought this 'reasonable', provided his staff were increased considerably (p. 209, para. 1705).

[82] Professor H. W. R. Wade, Minutes of Evidence, p. 553.

in 1973 in view of the continuing increase in the number and range of tribunals. Consistency need not amount to a standard code, which would be no more practicable now than it was in 1956. It would, however, ensure firstly that all potential procedural difficulties would be covered by the rules of all tribunals, not necessarily in the same form but in the form, so to speak, of a check-list; and secondly that where the intention was the same it would be expressed in the same words. Uniformity to this extent would appear to be an advantage – even a necessity.

## APPEALS

Discussion of appeals can run into cross-purposes because of a confusion as to what is meant by a one-, two- or three-tier system of appeal. There are several tribunals which can be regarded either as appeal tribunals or as tribunals of first instance according to whether a statutory officer who makes an *initial* decision is to be regarded as 'a tribunal'. Thus a supplementary benefit appeal tribunal will hear an appeal from a decision of a representative of the Supplementary Benefits Commission;[83] a rent assessment committee from that of a rent officer; a national insurance local tribunal from that of an insurance officer; or an immigration adjudicator from that of an immigration officer at a port of entry. Despite the name 'supplementary benefit appeal tribunal', the only one of these to incorporate the word 'appeal' in its title, we find it more logical not to regard the Commission as a tribunal, but to restrict the use of the word to tribunals scheduled to the Tribunals and Inquiries Act.

There are some tribunals from whose decisions there is no appeal (except review by way of the prerogative orders), namely supplementary benefit appeal tribunals, an independent schools tribunal, and the Betting Levy Appeal Tribunal. Most tribunals are not so self-contained, and a form of appeal either on facts or law and either within or outside the appeal structure is usually provided for a dissatisfied party.

In the more sophisticated tribunal systems appeals remain within

[83] To be accurate, SBATS have two minor jurisdictions (representing about 1·5 per cent of their total cases) which are strictly of first instance, concerning any recoverable overpayments and directions in cases of alleged wilful unemployment. The latter can result in an order for compulsory attendance at a training centre, and initial decision by a tribunal is clearly appropriate. The Child Poverty Action Group has urged that for analogous reasons, i.e. because the liberty of the subject is in issue, the decision to stop a woman's benefit on grounds of alleged cohabitation should also be a matter for decision by a first-instance tribunal and not by an official.

the system itself. National insurance is an example – for as we shall describe (p. 230), appeals on both fact and law lie from a decision of a national insurance local tribunal to the National Insurance Commissioner,[84] who also acts as the appellate authority on matters of law for medical appeal tribunals[85] (there being no appeal on the merits from these tribunals' determinations). Medical appeal tribunals are themselves appeal authorities, hearing appeals from medical appeal boards.[86] In the field of immigration there is a similar two-tier system of appeals, the initial adjudication normally being made by an immigration adjudicator. Any party dissatisfied with his determination may then appeal to the Immigration Appeal Tribunal provided that he obtains leave to appeal from either the adjudicator or the Tribunal.[87] If leave is granted the appeal almost invariably takes the form of a rehearing.[88] In both the national insurance and immigration fields the appeal system is self-contained.

A more common pattern is a right of appeal, on both law and merits, from the first instance tribunal to another, superior, tribunal or court (which often has an original jurisdiction of its own) with a further right of appeal on law only, to the High Court or the Court of Appeal. Both patterns are to be found in the industrial tribunals, whose varied jurisdictions have given rise to a somewhat complicated set of arrangements for appeal. There is a right of appeal in law to the National Industrial Relations Court from any decision of an industrial tribunal under the Contracts of Employment Act 1963, the Redundancy Payments Act 1965, the Equal Pay Act 1970, and on a complaint under the Industrial Relations Act 1971. An appeal in law lies to the Divisional Court from any decision made by an industrial tribunal under any other jurisdiction. The Industrial Relations Court has of course a considerable original jurisdiction of its own, and there is an appeal in all cases on a point of law to the Court of Appeal.[89]

Rating valuation appeals are another example – these are determined initially by local valuation courts: any person who appeared before a

[84] S. 70, National Insurance Act 1965.

[85] S. 42, National Insurance (Industrial Injuries) Act 1965. Leave to appeal must be sought, initially from the tribunal, and if refused, from the Commissioner.

[86] S. 39, National Insurance (Industrial Injuries) Act 1965.

[87] S. 7, Immigration Appeals Act 1969, and Rule 12, Immigration Appeals (Procedure) Rules 1970. Leave to appeal must be granted if the Home Secretary certifies that it is in the public interest for the Tribunal to decide the case, or if the appellant is already in possession of an entry certificate.

[88] Rule 18 provides for the determination of an appeal without a hearing, but in practice this only happens in a few exceptional cases.

[89] In Scotland to the Court of Session.

court and is aggrieved at the decision may appeal to the Lands Tribunal which conducts a rehearing on facts, law or merits.[90] The Lands Tribunal also has several original jurisdictions (e.g. in the assessment of disputed compensation under various statutes (see p. 53) and also as an arbitrator (by consent). In all its jurisdictions the decision of the Lands Tribunal is expressed to be 'final', subject however to the very important proviso that 'any person aggrieved by the decision as being erroneous in point of law' may require the tribunal to state a case for the decision of the Court of Appeal.[91] In substance the position in regard to transport licensing appeals is similar – applications for road haulage operators' licences are initially determined by the goods licensing authority[92] (the chairman of the local Traffic Commissioners) from whom there is a right of appeal to the Transport Tribunal[93] with a further right of appeal on a point of law to the Court of Appeal.[94]

For most tribunals arrangements are simpler – the tribunal is the final arbiter on matters of fact with an appeal to the High Court on a point of law. For many tribunals this was accomplished by section 9, Tribunals and Inquiries Act 1958 (now section 13 of the 1971 Act) which provides that any party to proceedings before the air operator's certificates authority, a children's voluntary homes tribunal, an independent schools tribunal, industrial tribunals (though their position was affected by the Industrial Relations Act 1971 – see above), a mines and quarries tribunal, the National Health Service Tribunal,[95] the National Insurance Adjudicator, a nurses' training institutions tribunal, the Prevention of Fraud Tribunal, rent tribunals, rent assessment committees and the Wireless Telegraphy Tribunal, who 'is dissatisfied in point of law with a decision of the tribunal' may 'either appeal therefrom to the High Court or require the tribunal to state and sign a case for the opinion of the High Court'.[96] It is clear from the Act that there is a further right of appeal to the Court of Appeal and House of Lords.

To this list must be added those tribunals which provide in their own statutes for a right of appeal on a point of law to the High Court, among them agricultural land tribunals, the Performing Rights Tribunal, mental health review tribunals, and the Commons Commissioners.

[90] S. 77, General Rate Act 1967.

[91] S. 34, Lands Tribunal Act 1949.

[92] Part V, Transport Act 1968. The decisions of the Traffic Commissioners are not appealable.

[93] S. 70, 80, and schedule 9, Transport Act 1968.

[94] Schedule 10, Transport Act 1962.

[95] Established under s. 42, National Health Service Act 1946.

[96] Whether proceedings are by way of appeal or case stated depends on the relevant High Court rules.

Sometimes the right of appeal is not to the High Court generally but to a particular or nominated judge. Two examples are the nominated judges dealing with appeals from the Comptroller of Patents (on facts and law) and the Pensions Appeal Tribunal (on law only) respectively. Although there may be no difference in procedure between appeals to the High Court and to a nominated judge the latter procedure can sometimes have advantages – for instance it enables representation by non-lawyers and a lower scale of costs and (as in the case of pensions appeals) a nominated judge's decision need not automatically be subject to appeal to the Court of Appeal. On the other hand a nominated judge being technically an 'inferior' tribunal may well be subject to the supervisory jurisdiction of the High Court which can mean that the decision of a judge who is an expert in patent law is reviewed by three of his colleagues who are never otherwise concerned with patent matters.[97]

As to the procedure on appeals to the High Court a word needs to be said about the distinction between an *appeal* on a point of law and proceedings by way of *case stated.* In an appeal the onus is on the parties to present the legal issues required to be determined by the court and the arguments in support of their position. The tribunal is not required to do anything to further the appeal, although the appellate court does have the advantage of being able to consider the record of the proceedings below (the notes of evidence or the chairman's record, if any). The case stated procedure on the other hand requires the tribunal to set out its findings (but not the evidence) together with a formulation of the issues required to be determined by the court, a procedure which presupposes a legally qualified chairman.[98]

There is, however, another practical distinction of some importance between these two avenues of appeal, namely that the case stated procedure enables a tribunal to adjourn a hearing when a point of law arises in the course of proceedings in order to send that special point up for a ruling with the intention of continuing the hearing after it has been decided.[99] To have issues clarified in the middle of a hearing in this way is obviously more convenient than an appeal after a decision has been made and can lessen the costs for the parties.

The Tribunals and Inquiries Act 1971 also provides for the case stated procedure to be used as an alternative to an appeal 'according as rules of court may provide'.[100] This is certainly the case with most

[97] See Report of the Banks Committee on The British Patent System (Cmnd. 4407), para. 165.

[98] See further Franks Committee, Minutes of Evidence, p. 205.

[99] See Tribunals and Inquiries Act 1971, s. 13(2) and R.S.C. Orders 56 and 94.

[100] S. 13(1).

tribunals but it may be that such an alternative does not exist for all tribunals.[101] The distinction has a practical consequence, since there is a time limit on appeals but none on a case stated, although in cases where the alternative methods are available, it is always open to a tribunal to refuse to state a case if it considers that this is being used to further an otherwise out-of-time appeal.

Lastly, in this catalogue of appeal structures, the avenue of appeal may not be to a tribunal but to the Minister. There is a small but specialized group of such appeals which we have already noted in passing, but which it may be convenient to summarize. Sometimes. particular questions are *reserved* for ministerial determination (e.g. national insurance contribution questions and immigration cases with a political or security flavour). In such cases issues which have been determined initially by a local official and which would otherwise be appealable to a tribunal are by statute diverted to the Minister. Alternatively the Minister may act as an appellate authority from *tribunal* decisions (as in the case of certain licensing decisions by the Traffic Commissioners and the Civil Aviation Authority and in respect of some National Health Service cases (p. 239). Moreover there is one 'tribunal', the Milk and Dairies Tribunal, which does not make a decision but a report to the Minister in the manner of a public inquiry (pp. 225–6).

[101] See *Middleton* v. *Vaux and Associated Breweries* [1972] (7 I.T.R. 129) in which the Industrial Court suggested that the proper method of appealing against a decision of an industrial tribunal is by way of notice of appeal rather than a case stated.

CHAPTER 7

# OPERATION IN PRACTICE

In earlier chapters we have tried to marshal the ascertainable facts about tribunals, and this has incidentally thrown some light on how they work. But what we have said needs to be supplemented in two ways. First, they are susceptible to atmosphere and are influenced by working relationships in ways which cannot be defined in statutes, regulations or reports, but which need to be defined at first hand. Second, there are some areas of the subject where information is still inadequate and which a comprehensive study of this kind can indicate but cannot explore very far – for example, the true nature of the cost of the system as compared with the cost of the courts or the exact reasons for delay in bringing appeals to a hearing. Enough information is available on such matters to show that more is needed, but the detail would be a study in itself.

Accordingly the purpose of this chapter is to supplement the preceding ones by discussing the 'imponderables' and by drawing attention to matters that would repay further research.

The chapter tends to seek out problems and difficulties, this being inevitable in a critical appraisal. To see these in perspective it must be remembered that tribunals dispose of many hundreds of cases on every working day of the year without encountering problems, without experiencing difficulties and without giving rise to complaint or question.

We discuss these matters under the following heads:

(1) Personal influences
(2) Relations with government departments
(3) Premises and 'stage-management'
(4) Advice and assistance to applicants or appellants
(5) Costs and expenses
(6) Speed of decisions, delays and case-loads
(7) Results
(8) Publicity.

## PERSONAL INFLUENCES

The way in which a tribunal operates in practice is of course influenced by a variety of things – for example the historical circumstances which led to its establishment, the way in which it is constituted and the rules of procedure which it is required to follow. But if there is one factor which more than any other influences both the way in which a tribunal works and the impression that it makes on those who have to appear before it, it is the personality of the individual chairmen and the influence (where there is such an appointment) of the President. The very nature of tribunal proceedings, and the fact that the applicant or appellant is often unrepresented, throws a heavy burden on the chairman and obliges him to play a much more active part in the proceedings than is normally expected of a judge in an English court of law. Moreover, tribunals are not so heavily encumbered with traditions as the courts, nor, on the whole, are their procedures so elaborately prescribed; so there is greater scope for innovation on the part of a President or chairman who is so inclined.

As we have seen, one of the advantages claimed for tribunals over the ordinary courts of law is that their proceedings are said to be far less formal. It is possible to make too much of this (and of the other advantages of tribunals) by failing to compare like with like – or, to be more specific, by comparing the way in which most tribunals operate with the way in which the High Court conducts its business; when a much fairer comparison would be with proceedings in the County Court or even, in some instances, with those in a magistrate's court. But, even so, the degree to which the proceedings of a particular tribunal or group of tribunals tend towards formality or to follow in this or that respect the rituals of the courts, often depends more on the views of the President or Chairmen as to the 'proper way of doing things' than on anything inherent in their constitution or rules of procedure. Certainly at the hearing it is the chairman's role which is crucial, and the way in which he handles the proceedings sets the tone of the occasion. At a different level the influence of a President can be decisive in setting the tone for a whole group of tribunals and an outstanding example of this can be found in the working of the Industrial Tribunal, which gives impressive evidence of an imaginative approach to a new field of adjudication. There are instances where, by contrast, a tribunal's way of working has been inclined towards something more formal and much more reminiscent of the courts, and it would be instructive to examine this aspect of the working of tribunals in more detail. However, this would mean enlarging the scope of the present study to an unacceptable extent and the most that can be done here is simply to emphasize the fact that more than on anything else the successful working of the whole tribunal system depends upon the selection of the right kind of people as Chairmen or Presidents.[1]

## RELATIONS WITH GOVERNMENT DEPARTMENTS

As we have seen the Franks Committee were perturbed by the extent to which tribunals were regarded by official witnesses as part of the machinery of the administration whereas, it was felt, they 'should properly be regarded as machinery provided by Parliament for adjudication rather than part of the machinery of administration'.

All tribunals which are properly so called[2] are of course wholly independent in the exercise of their judicial functions, and are 'the responsibility of' a government department only in the limited sense that appointments are in the hands of a particular Minister, who is, of course, responsible to Parliament, or that his department may be providing them with staff and administrative services. The point is not always made as clear as it might be. 'Home Office immigration tribunals', for example, is a common form of speech which is not only inaccurate but seriously misleading, since the adjudicators and the Appeal Tribunal are independent judicial bodies, and the latter is as likely to reject as to support an appeal by the Secretary of State against the decision of an adjudicator.

On the other hand the degree of working relationship between a tribunal and a department may vary both for historical reasons and because of the nature of the matters to be resolved.

There are some tribunals such as the Lands Tribunal and the Pensions Appeal Tribunals which, as if to emphasize their status and independence, have virtually no links with any of the executive departments. Their Presidents, chairmen and members are all appointed by the Lord Chancellor and they are 'serviced' on the administration side by the Lord Chancellor's Department in much the same way as the courts. Indeed, they appear in the Civil Service List as 'Lord Chancellor's Departments'.

Most tribunals, however, are linked fairly closely with one or other of the executive departments, for, although presidents and chairmen

[1] As we saw on p. 125 (*Tribunal staff and the general public*) there are circumstances in which the selection of the right kind of *staff* can be almost equally important.

[2] There are a few where appeal on final determination lies with the Ministers. See p. 239.

are often appointed by the Lord Chancellor, it is, as we saw in Chapter 4, by no means unusual for members to be appointed by a Minister in charge of an executive department: and most are dependent on these departments for the provision of staff and premises. Even tribunals such as agricultural land tribunals, mental health review tribunals, and the Immigration Appeal Tribunal, for which the Lord Chancellor is primarily responsible in that he appoints both the chairmen and members, depend nonetheless entirely on an executive department for their staffs and accommodation. Thus agricultural land tribunals are staffed and housed by the Ministry of Agriculture, Fisheries and Food, mental health review tribunals[3] by the Department of Health and Social Security, and the Immigration Appeal Tribunal by the Home Office.

Perhaps the closest relationship between a government department and a group of tribunals is that which exists between the Department of Health and Social Security and the social security tribunals. A variety of circumstances have combined to bring this about. There is the long association of previous ministries with previous kinds of machinery for adjudication, dating from the Poor Law, the Unemployment Assistance Board and the National Assistance Board on the one hand and the first Unemployment Insurance Act on the other, at times when opinion was not so sensitive on the issue of judicial independence. There is the corresponding fact that the structure has always been fragmented, with no full-time appointments on the adjudicatory side, so that in terms of servicing and staff, and even of physical accommodation, the tribunals have *in fact* been entirely dependent upon the Department,[4] even if the word 'appendage', which is sometimes used, does less than justice to their true status.

It should not be assumed that close links with an executive department inhibit a tribunal from acting independently in the exercise of its judicial functions. It is a matter of factual observation, for example, that an insurance officer presenting a case to a national insurance local tribunal enjoys no advantage whatsoever over the appellant. On the contrary the tribunal may well extend great indulgence to the latter, to help in what are to him adverse circumstances, while being almost ruthless to the former. Nonetheless problems do arise and it would be unrealistic to ignore them.

[3] In practice, hearings by these tribunals are normally held at the hospitals where patients are detained.

[4] It is true that these tribunals are not linked solely with the Department of Health and Social Security since their chairmen are selected by the Secretary of State from a panel to which appointments are made by the Lord Chancellor. But in all other respects they are closely tied to the Department, which is for all practical purposes the 'responsible' department.

In the first place there is the problem of 'departmental influence'. This is not necessarily harmful, and there is in fact a great deal in the history of the relations between departments and 'their' tribunals of which the departments have every reason to be proud, and through which a great contribution has been made to the general administration of justice in this country. Indeed without departmental influence in one form or another the tribunal system as we know it could neither have grown up nor been maintained.

On the other hand Ministers and their departments do have interests that they wish to safeguard and policies they are anxious to promote, and too close a connection with tribunals can lay them open to the criticism of being judges in their own cause. And if a tribunal depends entirely for its staff on officers seconded or attached to it from a department directly interested in the issues with which it has to deal, this in itself can make the association an uneasy one. The situation is aggravated when the clerk or secretary of the tribunal is a fairly senior officer of the department. It is even more so when he serves a part time or relatively inexpert tribunal which has to rely greatly on his advice. The old national assistance appeal tribunals, for example, were vulnerable to the accusation that through such means the tribunals were left within the firm control of the Assistance Board.[5] Nowadays it would be most surprising to find 'departmental influence' exercised on a tribunal in so crude a form. But 'departmental influence' in other forms can still cause problems. Staff on secondment to a tribunal do not lose all sense of loyalty to their old department and the influence of this should not be under-estimated, and occasionally it has been the cause of serious difficulty. We take up the point again in the concluding chapter.

Where things go wrong is where the different spheres in which tribunals and the departments operate are not properly distinguished. Boundaries are needed to protect the judicial integrity of tribunals and where these are disregarded or inadequately defined difficulties are almost certain to arise.

Thus procedures which blur the clear distinction between tribunals and departments can be a cause of trouble. The administrative review of supplementary benefit appeals, which we describe on page 353, is a case in point. In this particular instance the 'blurring' is made worse by the fact that the Department does not in practice attempt to distinguish sharply between a 'complaint' and an 'appeal', so that almost any expression of dissatisfaction is treated as an appeal – for example, no special form is required. Thus in substance this prior review by officials

[5] See R. S. W. Pollard (ed.) *Administrative Tribunals at Work* (Stevens, 1950), pp. 59–61.

is very much like, say, the steps taken to sort out differences between the taxpayer and the inspector without formal appeal to the General Commissioners of Income Tax. Nevertheless if disputes can be settled satisfactorily by either administrative or judicial review, and especially where (as with supplementary benefits) the number disputed is in any case a very small fraction of the total, it is natural that there should seem to be no clear dichotomy between the Department and 'its' tribunals.

A somewhat similar procedure in connection with the review of war pensions claims was at one time a cause of difficulty, and was eventually brought to the attention of the Council on Tribunals by the President of the Pensions Appeal Tribunals. Notice of Appeal has to be sent in the first instance not to the Tribunal but to the Department of Health and Social Security, which would then, on occasion, offer to review the case if the appellant agreed to defer his appeal. The President thought, and the Council supported his view, that although his acceptance of a review did not prejudice his right of subsequent appeal to the Tribunal the arrangement was 'liable to cause the appellant to confuse the role of the (departmental) medical board and that of the Tribunal and to feel that the Tribunal was merely a part of the Department or not entirely independent'.[6] In consequence a modified arrangement was agreed which leaves appellants in no doubt about their rights of appeal or about the independence of the Tribunal.

This was an interesting affair which illustrated not only the independence of the President of the Tribunal but also the importance of justice being 'seen to be done'. The Department's offer to review was always made because they thought it to be in the appellant's best interest, and it would be wrong to read any sinister connotation into their action; but equally the procedure violated a categorical recommendation of the Franks Committee (paragraph 73) that

> 'Documents relating to tribunal proceedings should be clearly designated as documents of the tribunal and should come from the tribunal and not from a Government Department.'

Secondly, there is a general problem of 'communication' which is most acute where there are a large number of part-time, relatively low-powered and essentially local tribunals which are directly linked with an executive department and have no President or regional chairman to act as an intermediary. We referred to this matter when discussing the structure of tribunals (p. 90) and suggested that one of the most solid advantages of the presidential system was that it went far towards

[6] Annual Report of the Council 1969–70 (paras. 62–3).

solving this particular problem. It is worth giving some account of what may happen in the absence of such a system.

Many members of social security tribunals, for instance, feel that they are working in almost total isolation;[7] and this situation has not been helped in the past by the reluctance on the part of the Department of Health and Social Security (which is in this case the 'responsible' department) to arrange conferences for chairmen.

It is true that although the case for holding conferences has been strongly urged by the Council on Tribunals not all the chairmen of national insurance local tribunals (who almost without exception are practising lawyers) are in favour of them. Yet even a proposal for a conference of chairmen of supplementary benefit appeal tribunals, which had received much support among chairmen, was at first opposed by the Department – apparently out of fear that such a conference might lead tribunals to operate along lines of common 'policy' instead of freely exercising such discretion as they had.[8] But conferences apart, there is also an absence of proper channels of communication which shows itself in various ways.

There is, for example, a difficulty in connection with the investigation of complaints about social security tribunals. The Department is, of course, concerned to know whether or not the tribunals are working satisfactorily, and there is therefore a certain amount of discreet supervision by the regional officers of the Department who are the main point of contact between the Department and the tribunals. This can make for friction and certainly makes it more difficult to investigate complaints. A tribunal chairman who is appointed for a three-year term will certainly be mindful of the fact that when his re-appointment comes to be considered the views of the regional office will be taken into account and may well be highly sensitive to anything which suggests to him that the Department is, to put it crudely, 'breathing down his neck'. In any event chairmen (and especially those who are lawyers) are likely to be on their guard against any attempts by the Department to exert some sort of influence on them. The Department for its part will be anxious to avoid any suggestion that such a thing is being attempted. In this situation any informal discussion between the Department and individual chairmen about the working of their tribunals

[7] It must be remembered in this connection that the Chief National Insurance Commissioner does not exercise any administrative functions in respect of national insurance local tribunals. His function is solely to act as a court of appeal from those tribunals.

[8] Now, however, the Department has withdrawn its initial objections and a number of conferences have been held.

tends to be inhibited. It also adds to the difficulty which some chairmen feel when there are matters which they wish to raise with the Department. It is not surprising therefore that members of the Council on Tribunals have encountered chairmen of social security tribunals who were 'clearly labouring under difficulties which they had no opportunity to discuss'.[9]

The lack of proper channels of communication also shows itself in the problems which face departments in connection with providing advice and information for chairmen and members of tribunals. Guidance on the law, and to a smaller extent on procedure, is available to national insurance and medical appeal tribunals in the published decisions of the National Insurance Commissioners. In the case of supplementary benefit appeal tribunals there is not quite the same problem because questions of law arise only rarely, but there are still occasions when one of the tribunals feels the need of a second opinion, and the lack of any recognized means of getting one must aggravate the feeling that they are working on their own. (It can happen that one chairman consults informally with the chairman of an adjacent tribunal but there is no official machinery to ensure that he even knows who his neighbouring colleagues are.) Exceptionally a supplementary benefit appeal tribunal which requires advice on a question of law has to look for this to a member of the legal staff of the Department of Health and Social Security who attends the hearing in a neutral role similar to that of an *amicus curiae* in court proceedings. Such an arrangement is unlikely to make a very happy impression on anyone doubtful about the independence of the tribunals. It has been accepted by the Council on Tribunals 'only with some hesitation', and the Department has been asked by the Council to make a report to them on each occasion the procedure is used.

Departmental circulars and memoranda which are a normal method of communication between the central departments and local authorities were at one time used by the former Ministry of Housing and Local Government to convey 'instructions' to rent tribunals on matters of procedure, but their use for this purpose was criticized as being an infringement of the tribunals' independence and they were subsequently used only to convey information and 'advice'. There are obviously dangers in any arrangement of this kind and there are also possibilities of abuse.[10]

[9] Annual Report of the Council on Tribunals 1968, paras. 14–16.

[10] In evidence to the Committee the then Permanent Secretary to the Lord Chancellor's Department said that in his view the use of departmental memoranda and circulars for this purpose was 'very dangerous'. Committee on Administrative Tribunals and Inquiries. Minutes of Evidence, days 6–7, p. 207: and see also days 3–4, p. 59.

The giving of 'informal guidance' to rent tribunals on points of importance for which there is no provision in the rules of procedure has also been criticized by the Council on Tribunals,[11] and now that rent tribunals have been brought into the presidential system of the rent assessment panels the use of departmental circulars and memoranda to give 'advice' seems to have died out.

This is a problem that need not have arisen, and which could now be solved, if procedural rules were more systematic and comprehensive, as we have suggested in Chapter 6.

The fact is that where there are close links between tribunals and an executive department, the department is in a dilemma. If it attempts to give advice and guidance to the tribunals for which it is generally 'responsible' it is open to the accusation that it is seeking to undermine the tribunals' independence. If it refrains from giving advice and guidance to them, it may equally be open to an accusation of neglecting them. A reflection of this dilemma is to be seen in the rather rudimentary provision for introducing new chairmen and members to the work of their tribunals. Usually the basic literature is made available, in the form of relevant Acts and regulations, and sometimes also an introductory note prepared by the responsible department or by the clerk or secretary to the tribunal. Opportunities are also provided for 'sitting in' at hearings.

Sometimes the provision goes a little further, but not always in a direction which reinforces the independence and status of the tribunals. For example, new chairmen of national insurance local tribunals are interviewed after appointment by a senior officer from the Department's regional office who gives them 'general information about their duties'; prospective members are interviewed by the manager of the appropriate local office; and a somewhat similar arrangement applies to the chairmen and members of supplementary benefit appeal tribunals.

But there is no settled general practice. Arrangements vary from one type of tribunal to another and mostly it seems to be a case of 'picking up the job as one goes along'. There is no systematic training for work on a tribunal, such as is now provided for magistrates; and, not surprisingly, there are occasionally members of tribunals who seem to have no clear idea of what their role on the tribunal is meant to be.

There also seems to be no settled practice which ensures that chairmen of tribunals are consulted as a matter of course about the drafting (or amendment) of rules of procedure, or that when they are their views are made known when the rules are submitted in draft to the

[11] Annual Report of the Council on Tribunals 1964 (paras. 56–9).

Council on Tribunals.[12] Still less is there any settled practice which ensures that they are consulted about proposals for legislation which would substantially affect the working of their tribunals. It is evident from the Annual Report of the Council on Tribunals for 1969[13] that the National Insurance Commissioners were consulted about the proposals in the abortive National Superannuation and Social Insurance Bill of 1970 only after the Council had suggested that they should be, whereas there was consultation in advance with the President of the Industrial Tribunals about the provisions of the proposed legislation on industrial relations which was in preparation at the same time.

It would be unfortunate if all that has been said about problems of communication were to give the impression that problems of this kind are confined to tribunals which have close links with the departments. Other tribunals, such as local valuation courts, the General Commissioners of Income Tax and Executive Councils and service committees of the NHS, which have only very loose links with the departments, also have to contend with problems of this kind. All these are local tribunals with a part-time membership consisting mostly of laymen which have to rely greatly on their clerks. In this they have some similarity to supplementary benefit appeal tribunals, but in fact they more closely resemble a bench of magistrates, for they are locally based and largely organize their own work, and do not depend on any of the central departments for the provision of staff or premises. Thus, as we have seen, the Clerks of the Valuation Panels (from which the members of local valuation courts are selected) are appointed by the Panels, the Clerks to the General Commissioners are appointed by the Commissioners themselves, and the Clerks of NHS Executive Councils and service committees are appointed by the Executive Councils.[14]

Some guidance on questions of procedure is received from the departments: for example notes of guidance in the form of a booklet are issued to each newly appointed general commissioner by the Lord Chancellor's Department, and circulars on specially important points

[12] A situation which is made even more unsatisfactory by the absence of any uniform arrangements for the drafting of such rules.

[13] See Appendices A and B to that Report. It could however be argued that the former did not directly impinge on the Commissioners' jurisdiction whereas the latter necessitated fundamental changes in the structure and working of industrial tribunals.

[14] The appointment of the Clerk to a Local Valuation Panel does not require Ministerial approval but the amount of his salary does. A Clerk to the General Commissioners can in certain circumstances be dismissed by the Lord Chancellor. Persons appointed as Clerks to NHS Executive Councils require the approval of the Secretary of State.

of procedure are sent out by the Department of Health and Social Security to NHS Executive Councils and service committees. But, in most matters, including questions of procedure, these tribunals have to look for advice and guidance to their clerks and it is the clerks who are mainly responsible for introducing new members to the role of the tribunals. Notes of guidance for new members of local valuation panels have been prepared by the Society of Clerks of Valuation Panels and valuable material for the briefing of new members has been prepared by individual clerks of the NHS Executive Councils.

In general the way in which these tribunals are organized makes for isolation, but in practice the part played by their clerks often makes up for this. All the clerks of these particular tribunals have professional associations through which they are able to keep in touch and to discuss problems of common interest. The Executive Councils Association (which also publishes a monthly journal) performs the same function for chairmen and members of the NHS Executive Councils and service committees. And though there are no similar associations of chairmen and members of local valuation panels or of General Commissioners of Income Tax, there are occasionally national or regional conferences (largely organized by the clerks) of the chairmen and clerks of Local Valuation Panels. Sometimes there are difficulties caused by lack of sufficient guidance from a central source and for this reason the Council on Tribunals have expressed the view that comprehensive notes of guidance for chairmen and members of NHS service committees ought to be issued by the Department of Health and Social Security.[15] The looseness of the links between the departments and the tribunals in this group also makes it hard sometimes to see where the real responsibility for their working lies.

Nevertheless, such evidence as is available about the working of these tribunals suggests that 'communication' is not so serious a problem for these tribunals as it is for the tribunals which have close links with the executive departments. Such difficulties as there are could probably be reduced by enlarging the boundaries within which the tribunals have to operate, as is at present being done for the 'divisions' of the General Commissioners of Income Tax (p. 81) and as it is proposed to do for the NHS Executive Council areas when they expand *pari passu* with the revision and enlargement of local government areas.[16]

Obviously the working of all tribunals will be greatly influenced by the way in which they are organized and by the structure within which they have to operate; and it is clear that if a group of local tribunals

[15] Annual Report of the Council on Tribunals 1968 (para. 42).

[16] National Health Service Reorganization, Cmnd. 5055, August 1972.

which depends upon an executive department for the provision of staff and premises can be organized under a presidential system many of the difficulties which we have listed under the general heading of 'relations with departments' and especially those which concern communication, will be greatly reduced. Indeed problems of communication in all their various forms seem on the whole to be quite remarkably absent in tribunals which are organized under a presidential system with their own central or regional administrative headquarters. Communication with the departments and between individual tribunals is made much easier, and there seems to be no difficulty in providing adequate information and advice for new members, or for individual tribunals where this is needed. Conferences and meetings of chairmen and members seem to be a normal feature of the tribunals' working. Communication between the tribunals and the Council on Tribunals is also more easily established.

However, difficulties of this kind cannot be altogether eliminated so long as there is no fundamental change in the situation in which most tribunals are rooted, namely their substantial dependence upon departments. Having stated the problems which arise from this relationship we will leave it to the concluding chapter to argue the solution.

## PREMISES AND 'STAGE-MANAGEMENT'

The premises on which tribunals meet, and the resulting effect on general 'stage-management', can have an important influence on their effectiveness. This is particularly true of the group of tribunals which deal with social security benefits, rents, redundancy payments or immigration, where a high proportion of appellants may feel at a disadvantage, and some may be inadequate or even illiterate. But it is true in some degree of all tribunals, since appellants, members of tribunals and members of their staffs alike are affected by the physical settings, which can be extraordinarily varied; for tribunals meet in buildings which are official or private, purpose-designed or makeshift, owned, rented or borrowed, modern or dilapidated.

It is axiomatic that appeals ought not to be heard on the premises of the department against whose decision the appeal lies, and efforts are always made to secure 'neutral' premises, where an appellant will not automatically feel that the dice are loaded against him. Such efforts are not always successful, and the DHSS in particular is often compelled to use its own local offices. Some people think that too much can be made of 'atmosphere', and that most appellants are too intent on their case to pay much attention to their surroundings. Others will maintain that friendliness on the part of the staff is what really matters. On the other hand it cannot be other than discouraging to an appellant against an insurance officer's decision to go to the same building which houses the insurance officer and his colleagues; even if he goes in by a different entrance, a device to which the Department resorts when it is compelled to use its own premises. Similarly an appellant against an income tax assessment might feel more confidence in going to the local town hall or to a hired room, as he usually does, than to premises of the Inland Revenue, a practice which the General Commissioners tend to discourage.

It is, of course, impossible to please everybody. In their early days industrial tribunals were occasionally compelled to meet in local employment exchanges, which was inappropriate and depressing; on the other hand an occasion has been quoted to us when in an emergency they hired a room in a somewhat luxurious hotel, which certain of their clients found equally disconcerting.

Apart from neutrality the main requirement in the tribunal room is as great a degree of intimacy as is consistent with the orderly conduct of the hearing. Magistrates' courts, which are often used, have the disadvantage that the dais is too high and the chairman too remote. The same considerations apply where, as is sometimes the case, county courts are used for tribunal hearings.[17] A low dais is less forbidding, and there are some tribunals, notably supplementary benefit appeals, where meeting on a level round the same table may have advantages.

Leaving aside the state of mind of the appellant, there are a number of desiderata for smooth working. Some tribunals need a medical examination and X-ray room, and thus at some of its provincial centres the Pensions Appeal Tribunals hire rooms in buildings owned by insurance companies. Again, where elderly or disabled people are likely to be involved stairs have to be avoided. Some tribunals can make considerable demands on space, since it is desirable that separate waiting rooms should be available for appellants and respondents, and if a department is represented its officer ought not to be accommodated with either, but should be found somewhere for himself. A separate room for consultation with a representative or advisers is often desirable and the tribunal itself may not need a retiring room as long as everyone else has somewhere to go while they consider their decision. There needs to be easy access to a telephone and to toilet facilities.

Attention to small detail is considered by some tribunal Presidents

[17] In their First Report (1959) the Council on Tribunals said that a county court seemed an 'unduly formal' setting for a rent tribunal hearing. They thought that a committee room in the local town hall was more suitable.

to be of great importance. Thus at the Immigration Appeal headquarters the room reserved for the Home Office representative had the door sign 'Home Office' removed in order not to suggest to the appellant that he was coming to a branch of the Department; and at the London headquarters of the Industrial Tribunals arrangements are made, locally and unofficially, for refreshments to be available, since the parties to a hearing almost invariably have to wait, often in a state of tension.

The Department of Health and Social Security also pay particular attention to the facilities provided for applicants and appellants to social security tribunals. For example, the choice of premises for supplementary benefit appeal tribunals takes into account whether the building can be easily reached, especially by the elderly or disabled, whether the tribunal rooms are accessible within the building, e.g. on the ground floor or reached by an attended lift, whether the rooms themselves are satisfactory as regards size, decoration and furniture, and whether toilet facilities are available.

This digression into the minutiae of accommodation is not irrelevant in a chapter on the working of tribunals, for it raises the question whether this important branch of the judicial system should continue to be housed in this *ad hoc*, sometimes makeshift, manner, or whether the physical needs of some tribunals have not enough in common to consider providing them with a more permanent habitation. Opportunities for this are doubtless restricted. As we have seen, there are at one end of the spectrum certain wholly London-based tribunals for whom accommodation is no problem,[18] and at the other there are a number, most of them not mentioned by name in this chapter, which meet so infrequently that *ad hoc* arrangements are all that are required. Or again the social security tribunals have exceptional needs in that they must get as close to their 'customers' as possible; to take another exceptional case, mental health review tribunals, which meet fairly frequently, must do so at the hospital in which the appellant is confined.

But a central block of tribunals have certain needs in common, which might be better satisfied than by the present arrangements, and the case for providing them with common premises is argued in the concluding chapter.

In general the responsibility for providing tribunal accommodation lies with the Estates Office of the Department of the Environment.

[18] Except for the normal problem of need outstripping the accommodation available. For example, the Lands Tribunal is at present stretched to its limit in Hanover Square, and new accommodation for the Patents Office has been accepted as a matter of urgency for some years. New premises for the Lands Tribunal in London have in fact been authorized, and may be available in about three years' time.

There are of course exceptions. Local Valuation Panels, which as we have noted earlier are exceptionally independent of the Department, are responsible for finding their own headquarters offices, and the courts themselves meet at a great many venues within panel areas, found by the Clerk. They are normally in local authority council chambers, committee rooms, village halls, etc., there being a provision in the General Rate Act that county councils and rating authorities may not unreasonably turn down a request for accommodation; most councils charge either nothing or a nominal fee. Clerks to the General Commissioners of Income Tax mostly conduct administrative work from their own private office (as, incidentally, does the Clerk to the Betting Levy Tribunal) and are responsible for finding suitable accommodation for hearings, though these also are customarily in town halls.

The minutiae of what might be called 'stage-management' are equally important; among other things it is important to ensure that the informal atmosphere of tribunal hearings is not abused.

For example, there is a strict understanding at national insurance tribunals that the insurance officer shall enter the room after the appellant and shall leave at the same time, thus making it manifestly clear that in spite of being a statutory officer he stands in the same relationship to the tribunal as does the appellant; and similar conventions exist in all tribunals.

It is, however, surprisingly easy for innocent slips to occur, and these can be more serious in the comparative intimacy of a tribunal than in the more formal atmosphere of a court.

## ADVICE AND ASSISTANCE FOR APPLICANTS AND APPELLANTS

That there are people 'who despite the official help of many kinds already provided, do not understand their rights or the procedure which will be followed if they decide to appeal to a tribunal' is probably as much the case today as it was over fifteen years ago when the existence of this problem was brought to the attention of the Franks Committee by evidence given on behalf of the then National Citizens Advice Bureaux Committee. No matter how much printed information is put out by departments, or how much care is put into its drafting, the message, all too often, seems not to reach the people for whom it was intended.

The difficulty of combining accuracy with brevity is familiar to anyone who has to draft an official statement. Where there is the additional need to achieve extreme simplicity of language such drafting requires a skill with which not all departments or tribunals seem to be equally endowed. Some 'hand-outs' to prospective appellants are admirable but some are much too long and involved. The ideal is perhaps one side of a sheet of paper giving the reader essential guidance but not attempting the impossible task of telling him all that he would need to know in all possible circumstances; it would be better to tell him exactly when and where to go for further information and advice. Incidentally, those who spend their lives with statutes and regulations, and see nothing alarming about them, tend to under-estimate the chilling effect they have on others, and it hardly seems necessary to quote the source, scope and text of the authority behind what is intended to be friendly advice.

The problem of explaining to people their right to apply or appeal to a tribunal is only one aspect of the difficulty of ensuring that applicants or appellants receive the advice and help they need. This is not a difficulty which affects all tribunals to the same extent, for there are some with a clientele which normally makes use of professional advice and representation. But it is a difficulty of first importance in the working of many of the more generally used tribunals, such as rent tribunals, rent assessment committees and social security tribunals and – in some of their jurisdictions – industrial tribunals, whose 'customers' are often not well off and probably are totally unused to proceedings in anything like a tribunal or court. Much can be done by radio and television to bring home to people their right to apply to a tribunal.[19] But even when a person is aware of his right to apply or appeal to a tribunal he may still be uncertain how to set about this, may well have difficulty in filling in the appropriate forms, and probably is very apprehensive about what will happen at the hearing. Almost certainly he will have little or no idea of how to present his case or how to challenge the evidence and arguments which may be put against it.

Leaflets can sometimes be of help in explaining how to apply to a tribunal and what to expect at the hearing. Clerks to tribunals and citizens' advice bureaux are often prepared to help would-be applicants and appellants in completing the necessary forms: and at the hearing some chairmen (but by no means all) will make a special point of explaining the order of events that will be followed. A good chairman will give considerable help to the applicant or appellant in the presentation of his case and will do everything he can to see that no points of importance have been missed. In some cases where the issue is between citizen and citizen the chairman's help is given to appellant and res-

[19] In 1971 there was a particularly good BBC television programme which showed how a supplementary benefit appeal tribunal was conducted. This had the dual advantage of being more effective than printed matter in informing people of their rights, and of showing them what they could expect – which was probably less formidable than they imagined – if they exercised them.

pondent alike – there are, for instance, many small employers at redundancy payment hearings or elderly landlords at rent tribunals who are as unsophisticated as the applicants, and as much in need of assistance. Indeed, at industrial tribunals it may be the respondent who needs the greater help, as the applicant may have a good trade union behind him who has instructed either a solicitor or a competent trade union official to present the applicant's case.

Often the principal need is for *personal* advice and an opportunity to discuss the case *beforehand* with someone who is both knowledgeable and understanding. Sometimes the only help beyond this which may be needed, and especially where the issue is straightforward and the proceedings are informal, is the presence of someone who can act as a companion for the applicant or appellant, rather than as a representative, at the hearing. Elderly people, in particular, who may feel nervous or confused by the proceedings can often be greatly helped by the presence at the hearing of some suitable person who can act as a 'hand-holder' for them and perhaps help to keep their papers in order. Help of this kind can somtimes be provided (and provided very effectively) by citizens' advice bureaux.

But often enough help of a more expert kind is needed. The applicant or appellant who is unable to afford the cost of professional assistance may then be faced with serious difficulties. If he is lucky enough he will be able to turn to one or other of the organizations which are equipped to give expert help free of charge, in some special field. The trade unions, for example, are pre-eminent in the service which they are able to provide for their members in connection with claims for industrial injury and unemployment benefit or redundancy, and the Royal British Legion specializes in giving help free of charge and on a comprehensive scale in connection with claims for war pension.

The Child Poverty Action Group and the National Council for Civil Liberties devote some of their resources to providing advice or representation, but they are primarily pressure groups whose purpose is to try to influence social policy, and the amount of help that they can offer to individual claimants is necessarily restricted to what they regard as key cases. From the tribunals' point of view the combination of political pressure group and appellant's advocate is not always a happy one. Often, when their advocate keeps to the point, his advocacy is of a high order, but too often he is concerned to inveigh against the existing law, which the tribunal must administer and which it cannot alter, and this does not further the interest of the appellant.

For many people, however, there is no organization from which help of this kind can be obtained. Legal advice in connection with tribunal proceedings is available under the Legal Aid and Advice Act 1949 but only, until recently, to an inadequate extent. Legal *aid* under the Act (which covers representation by a lawyer) is not available at all except in respect of proceedings before the Lands Tribunal, and recently the Commons Commissioners.

Two schemes of *lay* assistance which held out interesting possibilities have made disappointingly slow progress. A pilot scheme of Surveyors' Aid for applicants to rent assessment committees which was launched in the London area in 1967 by the Chartered Land Societies Committee in conjunction with the National Citizens Advice Bureaux Council has not come into large-scale use, in spite of its obvious usefulness. There is no single reason for this, but a combination of several – the total number of applications relating to unfurnished property has been less than was anticipated, the scheme may not have been well enough publicized, and to some potential applicants even the non-economic charge may not have appeared particularly cheap. A pilot scheme of lay assistance for applicants to mental health review tribunals sponsored jointly by the National Association for Mental Health and the National Council for Civil Liberties which received official approval in 1970, following lengthy discussions with the Council on Tribunals, has not yet begun to operate, because of lack of money.

There is on the other hand an unusually comprehensive advice scheme, statutorily grant-aided, for the assistance of immigrants. Section 23 of the Immigration Act 1971, which follows the recommendations of the Wilson Committee to which we have already referred, empowers the Secretary of State 'to make grants to any voluntary organization which provides advice and assistance for, or other service for the welfare of, persons who have rights of appeal . . .' under the Act. As a result of this the United Kingdom Immigrants Advisory Service, an independent, voluntary organization, provides a comprehensive service, including representation at a hearing by one of its 'counsellors', to anyone with immigration problems.

The Lord Chancellor's Advisory Committee on Legal Aid and Advice has supported a suggestion by the Law Society that citizens' advice bureaux and similar social agencies should be strengthened by having the services of qualified legal staff who could attend their sessions, advise them generally and put them in touch with solicitors accustomed to handling the types of problem involved, and arrangements of this kind are growing. They derive to some extent from the concept of the 'neighbourhood law centre', the equivalent, with modern improvements, of the Poor Man's Lawyer. The well-known North Kensington Centre seems to have been the pioneer of what is becoming a nation-wide movement, their example having been followed in varying guises in many parts of the country. For example, a comparable development of particular promise comes from two citizens' advice bureaux in the London Borough of Camden where, with the voluntary help of a team of young lawyers from both branches of the profession, an applicant or appellant can be provided with a written statement to hand to a tribunal. The statement sets out as fully as possible both the grounds of the application or appeal and the arguments in support of it, and these written statements have been welcomed by tribunal chairmen to whom they have been submitted.

There is obviously room for further experiments of this kind in which co-operation between lawyers, social workers and other people employed in similar work could be developed on a larger scale. Meanwhile, the Law Society's Legal Aid Scheme has been extended by the Legal Advice and Assistance Act 1972 to cover the first £25 of legal advice, but at the time of writing there has been insufficient experience to discuss the effect of this extension.

The benefit from such developments could be considerable. On the other hand it would probably be a mistake to think that the problem of providing advice and assistance would be solved simply by a wholesale extension of the Legal Aid and Advice Scheme to tribunal proceedings. Indeed, there is a great deal of suspicion of such extension and fear of what would happen if legal representation at tribunals came to be considered normal. Expense, increased formality and unnecessary delay are seen as some of the likely consequences, and with good reason.[20] The quality of legal representation at the group of tribunals we are considering leaves a great deal to be desired, and it is a common experience for those who attend tribunals as observers to see that an unrepresented appellant, who may be inarticulate and who may not have prepared his case at all well, often succeeds, whereas the appellant represented by an inexperienced barrister gains no discernible advantage.[21] Trade union representatives, who have no legal qualifications, appear to be better versed in this particular branch of the law than lawyers who have little to do with it. Moreover barristers in particular seem to suffer from an inflexibility of mind which inhibits them from adapting a style of advocacy suitable to the courts to the very different circumstances of a tribunal. Accordingly, the case for a wider use of

[20] See, for example, the facts quoted on p. 189 about the delays occasioned at industrial tribunals by lawyers' requests for adjournments.

[21] This statement is based on relatively superficial impressions. It is fair to add that it is not supported by statistics compiled earlier in the year by the Cobden Trust.

legal representation is not by any means generally accepted, nor has it been accepted by the Lord Chancellor's Advisory Committee; moreover it seems unlikely that its wider use would be welcomed by the majority of Presidents and chairmen.[22]

The probability is that insufficient is known about the nature of the assistance needed to help an applicant or appellant in the preparation and presentation of his case. The Council on Tribunals have paid much attention to the problem but lack the resources that would enable them to carry out research. For this reason they were unable to take up a suggestion by the Lord Chancellor's Advisory Committee that the Council or a University should initiate a research project 'to examine how far people appearing before tribunals are represented, by whom, and the extent to which people would avail themselves of a service giving their assistance in presenting their cases'. A programme of research and innovation in *legal* advice and assistance has, however, been put in hand by the Nuffield Foundation and will extend into the field of tribunals. An associated project in Birmingham by the Institute of Judicial Administration which involves an examination of the need in that city for advice and assistance 'both legal and non-legal' may also shed some light on the nature of these needs in connection with tribunal proceedings.

## COSTS AND EXPENSES

Although the advantages of 'cheapness, accessibility and freedom from technicality, expedition and expert knowledge of the particular subject' which were attributed to tribunals by the Franks Committee are not shared equally by all tribunals, there are at least some respects in which the average tribunal user is a good deal better off than the average litigant in a court of law of comparable standing.

One of these, undeniably, is absence of expense; for in the great majority of cases an application or appeal to tribunal costs nothing and involves the applicant or appellant in no danger of having to pay the costs of the other side if he is unsuccessful. Indeed it is this which most sharply distinguishes the working of tribunals from the working of the ordinary courts.

Some tribunals, it is true, can be costly to use; but this is not so much because of the way in which they operate (although a few, such as the Transport Tribunal and the Performing Rights Tribunal do have elab-

[22] See Annual Report of the Council on Tribunals 1967, para. 59, and the *New Law Journal* 19 Nov. 1970 (Report of an interview with the President of the Industrial Tribunals).

orate and 'courtlike' codes of procedure), but because the issues with which they are concerned involve, at least potentially, considerable sums of money; competing commercial interests are therefore prepared to pay large fees to lawyers and expert witnesses in order to ensure that their claims are presented as effectively as possible. The granting of a licence or other special right may also involve the payment of a fee.[23] But there are not many instances, even within this special field, in which an unsuccessful party can be made liable to pay the costs of the other side.

The same is true of most other tribunals. Very few have power to make an award of costs, and where they do the power can usually be exercised only in order to prevent abuse of the proceedings. Thus, costs can be awarded by industrial tribunals and agricultural land tribunals, but only in proceedings in which a party has behaved 'frivolously or vexatiously'.[24] Among tribunals with a jurisdiction clearly concerning the general public only the Lands Tribunal and the Commons Commissions have power to award costs at their discretion.[25]

If this power were to be extended at all widely to tribunals one of their main advantages would be diminished, for appellants of small means might be deterred by the fear of what it would cost them if they lost. The Lands Tribunal, which follows the practice of the courts and usually awards costs against an unsucessful party, has a particularly difficult responsibility in this regard, since its range of jurisdiction is so wide and the sums in issue are so variable. Sometimes they are of a very large order indeed, while the evidence and pleadings are highly complex and the hearings may last several weeks; in such cases costs may justifiably by very substantial. Moreover in some of its jurisdictions[26] the Tribunal is dealing with disputes between citizens, again of a substantial

[23] Although the fees payable are often small in relation to the benefits obtained. For example, an application to the Civil Aviation Authority may cost anything between £3 and £200 and the grant of a licence between £25 and £400. In addition there is an annual licensing fee.

[24] The Controller of Patents, for example, has the powers of an Official Referee in respect of costs, and costs can be awarded by the Performing Rights Tribunal and the Plant Variety Rights Tribunal. The Civil Aviation Authority, on the other hand, has no power to award costs. And an award of costs by the Transport Tribunal is in general restricted to cases in which a party has behaved frivolously or vexatiously. The same is true of the National Industrial Relations Court on appeal from an industrial tribunal.

[25] Except that in the case of the Lands Tribunal this discretion is sometimes fettered by statute (s. 4, Land Compensation Act). *Fees* are not discretionary but are prescribed in the Lands Tribunal Rules (second schedule). The application fee varies from 50p to £15 and the hearing fees from £1 to £250.

[26] E.g. s. 21 of the Leasehold Reform Act 1967 and s. 84 of the Law of Property Act 1925.

order, and the proceedings are indistinguishable from those of the High Court.

On the other hand realistic costs could operate harshly against an individual of small or moderate means, and it is said in criticism that the potential cost deters the individual ratepayer from appealing to the Tribunal against a decision of a local valuation court. This is to some extent mitigated by the fact that legal aid is now available in proceedings before the Tribunal and by the fact that it is the Tribunal's policy to assess costs at a modest sum if the values involved are small and the case reasonably conducted.

Nevertheless it may be said that as a general principle the power of a tribunal, other than a licensing tribunal, to award costs in reasonably conducted cases is an anomaly which needs special justification in each case.

In sharp contrast are the arrangements which apply in many of the so-called 'social service' tribunals. Not only is there no question of costs being awarded against an unsuccessful claimant,[27] but special provision is made to ensure that appeal to a tribunal does not put him out of pocket.

Parties who attend the hearing of a complaint by a service committee of a National Health Service Executive Council are normally paid their out-of-pocket expenses by the Council concerned. Claimants and material witnesses who appear before social security tribunals can both claim repayment of travelling expenses and receive subsistence allowance and compensation for loss of earnings. And the Pensions Appeal Tribunals can award travelling expenses and also, if the chairman considers there are reasonable grounds for the appeal, compensation for loss of earnings to the claimant, his representative and any medical specialist who examines the claimant.

An interesting point about industrial tribunals is that all these payments are made to both parties, their witnesses and representatives, on an equal basis. This applies to all their jurisdictions, with the sole exception of industrial training appeals, and is indicative not only of the fact that most of their proceedings are *lites inter partes*, and not claims against a Government department, but of the general shift from the original concept of an administrative tribunal to what in fact are now judicial tribunals.

The Franks Committee wished to see similar arrangements extended to a wider range of tribunals. They recognized that if tribunals were to be made truly accessible, 'the citizen must be able to have recourse to them without running the risk of being out of pocket his reasonable

[27] There is thus no sanction against an abuse of the right to appeal.

expenses'. They therefore proposed as a general principle that a successful applicant should be given a reasonable allowance in respect of his expenses (including, in some cases, an allowance of the costs of legal representation) and that an unsuccessful applicant should not only never have to pay any costs but should be entitled before both social service and most other tribunals to the same reasonable allowance as the successful applicant.

It was, however, envisaged by the Committee that the whole question of costs and expenses should be considered by the Council on Tribunals and it is, therefore, a matter of regret that though this particular proposal was accepted by the Government no action has as yet been taken to implement it. In consequence, an aspect of the value of tribunals which is of primary importance seems to have received attention from the Council only in connection with individual tribunals.[28]

Meanwhile, what is all too often overlooked is that the cheapness of tribunals for the user does in fact involve substantial costs for the taxpayer. Unfortunately, it is not easy to ascertain what these are, for in many cases a hidden subsidy is in operation in the form of assistance made available to applicants and appellants by trade union or other bodies such as the Royal British Legion.

In 1970, for example, the Legion provided representation for 2,247 appellants to pensions appeal tribunals at an average cost for each appeal of £7. Representation was also provided by trade unions on a much larger scale and over a wide range of cases at a cost which has not been quantified but which must have been considerable. The total cost to the unions is not ascertainable since there is no precise figure available of the number of members represented. There is, however, sufficient information available about the cost of individual cases to indicate that the costs to a union of representing one of its members before a national insurance tribunal in a case in which medical evidence was involved amounted on average to something between £10 and £20 in 1970.

Figures provided by the departments, however, make it possible to arrive at a rough calculation of the average cost to the taxpayer of a hearing before some of the more widely used tribunals. It works out as follows:

| | |
|---|---|
| National Insurance Local Tribunals | £16 |
| Industrial Tribunals (redundancy payments cases) | £40 |
| Rent Tribunals and Rent Assessment Committees | £40 |
| National Insurance Commissioners | £165–195. |

[28] See, for example, the Annual Report of the Council on Tribunals (1965) para. 39.

These figures, though fragmentary, do provide some indication of how large a proportion of the costs of individual proceedings are in fact 'hidden' costs so far as the average user is concerned. Were more known about these costs, including those hidden costs incurred by subsidized users, it might be possible to arrive at rough but not unreasonable comparison between costs in tribunal proceedings and those in the ordinary courts. But there is, of course, some relationship between the operating cost of a tribunal or court and the kind of adjudication which it provides, and any comparison would therefore be of value only if it were made between tribunals and courts of similar status. This no doubt would prove to be a difficulty. However a valid comparison should at least be possible between some tribunals (such as the industrial tribunals and rent assessment committees) and the county courts, and, perhaps, between the National Insurance Commissioners and the High Court, even though the equivalents of some tribunals might be hard to find.

## SPEED OF DECISION, DELAYS AND CASE LOADS

'Expedition' is one more of the advantages over the ordinary courts which are commonly claimed for tribunals and are perhaps far too much taken for granted.

No doubt it is true that compared with the general run of proceedings in the High Court the great majority of applications and appeals which come before tribunals are disposed of fairly quickly. But, as with costs, any useful comparison between courts and tribunals in regard to the speed with which their business is handled can only be made between courts and tribunals which have at least some similarity in the kinds of issue with which they deal, the standards of proof that they apply and the general levels of adjudication which they provide.

There are, as it happens, large differences between the various types of tribunal in the time taken to dispose of cases. For example, appeals to a supplementary benefit appeal tribunal (which more than any others are expected to provide speedy decisions) are normally determined within two to four weeks from the date of appeal. An application to a rent tribunal is determined in about four weeks, and an appeal to a national insurance local tribunal in about three to four weeks. Applications to rent assessment committees are usually determined in about two or three months, and to industrial tribunals under the Redundancy Payments Act 1965 in about ten weeks. The average time taken to dispose of an appeal to the National Insurance Commissioners is about twenty-two weeks, of which twelve are taken up by action in the Commissioner's office, and may be much longer where there is a contribution question which has to be determined by the Secretary of State. An investigation of a complaint by the NHS Executive Council and the appropriate service committee may well take several months to complete. And some appeals to local valuation courts immediately following a rating revaluation may have to wait years before they can be decided.

It is evident, therefore, that though most of the more widely used tribunals will usually provide their users with reasonably speedy decisions, some are not much more immune than the courts from the operations of 'the law's delays'.

Delays can, of course, sometimes lead to hardship. But where they do, means of complaint are not lacking, and so it might well seem reasonable to assume that any delays likely to be a serious cause of hardship would quickly come to notice. In practice, however, this is not so and instances of serious delay are sometimes slow to show themselves. The departments do keep a close watch on the time taken to dispose of cases when a new group of tribunals is starting work, and at all times for those tribunals where a department itself organizes the work, but it is doubtful whether adequate means exist at present to keep a close watch on delays generally.

To say this is not to under-estimate the value of the attention that has been paid to the problem by the Council on Tribunals, who have frequently brought delays to light either as a direct result of a complaint by a member of the public or of their own visits to tribunals, in the course of which they pay particular attention to any indications of delay in the day-to-day work of tribunals.

The Council are, however, handicapped by lack of staff and are not equipped to undertake research. What seems to be most needed at the present time, therefore, is some means which would enable them to monitor delays more effectively and, to supplement this, some more systematic study of the whole problem of delays than has yet been undertaken. The purpose of this would be not so much to establish the incidence of delay among particular tribunals as to identify the real causes of delay and the factors which contribute to this. If these could be clearly determined and their relative importance assessed, the work of minimizing delays would be greatly simplified.

Meanwhile an indication of the complexity of the problem can be obtained from some of the instances of delay which have already been investigated.

Changes in case loads, which may result from a variety of causes including new legislation, changed economic circumstances, or even increased publicity, are clearly one source of trouble.

For example, appeals to the former national assistance appeal tribunals averaged between 9,000–10,000 cases a year during the period 1961–5, whereas the load of comparable appeals after the Ministry of Social Security Act 1966 was over 12,000 from the very start and has risen sharply each year to its present level of nearly 30,000.[29] Applications to rent tribunals also rose sharply after the passing of the Rent Act 1965. Between 1961 and 1965 the average number of applications each year was 5,750. Thereafter it rose to an average of 16,000 and subsequently reached a peak of 19,267 in 1968.[30] Meanwhile the number of cases awaiting hearing by rent assessment committees in London began to mount up until there was a substantial backlog on hand. By 1967, therefore, there were some substantial delays in the hearing of cases both by supplementary benefit appeal tribunals and by rent assessment committees in London which attracted the attention of the Council on Tribunals.

In both instances, the situation was remedied as speedily as possible. A fairly substantial reorganization of supplementary benefit appeal tribunals was put in hand, and arrangements were made to provide additional members of staff for the London Area Rent Assessment Panel. The essential cause of delay in both instances seems to have been, therefore, the fact that the tribunals in question were not equipped with sufficient resources to enable them to cope with the effects of new legislation, doubtless because of the great difficulty of forecasting the effects of new legislation with any accuracy. It was not only this, however, for part of the delay in the hearing of cases by the London rent assessment committees turned out to have been due to an over-elaborate preliminary processing of applications. Streamlining the preliminary procedures thus helped to speed up the flow of cases.

Large fluctuations in case loads can also be a cause of trouble. In 1967 a complaint to the Council on Tribunals by a member of the public brought to light the fact that there were considerable delays in the disposal of rating appeals by local valuation courts in the Inner London area. Subsequent inquiries revealed that not only were there delays in such appeals elsewhere in England and Wales but that some appeals resulting from the general revaluation of rating which took place in 1963 were still outstanding in May 1968. The main cause of difficulty in this instance is that the general revaluations giving rise to the great bulk of appeals take place in England and Wales at lengthy intervals (the last were in 1965 and 1963 and the next is due in 1973). In consequence each revaluation gives rise to a great wave of appeals

[29] In 1971 there were 29,620 appeals.

[30] By 1971 the figure had declined to 15,793.

and this means that for several years afterwards most Local Valuation Panels (from whose members local valuation courts are constituted) are fully occupied in dealing with the appeals arising from it and current appeals have to take their turn in the queue.

This situation is evidently regarded as unavoidable under the present rating law; and Parliament has indeed made special provision for the amount at which rates are to be recoverable when an appeal is outstanding. But, here again, a heavy strain has been thrown on the Panels and their staffs and this is also reflected in the work of the Lands Tribunal to which appeals lie from local valuation courts. Hearings of appeals by local valuation courts which stood at 41,368 in 1966, have now dropped to 24,515 in 1971. They are, however, likely to rise substantially again after 1973. Unfortunately, it is apparently impossible to hold enough courts (the members being unpaid volunteers) or to appoint enough staff to deal with the periodic waves of appeals within, say, one year. The Department of the Environment regards it as doubtful whether enough suitable members could be found to man the courts and think that, if it were possible to do so, staffing the courts and Panels would provide a further obstacle, since even if suitably qualified people could be found to cope with the immediate rush of work after a revaluation, there would then be no use for most of them during the period up to the next revaluation. The Department have also pointed out that there is a limit to the number of appeals the valuation officer can cope with in a given time and that valuers in private practice instructed by appellants may be in the same difficulty.[31]

In so far as delays result from the difficulty of ensuring that tribunals are adequately equipped to deal with large or unexpected changes in case loads, it is tempting to say that much of the trouble would be avoided if there were a more unified tribunal system and more flexible arrangements for the provision of staff and members.[32] Unfortunately not all the problems of delay are amenable to a solution of this kind.

For example, the number of appeals in England and Wales awaiting disposal in the office of the National Insurance Commissioners has also caused some concern to the Council on Tribunals.[33] In this instance there

[31] Annual Report of the Council on Tribunals 1968, paras. 20–3.

[32] Case loads can, of course, decline or even disappear entirely. Between 1960 and 1966 the Transport Tribunal heard, on average, between 70 and 80 cases a year. After that year the number of cases fell off and by 1970 had sunk to 16. The number of cases heard by Agricultural Land Tribunals has also declined from 229 in 1960 to 70 in 1970.

Sometimes, too, an expected influx of cases simply fails to materialize.

[33] Annual Report of the Council on Tribunals 1968, para. 25.

has been very little change in the number of appeals in recent years,[34] but in the view of the present Chief Commissioner a substantial cause of difficulty seems to be the complication of the various statutes and regulations which have to be interpreted by the Commissioners as the ultimate court of appeal on national insurance and industrial injury cases. Indeed, the Chief Commissioner has said that as regards delays no substantial improvement is likely until there are changes in the law which has to be applied by the Tribunal. In the minority of cases which involve 'Minister's questions', i.e. questions of contribution which have to be resolved by the Secretary of State and not by the Commissioners, there is a serious additional delay which may occupy several months, and one over which the Commissioners have no control.

A final illustration of the rich variety of causes of delay suggests that there are some which not only are difficult to deal with but also carry disturbing implications for the future. In 1970 the average time taken to dispose of an application to an industrial tribunal under the Redundancy Payments Act 1965 was found to be ten weeks. This rather high average figure was queried by the Council on Tribunals and it then came to light that this was mainly due to the fact that in about 28 per cent of the cases there was legal representation and that one or more adjournments were invariably required to enable legal representatives (who were often instructed at a late stage) to prepare their cases.[35] Adjournments were also sought because of other commitments of legal representatives.

## RESULTS

Tribunals cannot be judged by the results of their decisions, in terms, for example, of the proportion of appeals or applications that succeed or fail. In some important instances, notably those relating to rent and rates, their outcome cannot even be considered in such terms. The purpose of rent assessment committees or tribunals, for example, is to determine fair or reasonable rents, and landlords or tenants only succeed or fail in the sense that one may be more or less dissatisfied than the other; similarly in local valuation courts 'success' may range from the absolute to the minimal. Again, the vast majority of the cases of the General Commissioners of Income Tax is of an interlocutory kind and only in a tiny proportion of them (about 3,000 annually out of a million) is there what is officially recorded as a 'contentious' matter.

Even in cases where there is an appeal against a specific decision,

[34] On average, the Commissioners deal with about 2,500 cases a year.

[35] Annual Report of the Council on Tribunals 1970–1, para. 60.

and where judgment has got to be given in favour of one party or the other, extraneous factors may detract from the apparent statistical significance of results. A low proportion of successful appeals might reflect the fact that it is cheap and easy to appeal, and that people will 'have a go' without too much soul-searching about the merits of their case; for example an intending immigrant turned back by an immigration officer would seem to have nothing to lose and everything to gain by appealing to an adjudicator. A high proportion of successful appeals, on the other hand, might suggest that tribunals are the citizen's good friend, but could equally well mean that the officials against whose decisions appeals were made were not doing their job properly. In this connection a more significant figure would be the proportion of decisions by statutory officers against which any appeal is made at all, for in such matters as social security and rents it is usually very small indeed.

Again, with many kinds of application, as distinct from appeal, the proportion which succeed may tell us very little unless supplemented by background information. Fewer than 1 per cent of applications for road service licences are refused by the Traffic Commissioners, but perhaps 15 per cent for air transport licences by the former Air Transport Licensing Board.[36] On the other hand applications to the agricultural lands tribunals, which are predominantly made either by landlords for permission to give notice to quit or by tenants to compel owners to carry out drainage works, only succeed in some 40 per cent of the cases heard. Some jurisdictions of the industrial tribunals do not lend themselves to having their results recorded in terms of success or failure, but a recent sample of redundancy payment applications showed about 40 per cent successful; to assess the significance of this, however, we should need to know a good deal about the various employment situations, e.g. the size and standing of the firms concerned, the nature of their work and the extent of their trade union membership.

Having said all this as a *caveat* against attaching too much significance to statistical evidence of success or failure, we may nonetheless be justified in quoting a few figures, for what they may be worth, relating to some of the major tribunals in which the citizen is appealing for a right or benefit.

Insurance officers customarily make between 17 and 18 million decisions in a year, of which between 35,000 and 40,000 are the subject of an appeal. Of this remarkably low figure the number which succeed varies according to the subject matter, i.e. 39 per cent when it is

[36] Though this greater rate of refusal probably reflects the care that has to be exercised in regulating air transport rather than the inability of applicants to meet standards of fitness.

industrial injury to 7 per cent when it is family allowances, while the ordinary run of cases average 20 per cent.[37] Appeals from local tribunal decisions to the National Insurance Commissioners average about 2,500 annually, of which about 29 per cent succeed under the National Insurance and Industrial Injuries Acts and about 12 per cent under the Family Allowances Act.

Figures for successful supplementary benefit appeals, which now approach 30,000 a year out of a total number of decisions by the Supplementary Benefits Commission of about 8 million, show a quite remarkable consistency, namely 19·7 per cent, 19·3 per cent and 19·6 per cent for the three years 1968–70. Consistency also appears in the decisions of the mental health review tribunals over what are technically applications, rather than appeals, for discharge from detention or guardianship; the figures for the same three years were 14 per cent, 20 per cent and 17 per cent respectively.

In war service pension appeals there is a striking discrepancy between success in entitlement appeals and assessment appeals, though an equally striking consistency within each category, the former being 26 per cent, 18 per cent and 24 per cent for the same three successive years and the latter 45 per cent, 46 per cent and 43 per cent.

In the first two years' operation of the Immigration Appeals Act (July 1970 to June 1972) the numbers of appeals lodged by Commonwealth citizens (the additional number of aliens being shown in parentheses) were 6,112 (541), of which 850 (27) were allowed and 2,757 (94) dismissed, the balance being either withdrawn – 673 (70) – or still outstanding when the figures were published. Appeals to the Appeal Tribunal were 213 (29) by individual appellants and 72 (5) by the Secretary of State. Setting aside those withdrawn or outstanding, a total of 60 individual appeals were allowed and 116 dismissed, and 31 appeals by the Secretary of State were allowed and 27 dismissed.

The National Insurance Commissioners and the Immigration Appeal Tribunal are the only higher appellate tribunals which are relevant in this context, but there are of course a number of instances where tribunal decisions in other fields can be reviewed by the courts.[38] Three are perhaps worth mentioning, for contrasted reasons.

In the three years 1968–70 a total of 225 appeals were made from decisions of the industrial tribunals to the Divisional Court, of which

[37] Figures given by the DHSS as representing the average for the three years 1967–9 inclusive.

[38] Or occasionally by the Minister. Review by the Minister is most usual in air transport licensing, and in 1970 he reviewed 30 of the ATLB's decisions on appeal, of which he allowed 17.

55 succeeded, although 3 were subsequently reversed; and in 1969 three unsuccessful appeals to the Divisional Court were reversed by the Court of Appeal.

The Pensions Appeal Tribunal happens to be a wholly untypical example, but we quote it for the interest of a legal point concerning standard of proof. Here appeals to the High Court lie only in entitlement (not assessment) cases, and then only on the ground that a decision of the Tribunal is erroneous in point of law. The bare figures give the surprising information that in the years 1968–70 there were 84 such appeals, of which 71 succeeded. The explanation is that most of these cases were remitted by the High Court to the Tribunal for rehearing, with the consent of both parties, as a result of a particular decision by the Court in 1966.[39] Here it was held that in determining whether a disability should be attributed to war service the Tribunal had a duty to satisfy itself that the Minister had established 'beyond reasonable doubt' that it could *not* be so attributed, whereas in this and previous cases the Tribunal had been guided by a previous decision of the High Court[40] which held that the Tribunal had to decide the class of case concerned 'on the balance of probability'. It was accordingly necessary for all comparable cases to be reviewed.

Finally the Commissioners of Income Tax (both General and Special) may be required either by the taxpayer or the Inspector of Taxes to state a case to the High Court on a point of law (their decisions on fact being final). In the five years ended December 1969 there were 81 cases stated by the General Commissioners and 94 by the Special Commissioners, of which the Court upheld 43 and 53 respectively, over-ruled 30 and 34, varied 2 and 2, and remitted 6 and 5. The point of mentioning this is that it reveals a curious anomaly. Hearings before the Commissioners are strictly private, on the ground that people should not be required to discuss their private financial affairs in public; yet if a case is stated it is heard in open court.

One ought not to leave the subject without mentioning an imponderable result of tribunal hearings in the social security field, namely the satisfaction which people gain from having had their say and receiving a fair hearing. Just as good news is no news, so does one hear less of courtesy and consideration at tribunals than of alleged harshness and prejudice, especially by critics of supplementary benefit appeal tribunals. This is not a matter that can be quantified, but there is ample evidence[41] that people appreciate, and are often surprised by, the trouble

[39] *Judd* v. *Minister of Pensions and National Insurance*, [1966] 2 Q.B. p. 580.
[40] *Miller* v. *Ministry of Pensions*, [1947] 2 All E.R. 372.
[41] E.g. from the citizens' advice bureaux. The more limited experience of

that is taken over their cases, even when they lose them. The careful explanation of why rules prevent the granting of the benefit sought, in a calm atmosphere away from queues of applicants and hard-pressed officials, makes a good impression. To consider such tribunals as safety valves may not be to rank them very high, but even safety valves have their uses.

## PUBLICITY

Publicity is not one of the most conspicuous features of the working of tribunals except in so far as it is often conspicuous by its absence. But it is something which may well become increasingly important and therefore deserves some comment in this chapter, even if only briefly.

Licensing tribunals and the like are of course concerned with issues likely to attract public notice, and their proceedings are anyhow of considerable importance to business interests. Notices which give information about pending and completed applications are therefore published by the Civil Aviation Authority and the Traffic Commissioners[42] at regular intervals and are circulated to the press or to anyone else who might be considered to be an interested party. Similar notices are put out by the Patent Office and the Plant Variety Rights Office; and the proceedings of the Transport Tribunal are also published in the trade press.

A number of other tribunals such as the industrial tribunals, rent assessment committees, the Lands Tribunal and the National Insurance Commissioners keep in close touch with the press and notify them of their hearings. In practice, therefore, their proceedings are quite widely reported, particularly in the local press. Hearings by local valuation courts are often well reported in the local press, whose readers have a keen interest in local property values.

On the other hand most of the tribunals which sit in private, such as the supplementary benefit appeal tribunals, the mental health review tribunals, the General Commissioners of Income Tax and the Betting

the authors in visiting such tribunals bears this out; they have encountered dissatisfied customers, especially at supplementary benefit appeal tribunals, but their dissatisfaction has been with the rules rather than with the tribunal.

42 Though the 'Notices and Proceedings' of the Traffic Commissioners are not the simplest of reading. The ordinary member of the public is intensely interested in applications to increase bus fares, but in the unlikely event of his knowing of this publication he would have to look for them in the small print among a mass of other matters under the discreet heading 'Applications to Vary Conditions'.

G

Levy Appeal Tribunal, normally have no contact with the press. Information about cases of complaint investigated by service committees is however made available to the press by NHS Executive Councils but in such a form that the parties to the proceedings are not identified.

National insurance local appeal tribunals, which are among the most widely used of all, are in a rather special situation, for though hearings are normally held in public,[43] publicity of any kind would probably be most unwelcome to many of the appellants and might indeed act as a deterrent to some. The tribunals therefore do not go out of their way to court publicity, although information about times and dates of hearings can always be obtained by inquiry from the local national insurance offices to which the individual tribunals are 'attached'.

'Official' reports of selected decisions of the kind usually associated with court proceedings are not very common where tribunals are concerned. Selected decisions by the National Insurance Commissioners are regularly published by the H.M. Stationery Office and there is also a separate series of reports of selected decisions by industrial tribunals and by the Immigration Appeal Tribunal (including some adjudicators' decisions which have not gone to appeal). Otherwise, reports of the more important decisions by other tribunals are usually to be found only in professional journals and the like. For example, reports of cases of particular importance which have been investigated by service committees of NHS Executive Councils are regularly published in the journal of the Executive Councils' Association and reports of similar cases decided by rent assessment committees are to be found in the 'Estates Gazette'. The legal journals, however, seem uncertain whether reports of tribunal proceedings qualify for inclusion, and, if so, which tribunals it would be proper to report.

Although most tribunals seem hardly likely to provide the stuff of which newspaper reports are made, some newspaper editors feel that more could be done to provide coverage of tribunal proceedings in the local press and to let more people know about the work of tribunals generally. There have been discussions with the Council on Tribunals about this,[44] and it has been suggested that greater use could be made of the Central Office of Information as a means of informing the press about tribunal hearings, that more attention should be paid by tribunals to the facilities provided to the press at hearings and that tribunal chairmen should be encouraged to take a more forthcoming attitude towards the press generally, particularly in providing information of a general kind about the work of their tribunals.

[43] There is provision for private hearings in certain circumstances.

[44] Annual Report of the Council on Tribunals 1968 para. 33.

Better informed press reports would certainly be helpful, since very few people seem to have any clear idea of what most tribunals do or how they fit into the scheme of things, particularly in relation to the courts and government departments. But something more than better press reporting is needed to remedy this situation. A major obstacle to the ordinary citizens' understanding of tribunals is the confusing variety of separate jurisdictions and the fact that many tribunals seem to lack any definite identity, and in this respect, as we remarked on p. 91, tribunals organized under a presidential system have a distinct advantage.

Meanwhile a good deal of missionary work has been done by the Council on Tribunals; and interest in tribunals generally is far more widespread than it used to be. Some tribunals now have a steady flow of visitors, many of whom are students, and through this there is a growing appreciation of just how valuable a contribution is being made to the life of the community by what is even now occasionally referred to as 'Star Chamber justice'.

## CHAPTER 8

# SUPERVISION AND CONTROL BY PARLIAMENT AND THE COUNCIL ON TRIBUNALS

### TRIBUNALS AND THE MACHINERY OF GOVERNMENT

Although tribunals were envisaged by the Franks Committee as 'independent organs of adjudication' and do indeed mostly operate as such, the principle of ministerial responsibility to Parliament for their proper functioning has been preserved; and they are thus subject, like any other part of the administrative machinery of government, to control and (in a very general sense) supervision by Parliament.[1]

Parliamentary supervision of tribunals does not, of course, involve any interference with their judicial independence. Discussion of matters which are *sub judice* will not normally be permitted in either House, and Ministers are usually quick to disclaim any responsibility to Parliament for the decisions of tribunals. It does mean, however, that there is ample opportunity for Members of Parliament to air criticisms and to raise questions about the functioning of particular tribunals or groups of tribunals. Indeed some of the more widely used tribunals are quite frequently the subject of Parliamentary Questions and from time to time individual cases are specially discussed.

Parliamentary supervision is therefore by no means simply a convenient piece of constitutional mythology, but can often be a means of exerting considerable pressure upon the responsible Ministers. Nevertheless, where tribunals are concerned there are severe limits to the effectiveness of the classical Minister/Parliament system of control and supervision.

In the first place, as we have seen in the preceding chapter, Ministers are by no means well placed to 'supervise' the tribunals for which they are responsible. They may control (by the power to make appointments, to supply staff and premises and to prescribe rules of procedure),

[1] The extent to which the decisions of tribunals are subject to supervision by the Courts is discussed separately in Appendix I under the heading of Review.

many aspects of their functioning; but they can never disregard the fact that the whole purpose of establishing a tribunal is to provide a means of obtaining decisions free from ministerial influence.[2]

So far as Parliament is concerned, debate about the working of particular tribunals tends to be only incidental to the discussion of some larger problem such as rent control, industrial relations or social insurance in which tribunals happen to be involved. Members are mostly more intent on debating, on party lines, the issues of policy which underly the tribunals' operations (including the extent to which particular policies have been furthered by the use of tribunals) than in trying to examine objectively the details of their working.

Lastly, the division of responsibility for tribunals among a number of different ministers tends to confine discussion of problems within departmental boundaries, although quite often a certain type of jurisdiction is common to a number of departments and gives rise to problems which could profitably be discussed 'across the board'.

## THE DEVELOPMENT OF SUPERVISION AND CONTROL

### *The Situation facing the Franks Committee*

The weakness of this 'classical' system of control and supervision (such as it was) which existed up to 1958 has nowhere been more accurately diagnosed than in the memorandum submitted by Professor W. A. Robson to the Franks Committee in 1956:

> 'At no time has Parliament or the Government or individual Ministers discussed the principles which should inform a system of administrative justice. The number and variety of tribunals have grown continually but they have remained strictly *ad hoc.* Neither Parliament nor the government has felt able to rise to the height of a general proposition on this vital subject. In consequence while we have a multitude of administrative tribunals we have not evolved a coherent system of administrative justice.'

As a remedy for the disorderly development of tribunals Professor Robson suggested the establishment of a Standing Council on Administrative Tribunals with two principal functions. One of them would be to consider and report from time to time on the remuneration, qualifications and conditions of appointment of members of tribunals. The other would be to keep administrative tribunals under review and to consider all proposals to establish new ones, to amalgamate or

[2] Though the fact that departments supply tribunal staff may have its pitfalls, as we suggested on p. 127.

abolish existing ones, or to amend their jurisdiction. Such a body, he suggested, might also draw up or approve rules of procedure and regulations applying to administrative tribunals.

The grounds for this proposal were subsequently explained to the Committee by Professor Robson as follows:

'I think that a feature which explains the irregular and unsystematic development of administrative adjudication in almost every respect has been the absence of any sort of scrutinizing body which is continuously in existence. That is the fundamental weakness, and I think that no matter what may result from occasional inquiries such as that on which this Committee is now engaged, there will still remain the need for a continuing scrutiny over the whole field particularly in regard to day to day work. I think this is exemplified by some of the recent discussions in Parliament. For instance, the discussion on the tribunal[3] which it is proposed to set up in the Restrictive Trade Practices Bill took place purely *ad hoc* without any sort of consideration of the relation which a tribunal of that sort would bear to any existing tribunals or to the courts. I am sure that is wrong. There should be some focal point from which really knowledgeable advice and guidance could be maintained.'

The circumstances in which such a focal point was eventually created form part of the history of the Council on Tribunals which is now the main instrument of supervision of tribunals as a whole.

### *The Franks Committee's Response*

The report of the Franks Committee which was published in July 1957 accepted the case for some better system of supervision. The Committee's view of the situation is summarized in the following extract from Chapter 11 of their report.

'These difficulties [about tribunals] are not met by review at an interval of about 25 years by *ad hoc* committees like ourselves or the Donoughmore Committee, which in the nature of the case must inevitably concentrate their attention upon general principles.... Perhaps the most striking feature of tribunals is their variety not only of function but also of procedure and contribution. It is no doubt right that bodies established to adjudicate on particular classes of case should be specially designed to fulfil their particular functions and should therefore vary widely in character. But the wide variations in

[3] The Restrictive Practices Court established under s. 2 of the Restrictive Trade Practices Act 1956.

procedure and constitution which now exist are more the result of *ad hoc* discussions, political circumstance and historical accident than of the application of general and consistent principles. We think that there should be a standing body, the advice of which would be sought whenever it was proposed to establish a new type of tribunal and which would also keep under review the constitution and proceedings of existing tribunals. . . . We consider that if a standing body of this kind is to be effective it should be for the most part advisory in nature and its advice should be given to a Minister or Ministers.'

The similarity between the Committee's views in this respect and those put forward by Professor Robson is striking; indeed, the influence of Professor Robson's evidence on their own proposals was acknowledged by the Committee. However, it was made clear that the Committee's views had also been much influenced by the evidence of Mr (now Professor) H. W. R. Wade. This laid less emphasis than Professor Robson's on the organization of tribunals, but made a powerful case for action to ensure that the proceedings of all tribunals were conducted according to certain generally accepted and consistently applied standards of procedure. To this end it included a proposal for the establishment of a standing body which would have power to make rules of procedure for tribunals in much the same way as the Rules Committee of the Supreme Court.[4]

*Proposals for Councils on Tribunals*

In the end, both points of view were reflected in the Franks Committee's recommendations. The Committee's main proposal for reform of the system of supervision was that two standing Councils, one for England and Wales, and one for Scotland, should be set up to keep the constitution and working of tribunals under continuous review. The Council for England and Wales should be called the Lord Chancellor's Council on Tribunals and should be appointed by and report to the Lord Chancellor. The Scottish Council should be appointed by and report to the Secretary of State for Scotland. The chairman of the

[4] What mainly concerned both these distinguished academic lawyers was how best to establish a proper system of 'administrative justice' which would not only ensure a more orderly development of tribunals but which would also ensure the application of minimum standards of conduct over the whole field of administrative and quasi-judicial procedures. Much of their evidence was concerned therefore with problems arising in connection with ministerial inquiries (which formed one part of the Franks Committee's terms of reference), and Professor Robson in particular was interested in the possibility of providing more effective means of redress for 'maladministration' (a matter excluded from the Franks Committee's terms of reference but now the concern of the Parliamentary Commissioner for Administration).

Scottish Council should sit as an additional member of the Lord Chancellor's Council, and reports by the Scottish Council relating to tribunals established on a basis common to Great Britain should be referred by the Secretary of State to the Lord Chancellor. The Secretary of State should retain sole responsibility for action on purely Scottish matters.

The choice of the Lord Chancellor as the Minister to whom the Council for England and Wales should report was determined by the Committee's view that tribunals ought properly to be thought of as 'independent organs of adjudication' and not as part and parcel of the ordinary machinery of administration (which the Committee believed to be the view of certain distinguished representatives of the Civil Service). For this reason the Committee rejected the view expressed by the then Joint Permanent Secretary to the Treasury that the Council should report to the Prime Minister, even though they acknowledged that if the Council were responsible to the head of the Government its reports would acquire additional prestige. It must be emphasized, however, that the Committee envisaged that, as a result of his responsibility for the Council and the somewhat wider responsibilities for appointments to tribunals which the Committee had suggested should in future be vested in him, the Lord Chancellor would 'come to exercise a supervision over the proper functioning of tribunals as a whole'.

Overall, the Committee's proposals for the future administration of tribunals can be summarized as follows: Ministerial responsibility (except in regard to purely Scottish matters) would rest mainly with the Lord Chancellor advised by the Council on Tribunals, which would keep the constitution and working of tribunals under continuous review. In order to secure the independence of the personnel of tribunals from the departments concerned with the subject matter of their decisions, the chairmen of tribunals would in future be appointed by the Lord Chancellor (or, alternatively in Scotland, by the Lord President of the Court of Session or the Lord Advocate), and members would be appointed by the Council on Tribunals. Responsibility for the removal of both chairmen and members would rest with the Lord Chancellor (or alternatively in Scotland with the Lord President of the Court of Session or the Lord Advocate). In addition detailed procedures for each tribunal would be formulated by the Council on Tribunals in the light of the general principles enunciated in the Committee's report.

*Parliament's Reaction to the Proposals*

The Report of the Franks Committee was published in July 1957 and was discussed in both Houses of Parliament in the autumn of that year.

There was a general welcome for its proposals and the Government announced that they had accepted the great majority of the Committee's recommendations including, in particular, the proposal to establish a Council on Tribunals. There were two substantial points on which the Government were not prepared to go along with the Committee. In the first place the proposal to set up a separate Council for Scotland was not accepted, since many tribunals were organized on a basis common to Great Britain as a whole, and it therefore appeared to the Government better to set up a single Council with a separate panel or Committee of the Council to deal with matters of special concern to Scotland. Secondly, the Government, although sympathetic to the object of the Committee's recommendations in regard to the appointment of chairmen and members of tribunals, were not prepared to agree that members should be appointed by the new Council. The Government accepted that 'in general' chairmen should be appointed by the Lord Chancellor in England and Wales and by the Lord President of the Court of Session in Scotland; but, as regards members, they held firmly to the view (in the face of some criticism) that, in order to preserve proper accountability to Parliament, appointments generally should be made by the Minister of the Department concerned, 'after consultation with the Council'.

The way in which the matter was put by the Lord Chancellor in the House of Lords[5] ('what we propose . . . is that before appointing members, ministers should consult the Council, so that the Council will be able to see whether the panels are on the right lines and broadly representative of people having the proper knowledge and qualities . . .') could be taken to suggest that there had been a less complete rejection of one of the Committee's major recommendations than proved to be the case. In due course, however, when the Tribunals and Inquiries Bill was introduced in the House of Lords on 11 March 1958, it became clear that there was a substantial departure from the arrangement proposed by the Committee and that it was intended that the Council should have power only to make to the appropriate Minister 'general recommendations as to the making of appointments to membership'. By then, however, the Government's thoughts about the Council had taken clearer shape, and the case for preserving accountability to Parliament, which was now reinforced by the argument that in practice it would be beyond the resources of the Council to undertake the duty of making the large number of appointments that would be involved, seems to have won general acceptance.[6]

[5] Official Report, House of Lords, Vol. 201, Col. 580.

[6] Official Report, House of Commons, 3 July 1958, Vol. 590, Cols. 1615–16.

There was also a further departure from the recommendations of the Franks Committee in that it had been proposed by the Committee that the rules of procedure for tribunals should be *formulated* by the Council, whereas the Bill provided only that the Council should be *consulted* about the making of such rules. This change, it was explained, was made because the Government felt that empowering the Council to formulate the rules would give it an executive function which would not be appropriate to such a body. Possibly, the Government were concerned at the extent to which the various bodies in charge of the nationalized industries were free from accountability to Parliament for their actions, and for this reason had decided as a matter of principle that the new Council on Tribunals should be confined to a purely advisory role.[7] If so, it was only logical that they should reject those recommendations of the Franks Committee which seemed to tend in a different direction. Unfortunately the effect of their decision was to remove a large part of the ground on which the Franks Committee had hoped to establish tribunals as 'independent organs of adjudication' and to return them to much the same position as they had occupied before.

However, although tribunals had failed to achieve entire respectability and continued to inhabit a curious sort of 'demimonde' between the administration and the judiciary, they were not now so unprotected as they had been, and Parliament was not disposed to be too anxious about their precise status in society. The Bill gave effect to the greater part of the Franks Committee's recommendations about tribunals and did in fact represent a notable advance along the road towards administrative justice. Moreover it must not be forgotten that many of the recommendations in the Franks Committee's report were directed towards ministerial inquiries (which formed the second part of the Committee's terms of reference) and much of the debate in Parliament was therefore concerned with the Government's attitude towards these.

In the event therefore the Bill had a smooth passage through Parliament. References to 'Magna Carta' and the 'first chapter of a new Bill of Rights' added a pleasant touch of euphoria to the Second Reading debates. No one asked the awkward question whether it was really intended that the Lord Chancellor should 'come to exercise a supervision over the proper functioning of tribunals as a whole', and, if so, how this would come about. And since all parties were anxious to see the Bill brought into operation as quickly as possible, pressure by the Government to have it passed before the Summer Recess succeeded in

[7] As to this, see Official Report, House of Lords, 27 Nov. 1957, Vol. 575, Col. 379.

getting it through all its stages in less than five months from the date of its introduction in the House of Lords.

The Bill received Royal Assent on 1 August and on 3 December 1958 Section 1 of the new Act was implemented. The Council on Tribunals, now widely hailed as 'watchdog for the public', was launched into existence under the Chairmanship of the Marquess of Reading, a distinguished lawyer with considerable political and ministerial experience, who was well known as a champion of the liberties of the subject.[8]

*The Establishment of the Council*

The circumstances in which the Council came into being have been described at some length in order to make clear how far it differed from the kind of body which had been originally conceived by the Franks Committee. The differences were certainly substantial but it would be wrong to imply that the new watchdog had been bewitched by Whitehall into ineffectiveness. It now 'lacked teeth' in the sense that all executive power had been withheld from it, but in some respects its position had been greatly strengthened though admittedly more in regard to ministerial inquiries than to tribunals. Moreover the membership of the Council was unusually strong. The Act provided that it was to consist of not more than fifteen nor less than ten members, and initially, fourteen were appointed to it. A majority was broadly representative of the interests of landowners, agriculturalists, industrialists, local government, the social services and public administration but there was also a small (though high powered) group of lawyers including one of the original authors of the proposal to establish such a body, Professor H. W. R. Wade, and a distinguished solicitor Mr H. Wentworth Pritchard who had been a member of the Franks Committee.[9]

It was evidently a body which would not be afraid to take an independent line; and it was made clear from the outset by the Government that it would have considerable freedom of action. The most serious cause for concern, and eventually a real cause of difficulty to the Council, was the relative smallness of its resources in relation to the size of its jurisdiction.

Under the Act, one of its principal functions was 'To keep under

[8] In May 1947, as spokesman for the Liberal Party, he introduced in the House of Lords a Bill for the Preservation of the Rights of the Subject and subsequently in June 1950, supported Lord Samuel's Liberties of the Subject Bill. He introduced the debate in the House of Lords on the Report of the Franks Committee.

[9] Mr Wentworth Pritchard retired from the Council in December 1970, Professor Wade (the last remaining of the original members) in December 1971.

review the constitution and working' of the assortment of tribunals listed in the First Schedule to the Tribunals and Inquiries Act, a list having been found necessary because, as the Home Secretary had explained on Second Reading, 'tribunals defy definitions in general terms'.[10] But the intention of the Government had been to include all tribunals of the type which the Franks Committee took to be within its purview,[11] and some fifty-five different categories were included.

Additionally, it was provided that the Council should be consulted by the appropriate rule-making authority before procedural rules were made for any tribunal specified in the First Schedule to the Act, and should also be consulted before any of the scheduled tribunals might be exempted from the requirement to give reasons for their decisions when requested to do so. The Council, as we have seen, was also empowered to make general recommendations to ministers concerning appointments to membership of the scheduled tribunals.

To undertake this task the Council was certainly well equipped with personal ability and devotion to duty. But it cannot be said that, as a task-force to patrol so considerable (and so largely unmapped) an area, it was notably well equipped in other respects. Service on the Council (except in the case of the Chairman) was part-time and unpaid and the entire staff at the outset consisted of only four people, the Secretary (a lawyer who had been previously Legal Secretary to the Law Officers of the Crown) an Executive Officer, a typist and a messenger/attendant.

An indication of how the Government envisaged the Council's operations is to be found in what was said by the Attorney General during the course of the consideration of the Tribunals and Inquiries Bill in the House of Commons.[12]

> 'For the first two years or so there will be a lot of new ground to tread and the Council will need to put in a good deal of time. It will need to study the question of costs [of tribunals], the necessity or desirability of swearing witnesses and to the need for more appellate tribunals. After that we think the work is likely to get less strenuous. . . .'

As a long term forecast of the Council's work, this proved to be even

[10] Official Report, House of Commons, 3 July 1948, Vol. 590, Cols. 1612–13.

[11] This is to say bodies other than the ordinary courts which hear and determine disputes or differences and which are constituted under an Act of Parliament by a Minister or for the purpose of a Minister's functions but excluding (i) tribunals which do not make decisions (subject to the exception of Service Committees of NHS Executive Councils) and (ii) tribunals in the industrial field (which were at the time mainly concerned with wage negotiations). See Appendix II to the Report of the Franks Committee.

[12] Official Report of Standing Committee B. 10 July 1958, Cols. 34–35.

more inaccurate than the usual run of such forecasts for the weather. But the Attorney General's subsequent comments were nearer the mark and certainly pictured fairly accurately the way in which the Council would have to work:

> 'It is envisaged that apart from meetings in London, members will attend sittings of tribunals in various parts of the country to watch them at work . . . they will need to become familiar with tribunals and will need to visit them . . . most of the Council's work will be done by the Council itself, that is to say, the general supervision of tribunals, special studies and the general recommendations on membership of tribunals, but it will clearly need a staff to answer enquiries, to do typing, etc.[13] It will need a legally qualified secretary with one or two assistants to obtain and analyse information, to draft reports and to help the Council in the examination of draft regulations submitted by departments. The staff will be part of the Lord Chancellor's Department in London. There will be a smaller staff in the Scottish Home Department in Edinburgh. These staffs will presumably be civil servants seconded to the Council and who will have the normal Civil Service careers open to them.'

*The Council's work – Initial Limitations and Difficulties*

Curiously enough, the tide of goodwill which appeared to be flowing so strongly when the Council was first launched soon seemed to have lost its force (at least so far as the Government and Parliament were concerned) and the Council were at first obliged to put in some fairly hard rowing merely to maintain their position.

An early indication of difficulty arose in connection with the setting up of new tribunals. The Franks Committee had recommended that any proposal to establish a new tribunal should be referred to the Council for their advice and the Home Secretary had confirmed in the Commons when the Report was first discussed that the Government 'proposed to consult (the Council) before establishing any new tribunal'. Section 1(1)(b) of the Tribunals and Inquiries Act requires the Council to 'consider and report on particular matters referred to them by the Lord Chancellor and the Secretary of State with respect to tribunals other than the ordinary courts of law, whether or not specified in the First Schedule to the Act, or any such tribunal', and presumably there would be scope within this provision for any proposal by the Government

[13] The fact that the Attorney General thought it necessary to tell the Standing Committee that there would have to be someone to do some typing vividly illustrates the scale to which the original Franks proposal had been reduced in the mind of the Government.

to establish a new tribunal to be made the subject of a formal reference to the Council by the Lord Chancellor and the Secretary of State. But nothing was said about this during the passage of the Bill through Parliament, and no action was taken by the Government to make effective what subsequently proved to be one of the Council's most important functions. In the end it was on the Council's own initiative that an arrangement was agreed under which the Council is consulted informally about draft legislation involving the setting up of new tribunals. Even so, it remains an arrangement which follows no settled procedure and which lacks any statutory basis.[14]

Again, when members of the Council actually attempted to visit certain of the tribunals which met in private, for example those of the national health service, they found that they could only do so 'on sufferance and not as of right', and that they were debarred altogether from retiring with members of a number of tribunals, notably national insurance tribunals, when they were considering their decisions. This was perfectly proper in terms of rules of procedure drawn up before the Council's existence, but no thought had been given to recognizing the Council's special position and it was no less than six years before the matter was regularized.[15]

To these initial handicaps was added another of a different kind, namely that for two largely unforeseen reasons the Council's energies in their early years were diverted away from the supervision of tribunals, which had been their original *raison d'être.*

First, their responsibilities towards ministerial inquiries, which had been accorded to them by Parliament almost as an afterthought, proved to be unexpectedly demanding, and indeed until 1968 occupied the greater part of their time.[16] This was a mixed blessing for the Council. It considerably enlarged their horizon and added to their prestige, which was enhanced by their evident determination to stand up for the rights of the ordinary citizen even if this brought them into head-on collision with departments; moreover it brought their work to the

[14] This matter is discussed further on p. 320.

[15] Annual Report of the Council for 1965, para. 6. The point appears as a matter of complaint in the five preceding Annual Reports. Rules of procedure since 1965 normally provide that where sittings are held in private the rule shall not exclude 'members of the Council on Tribunals in their capacity as such'. Today members of the Council are excluded only from the Betting Levy Appeal Tribunal, where the rules are in conflict with the statute, and where, according to the tribunal's Chairman, they could only be present if they could persuade a bookmaker to request their attendance.

[16] This development is described in detail in Wraith and Lamb, *Public Inquiries as an Instrument of Government*, 1971, George Allen & Unwin (for the Royal Institute of Public Administration), p. 220 ff.

attention of a wider public than might otherwise have been aware of it. But it meant also that they were very slow to tackle systematically some major problems of tribunals, especially as the growth of their staff remained wholly unrelated to the growth of their work.

A connected difficulty was a certain misunderstanding of the Council's role by many members of the public. It was public concern over the problems of 'maladministration', or, to be more precise, the lack of sufficient protection of the individual against unfair or wrong decisions by authority in which no ministerial inquiry or proceedings by a tribunal were involved – which led to the setting up of the Franks Committee. Yet as the Committee put in their report

> 'We have already said that our terms of reference do not instruct us to consider the vast majority of what we have termed further decisions – because they do not result from a formal procedure involving a tribunal or inquiry. It may be thought that the individual is less protected against unfair or wrong decisions. But we are not asked to go into questions of maladministration which may arise in such cases. It follows that the celebrated case of Crichel Down, which is widely regarded as a principal reason for our appointment, itself in fact falls outside the subjects with which we have been asked to deal' (para. 14).

It was also about the time of the publication of the Report of the Franks Committee (July 1957) that public interest began to be drawn towards the work done by the 'Ombudsman' in some Scandinavian countries as a protector of the rights and interests of the ordinary citizens against wrong-doing by the administration.[17] It came about, therefore, that the Council was born and lived its early years very much under the influence of the 'Ombudsman idea'. The Council made it clear that they would welcome complaints from members of the public, and it was accepted as a matter of principle that complaints should not be used merely as 'pointers' to defects in the machinery but should be pursued with the responsible departments to the fullest possible extent in case (where it was apparent that a wrong had been done) some redress could be provided. This is a policy which, without question, had produced some very satisfactory results.[18] But it may have encouraged a

[17] In July 1957 an article about the Ombudsman by Professor David Mitrany was published in the *Manchester Guardian* and was perhaps the first reference to this institution to appear in the British Press.

[18] There was indeed some hope during the Council's early years that the Council might eventually turn into a form of British Ombudsman. The opinion was also expressed by the distinguished Danish Ombudsman (Prof. Nils Hurwitz) that the Council contained the germ 'of his office'. See 'The Council on Tribunals', Professor H. W. R. Wade. *Public Law*, Winter 1960, p. 351. The

tendency to look to the Council as a 'court of appeal' against the decisions of tribunals and to feelings of disappointment among complainants when it had to be made clear that the Council had no power to function in this way.[19] In consequence the Council has always had the difficult task of keeping alive in its work the spirit of an Ombudsman while being mindful that the limits within which it can act as such are severely circumscribed.

*The Council's Growing Jurisdiction*

Difficulties such as these impeded the Council's work but did not prevent them from making steady progress, and the area of their jurisdiction has extended from 55 tribunals scheduled to the original Act to 74 in the Act of 1971. They include the important industrial tribunals and rent assessment committees as well as longer-established tribunals such as the local valuation courts which previously had been outside the Council's jurisdiction. The character of the jurisdiction, however, has not changed in any essential. In 1961, the Whyatt Report,[20] which foreshadowed the appointment of a Parliamentary Commissioner for Administration in 1967, proposed that the powers of the Council should be extended to enable it 'to survey those areas of discretion where decisions are made which are not at present subject to appeal and to make proposals for bringing such areas within the tribunal system whenever it is appropriate to do so'. But nothing came of this. When it was announced by the Lord Chancellor that the Government of the day saw serious objections in principle to the proposals,[21] but that they had themselves undertaken a detailed review of the extent to which aggrieved persons could appeal against discretionary decisions, and were examining in greater detail a few instances in which it appeared that provision for appeal might well with advantage be introduced as an

Council's relationship with the Parliamentary Commissioner for Administration is discussed at p. 217.

[19] A further cause of misunderstanding is that in the body of the Tribunals and Inquiries Act there is no mention of the Council 'supervising' the tribunals within their jurisdiction (and clearly it was intended by the Franks Committee that this should be a function of the Lord Chancellor). Yet the Schedule listing the tribunals, the constitution and working of which the Council is required to 'keep under review' refers to those tribunals as being under the Council's 'supervision'. It would be difficult to find a more appropriate word, but it is ambiguous enough to be misleading sometimes.

[20] 'The Citizen and the Administration': A report by Justice prepared under the direction of Sir John Whyatt, formerly Chief Justice of Singapore.

[21] House of Lords Official Report, 8 November 1962, Cols. 384 and 385. The Government also saw serious objections in principle to the proposal to appoint a Parliamentary Commissioner.

additional safeguard to the person affected by the decision, the Chairman of the Council[22] expressed the hope that there would be the earliest possible consultation with the Council if any new tribunals were to be established. The Lord Chancellor replied that the Council would be consulted 'in accordance with the arrangements which were made some time ago as regards any proposals which may lead to the setting up of new tribunals', but (as a subsequent Report of the Council drily puts it) 'he did not offer any opportunity to the Council to see the results of the survey in which the Council had expressed an interest, or to express a view as to the cases in which appeal to a tribunal should be allowed'.[24] The Government, it was clear, wished the Council to cultivate their own garden and not to meddle with the management of the estate. Fortunately, as Candide found, 'the piece of ground, though small, yielded them a plentiful crop'.

*Approval of Procedural Rules*

Such time as the Council could allocate to tribunals, as distinct from inquiries and general complaints from the public, was in fact to be rapidly absorbed by questions of tribunal procedure and by visiting tribunals to obtain first-hand information. Fourteen different sets of rules (or amendments to rules) had been submitted to them by the end of their first year and 148 by July 1971.[25]

The Council's approach to these rules has been based on the general principles enunciated in the Franks Report – that before the hearing the applicant or appellant should be aware of, and fully understand, his right to apply to the tribunal and should know in good time the case he would have to meet; that the hearing itself should take place in public except in special circumstances; that there should normally be a right to legal representation; that after the hearing the decision of the tribunal and the reasons for it should be stated as fully as possible; and that the parties should be adequately and promptly notified of the decision, the findings of fact, the reasons for the decision and any right of appeal. But the approach has not been solely dictated by the Franks Committee's recommendations and the Council have developed their own jurisprudence in these matters.[26] Generally, they have avoided any

[22] Viscount Tenby (formerly Major Gwilyn Lloyd-George, M.P.) former Home Secretary and Chairman of the Council 1961–7.

[24] Annual Report of the Council on Tribunals for 1962, para. 18.

[25] Under s. 8 of the Tribunals and Inquiries Act 1958 (now s. 10 of the Act of 1971). An account of the Council's *modus operandi* is given in Professor J. F. Garner's article 'The Council on Tribunals', *Public Law*, Winter 1957 (subsequently reprinted by Stevens & Son Ltd).

[26] An indication of this is to be found in paras. 37–57 of the Council's Annual Report for 1965 (pp. 9–14).

detailed prescription of the procedure to be followed at the actual hearing (since experience has shown that it is important to allow for considerable flexibility, particularly where the parties are unrepresented) and have left scope for innovation. Among the points over which they have developed new lines of policy are the hearing of proceedings in private, the giving of reasons for decisions and the right of representation and appearance. On this last point, they have on many occasions questioned draft rules restricting the right of representation to counsel or solicitor and have usually succeeded in getting the draft altered. The Council prefer to leave the door open to applicants and appellants to be represented by a person of their own choice unless there happen to be strong reasons for restricting the right of representation in some way. In one instance which was wholly exceptional, they were obliged to support a rule of procedure which contained a ban on legal representation, but this was mainly because in the absence of such a rule (which applied to proceedings before service committees of National Health Service Executive Councils) complainants would have been deterred from coming forward.[27]

The Council have had the great advantage that consultation with them on procedural rules is a statutory requirement, unlike, for example, the scrutiny of draft legislation. Departments have come to appreciate the kind of points to which the Council attach importance, and consultation has worked smoothly. Exceptionally, where there is no statutory obligation on a department to promulgate comprehensive procedural rules, the Council have had the additional task of persuasion that such rules are desirable and necessary.[28]

Cases of actual disagreement between the Council and government departments or rule-making authorities are, however, unusual. In their Annual Report for 1964 the Council stated that they had, in general, found them constantly helpful and appreciative on receiving the Council's suggestions and expressed the opinion that 'the real problem lies not in difference of opinion but in devising departmental machinery for producing simpler, clearer and more uniform rules'.[29] Nevertheless there have been a few serious differences of opinion,[30] and since it is normal for rules about which the Council have been consulted to

[27] Annual Report for 1960, paras. 37–44.

[28] See Annual Report for 1967, para. 72 and Appendix B, in which the Council persuaded the Ministry of Housing and Local Government to prepare rules for rent assessment committees.

[29] Annual Report for 1964, para. 34.

[30] See, for example, Annual Report for 1964: where the Council record difficulty in getting agreement on time limits (para. 28(3)) and also on rights of

contain some reference to the fact that there has been such consultation, it has been regarded by the Council as a matter of great importance that there should be an arrangement which would ensure that Parliament and the public were informed, before such rules were made, that a Minister or other rule-making authority had rejected the Council's advice. It was raised with the Government in the Council's first year of operation, but the Council's proposals for meeting the difficulty proved unacceptable. Eventually it was decided that in a case of disagreement between the Council and the Government on a matter of importance a note of the Council's advice would be published, by the Minister concerned, simultaneously with the publication of the rules. It was, however, agreed by the Council that they would only ask for publication in exceptional cases and where the issue between the Council and the rule-making authority was serious; and it was accepted that the Government should reserve the right to publish rules in advance of any note of the Council's advice where the circumstances made this necessary. So far it has not proved necessary for the Council to make use of the arrangement but it remains as a valuable safeguard against any danger of being put in a false position.

The Council's supervision of procedural rules has not been confined to new drafts submitted to them by statutory requirement, but has arisen also from complaints by the public, from their own visits to tribunals and from informal reference by ministers or judicial authorities. For example, the ban on legal representation at some national health service tribunals (p. 206) was considered because of a complaint by a doctor; in 1964 the Council were asked by the Minister of Health to consider one of the recommendations of the Franks Committee covering appeals to (and from) the National Health Service Tribunal itself;[31] in the same year an important point of procedure about the disclosure of information supplied to a rent tribunal by a landlord, but withheld from the tenant, was brought to the Council's attention by the Lord Chief Justice;[32] and in the following year the President of the Pensions Appeal Tribunal raised a difficult matter concerning the internal review of appeals by the Department of Health and Social Security in a manner which caused appellants to feel that the Department and the Tribunal were indistinguishable; this was not finally settled until 1969.[33]

representation and admissibility of evidence in Independent Schools Tribunals in Scotland.

[31] Annual Report for 1964, paras. 44–9.

[32] Annual Report for 1964, paras. 56–9.

[33] Annual Report for 1969–70, paras. 62–3.

*Matters referred to the Council for Advice*

A *formal* reference to the Council under the Tribunals and Inquiries Act can only be made by the Lord Chancellor and the Secretary of State for Scotland (acting jointly or severally) and such references are now infrequent. A particularly difficult one was made in the Council's first year of office on the question whether any exemptions should be allowed from the general obligation laid on tribunals by s. 12(1) of the Act to give reasons for their decisions when requested to do so.[34] There was also a joint reference by the Lord Chancellor and the Secretary of State in 1960 on two other questions arising out of the Franks Committee's recommendations – whether evidence given before tribunals should be absolutely privileged and whether tribunals should have power to subpoena witnesses to give evidence or produce documents.[35] Since then there have been no formal references and it now seems to be normal practice to consult the Council informally.

One of the most important informal consultations has been about the *membership* of tribunals. The Council is empowered by s. 5(1) of the Act to make 'general recommendations' to ministers about the appointment of members, and it was indicated in Parliament[36] that recommendations might include such things as the balance of men and women or the average age. It appears from the Council's Annual Reports, however, that they have not used the *initiative* which the Act allows them in making recommendations, but that their advice has only been given in response to requests for it from the Lord Chancellor. A good example concerned agricultural land tribunals, both as to age limits for

[34] First Report (1959) paras. 56–8: see also Annual Report for 1960 paras. 86–90. Since then the Council appears to have had some qualms about the exemption of Revenue tribunals from this provision – see Annual Report for 1965, paras 68–9.

[35] Annual Report for 1960, paras. 66–85.

[36] 'We came to the view that the right thing to do was to give the Council what one may call a fairly general power regarding the appointment of members by saying this kind of thing – it is for the Council to interpret, but this is what we had in mind – "on this particular type of tribunal we recommend that you should alter the balance". Perhaps there may be too many ladies on a tribunal or perhaps more lady members are needed. Perhaps the average age may be getting too high. Such things are relevant factors which the Council may usefully bring to the notice of a Minister not only in relation to a member of tribunals but to a particular tribunal. Although it may not come within the definition of a general recommendation the Council might draw the attention of a Minister to the fact, if it were the fact, that one or two members of a tribunal had the unfortunate habit of dropping off to sleep on a hot summer afternoon – although, as I say that might not come within the definition of a general recommendation.' Attorney General. Official Report, House of Commons Standing Committee B. 10 July 1958, Cols. 50–1.

their legal chairmen and landowner/farmer members and as to whether land agents who were tribunal members should be allowed to appear in a professional capacity in agricultural land tribunals other than their own. But very little has been said in the Council's Reports about, for example, remuneration, and the general impression is that by comparison with procedural matters membership has been a neglected subject.

*The Investigation of Particular Tribunals*

A passage in one of the concluding paragraphs of the Council's Annual Report for 1961 reads:

> 'Most of the tribunals under the Council's supervision already have satisfactory rules of procedure and on many of the points which were the subject of specific recommendations by the Franks Committee the Government have already taken action. What is now needed in this field is some closer and more systematic examination of the working of tribunals than could be undertaken by the Franks Committee.'

About the closeness with which many aspects of the working of tribunals have been examined since then there can be no doubt, the Annual Reports being laden with points of detail that have been explored with the utmost care. Unfortunately, for the reasons we have mentioned (staff shortage and preoccupation with statutory inquiries) the systematic examination of their working has been limited. Nevertheless rent tribunals were examined in some detail in the Council's early years;[37] a special section of the Annual Report for 1963 was devoted to the working of mental health review tribunals following a complaint by the National Council for Civil Liberties; and disciplinary procedures and the investigation of complaints in the national health service were the subject of a special section in the Report for 1968.

Judged from the Annual Reports the Council's work inevitably seems fragmentary, since they must record the more immediate events of each year, even though they may amount to no more than minor adjustments of machinery which on the whole is operating smoothly and well. It is regrettable that no means has been found of publishing the mass of more significant information which has by now accumulated in their records.

One of the Council's most effective means of 'supervision and control' has been their practice of visiting as many tribunals as possible, sometimes – according to members' personal predilections – unobtrusively

[37] Annual Reports for 1961, paras. 40–54 and for 1962, paras. 40–50. In this instance alone systematic investigation was assisted by a questionnaire.

and almost as members of the public. This has been extremely time-consuming and there is a limit to what can be done by busy people in addition to their regular commitments to Council and committee meetings, and they have themselves pointed out that their visits 'ought not to be regarded in any sense as a substitute for regular departmental inspection'. However, the visiting that has been possible – and over the years it has been considerable – has been instrumental both in bringing to light deficiencies and in passing on practices which seemed commendable; and reports by members of the Council do have a special value in that they come from an entirely independent source and pay special attention to the needs of the users of tribunals as well as to those of the tribunals themselves.

*Consultation on Proposed Legislation*

One of the more encouraging aspects of the Council's work which emerges from their Annual Reports is that departments have increasingly consulted them about proposed new legislation. Such consultation is not subject to any statutory procedure, and *ad hoc* arrangements have not been altogether satisfactory; indeed it has sometimes been necessary to remind departments that the Council should be consulted at all. Admittedly departments have sometimes hesitated to consult the Council at the drafting stage because it would traditionally be regarded as a breach of Parliamentary privilege, but this has only proved to be an initial difficulty with departments with whom consultation has been most frequent; and in any case, as we note on page 320, the Treasury have approved – indeed encouraged – the practice.

But there is no firm arrangement by which the Council are consulted about proposed *changes* in the constitution and working of tribunals already under their supervision. Moreover there is nothing to ensure that the Council are consulted *in good time.* All too often, as they have pointed out, departments do not consult them until they have 'taken their decisions and printed their Bill, hence they are then most reluctant to change',[38] and in spite of pressure from the Council failures still occur. For example, in 1968 they were not consulted about the Transport (London) Bill until shortly before it was presented, and a provision in the Finance Act 1967 reducing the size of the quorum for certain hearings by the Special Commissioners was not mentioned to the Council at all until after the Act had been passed. The Inland Revenue 'apparently considered that consultation with the Council was unnecessary' – in spite of the fact that they had consulted the Law

[38] As happened with the abortive National Superannuation and Social Insurance Bill of 1970.

Society and the main accountancy bodies about their proposals beforehand.[39]

*Positive Appraisal*

The Council have always looked on the scrutiny of prospective legislation as an 'essential corollary' of a wider duty, and have been dissatisfied with the absence of any machinery which would assist them to play a more positive role. They have been dissatisfied also by the absence of any mechanism which would make their views publicly known when Bills are before Parliament, for as matters stand important provisions about tribunals may be enacted without either Parliament or the public knowing that the Council have studied them and made recommendations.[40]

But in spite of shortcomings the Council's consultative role has grown, and they have always tried to use the process of consultation – often about detail – as a means of raising wider questions, such as whether the work proposed for a new tribunal could reasonably be undertaken by an existing one, or whether a proposed national or regional organization was appropriate. For example, a suggestion made by the Council in 1963, in connection with what subsequently became the Industrial Training Act of 1964, encouraged the eventual organization of the industrial tribunals on a regional basis and the development of the presidential system; and in 1965 they pressed very strongly (and not altogether without success) for an amalgamation of rent tribunals and rent assessment committees.

Recently there has been evidence that the Council at last feels in a position to undertake a more fundamental appraisal of proposals to establish new tribunals than in the past, and in particular they have taken a stand against the practice of legislating about tribunals without considering the consequences.[41] It may well be that this indicates the opening of a new chapter in the Council's affairs.

*The Council and the departments*

In earlier years there was uncertainty and suspicion about the Council's activities, and even, one may suspect, a determination to keep them at arm's length – a determination which was probably strengthened by the furore generated by the Council's first clash with Whitehall.[42] Here and

[39] See Annual Report for 1970–1, paras. 15–17 and Appendix A.

[40] Their views on this matter are set out in their Annual Report 1969–70, para. 48.

[41] See Annual Reports for 1969–70 (paras. 43–8 and Appendices A and B) and for 1970–1 (paras. 15–21 and Appendix A).

[42] This was not about a tribunal, but about the public inquiry into the so-called 'Chalkpit' case near Stanstead in Essex.

there this attitude still exists, but it is no longer common and on the whole the Council have now built up a satisfactory working relationship with departments. An important part of the work of the Secretariat consists of building bridges with Whitehall, and a factor which has enhanced good relations is the presence on the Council of a distinguished ex-member of the Civil Service. This gives departments an assurance that the Council will act with some understanding of their situation, an assurance strengthened by the occasional presence by invitation at their meetings of ministers and departmental officers.

This does not necessarily diminish the conflict which is inherent in the fact that the Council is a 'watchdog' defending the public interest, and that departments are unwilling that the Council should seem to encroach on the sacred ground of policy. It does mean, however, some measure of mutual confidence.

Another factor which has helped good relations is that the Council have always been ready to respond to any genuine request for speed in connection with draft legislation, when departments are usually obliged to work to a strict time-table; and that complaints received by the Council from the public and from professional bodies are quickly referred to departments, whose answers on the whole deal very adequately with them. There is, however, a comment in the Council's First Report in 1959[43] which is worth recalling:

> 'Whenever it has seemed necessary, we have sought and received the assistance of departments in investigating complaints by members of the public about the constitution and working of particular tribunals. But we draw attention to the need for a two-way traffic on these matters and consider we should be similarly informed by the Departments of any complaints received by them concerning the tribunals placed under our supervision.'

There is no doubt that over the years excellent roads have been built between the Council and the departments, but so far most of the traffic seems to flow one way.

*The Council and Parliament*

The Council's relations with Parliament are indirect, since the channel of communication is through the Lord Chancellor and the Secretary of State for Scotland. Quite possibly if the administrative view of tribunals had prevailed with the Franks Committee, so that Reports by the Council were made to the Prime Minister as head of the Administration, the subject would have received more attention in Parliament than has

[43] Para. 118.

been the case. Nevertheless points raised in Annual Reports are from time to time the subject of Parliamentary Questions, and it is now normal for ministers, in order to assist the passage through Parliament of new proposals for tribunals, to pray in aid the Council's stamp of approval. A debate on the work of the Council took place in the House of Lords some years ago.[44] On the other hand, battles over planning inquiries in which the Council have been involved have received a greater share of Parliamentary attention than the less spectacular but in some respects more important work in connection with tribunals.[45]

Meanwhile the absence of any formal links with Parliament has to some extent been compensated by the presence on the Council of members with knowledge and experience of Parliamentary affairs, and the practice which has been followed so far of appointing as Chairman a member of the House of Lords.

*The Council and the Parliamentary Commissioner for Administration*

Another important but less direct link with Parliament has been added in the person of the Parliamentary Commissioner for Administration who is *ex officio* a member of the Council.[46] That the work of the Council and that of the Parliamentary Commissioner should be linked through the person of the PCA, and not by means of any institutional arrangement, can be seen as a typically British, *ad hoc*, solution of the constitutional difficulty posed by the fact that there is an overlap between a part of the work of the Council (which reports to the Lord Chancellor and the Secretary of State) and the PCA (who reports directly to Parliament). It can also perhaps be seen as an instance of the working of the British political genius – a compromise solution of a problem not yet ripe for any more drastic resolution.

In practice the arrangement seems to have worked out surprisingly well. To all intents and purposes tribunals are excluded from the jurisdiction of the PCA,[47] but his presence on the Council has proved very valuable and has undoubtedly made the Council more competent to deal with the administrative machine. At the same time the PCA

44 Official Report on a motion by Lord Lucas of Chilworth (House of Lords) 12 July 1961, Vol. 233, Cols. 153–220.

45 One report (on the Packington Estate in Islington) gave rise to a debate on a vote of censure on the Government. Official Report (House of Commons) 2 March 1966, Vol. 725, Cols. 1311–96.

46 S. 1(5), Parliamentary Commissioner Act 1967 and s. 2(3), Tribunals and Inquiries Act 1971.

47 Although allegations of maladministration by departmental officials in connection with matters which have become the subject of proceedings before a tribunal can (and have been) investigated by the PCA.

has introduced arrangements which help to ensure that complaints which reach him about tribunals are redirected towards the Council. A friendly relationship is also maintained between the two Offices, but the statutory basis on which the PCA has been established makes it impossible for any closer links to be developed. Constitutionally the Council and the PCA have been placed in separate compartments and it has been left to the two bodies themselves to arrive at some satisfactory arrangements for working together. So far as personal goodwill permits this has been done; but it is to be hoped that sooner or later some thought will be given by Parliament to the possibility of a greater degree of fusion, or at least partnership, between the Council and the PCA, which would express better than is possible at present the affinity which exists between them.

*The Council's Other Relationships*

Within the limits of the resources available to them, the Council have been free to develop whatever links they please with the public and the professions. There was an early move to establish relations with the National Citizens Advice Bureaux Council, who perhaps know better than most where the tribunal shoe pinches for the more vulnerable members of society; later, links were forged with the Trades Union Congress, which has a special interest in social security tribunals and many of whose constituent members have their own insurance departments, and with various professions, including both branches of the legal profession, on whose work tribunals impinge. They have also made themselves readily accessible to such ordinary members of the public as have approached them.

The Council are of course largely unknown to the general public, as indeed they are in some areas of the Civil Service, and the relatively small number of complaints about tribunals[48] probably indicate that the Council is not well enough known rather than that tribunals work exceptionally well. There has been no staff or money for publicity or systematic public relations, and the Council's only recourse has been to let the result of their work speak for itself. It is not a satisfactory position.

Even less satisfactory is that money and staff have equally been lacking for research, a serious omission in a body of the Council's particular purposes. In recent years links have been made with research bodies, and the subject of research is mentioned with increasing

[48] An average of about 40 complaints a year in relation to the 185,000 or so cases which were heard by tribunals in the period covered by the Council's Annual Report for 1970–1.

prominence in Annual Reports;[49] but the Council is helpless to undertake research itself, and it is one of its principal limitations.

## WALES AND SCOTLAND

Welsh, as well as Scottish, interests are specially represented on the Council, since the Act under which it was established requires that 'regard shall be had to the need for representation of the interests of persons in Wales'.[50]

In establishing the Scottish Committee the Act provided for 'either two or three members of the Council designated by the Secretary of State' and 'either three or four persons not being members of the Council appointed by the Secretary of State'. The Parliamentary Commissioner for Administration is also an *ex-officio* member of the Scottish Committee[51] and his representative in Scotland (who normally attends meetings of the Scottish Committee on his behalf) shares office accommodation with the Committee in Edinburgh.

Under the Act, a number of the tribunals under the Council's general supervision which have been separately constituted for Scotland (such as the Scottish rent tribunals and industrial tribunals) are designated as being under the supervision of the Scottish Committee; and no report on any of these tribunals or on any matter specially referred to the Council by the Secretary of State can be made by the Council without prior consultation with the Scottish Committee. The Committee also have the right to report directly to the Secretary of State in certain circumstances.

By comparison with the Council the scale of the Committee's operations is small, and the Secretary, who is seconded from the Scottish Home and Health Department, normally continues to undertake some duties for that Department.[52]

Some twenty different categories of tribunal come under the supervision of the Committee, but the number of cases is much fewer than

[49] See especially the Report for 1970–1, paras. 94–100.

[50] In practice, one Member of the Council has always been appointed primarily to represent Welsh interests. In 1964 a memorandum on the use of the Welsh language in tribunal proceedings was submitted by the Council to the Committee appointed under the Chairmanship of Sir David Hughes Parry QC to clarify the legal status of the Welsh language (see Appendix A to the Annual Report of the Council for 1964).

[51] Normally, the Committee consists of three designated members of the Council plus the PCA and three other members appointed by the Secretary of State – a total of eight members in all.

[52] But these are outside any area of departmental business with which the Committee is likely to be concerned.

those handled by their equivalents (where they exist) in England and Wales[54] and hearings are mostly concentrated in the Edinburgh/Glasgow area. The task of supervision is therefore made much easier. Moreover, the smaller size of population means that the machinery of government is nothing like so large or elaborate as it is south of the Border, and therefore such problems as do arise between the Committee and the Scottish departments are of more manageable proportions and can usually be settled without great difficulty. Occasions for consultation between the Committee and the Scottish departments either about draft legislation or rules of procedure are also fewer.

Even so, within its much more restricted field of operations the Committee has probably operated no less effectively than the Council and has performed an equally valuable function.[55] In procedural matters the Committee follows much the same lines of policy as the Council but is evidently not inhibited from adopting a distinctively Scottish approach.[56] From time to time too, the Committee has to advise on the procedure of tribunals which are peculiar to Scotland, such as the Crofters Commission and children's hearings.

In the light of experience it seems clear that the Government's decision not to set up a separate Council on Tribunals was the right one, and there is no doubt that both the Council and the Scottish Committee have benefited from the present arrangements. Within what is, in effect, a 'federal' structure, the Scottish Committee is able to function with a considerable degree of autonomy and yet in close co-operation with the Council.[57]

The Committee has several times been able to look to the Council for support and the Scottish point of view has been much better represented on the Council than would otherwise have been the case.[58]

[54] In 1970 the number of redundancy payment cases heard by Industrial Tribunals in England and Wales was 7,158; in Scotland the corresponding figure was 793. In the same year the number of cases which came before rent assessment committees in England and Wales was 3,240; in Scotland, 465. With Rent Tribunals the discrepancy was much greater; there were 14,923 cases in England and Wales and only 350 in Scotland.

[55] For instance, pressure by the Committee has recently been instrumental in bringing about for the first time a conference of Chairmen and Clerks of Valuation Appeal Committees in Scotland.

[56] As it did, for example, in regard to rules of procedure for the Lands Tribunal for Scotland (see Annual Report of the Council for 1970–1, paras. 43–4).

[57] On two occasions (following the deaths of Lord Reading and Lord Tenby) the Chairman of the Scottish Committee has been elected Acting Chairman of the Council.

[58] The Franks Committee recommended only that the Chairman of the Scottish Council should sit as an additional member of the other Council.

## CONCLUSION

In the Report for 1960 there is the following perceptive comment:

> 'The Council has now been established for two years. It has had to undertake what is a new constitutional function, the ultimate nature of which cannot be foreseen at all clearly. It is, however, already clear that the work will grow.'

If for 'two' years were substituted 'fourteen' it would still be as valid an observation as when it was first made. In the present chapter it has only been possible to sketch in the Council's background and to give some indication of the lines on which it works. Yet as a picture of the Council's work it remains inadequate. For one thing the work can be seen only in a right perspective when one appreciates how heavy are the demands which are made on the members individually, and particularly on those who are members of the Council's specialist committees – all of whom are unpaid and all of whom have other demands on their time.[59] For another, it is extremely difficult to convey to anyone not familiar with the work of tribunals or its previous history to appreciate that, as has been often said, one of the most important things about the Council is that it *exists*.

It is true that a large part of the Council's time (perhaps too large a part) which could otherwise have been devoted to tribunals has been taken up by problems arising in connection with inquiries. But much of great value has been unostentatiously achieved. Not least, the independence of tribunals has been strengthened and many of the departmental boundaries which have acted as a barrier to the development of a coherent (and comprehensible) system of tribunals have been broken down. To a very large extent the Council has succeeded in becoming 'a permanent focus of interest, knowledge and scrutiny concerning administrative tribunals'[60] and in so far as it has done so, it may claim to have achieved the purposes for which it was originally established.

[59] Not until 1972, after twelve years, was a small honorarium made available to those who wished to claim it.

[60] Professor W. A. Robson: 'The Franks Report', *Journal of Public Law* (1958), p. 30.

CHAPTER 9

# THE ADMINISTRATIVE–JUDICIAL SPECTRUM

Tribunals are concerned with claims or disputes arising from social policies. They occupy a large part of a spectrum at one end of which is the everyday administrative decision taken in an office and at the other a judicial decision taken by a court. The metaphor of a spectrum is helpful to an understanding of the role played by tribunals in the making of decisions, for in the bands of colour which comprise a spectrum one can discern clearly enough a progression from one pole to another, but at the same time find it difficult to say at what point one colour passes over into another. This is a fairly accurate simile for the various kinds of decision-making process which we shall be describing among which lawyers have for a long time tried unsuccessfully to distinguish between the 'administrative' and the 'judicial'. However, we are less concerned with legal philosophy than with the institutions which exist on the frontiers of law and administration. More specifically, we discuss, first, the varieties of choice which are open to Parliament as to how decisions shall be made, and second, the factors which appear to govern the choice.

It may be helpful to recall how the Donoughmore and Franks Reports approached the matter. One's impression is that both allowed too little for the subtler gradations of colour in the spectrum.

The Donoughmore Report, which incidentally often speaks of justiciability but nowhere defines it, says at one point:[1]

> 'If a statute is in general concerned with administration an executive Department should be entrusted with its execution; but if the measure is one in which justiciable issue will be raised in the course of carrying the Act into effect, and truly judicial determinations will be needed in order to reach decisions, then *prima facie* that part of the task should be separated from the rest, and reserved for decision by a Court of Law – whether ordinary or specialised, as in the circumstances Parliament may think right.'

The Franks Report says in a much quoted passage:[2]

[1] Report p. 92–3.
[2] Report p. 9 para. 40.

'Tribunals are not ordinary courts, but neither are they appendages of Government Departments. Much of the official evidence... appeared to reflect the view that tribunals should properly be regarded as part of the machinery of administration, for which the Government must retain a close and continuing responsibility. Thus, for example, tribunals in the social service field would be regarded as adjuncts to the administration of the services themselves. We do not accept this view. We consider that tribunals should properly be regarded as machinery provided by Parliament for adjudication rather than as part of the machinery of administration.'

In each case the dichotomy seems over-simplified and assumes that in the last analysis it is possible to separate law from policy. Clearly some decisions are administrative and others judicial, but in between there is a large area in which the concepts pull against each other with varying strengths, and thus produce the 'colours of the spectrum'.

It follows that the phrase 'administrative tribunals', which has come into common use and is indeed the title of this book, is inadequate and can even be misleading, for the only factor common to all tribunals is that their members are in some degree expert in the subject matter of the adjudication. If tribunals need a qualifying adjective it should be 'special' rather than 'administrative', both because of their membership and their infinite variety.

Another way in which they are special is that the constituent elements of each may be unique. The exact place of any one of them in the administrative-judicial spectrum will be determined by a number of variables, which may be seen in the various tribunals in every possible permutation and combination. The chairman may be a civil servant, a part-time lay adjudicator or a full-time legally qualified President; the proceedings may be as formal as in a court or may resemble a conversation round a table; a tribunal may have to apply rules so closely drawn that its function is simply to determine the facts and apply the law, or it may exercise wide intuitive discretion; and its decision may be final or subject to appeal. Seen from a quite different viewpoint, a tribunal may be determining an issue between citizen and citizen or citizen and public authority.

Moreover it is impossible to predict that particular *kinds* of tribunal will have common characteristics so far as chairmanship, procedure, discretion or finality are concerned; the pattern of these 'variables' changes disconcertingly from one tribunal to another, even within what might seem to be natural groupings. In such cases it is sometimes difficult to judge whether the variables are arbitrary or whether the grouping is in fact an unnatural one. There is, by contrast, a certain homogeneity in these matters in the courts of law.

1. *Administrative Decision*

At the administration end of the spectrum Parliament[3] will have conferred upon a Minister, a local authority or a public corporation authority to decide on policy grounds alone. A Minister in turn will devolve authority within his Department to be exercised as part of its day-to-day administration, since although there will always be cases which come to him for his personal decision there will be an obvious limit to their number. Guidelines or administrative instructions will be circulated within the Department as to how discretion is to be exercised in his name.

An example is the discretion given to the Minister of Transport by section 48 of the Town and Country Planning Act 1959 in regard to the purchase of properties affected by planning blight. In the terms of the Act the Minister's power to acquire such land by agreement 'shall be exerciseable in respect of any land which, *in the opinion of the Minister, may* be required for that purpose, notwithstanding that the land is not immediately required for that purpose'. This is clearly an unfettered discretion, but among the Department's internal guidelines for its exercise is a directive that it is generally to be used to relieve owner-occupiers from hardship caused by proposals which are public knowledge, and only very exceptionally to relieve non-resident owners, and then only those who are suffering a substantial degree of personal financial hardship.[4]

From the point of view of a department such arrangements have the advantages of flexibility and control, but from that of the man in the street they have the disadvantage that decisions may seem arbitrary, in the sense that the manner in which they are reached does not have to conform to published rules and that he may be given no indication of the case he has to meet or the criteria that he must satisfy.[5]

[3] The decision is ultimately made by Parliament, and it is conventional to attribute it to Parliament, since no other attribution is constitutionally possible. Clearly, however, the question whether potential conflict is to be resolved administratively in a department or judicially by a tribunal is a matter which is recommended to Parliament as a result of departmental advice and ministerial decision.

[4] Second Report of the Parliamentary Commissioner for Administration, Session 1969–70 (Annual Report for 1969). Case No. C458/L p. 176, Cmnd. 138.

[5] There may even be circumstances in which guidelines take on the character of delegated legislation rather than mere administrative instructions. Cp. Scott L. J. in *Blackpool Corporation* v. *Locker*, [1948] 1 K.B. 349. In this case a circular to a local authority which the Department thought merely explained the

The disadvantage may be overcome to some extent by making the criteria governing the administration of a particular policy available to the public. Thus, the Department of the Environment issues occasional 'Development Policy Control Notes', which set out current Ministerial policy in considerable detail for the guidance of intending developers; while instructions to immigration officers on the exercise of the Minister's discretion are made known by being laid before Parliament.

2. *Administrative Decision Subject to Inquiry*[6]

Alternatively, Parliament may confer powers upon a Minister or statutory authority subject to the requirement that in certain circumstances an inquiry shall be held before a final decision is made. This is normally a public hearing before a single individual, most commonly a departmental 'inspector', to whom interested parties may make representations. The hearing authority is not empowered to make a decision, but acts as a clearing-house of evidence, and finally makes a recommendation to the Minister, who may or may not follow it in making his decision.[7] Public inquiries are always held into planning appeals unless the appellant agrees to settle the matter through 'written representations', and they are also held increasingly, whether there is a statutory requirement or not, into objections to any development which may adversely affect the environment. Generally the Minister must give the appellant or objector 'an opportunity to be heard by a person appointed by him for the purpose'; in practice the inquiry he holds is almost invariably a public one.

There is a small ambivalent area where the distinction between tribunal and inquiry becomes blurred. For example, certain 'tribunals' do not necessarily have the power of final decision, since there is provision for appeal to the Minister himself – though should no appeal be made the tribunal's decision does stand as final. Examples are the refusal

procedure for requisitioning houses was held to be a piece of delegated legislation because of the Minister's power to delegate any of his functions to such extent and subject to such restrictions as he thought proper. As delegated legislation the circular was not merely advisory but binding on the authority. The judge said 'Of such secondary or sub-delegated legislation . . . neither the general public . . . nor the legal adviser of an affected member of the public, however directly he may be affected, has any source of information about his rights, to which he can turn as of right and automatically'.

[6] The subject of inquiries, as distinct from tribunals, is dealt with comprehensively in *Public Inquiries as an Instrument of Government* (George Allen & Unwin for the Royal Institute of Public Administration, 1971).

[7] Though since January, 1969, relatively small planning appeals, comprising nearly three-quarters of the total, have been *decided* by the inspector (Town and Country Planning Act 1968).

or withdrawal of a licence by the Traffic Commissioners or the Civil Aviation Authority. The Milk and Dairies Tribunal, on the other hand, is almost indistinguishable from a public inquiry in that its sole function is to examine the facts and report to the Minister; it differs only in its membership, i.e. instead of an *ad hoc* 'inspector', with or without an assessor, there is a permanent legal chairman with a balanced membership drawn from panels representing milk producers, consumers and retailers.

Conversely, there are instances where the conclusions of a hearing authority may be binding on a Minister in certain respects, e.g. findings favourable to the appellant by a 'tribunal or inquiry' under the Prevention of Frauds (Investments) Act 1958.

It is at about this point in the spectrum that administrative discretion begins to shade into adjudicatory procedure, and from now onwards we shall be moving into the area of judicial decision.

### 3. *Decision by a Regulatory Body*

The next 'colour' in the spectrum is seen when Parliament grants the power of decision to a commission, board or similar authority (either at national, regional or local level), which has administrative or advisory (as well as adjudicatory) functions delegated to it. Where the delegation is to a local authority appeals may lie to a variety of sources – for example, to magistrates under the Public Health Acts, to the Minister in the case of planning, to the Crown Courts in some highway cases and to County Courts under the Housing Acts.

In general this pattern is characteristic of regulatory bodies whose main adjudicatory function is one of issuing, varying or revoking various kinds of licence. Decisions may be taken either with or without a formal hearing, or after a hearing conducted by the authority itself or one or more of its members (as with the Traffic Commissioners or a road haulage licensing authority) or a specially appointed committee of the authority (e.g. a service committee of a National Health Service Executive Council). An example of this type of authority was the Air Transport Licensing Board, which was both a licensing and an advisory body.[8] It exercised an advisory function by considering representations

[8] Its predecessor, the Air Transport Advisory Council, was of course purely advisory. Its successor, the Civil Aviation Authority, does not have a statutory duty to receive representations from the public, but procedural regulations provide for consumers to make representations about licensing. It is also required to take account of consumer interests and to develop consultative arrangements by the Civil Aviation Guidance White Paper (Cmnd. 4899), paras. 7 and 28, and has a statutory duty to advise on airport planning. The Mental Health Review Tribunal, an adjudicatory body, also advises the Home Secretary on patients

from any person regarding the adequacy of the facilities provided by airline companies and reporting to the Minister on those representations. It exercised a licensing function by issuing air service licences in the United Kingdom or revoking, suspending or varying existing licences – and in each case the applicant or licence holder was entitled to a hearing before the Board took action. This is not to say that the whole of air transport licensing was delegated to the Board; there was a general right of appeal to the Minister by any party to a case who disagreed with the Board's decision; the Minister's confirmation of the Board's approval of tariff provisions was required in the case of external services and his consent was required for the grant of a licence to a foreign person or company; and if the Minister directed in writing that an application would involve negotiations with another state (e.g. for reciprocal landing rights) and that it was inexpedient to commence those negotiations, the Board was required to refuse the application without a hearing.

4. *Decision by a Tribunal on Appeal from a Minister's Determination*

The clearest example of this group is when the Secretary of State for Education and Science considers an independent school to be 'objectionable' because of inadequacies in the premises, facilities, staff or quality of teaching, and when he may serve a 'notice of complaint' on the proprietor (with a copy to any teacher alleged not to be a proper person to be employed for that purpose). Appeal then lies to an independent schools tribunal, which decides whether the Secretary of State's complaint is justified. If the tribunal upholds the complaint, or if no appeal is lodged, the proprietor then has six months to remedy the deficiencies set out in the complaint, and if the tribunal or the Secretary of State (in the case of no appeal) consider the complaint to be irremediable they may order the school to be struck off the Register of Independent Schools.

5. *Decision by a Tribunal on Appeal from the Determination of a Designated Officer*

The next variation, which is both more common and more complex, occurs where Parliament has given authority to make an initial determination to officers designated in an Act of Parliament and working at a local level. These, e.g. rent officers, rating valuation officers, insurance officers and immigration officers, are the first in an ascending hierarchy of authorities.[9] Normally they will make their determination on a case

whose discharge is subject to restrictions. Metamorphoses of this kind within tribunals, whereby they change or add to their function, were mentioned on p. 55.

9 The same is true in effect of the officer who handles claims for supplementary

without a formal hearing and without recourse to their department, panel or local authority. The sheer size of the case-work would normally preclude this, for to give but one example insurance officers handle over 17 million cases each year. Certain questions, e.g. eligibility or insurability, may be reserved to a Minister, to whom there might also be a right of appeal, but normally appeal will lie to a *local* tribunal, e.g. a rent assessment committee, local valuation court, national insurance local tribunal, medical appeal tribunal or immigration adjudicator.

As will be apparent, this method is normally chosen when legislation gives rise to very large numbers of individual claims or appeals, and the emphasis is on the rapid processing and disposal of cases by local officials; the functions of tribunals of this kind may be to act as a safety net for mistakes or errors of judgment by local officials, or conversely to allow officials to refer to the tribunal for guidance.

6. *Decision by a Tribunal having the Attributes of a 'Special Court'*

Next, Parliament may resolve the problem of disputes by handing it over to a tribunal especially created for the purpose. A frequent characteristic of such tribunals is that the cases they hear are disputes between citizen and citizen, rather than between citizen and State.

The most important example, though not the most clear-cut, is that of the industrial tribunals, whose various jurisdictions are concerned either with disputes between employer and employed or with definitions of categories of employment. The example is not clear-cut because the Department of Employment may be one of the parties, or it may intervene and take part in the proceedings, but all its cases consist of *lites inter partes* and its decisions are reached on issues of fact and law.

A clearer example of the use of this alternative is the Performing Rights Tribunal, which is a statutory body set up to settle what are in effect private disputes between the owners of copyrights (or professional organizations which act as private licensing bodies on behalf of the owners) in literary, dramatic or musical material, or recordings or TV material, and those who wish to use that material in public (including performances on radio and TV). Sometimes the delegation does not progress this far – an example is a tribunal having a similar function of arbitrating in private disputes between the owners of certain private rights, namely the Plant Variety Rights Tribunal, which considers

benefit, except that he is not designated in the Act, and in form an appeal is an appeal against a determination of the Supplementary Benefits Commission. The Commission is in some sense an example of our third alternative, where Parliament gives statutory authority to an independent body. On the other hand it could hardly be called 'regulatory' in the same sense as the Traffic Commissioners. Indeed the SBC is a 'specimen' which is difficult to classify.

applications by plant breeders to register their rights in a new plant variety, or by growers who consider that the holder of plant breeders' rights has unreasonably refused to grant a licence to grow the new variety or has imposed unreasonable terms in a licence. However, unlike the Performing Rights Tribunal, these applications are first considered by a government official, the Controller of Plant Variety Rights, who makes the initial decision on any application after considering written representations or, if requested, holding a formal hearing. Any party to the proceedings who disagrees with the Controller's decision then has a right of appeal to the Plant Variety Rights Tribunal. By contrast a much more complicated structure exists in the general field of patents, where the determination of disputes has been delegated to a specially constituted office of the Department (the Patent Office, which is a branch of the Department of Trade and Industry). Hearings are held before a specially authorized member of that office but decisions are taken in the name of the Controller of Patents. From these decisions there is a right of appeal to the Patents Appeal Tribunal (which in fact consists of a nominated Judge of the High Court sitting as the tribunal) with a further right of appeal to the High Court on a point of law.[10]

7. *Decision by a Superior Tribunal*

In a few cases there is a two-tier structure in which one tribunal may hear appeals from another. The principal higher tribunals are the Transport Tribunal, which hears appeals from decisions of Road (Goods) Traffic Licensing Authorities; the Lands Tribunal, from decisions of local valuation courts;[11] the National Insurance Commissioners, who hear appeals against determinations of national insurance local tribunals; and the Immigration Appeal Tribunal, which hears appeals, either from appellants or from the Secretary of State, from the decisions of adjudicators.

8. *Decision by the Courts Themselves*

Finally, the courts themselves may be used as a means of settling disputes, usually between individuals, or of furthering a policy which has been embodied in the law of the land.

'The Courts' in this context is a versatile expression – it may mean

[10] Previously, appeals lay to the Law Officers of the Crown (i.e. the Attorney General and Solicitor General) – a sort of half-way house.

[11] An extraordinary example of the confusion which exists in the nomenclature of the subject is that the Lands 'Tribunal', which is in effect a National Valuation Court, hears appeals from a local valuation 'court', which is a tribunal.

the county courts, or branches of the High Court sitting with assessors, or Special Courts of High Court status, or the High Court itself, though in the general context of tribunals the last-named is simply a means of appeal on points of law.

It seems more common nowadays for new jurisdictions arising from social policy to be given to *ad hoc* tribunals than to the county courts, but under the 1965 Rent Act proceedings for possession or arrears of rent or other disputes arising out of the terms of tenancy are left to the county courts, even though questions of rent and security of tenure for furnished premises remained with rent tribunals and fair rents for unfurnished premises are determined by rent assessment committees.

Branches of the High Court sitting with assessors are the Admiralty and Commercial Courts, whose expertise in the subject matter of the adjudication is one of the main distinguishing marks of what is commonly called a tribunal; close to them in this regard are two Superior Courts of Record – the Restrictive Practices Court[12] and the National Industrial Relations Court, which consist of a High Court Judge with lay members; and – something of an anomaly in this regard – there is the Transport Tribunal, which is a tribunal in the sense that it comes within the purview of the Council on Tribunals (as the others do not) but a court in that it is a Court of Record with rules of procedure similar to those of the High Court.

### *Alternatives in Combination*

The various alternatives which we have postulated are not mutually exclusive but can sometimes be found in combination. The machinery for settling industrial injuries claims under national insurance legislation provides a good example. Claims for compensation are first considered by the local national insurance officer. If, however, there are doubts about the applicant's eligibility in terms of his contributions, or his insurability, in terms of the precise nature of his occupation, the claim is referred to the Secretary of State, who determines the matter and refers the claim back to the insurance officer, who then has to decide whether the accident was one 'arising out of and in the course of the applicant's employment'. The insurance officer's decision on this point is subject to a right of appeal firstly to a national insurance local tribunal (a three-man tribunal with representatives from an employer's panel and an employee's panel) and then to the National Insurance Commissioner. Having established a *right* to benefit the applicant will then be entitled initially to an 'injury benefit' payable weekly while off

[12] Though, as we argue on p. 252, the Restrictive Practices Court has most of the attributes of a tribunal.

work temporarily, the amount of this benefit likewise being determined through the insurance officer/local tribunal/Commissioner structure. If, on the other hand, it appears that the injury might result in permanent disablement, and in any event at the end of six months on injury benefit, the insurance officer is required to refer the case to a medical board (which in practice consists of local doctors retained by the Department for the purpose) for assessment of the extent of the permanent disablement.[13] There is a right of appeal from the medical board's assessment to a medical appeal tribunal (a three-man tribunal of two medical specialists with a chairman, usually a lawyer, appointed by the Lord Chancellor), with a further right of appeal on a point of law to the National Insurance Commissioner.

A somewhat similar example may be seen in the administration of supplementary benefits, where the scales are set (i.e. increased from time to time over those in the Act) by the Secretary of State, but responsibility for decisions is vested in a body which he appoints in terms of our third alternative, i.e. the Supplementary Benefits Commission, working through a local staff assigned to them by the Secretary of State, and having in practice much in common with the local officer of our fifth.

## FACTORS GOVERNING CHOICE

Having reviewed the various ways in which claims or disputes may be settled it is natural to ask what factors cause one alternative to be preferred to another. Why, subject to Parliament,[14] should government departments wish to retain certain matters in their own control and deal with them administratively, but prefer others to be decided judicially? And if judicially, how do they differentiate between the courts and one of the several kinds of tribunal?

### JUSTICIABILITY

The first of these two questions turns on what is to be regarded as a justiciable issue, and who in the last analysis decides whether any issue is justiciable or not. Justiciability, however, is a notoriously elusive concept. On the one hand, according to Professor Wade:

> 'The fundamental question . . . is whether the subject matter is suitable for pre-ordained rules'

[13] Special arrangements exist for certain industrial diseases, such as pneumoconiosis and byssinosis.

[14] The ascription to Parliament of the actual decision is by no means mere convention. There have been occasions, examples of which are given on p. 248, when Parliament has radically altered a proposed method of adjudication.

but after giving two examples he continues:

'But this is simply to say that these are fields where decisions can be taken according to law rather than according to policy, and that there are some standards which are intended to operate regardless of the policy of the day. In a word the subject matter is justiciable.'[15]

On the other hand there are academic lawyers who share Dr Geoffrey Marshall's view that 'no dispute or issue is inherently justiciable or suited to judicial solution.'[16] Dr R. M. Jackson, in evidence to the Franks Committee, took up a position on the fence:[17]

'Q. Is it possible to define justiciable and non-justiciable? – No, I do not think so.

Q. What is non-justiciable or political is really what the Minister feels is to be decided by him rather than by anybody else, is that fair? – No, not quite. I think it is pretty clear, and there is a general concensus of opinion, as to what falls on either side of what is rather a no-man's-land. When I say you can't define it, I mean that I do not think you can get anything which shows you a clear distinction.'

Certainly when one examines the actual ways in which decisions are taken it seems that not only principle but tradition, changing circumstances – even chance – may help to determine whether they are taken administratively or judicially; a view which is supported by the Whyatt Committee, which applied itself to this precise question in 1961.[18]

Moreover the frontier which divides administrative from judicial decision-making is one which moves with changing social and political circumstances. Thus in comparatively recent years local valuation courts have replaced local authority assessment committees, mental health review tribunals have replaced the Board of Control, the Air Transport Licensing Board and the immigration appeals machinery have replaced discretionary decision. The last-named is of particular interest, as the Whyatt Committee quoted the admission of aliens as a subject *unsuitable* for a tribunal:

'. . . no provision has been made for appeal to a tribunal since the

[15] H. W. R. Wade, 'Anglo-American Administrative Law: Some Reflections', *Law Quarterly Report* (1965) 357 at 373.

[16] Essay 'Justiciability' in *Oxford Essays in Jurisprudence* (ed. A. G. Guest. Oxford University Press, 1961) p. 278: see also W. A. Robson, *Justice and Administrative Law* (3rd ed.) p. 14.

[17] Evidence, Day 11–12, p. 455.

[18] Lord Shawcross (ed.) *The Citizen and the Administration: The Redress of Grievances* (Stevens & Sons, see especially p. 27).

Minister is responsible for policy and therefore must retain the final decision on such matters within his control.'

These particular decisions to 'tribunalize' sprang from various sources – those affecting immigration and mental patients from changing social attitudes and informed public opinion;[19] rating appeals from the decision to nationalize the valuation of property for rating purposes, since it would have been inappropriate for a committee of a local authority to review a decision of the Inland Revenue; air transport licensing from the growth of a new industry. The essential point is that these issues became justiciable when Parliament accepted that for one reason or another they *ought* to be justiciable; they were not inherently so. Judicial decision was not originally *chosen* at all, but came as a result of pressures of opinion or from changes in administration or technology. The circumstances in which a department or Minister might initially choose to propose a judicial form of decision to Parliament would be when there was no policy interest in the outcome. For example it would not matter to the Department concerned which of two contestants succeeded in a copyright case, or, in the instance of a dispute between a citizen and the state, whether an individual succeeded in establishing a claim to benefit. This would be very nearly true also of a redundancy payment appeal to an industrial tribunal, where the issue is between private citizens, but where the Department has an indirect financial interest.

The frontier is not one which is likely to move at any great speed, partly because if it did so the result would be chaotic, but largely because the need for it to do so does not seem to be pressing. One of the avowed purposes of the Whyatt Committee, for example, was to review 'areas of discretionary decision' in government and, *inter alia*, to determine whether an individual ought to have an impartial adjudication of his dispute with authority. It cannot be said that they found that the public were particularly ill-served by the Administration in this matter, for a survey of seven departments disclosed comparatively few instances where in their view discretionary decisions by administrators ought to have been subject to external review.[20] The most interesting, which still have force today, were to be found in the then Ministry of Education, and concerned decisions by local education authorities, against which the only appeal is to the Minister, such as the placing of children

[19] In the allied field of public inquiries this is also true of planning appeals.

[20] At this point the Report, which is of course normally associated with the 'Ombudsman', was not thinking of decisions taken in the context of alleged maladministration, but simply of decisions which might be challenged because they were not the right decisions.

in particular schools against their parents' wishes;[21] and in the then Ministry of Health, which the Committee described as 'a highly tribunalized Department', in the matter of the award of marginal benefits such as invalid chairs, hearing aids, surgical equipment etc. There were of course other examples, but these perhaps indicate better than most the kind of situation in which the frontier of tribunal provision could appropriately be extended.

The difficulty is that once launched on this most slippery slope it becomes difficult to stop, and if the quality of every discretionary decision were open to challenge nothing would ever get done. There seems to be no difference in principle between some matters which are already tribunalized, those which the Whyatt Committee thought *ought* to be tribunalized and those which it would be manifestly impracticable to tribunalize – for example the allocation by a local authority of council houses, or accommodation for old people, or indeed anything in which demand exceeds supply. Principle must be modified by common sense in deciding where to call a halt.

The Whyatt Report itself, conscious of the need for moderation in limiting the area of administrative discretion in the day-to-day work of government, quoted with approval the Swedish notion of a 'General Tribunal'; for there is in that country a body, whose name can be variously translated, which deals with appeals against all types of discretionary decision which are the occasion of sufficient friction with the public to justify being on a list, which is annually revised and brought up-to-date in the light of the previous year's demands upon its services.[22]

Meanwhile, there can never be a completely clear distinction between administrative and judicial. At one end of the spectrum a number of tribunals (notably those concerned with regulation and licensing) are so 'policy-oriented' as to be almost an extension of the administrative process; they step across the invisible line which may perhaps be said to divide an administrative from a judicial decision by virtue of holding a *hearing*. Others, for example industrial tribunals, are 'court-substitutes',[23] or courts in all but name. Between the two extremes rent assessment committees, for example, both settle disputes (between

[21] The Report unhesitatingly said that such decisions should be made, on appeal, by an independent tribunal outside the Department. It is interesting that in Scotland comparable decisions are in fact made by the Sheriff, i.e. by an independent judicial authority who nevertheless has the advantage of local knowledge, which the Minister has not.

[22] Proposals by Professor Robson and others for a reform of the appellate system, as it affects tribunals, are mentioned on p. 349.

[23] The expressions 'policy-oriented' and 'court-substitute' were coined by

landlord and tenant) and implement policy (by determining an objectively 'fair' rent). Moreover the justiciable element in the various tribunals, that is to say the element for which a proper decision requires the training of a judge, is immensely variable. To give some examples: in the *valuation* group, the rent of an unfurnished house must be judged by criteria which take account of market price less scarcity value, with attention paid as far as possible to consistency, and its rateable value must be judged by criteria similar in principle though differing in detail; but these decisions rest on expert knowledge and visual evidence as much as on the judicial mind. Very close to them, in justiciable terms, is a small group which must ascertain that *minimum standards* are maintained, for example of teaching and equipment in schools or hygiene in dairies; here again expert knowledge is required, though there is somewhat more scope for subjective judgment. In the *licensing* group the issues turn both on the fitness of an applicant and on the existing supply of what he wishes to provide, whether it be an airline or a public house, the former a matter of personal judgment and the latter one of policy. In *revenue tribunals* the judicial element may vary from interpreting a sophisticated point of income tax law to guessing the probable income of a self-employed man whose book-keeping is rudimentary; in *medical assessment* it may amount to splitting the difference between two doctors' estimates of percentage disability; in a mental health review tribunal, to whether it is reasonable public risk to relax restrictions on a mental patient; in a supplementary benefit appeal tribunal, to whether some article is a luxury or a necessity; in a rent tribunal, as to whether a tenant's behaviour and associates are tolerable.

Only in a minority of subjects, of which national insurance and redundancy payment claims are perhaps the clearest examples, is judgment based strictly on the application of law to a given set of facts.

## COURT OR TRIBUNAL?

The second question that we asked on p. 231 – how do departments, Ministers or Parliament differentiate between the courts and one of the several different kinds of tribunal? – raises the wider topic of whether there is in fact any difference between the two, and if so wherein it lies. The discussion of this is likely to be as elusive as that of the concept of justiciability, but we try to deal with it at the beginning of the next chapter. Meanwhile, accepting for the moment that some

B. Abel-Smith and R. Stevens, *Lawyers and the Courts* (Heinemann, 1970), to denote the two ends of the spectrum.

difference exists, it is remarkable how far we have travelled since Donoughmore, or even since Franks. As we have seen (p. 38) the Donoughmore Committee recommended that judicial functions should

> 'normally be entrusted to the ordinary Courts of Law and their assignment by Parliament to a Minister should be regarded as exceptional and requiring justification in each case' (p. 115).

This was reiterated by Franks:

> '... in deciding by whom adjudications involving the administration and the individual citizen should be carried out preference should be given to the ordinary courts of law rather than to a tribunal unless there are demonstrably special reasons which make a tribunal more appropriate ... namely the need for cheapness, accessibility, freedom from technicality, expedition and expert knowledge of a particular subject' (paragraph 406).

Yet repeatedly since then Parliament has preferred tribunals to the courts.

## THE TREND TOWARDS TRIBUNALS

### *The Recommendations of Commissions and Committees*

Although there must be an element of speculation as to why government departments prefer one course to another we are not entirely without guidance, since the method of adjudication has often followed the recommendations of a Royal Commission, committee of inquiry or departmental committee.

Thus in 1945 the Ridley Committee on Rent Control[24] believed that the incidence of the Rent Restriction Acts had become so uneven that controlled rents could only be adjusted by

> 'a body which devotes itself exclusively and continuously to the task which a regular court could not do without neglecting its other suitors.'

In 1957 the Royal Commission on Mental Health[25] discussed the alleged deficiencies of the Board of Control and concluded that their shortcomings were due to the fact that they had originally been created for administrative purposes and were not qualified to act judicially, and that moreover they were inappropriately centralized in London. The

[24] Report of an Inter-Departmental Committee on Rent Control: Cmd. 6621/1945.

[25] Report of the Royal Commission on the Law relating to Mental Health and Mental Deficiency: Cmnd. 169/1957.

Commission's Report was also critical of the part played by local magistrates in admissions and visits; they did however consider whether applications for removal of restrictions on patients should be dealt with by three local Justices sitting elsewhere than in court, but concluded that for various reasons, including the inevitable association of the magistrates with crime, this would be unsuitable. What was needed was a legally qualified chairman, the appropriate medical and psychiatric experience and an association with a locality through a well-known local figure; and this pointed clearly to a tribunal.

The Wilson Committee on Immigration Appeals[26] in 1967 was equally specific. Having discussed (paragraph 105) whether appeals could be heard by the courts they concluded:

> 'Neither the procedure ordinarily followed by the courts, nor the rules of evidence which they observe, are in our view appropriate for immigration appeals. The appeals would in any case relate to a special and highly technical code of rules for the application of which the magistrates' court would be less appropriate than, say, a tribunal dealing only with such rules.'

As a final example of a somewhat different kind the Donovan Commission[27] drew attention to the divided jurisdiction, in the field of disputes between employer and employee, between industrial tribunals and county courts, by which the same claimant might have to take a claim for a redundancy payment to the former and one for wrongful dismissal or holiday pay to the latter. It concluded that all such disputes ought to be within the jurisdiction of the industrial tribunals, though in matters other than redundancy pay and 'unfair' dismissal the claimant should be able to choose between the tribunal and the court.

An even more striking example of preference for tribunals over the courts was in the transfer of workmen's compensation disputes, after fifty years, from county court judges to the industrial injuries tribunals. This was of course a corollary of the absorption of workmen's compensation into the wider national insurance scheme, and the Beveridge Report was as much concerned with the deficiencies of workmen's compensation as such, with its lump sum settlements and absence of constructive or remedial measures, as with the shortcomings of the courts. Nevertheless the Report was critical of the courts as an agency for this particular jurisdiction:

[26] Report of the Committee on Immigration Appeals: Cmnd. 3387/1967.

[27] Report of the Royal Commission on Trade Unions and Employers' Associations, June 1968.

'The authors of the original Acts (i.e. of 1896 and 1906) contemplated that disputes would be settled by friendly and informal arbitration, but this has not been realized and disputes are now generally settled by formal proceedings in the courts.'[28]

Most recently, as we have noted elsewhere (p. 45), children's hearings before a 'tribunal' have replaced the juvenile courts in Scotland for children under 16, except for a few serious offences. One might have supposed that the juvenile courts themselves were so informal, and savoured so little of the magistrates' court, that the change would be nominal. Nevertheless it was thought necessary, by yet another departmental committee,[29] that the change should be made, and these hearings now come under the oversight of the Council on Tribunals. They represent, along with the mental health review tribunals, an incursion by the tribunal system into the field of remedial social work.

*Advisory to Adjudicatory – a Thin Dividing Line*

These are instances where we can look for evidence to official reports. For the reason why the licensing of air transport was originally tribunalized we have to rely on a ministerial statement to Parliament, from which it appears that the former Air Transport Advisory Council, in a manner of speaking, tribunalized itself. After referring to the fact that he and his predecessor had frequently turned to the Council for advice, the Minister went on to say:

'As a result this body, which had originally been designed as nothing more than a consumers' council, gradually assumed the functions of a licensing authority.'[30]

He was accordingly proposing to legitimize the position by creating the Air Transport Licensing Board.

*Transfer from Local to Central Government*

The other example that we quoted of a former administrative decision being made judicial was the local valuation courts, which followed on what might be called the nationalization of rating valuation, i.e. the substitution of Inland Revenue valuers applying a uniform code throughout the country for valuation by rating authorities with its

[28] The Beveridge Report – Social Insurance and Allied Services, November 1942, pp. 77–9.

[29] Report of the Committee on Children and Young Persons (Scotland) 1964, Cmnd. 2306, and the Kilbrandon Report 'Social Work and the Community' 1966, Cmnd. 3065.

[30] 618. H.C. Deb. col. 1227.

resultant discrepancies between rich and poor areas. Objections to draft lists were previously heard by local authority assessment committees, acting administratively, though there was an appeal from their rulings to Quarter Sessions, and in turn from there on a point of law to the Court of Appeal. When valuation came to be made by the Inland Revenue the judicial process was localized in the valuation courts, with an appeal to an expert appellate body, namely the Lands Tribunal.

## RETENTION OF FINAL ADJUDICATION BY MINISTER

The Donoughmore Report, in arguing that Parliament should always be extremely reluctant to entrust 'Ministers or Ministerial Tribunals' with purely judicial powers, conceded that there might have to be exceptions, in which case the decision of Parliament should normally depend on what is 'the dominant aspect of the problem or class of problem to be solved'.[31] The more that policy was the dominant aspect the more probable it is that adjudication – certainly appellate adjudication – would be kept within a Department. At the time this was written the future importance of *licensing* as a class or type of adjudication was not appreciated, and today the most notable examples of the retention by a Minister of appellate jurisdiction relate to the Traffic Commissioners and the Civil Aviation Authority. The former have indeed been responsible for generating the most comprehensive of all discussions by a departmental committee of the advantages and disadvantages of administrative adjudication in this field. In 1952 a committee known as the Thesiger Committee[32] was appointed to

> 'enquire into the operation of the provisions of the Road Traffic Act 1930, relating to the licensing of public road passenger services and to make recommendations.'

The Committee say (paragraph 182) that on no aspect of their task were they asked to consider more evidence than on whether appeals from Traffic Commissioners should continue to be determined by the Minister or whether jurisdiction ought to be transferred to a tribunal such as the Transport Tribunal, which already dealt with the carriage of *goods* by road.

Since the Committee discuss the point in some 5,000 words, half of which comprise a dissenting opinion by one of the six members, it is

[31] Report, p. 96.

[32] Committee on the Licensing of Road Passenger Services, HMSO 1953. The curious differentiation between passenger and goods services is discussed in another context later in this chapter (p. 243).

clearly impossible to summarize the arguments without distortion. For present purposes it is perhaps sufficient to say that the majority believed that the Minister, and not a tribunal, should be the appellate authority since the decisions which licensing authorities had to make differed fundamentally from those which judges had to make, i.e. they had to decide 'what is the desirable decision . . . as tested by representations as to the public interest'. While it was important to reach decisions in a judicial manner 'the decision is largely determined by policy', and it is appropriate that the appellate authority should be one which 'approaches the matter from a similar point of view to that which the Statute requires from the Licensing Authority' (paragraphs 196–7). The fundamental point (paragraph 200) was that the primary purpose of the licensing system was to provide the country with suitable and efficient transport services and not to determine claims between individuals.

The arguments in favour of transferring appellate jurisdiction from the Minister to a tribunal, which were developed at very great length, rested on two basic assumptions. First, 'that it was inappropriate for a quasi-judicial function to be performed by a Minister who as a politician may either be influenced, or appear to be influenced, by political considerations'. Second, that it was wrong that appeal made from 'the decision of an Authority appointed by the Minister and heard by an inspector appointed by the Minister should finally be determined by him; this was held to constitute 'appeal from the servant, through the agent, to the master, whereas the appellate authority should both be independent and be seen to be independent' (paragraph 191).

A point of view similar to that of the majority was expressed by another Minister in introducing the Bill to establish the Air Transport Licensing Board:

> 'I considered most carefully the possibility of setting up some independent appeal machinery. But since, at times, issues of Government policy and of public interest are bound to be involved I felt that Hon. Members would not wish these matters to be settled by anyone except a Minister accountable to the House of Commons.'[33]

The argument of ministerial accountability, which is encountered elsewhere, and notably in the field of planning inquiries, is one which needs to be treated with reserve. If a tribunal *is* established accountability to Parliament disappears, and in the case of planning appeals the principle of accountability has been diminished by transferring the

[33] 618. H.C. Deb, col. 1227.

Minister's jurisdiction in the majority of appeals to his inspectors.[34] What the argument means is that there are categories of decision for which ministers *choose* to remain accountable politically.

Air transport licensing is a particularly clear example of policy being 'the dominant aspect', an aspect which could very easily have international as well as domestic implications. Incidentally, the Civil Aviation Authority is not subject to the scrutiny of the Parliamentary Commissioner for Administration, since the Minister is no longer accountable to Parliament on many day-to-day licensing decisions.

As we have seen, this is the area where tribunals come closest to being public inquiries. The Milk and Dairies Tribunal, which we also quoted in this context, originated in an almost accidental way. When the enforcement of hygiene regulations was to be transferred from local authorities to the Minister of Agriculture (by the Food and Drug (Milk and Dairies) Bill 1943), no appeal machinery was envisaged. It was introduced at the Committee stage as an informal arrangement by which a 'tribunal' to advise the Minister was to be chaired by an officer of the Department. In debate this was amended, and it was finally agreed that the Chairman should be a man of good public standing, not a milk producer, but with an interest in agriculture and public affairs. This was a good example of a decision which was intended to be administrative being made *to some extent* judicial by the pressure of the agricultural interests in Parliament.

A quite different sphere in which the Minister retains final jurisdiction is in national health service matters, where however there is a complicated system by which he is advised by a three-man 'tribunal' over complaints about the service, and by advisory committees if matters reach the point of a doctor's or dentist's remuneration being stopped.

An important example of the *recovery* of ministerial control of a matter which had previously been tribunalized is the provision in the Immigration Act 1971 (sections 14(3) and 15(3)) whereby the right of appeal by an alien is withdrawn if deportation, or refusal of permission to remain, is contemplated on grounds of security or for political reasons, and which stemmed from the case of Mr Rudi Dutschke. In that case the Home Secretary had felt it necessary to direct, in terms of

[34] There is an interesting anomaly here. In dealing with a transferred appeal the inspector's powers are equivalent to those of the Secretary of State, of whom he is independent (para. 2 of 9th Schedule, T. & C.P. Act 1971), and he issues his decision in his own name. For all other purposes of the Act, however, including the right of appeal to the courts, the inspector's decision is treated as that of the Secretary of State (para. 2(3) 9th Schedule). The Secretary of State would also be accountable to Parliament for the inspector's decision on a transferred appeal.

the Alien (Appeals) Order 1970, that the appeal should be heard by a special panel and that certain matters relating to the decision not to allow the appellant to remain in this country could not be disclosed to him, since to do so would be contrary to the interests of national security. In the event these matters were also withheld from Mr Dutschke's counsel. Much of the strong public interest in the case was hostile to the Home Secretary's decision, a hostility which was exacerbated by the hearing arrangements, which only allowed a fraction of those who attended to hear what was going on. There was general agreement that the conduct of arrangements was unsatisfactory and that the hearing itself could hardly be considered a judicial tribunal.

In the context of this book the point of interest is not whether Mr Dutschke received justice but whether the issue was in a true sense justiciable. Certainly the Government felt that a mistake had been made in removing such highly sensitive matters from the sphere of administrative decision, for in the special Debate in the House of Commons the Home Secretary did not seek to defend the Tribunal procedure from criticism:

> 'The present situation with regard to the Appeal Tribunal is not right. I know that the Attorney General feels that it is not satisfactory . . . it is not working out as the House thought it would, and I think further thought should be given to the matter.'[35]

## THE USE OF EXISTING MACHINERY OR THE CREATION OF NEW

One of the choices which will often be open to Parliament is between the use of some existing machinery of adjudication and the creation of new machinery to meet new situations, and here we may note two interesting contrasts in recent years. Under the Rent Act 1965 machinery had to be devised for determining a 'fair rent' for unfurnished accommodation. The Minister of the day considered proposing that the jurisdiction of the Lands Tribunal should include this, but decided that although the expertise of the Tribunal was appropriate its organization was not, since although it was frequently on circuit in all parts of the country where there was an accumulation of cases the operation of the Rent Act needed a network of static local tribunals. He considered also the existing rent tribunals, whose organization was appropriate and whose jurisdiction, *prima facie*, lay in much the same field. He

[35] 809. H.C. Deb. col. 799. For a critical but balanced account of the case itself see B. A. Hepple, 'Aliens and Administrative Justice: The Dutschke Case', *Modern Law Review*, September 1971. See also Annual Report of the Council on Tribunals 1970–1, paras. 30–1.

concluded, however, that the emergency legislation of 1948 over furnished rents, by which the tribunals could take into account such matters as security of tenure and personal circumstances, was of a different order from the objective economic criteria of the fair rent formula. Local valuation courts might also have seemed appropriate, since in this country rent and rates are related to each other, but their suitability was thought superficial as they worked, so to speak, with a much broader brush than was needed for the new formula, and being a legacy from local government they were somewhat outside the Department's direct sphere of influence. Accordingly he proposed to Parliament that the new rent assessment committees should be created, in a situation where on the face of it other existing machinery could have been employed, and in spite of strong representations from the Council on Tribunals that a unified system should be established for furnished and unfurnished rents.[36]

By contrast, jurisdiction in several industrial matters was added between 1964 and 1966 to the existing industrial tribunals, whose original function of determining disputes arising from the industrial training levy soon became a relatively minor one. Their jurisdiction, and organization, was greatly extended by the Industrial Relations Act 1971, and the Equal Pay Act will add to it still further as it becomes operative.

These are examples of reasoned choice, but patterns of adjudication may be determined by more fortuitous circumstances. The seemingly illogical arrangements which govern traffic licensing are a good example. Briefly, passenger vehicles are licensed by the Traffic Commissioners, with an appeal to the Minister; goods vehicles by the Chairmen of the Commissioners sitting alone as 'Licensing Authorities', with an appeal to the Transport Tribunal. The difference arose from two historical accidents – first that buses and coaches were becoming a serious problem some time before trucks and lorries; second, that between the Road Traffic Act 1930, which established the Traffic Commissioners, and the Road and Rail Traffic Act 1933, which established the Licensing Authorities, the publication of the Donoughmore Committee's Report had brought the growing judicial powers of ministers into question; in these few years, also, goods haulage had begun the spectacular rise which was to result by 1971 in 85 per cent of all freight ton-miles being carried by road.

[36] In recent years rent tribunals and rent assessment committees have in fact drawn closer together (p. 96) and future legislation in the light of the Report of the Francis Committee may draw them closer still. See Annual Report of the Council on Tribunals, 1965, paras. 18–28.

The Royal Commission on Transport, from which both measures arose, had in its *Second* Report in 1928,[37] dealing with passenger traffic proposed the Minister as the appellate tribunal, but in this they were doing no more than continuing the judicial powers given to him in the first statute that ever attempted to deal with the new traffic problem – the Roads Act 1920. In their *Final* Report in 1930,[38] dealing with goods traffic, they proposed a similar arrangement for goods licence appeals, but when the Bill came to be published the Government had substituted a new 'Appeal Tribunal' for the Minister:

> '(In the case of passenger vehicles) Parliament, while widening the rights of appeal, retained the appellate position of the Minister. In the licensing of goods vehicles we are entering a new field, and the Bill proposes a separate tribunal to hear appeals.'[39]

The new Appeal Tribunal was subsequently merged with the Railway Rates Tribunal by the Transport Act 1947 under the new name of 'Transport Tribunal', though subsequent legislation has eroded its functions to the point when its work is residual.

The Thesiger Report of 1953, to which we have already referred, was a postscript to these events. As we have seen, it recommended that the Minister should continue as the appellate tribunal. It was argued at the time in support of this recommendation that the increase or diminution of passenger services was a matter of public policy, directly affecting the convenience of the travelling public, whereas only operators were affected by the licensing of goods vehicles. This was doubtless truer in the early 1950s than it is today, but even in 1953 it is questionable whether any committee starting with a clean slate would have argued that buses should in the last analysis be authorized by a Minister but trucks by an independent tribunal.

*Rent Assessment Committees and Rent Scrutiny Committees*

A difficult choice faced the Minister of Housing in the Housing Finance Bill in 1971, one of whose purposes was to extend the 'fair rent' concept into the public sector, thus requiring housing authorities to fix rents in accordance with the criteria prescribed for private landlords in the 1965 Rent Act. His final proposal was unusual in that it involved associating an administrative type of jurisdiction with a judicial tribunal. It would have been logical to expect – and indeed the Secretary

[37] Cmd. 3416 of 1929.
[38] Cmd. 3751 of 1930.
[39] 89. H.L. Deb. 1932–3. Col. 13. Introductory speech by the Secretary of State for Air.

of State first proposed – that rent assessment commitees should undertake the new jurisdiction, the panels being increased in size to make this possible. But the kind of decisions that were going to be called for would be administrative rather than judicial. Vast numbers of houses would fall within the new provisions overnight, and the task of adjudicating on each one individually (assuming a high proportion of appeals) would have been physically impossible. The alternative of setting up some completely new machinery would have been open to criticism on the grounds of confusion, complexity and cost. Accordingly it was decided in principle that the provisional fair rents fixed by local authorities should be 'scrutinized' in the light of all relevant circumstances, but without obligation to consider individual dwellings or to hear appeals from aggrieved tenants; houses would, instead, be considered on the basis of samples or types. Clearly this approximates to administrative review rather than judicial determination.

Rent assessment committees appeared to be the proper and convenient agencies through which it should be done, but the Council on Tribunals objected to a judicial tribunal being used for an administrative purpose; they thought that not only was it wrong in principle that the judicial and administrative function should be thus confused, but that it would weaken confidence in the impartiality of rent assessment committees in the private sector.[40] To meet this objection the Secretary of State decided to add to the membership of the panels, but to require panel presidents to appoint from their increased number 'rent scrutiny committees' – the title was later altered to 'boards' – *in addition to* rent assessment committees; these boards would sit with a chairman and *six* members (instead of two) in order to discharge this new responsibility. Thus although it would be possible to distinguish between assessment committees and scrutiny boards at an actual meeting there would be a manifest association on the panel between a judicial body determining disputes between landlord and tenant and an administrative review body deciding from their own inquiries whether to confirm or to propose amendments to a local authority's provisional determination.

Curiously enough, history was repeating itself after more than half a century. The first of all departmental investigations into rent restriction, the Hunter Committee of 1919,[41] considered but rejected the idea of special tribunals and came to the conclusion that aggrieved tenants must continue to look to the courts. Their reason was that tribunals would be:

[40] Annual Report 1970–1, paras. 38–40.

[41] Ministry of Reconstruction Committee on the Increase of Rents and Mortgage Interest, Cd. 9235.

'impracticable because of the enormous number of houses on which practically simultaneous decisions would be required, involving an immense amount of labour'.

*National Superannuation and Social Insurance – 'Minister's Questions'*
The most recent example at the time of writing of a choice between new and existing machinery relates to questions of national insurance contributions and eligibility which had hitherto been decided by the Minister. In the National Superannuation and Social Insurance Bill in 1969 it was proposed that these traditional 'Minister's questions' ought to go to a new independent tribunal with a right of appeal to the High Court on a point of law. The Council on Tribunals urged that this was misguided, and that use ought to be made of the existing machinery of national insurance local tribunals with an appeal to the National Insurance Commissioner, which accords with the Council's view that there should in principle be fewer and stronger tribunals. The opposing points of view need not detain us here;[42] all that we are concerned to establish is that this particular kind of choice is constantly recurring and that decisions to proceed *ad hoc* continue to add to the complexity of the subject.

## EXTERNAL INFLUENCES ON CHOICE

Apart from advice which may reach him through formal and official channels, such as a Royal Commission or departmental committee, a Minister's judgment as to the appropriate method of adjudication is often influenced by consultations, in the course of formulating policy, with professional bodies or other associations which have special knowledge of a subject.

For example, over a very wide range of legislation, emanating from various departments, the associations of local authorities are informally consulted. Such consultation is particularly important in this country, where the point of contact – and potential conflict – between the citizen and the state is as often a local authority as a government department, and indeed local authorities will often be responsible for implementing policy. Consultation with the associations is so regular that their 'parliamentary' work is one of their most important activities. Similarly

[42] They are difficult to summarize briefly, and may be found in a letter from the Council on Tribunals to the Lord Chancellor, published as Appendix B to the Council's Annual Report for 1969–70. At the time of writing the matter is in suspense, the proposed legislation having lapsed on the change of Governments in June 1970.

in preparing most agricultural legislation account would be taken of the views of the NFU, or in industrial legislation of the CBI and TUC. The British Medical Association was a powerful influence in determining the complex arrangements for adjudication in the national health service, though this was perhaps only to be expected when the matter under discussion so very closely concerned the profession on which the service was to depend. More typically, there is consultation, as occasion may arise, with the Law Society, the Magistrates' Association, the Royal Institute of Chartered Surveyors, and a wide variety of voluntary organizations.

Consultation of this kind may sometimes rest on the observance of strict confidence, since there are matters in which departments must be discreet in discussing Government policy outside Parliament, and it tends in any case to diminish as policy crystallizes into legislation. On the other hand the recent trend has been towards overt consultation and open discussion at the policy-forming stage, as is instanced by the practice of issuing 'Green Papers' and 'Consultative Documents'. This is perhaps especially welcome in the context of adjudication, since the public and the professions will have had an opportunity to say in advance what they consider to be fair ways of settling disputes which may arise between themselves and public authorities.

## LIMITATIONS ON CHOICE

We have tried to distinguish the different kinds of choice which may be open to ministers and to Parliament and to adduce, where there is sufficient evidence, why one choice has been made in preference to another. Over a large part of the field, however, the element of choice hardly arises, for the manner in which disputes will be settled is largely determined by the surrounding circumstances.

This is true of any *appellate* tribunal where the point at issue is a denial of an individual's claim to be qualified to receive a particular kind of benefit (e.g. a pension or unemployment pay); or where he is threatened with loss of livelihood by being judged unsuitable or incompetent professionally (e.g. as the head of an independent school or a producer of hygienic milk); or where he is caught up in a dispute which arises from an administrative operation prescribed by statute (e.g. the hearing of complaints by a service committee on behalf of a National Health Service Executive Council). In such cases there is a manifest need for an impartial and independent review, and 'choice' becomes a question of *how far* it is desirable to go in order to give the individuals concerned the feeling that they have been treated fairly.

Or again, any element of choice may have been excluded at a very early stage by a political decision that a certain structure of adjudication is essential to a policy; the extreme example of this is seen in the fact that the role of industrial tribunals and an Industrial Court, to be embodied in an Industrial Relations Act, had been part of the electoral programme of the present (1973) Government.

### THE FINAL DECISION OF PARLIAMENT

Since appointing the Council on Tribunals to be its watchdog in these matters Parliament has found few occasions to concern itself with adjudicatory provisions, unless they have been central to a Bill's purposes, as with the Industrial Relations Bill. Normally such provisions will have been scrutinized by the Council before Parliament sees them.[43]

In earlier years, however, as we indicated on p. 231, Parliament has not always accepted the judgment of Ministers and departments. Two examples from the past are of interest, since they deal with fundamentals.

In 1944 no provision for appeal was made in the Food and Drugs (Milk and Dairies) Bill, by which the Minister would withhold or withdraw a licence from a dairy farmer on the ground that his method of production was unhygienic. The agricultural interest in Parliament made strong objection, and in the course of debate the merits of a county court judge were set against those of an 'appeal to equals . . . people who understand the business'. The Minister was disposed to accept an *advisory* tribunal (which is what the Milk and Dairies 'Tribunal' is today) but to resist an independent tribunal over whom he had no control on the familiar ground of accountability to Parliament:

> 'He might have to prosecute for producing dirty milk a man whom the Tribunal said was producing clean milk.'

He was prepared to ask the Milk Marketing Board and the National Farmers' Union to nominate panels for a tribunal, but not to accept an independent chairman, a post which he thought should be held by a senior Veterinary Officer of his Ministry.[44]

[43] The Council have no statutory right to scrutinize draft legislation, as they have over procedural rules, but it has been the growing practice of departments to consult them over the drafting of Bills. The point is discussed in the Council's First Annual Report (1959) at para. 124. But see also their Report for 1970–1, in which they complain that it is not always made clear to Parliament that they may have been critical of certain points but have been unable to persuade a Department to their way of thinking.

[44] 400. H.C. Deb. col. 1813 ff.

At the Report Stage the Solicitor General justified this on the ground that:

> 'We have left the truly justiciable issue to a tribunal and left what is truly a matter of fixing national standards to the Minister.'[45]

He also sought to justify the retention of a civil servant as chairman, but Members continued to be critical of this, and when the Act became operative in 1949 the Regulations provided for 'a man of good public standing, not a milk producer, but with an interest in agriculture and public affairs'.

This was an example of Parliament introducing an element of adjudication where none existed. An example of Parliament *improving* a Bill is provided by the Lands Tribunal Bill 1949, the purpose of which was to strengthen and codify the statutory arrangements for settling disputes about the valuation of land. In the previous year the Local Government Act 1948 had transferred appeals against the decisions of local valuation courts from Quarter Sessions to the county courts, though the Act was not yet in operation. A private Member (the then Mr Selwyn Lloyd) proposed that this provision should be rescinded and such appeals transferred to the new Lands Tribunal, on the grounds that not only were the county courts already over-burdened with work but that 'it was unreasonable to expect a county court judge to be expert in rating law' – a vivid example of two of the Franks Committee's criteria for tribunals, expedition and expert knowledge.[46] The amendment was welcomed by the Attorney-General and subsequently implemented, and rating valuation appeals now form a substantial part of the day-to-day work of the Lands Tribunal.

The place which any particular tribunal may occupy in the spectrum is determined by various factors – deliberate choice, force of circumstances, accidents of history, parliamentary pressures, and of course the nature of the issue to be settled. The spectrum itself derives its colours from the interplay of law, policy and administration, rather than from any coherent set of principles.

[45] 401. H.C. Deb. col. 1370.
[46] 462. H.C. Deb. col. 46.

CHAPTER 10

# COMPARISON WITH THE COURTS

> 'As a purely theoretical proposition in constitutional law I suppose I should have to condemn the proliferation of *ad hoc* tribunals as unhealthy.'
>
> *The Lord Chancellor*[1]

During the course of this speech Lord Hailsham went on to regret that during his lifetime Parliament had established so many local and specialist 'courts' outside the Queen's Courts, and wondered why they had preferred tribunals to the established network of the county courts. He judged the answer to this question to lie principally in the distrust by Parliament and the public, in an age of experts, of a judge sitting alone, and, as we shall see, expressed himself in favour of more advisers and assessors.

In our opening survey of tribunals in Chapter 2 we noted that there was an ill-defined watershed – perhaps a 'no-man's-land' would have been a more appropriate simile – between tribunals and the courts. Although in this chapter we are more concerned with their practical working than with their constitutional differences, the points we made on page 67 are perhaps worth elaboration.

The Franks Committee's repeated use of the expression 'tribunals other than the ordinary courts of law' might imply that there was little difference, and certainly no fundamental difference, between the two. While this may be broadly true, it is instructive to recall the analysis of the Donoughmore Committee, which identified a large number of bodies outside the ordinary courts which they categorized as 'Specialized Courts of Law',[2] and others – a sub-category, so to speak – which they called 'ministerial tribunals'. Their specialized courts ranged wide, from the domestic courts of the medical and legal professions to various referees not appointed by ministers and the Chief Registrar of Friendly Societies appointed by the Treasury, and including the now defunct

[1] The Holdsworth Lecture, given to the Holdsworth Club in the University of Birmingham, 3 March 1972.

[2] Report pp. 83–7.

Railway and Canal Commission and Railway Rates Tribunal. Today they would have included the Restrictive Practices Court, the Commercial Court and the National Industrial Relations Court. Their ministerial tribunals embraced unemployment insurance and war pensions tribunals and would now presumably embrace all the later tribunals dealing with claims and licences.[3] It is apparent that as happens in discussing almost any aspect of tribunals we are looking at the colours of a spectrum, though so much do the colours run into one another that the Donoughmore Committee included the Special Commissioners of Income Tax, a modern 'tribunal', as a specialized court, and admitted that their distinction between ministerial tribunals and specialized courts was 'essentially one not of kind but of degree'.

What we have in fact are on the one hand the ordinary courts of law, distinguished by broad and general jurisdictions; and on the other the specialized courts and the ministerial tribunals of the Donoughmore Report, whose jurisdictions are narrower and more specific. From this it would perhaps seem to follow that the wider the jurisdiction of a tribunal the more it will take on the attributes of a court, and it is interesting that of the two tribunals which enjoy the widest jurisdictions the Lands Tribunal does in fact most nearly resemble a branch of the High Court and the Industrial Tribunals have come to approximate to the 'Labour Courts', analogous to the county courts, adumbrated in the Donovan Report (see p. 87).

If we used the word 'tribunal' in its true generic sense we could turn the argument round, and say that the real watershed lies between tribunals which have a *generalized* jurisdiction (which are in fact the ordinary courts of law) and those which have a *specialized* jurisdiction (which would include both the special courts and ministerial tribunals of the Donoughmore nomenclature). A characteristic of the specialized jurisdictions is that they may not only be specialized but temporary or sporadic, as instanced by the various national service tribunals which have long been redundant, or by those tribunals which we mentioned on p. 58 which may only meet once in a number of years.

An analysis which is difficult enough is made more so by confused nomenclature. We have already noted, among what are statutorily called tribunals, the confusion whereby for example a local valuation 'court' is inferior to the Lands 'Tribunal', which as we have said bears some resemblance to a branch of the High Court; or whereby a rent

[3] Including so far as the nature of their jurisdiction is concerned the local valuation courts, although for historical reasons these have never been 'ministerial' tribunals, and have to this day a far more tenuous Departmental connection than the tribunals which are concerned with rents.

assessment committee is a tribunal although there is something else called a rent tribunal. There is equal confusion on the frontier between 'specialized courts and ministerial tribunals'. In the jurisdiction of the Restrictive Practices Court there is not, strictly speaking, a *lis inter partes*. Moreover in deciding whether or not an agreement is restrictive the Court must, among other things, judge as best it can the future effect of the agreement, whether it will benefit purchasers, consumers or users (which, as a former President of the Court has admitted, involves a value-judgment coloured by the economic theories held by the evaluator),[4] and whether the restriction is reasonable having regard to the balance between its advantages to purchasers and any detriment to persons in the same trade. This sounds very like a regulatory tribunal, and indeed the authors of *The Restrictive Practices Court*[5] say that it would almost certainly have been called a tribunal but for pressure on the Government to create an 'impartial court' in contrast to the unpopular tribunal known as the Monopolies Commission. In fact it is not only called a 'Court' but ranks as a 'Superior Court of Record'.

When we leave this uncertain area of comparative analysis for the firmer ground of comparing how the two institutions work in actual practice, we find that there are certain attributes which broadly distinguish one from the other, though even here the distinctions are not always clear-cut. These attributes are the greater use by tribunals of adjudicators expert in the subject matter of the adjudication; and their greater reliance on independent investigation to supplement the adversarial presentation of a case, which allows them to reach decisions in the light of criteria other than the actual evidence submitted to them. Perhaps more important than either, though more difficult to define, is a difference in atmosphere, whereby the applicant or appellant is treated more as a 'customer', in whose problems the tribunal is involved, and less of a 'suppliant', whose affairs the court views with detachment. The point is referred to again on p. 282.

## EXPERTISE

Tribunals employ – as decision-takers and not just as witnesses – large numbers of experts such as valuers, psychiatrists and botanists, or persons with specialized experience such as trade unionists, em-

[4] Lord Diplock, *The Role of the Judicial Process in the Regulation of Competition* (Oxford University Press, 1967), p. 17.

[5] R. B. Stevens and B. S. Yamey (Weidenfield & Nicolson, 1965), p. 18–19. See also R. M. Jackson, *The Machinery of Justice in England*.

ployers or economists. This contrasts with the traditional notion of a judge as an 'all-rounder', expert only in the law, for whom the parties provide expert knowledge, should he require it, by putting expert witnesses in the box. Apart from the common dilemma of the judge faced with experts from each side who differ, there is the problem that neither he nor the lawyers may be sufficiently well-versed in a particular subject to ask the right questions of expert witnesses, whose potential value in assisting in a decision is thereby diminished.

Tribunals on the other hand are ideally the embodiment of expert adjudication, for even if their members are not selected for a particular expertise the very fact of being restricted to a narrow field means that they soon become expert in it. An important minority of tribunals do not in fact have definable experts among their members, not even a lawyer-chairman. The General Commissioners of Income Tax are usually served by a Solicitor-Clerk, the Commissioners themselves being mostly local businessmen of good standing in the community but with no claim to expert knowledge of taxation. Local valuation courts, the other unpaid amateurs of the tribunal world, are also advised by an expert Clerk, though his training is normally in valuation and not in law. And supplementary benefit appeal tribunals and some rent tribunals (though not rent assessment committees) are without legal expertise. In all these cases chairmen and members alike rapidly acquire an all-round knowledge of their field of adjudication (although not necessarily the specific expertise of members of other tribunals or assessors in the courts), while retaining, one supposes, the 'expertise' for which they were appointed, namely common sense and balanced judgment. They may be likened to a jury elevated to the bench, save that they are chosen not by chance but by reason of a certain experience.

But 'expertise', other than legal expertise, can be an elastic term. Medical expertise, in the group of tribunals where medical assessment is crucial, is obviously a straightforward notion, though at mental health review tribunals the psychiatric expert is balanced by the elusive 'layman'. In other groups expertise may be variously regarded. Industrial tribunals, for example, demand of the non-legal members a general knowledge of industrial, manufacturing and commercial background and employment, from the standpoints of employer and employed; but this background experience must be brought to bear on questions which are juridically unrelated – redundancy, taxation, job definition, or unfair industrial practice. The matters which the non-legal members of national insurance tribunals must consider are less varied, but are far from homogeneous, and call for a knowledge of working-class life and problems sufficiently wide to embrace the full range of social security benefits. Entitlement to unemployment benefit is, so to speak, their staple diet, but problems of a very different order may arise in determining entitlement to family allowances, retirement pensions, industrial injuries or sickness benefits. In the valuation group on the other hand, people of very different backgrounds are called upon to adjudicate on furnished rents, unfurnished rents, rates and compensation for compulsory purchase, even though a knowledge of property valuation is obviously common to them all.

The courts themselves are, of course, no longer immune from specialization.[6] An early example was the setting apart of the Commercial List within the Queen's Bench Division in 1895 in response to the needs of the commercial community – the genesis of the Commercial Court. Other facets of specialization within the courts are the nominated judge who deals with patents appeals, and the Divisional Court which hears nearly all applications under the prerogative orders.[7] But such specialization is rather different to the use of an original expertise: as in the case of non-expert tribunal members, a specialist judge may very well become an expert in the field because of his continual acquaintance with it, but he may not necessarily have been an expert when assigned to that field.

There are two fields in which experts have in fact been introduced to the courts, though in each instance it was a 'specialized' and not an 'ordinary' court, these being the Restrictive Practices Court to which we have already referred and the Industrial Relations Court. As Lord Justice Diplock has noted in regard to the former:

> 'But if value judgments upon matters of economics are to be made by a judicial tribunal it is evident that its composition should not be limited to judges whose experience is restricted to the profession of the law. It should include, either as members or assessors, persons with knowledge and experience of commerce and industry – persons who know how the economic system works in practice'[8]

Accordingly the Court sits in divisions consisting usually of one judge[9] (the President) and between two and four lay members chosen for

[6] There has always been a degree of specialization if only in the division between the chancery and common law sides of the legal profession.

[7] The unplanned specialization of county courts may also be noted – in theory their jurisdiction is very wide, in practice they are overwhelmingly concerned with debt collection.

[8] Diplock, *Role of the Judicial Process*, p. 19.

[9] There are five judges assigned to the court, three in England, one in Scotland and one in Northern Ireland. When not sitting in the Restrictive Practices Court they perform their ordinary judicial duties.

their knowledge or experience of industry, commerce or public affairs.

Similarly, the Industrial Relations Court comprises a judge or judges from the High Court and the Court of Appeal, together with members appointed by Her Majesty on the joint recommendation of the Lord Chancellor and the Secretary of State by virtue of their 'special knowledge or experience of industrial relations'.

A recent Departmental Committee on the British Patents System recommended that the specialist patents judge in the Chancery Division should be replaced by a Patents Court of three judges having jurisdiction for the whole of the United Kingdom, either on its own or as part of an enlarged national Commercial Court, and hearing all patent actions including appeals from the decisions of the Comptroller. It had been proposed to this Committee in evidence that there should instead be a Patents Judge as chairman with two lay members on the precedent of the Restrictive Practices Court, but it rejected this suggestion. In doing so it drew attention to the fact that the present law allows for a 'scientific assistant' to assist the judge, not as an assessor but as an 'elucidator', but that this provision had been scarcely used.

The use of assessors is of course another way in which the courts may have the advantage of expert knowledge, but although county courts, all Divisions of the High Court and the Court of Appeal may summon assessors in any civil proceedings, few have ever done so.[10] The Admiralty Court is the only exception.

Once again, therefore, the distinction between courts and tribunals is one of degree rather than kind – experts, whether appointed as such or 'trained on the job' are much more common on tribunals than in the courts. This may well be a matter on which courts and tribunals will draw closer together in the future, for in the speech referred to the Lord Chancellor advocated greater participation by laymen in judicial decisions in the courts:

> 'May it not be that a judge sitting alone has his limitations, and that the public instinctively recoils from giving its confidence to a system which places too much power in the hands of a single man, however expert?'

He went on to say that the distinguishing mark of the modern *ad hoc* tribunal which had so vastly proliferated was the presence of a lawyer-chairman, supported by two lay members who could overrule him.

> 'Could it be that the courts would be more acceptable for some kinds of disputes if some of them had lay members sitting beside the judge?'

[10] Anthony Dickey, 'The Province and Function of Assessors in English Courts', *Modern Law Review*, September 1970.

A comparatively recent example flows from the Race Relations Act 1969. If the Race Relations Board is unable to resolve a dispute by conciliation, which is its principal purpose, it may institute proceedings before a county court judge assisted by two assessors appointed by the Lord Chancellor from a list of persons 'appearing to him to have special knowledge of race and community relations' (s. 19(7)). But if this can be said to illustrate a drawing together of court and tribunal it also serves to draw attention to a factor which keeps them apart, namely that the court in this instance has the power to inflict a penalty, which is not a function of tribunals.[11] This is perhaps one of the more fundamental differences between them.

## ADVERSARIAL PRESENTATION

Most courts (the juvenile courts are an obvious exception) adhere to the adversarial system, which pre-supposes a judge sitting above the contest, ensuring that the contestants observe the rules, assessing their performance and at the end of the day giving judgment according to the evidence put before him.

This is also true of some tribunals, but often the issues before them would not be amenable to this method. The adversarial system pre-supposes a contest, in which one party wins and one loses. But the issues before some tribunals are non-combative[12] – does this school or dairy reach a required standard, is that person entitled to a service pension or supplementary benefit, is a person well enough to be released from restriction in a mental hospital, what is a fair rent for a particular property? Sometimes there may indeed be opposing persons interested in the outcome (as in rent disputes), so that there is the appearance of a *lis inter partes*, or a supposed *lis* may be manufactured by putting forward a departmental officer to oppose an application. In other cases it may be debatable whether a tribunal is adversarial or not. For example, at a mental health review tribunal it could well be that the hospital psychiatrist opposes an application for release, but if he were to do so in the patient's presence the doctor–patient relationship would be irreparably damaged. For this reason the tribunal hears the psychiatrist and the patient separately. This may or may not suggest that there is a *lis*, but what is certain is that expert evidence is not necessarily the

[11] An exception is the General Commissioners of Income Tax, who may penalize, i.e. fine, taxpayers in delay cases who continue to be recalcitrant.

[12] Except in so far, in the words of Dr Geoffrey Marshall, they 'compete against a standard'. 'Administration, Administrative Law and Administrative Discretion': a paper given to the International Political Science Association, 1967.

deciding factor. If it were one would expect the hospital psychiatrist to have the final say, or for the case to be reviewed by a panel of experts. In fact mental health review tribunals contain only one expert, the others being a lawyer-chairman and a local layman, whose combined judgment may in fact override that of the psychiatrist.

But in many cases there is no pretence of an adversarial contest, and the courts have decided that in national insurance cases there is no *lis*.

Even when there is the appearance of a *lis* and therefore of an adversarial contest, tribunals – to a far greater extent than judges – go outside the hearing room and try to ascertain facts for themselves. Those concerned with valuation, tenancies or standards of husbandry on agricultural land invariably examine the property concerned, and their visit is frequently the determining factor; an agricultural land tribunal, for example, will normally reach its formal decision on the farm and not 'in court'. Those concerned with licensing or standards will normally visit garage, school or dairy, and will take account of facts not necessarily presented in evidence. Those in which a medical examination is crucial, for example a pensions appeal tribunal in an assessment case, will if they think fit seek specialist medical opinion over and above the medical evidence presented to them by the appellant's and the Department's doctors, or in the case of medical appeal and mental health review tribunals, may prefer to rely on the opinion of the expert on the tribunal itself. A rent assessment committee may even ignore the evidence presented to it completely; the point is developed on p. 89 and more specifically on p. 273 when we discuss the rules of evidence more fully.

It remains a fact that some of the most important tribunals adhere to adversarial procedure, whether or not they also go beyond the evidence presented by the adversaries. This has long been so, and indeed a distinctly critical reference was made to the fact in evidence to the Franks Committee by the Law Society of Scotland,[13] who maintained that 'testing by controversy of adversaries' was neither typical of the legal process, as was popularly supposed, nor was it necessarily as suitable for tribunals as 'the sympathetic and patient investigation of private persons' difficult circumstances'. They stressed that 'the day-to-day work of a solicitor was concerned with social rather than with purely legal matters' and that 'most legal work, especially in the solicitor branch of the profession, was very far removed from the adversarial.'

### *The Justification for Tribunals*

We began by quoting the Lord Chancellor's question why tribunals

[13] Evidence, Day 23, p. 1055.

continued to be preferred to the courts (specifically to the county courts). What we have seen so far is that they are capable of greater flexibility. To a far greater extent than a court a tribunal may be dealing with a more or less justiciable issue; may have a more or less expert membership; may be more or less formal in its procedure; may permit of a greater or less degree of subjectivity in reaching a decision; may reach finality, be subject to appeal or may indeed be merely advisory to the executive. Their justification goes beyond what the Lord Chancellor apprehended as Parliament's mistrust of a judge sitting alone to determine the sort of issues that arise from modern social legislation, though this is undoubtedly important. For example, a court may determine a legal issue between landlord and tenant, but a tenancy dispute at an agricultural land tribunal may turn on whether land is being efficiently farmed, or at a rent assessment committee on an intimate knowledge of local property values. It is improbable that a judge in an ordinary court, sitting alone, would be equipped with either kind of knowledge. Again, a court will determine contractual issues between employer and employed, but a knowledge of manufacturing and commercial processes may be needed to determine whether in particular circumstances a man became redundant or was dismissed.

But there are other justifications than this. At one extreme no court would wish to determine claims for supplementary benefit, which have much of the character of an administrative review; nor, at the other, would a court wish to license traffic or enforce standards of milk production, which are matters of expert judgment and the application of policy. The courts do not wish to become burdened with 'policy-oriented' matters any more than their nineteenth-century predecessors wished to be burdened with fixing railway rates.

There is furthermore the important point made by the Permanent Secretary to the Lord Chancellor in evidence to the Franks Committee,[14] when he himself was contemplating the prospect of what would be necessary if the business of the tribunals were to be added to that of the courts. He added the further consideration that in his judgment

> 'many of the disputes in question do not warrant . . . the services of a highly remunerated judge; they are of a nature in which justice can be done just as fully by a practising or retired member of the legal profession, or by a layman whose specialized knowledge more than compensates for the lack of training in the impartial examination of facts which is acquired by practice at the Bar or as a solicitor.'

[14] Evidence, Day 7, pp. 191–2.

Remuneration apart, they do not require a judge's training, knowledge and experience.

Finally, there are several matters which come before tribunals which, provided that natural justice is observed, are better investigated by methods other than the adversarial, and outside the rules of evidence of the courts.

The Donoughmore Report, echoed by Franks, found much of the justification of tribunals in more mundane matters, such as cheapness, simplicity, accessibility, speed and informality. Today some of these considerations have much more weight than others. The county courts are more informal than they used to be, and as we shall see later in this chapter are further simplifying their pre-trial procedures; nor are they necessarily less expeditious than tribunals. On the other hand the approach to them is tortuous compared with the straightforward path to a tribunal hearing, and far more expensive to the individual with a relatively small financial claim. Indeed, cost is undoubtedly the deciding factor in discouraging the ordinary person from using the county courts.

The reasons for the retention and growth of tribunals, alongside the 'ordinary courts', are accordingly varied and substantial.

## PROCEDURAL DIFFERENCES

But although there may be no fundamental difference between courts and tribunals, and although tribunals represent an extension of the judicial system rather than a radical departure from it, there are some major procedural differences between the two, some of which may indeed go beyond procedure into the realm of principle. There are more concrete matters than those we have been discussing, and we may deal with them more specifically. They comprise:

Study of the papers before hearing,
Order of events,
Representation,
Privilege for witnesses,
Burden and standard of proof,
Rules of evidence,
Precedent,
Public and private hearings,
Withholding of evidence and exclusion of parties.

We will conclude with some observations on the general atmosphere surrounding courts and tribunals, and on their respective roles in the matter of conciliation.

*Study of the Case Before Hearing*

We have already described (pp. 135–9) the kind of written information that is required of parties in advance of a hearing – what in a court of law would be known as pleadings. We saw that these took a variety of forms and went by various names.

A common feature was that where the claimant was likely to be an individual aggrieved by an adverse decision, and probably without legal representation, the requirements should be of the simplest, and that he should merely be asked to say in his own words why he thought the decision was wrong. Even this can cause difficulty to people unaccustomed to marshalling their thoughts on paper, and it is significant that the industrial tribunals have found that a questionnaire which keeps the appellant to the point and indicates the kind of information that is relevant is an improvement on the original statutory form which gave him a free hand. Furthermore, it is a convention among the principal tribunals dealing with individual claims that if a statement is inadequate it is their responsibility to help the unrepresented claimant to make good its deficiencies.[15]

Pleadings and case papers raise the question of how much information ought the parties be required to disclose to a tribunal before the hearing. It can be argued that pleadings, however simple they may be in practice, do have the benefit of isolating the issues for the tribunal and informing the parties (particularly the appellant in 'citizen *v.* state' issues) of the case they are likely to meet. More specifically, if a tribunal is given some indication in advance of the facts and issues which are likely to be raised and argued, the tribunal may be able to shorten the hearing time by cutting short irrelevant arguments, the members can brief themselves beforehand on particular legal points which might arise, and the tribunal might be in a position to suggest to an appellant how his case could be better presented. On the other hand it might be suggested that a preliminary consideration of the papers might lead to pre-judgment by the tribunal, and that if the preliminary papers were to be of any real assistance to the tribunal it would be difficult to keep them simple enough for the average appellant to cope with, without employing a solicitor.

The normal practice in tribunals *is* for the papers to be read in

[15] The National Insurance Commissioners take the view that to strengthen or formalize what is required of a claimant in advance of a hearing would be a seriously retrograde step, and could on occasion lead to a miscarriage of justice. It is their practice to extend the utmost liberality to a claimant, to the extent of drawing his attention to a point he may have missed, and which, after giving the insurance officer or the Secretary of State an opportunity to comment, they will take into account.

advance, a practice which seems to stem from common sense practicalities rather than from any particular theory, since most tribunal members and some chairmen are busy people fitting in the work with other commitments and dealing with a large number of cases at a sitting. A Statement of Case before the Pensions Appeal Tribunal, for example, can be an extremely formidable document with complex medical reports from both sides; papers are circulated seven or ten days in advance and members are *required* to study them beforehand. Outside the normal circle of statutory tribunals the documentation presented to an area committee of the Legal Aid Scheme is such that it would be impossible to get through the work if members had not familiarized themselves with the cases beforehand. Moreover, as we have frequently remarked, the social security tribunals suffer from a very high proportion of non-attendance, and where a decision has to be arrived at on the papers it is as well to have read them in advance.

On the other hand the view is not universal. The Lands Tribunal, which incidentally is one of the most 'court-like' tribunals in status and its form of pleadings, hears a case without a preliminary perusal of the papers, as do the Special Commissioners of Income Tax.

*Order of Events*

The order of events at tribunal proceedings was one of the matters which the Franks Committee was called upon to consider:

> 'A definite order of events at a tribunal hearing promotes clarity and regularity. It has, however, been urged upon us that adherence to a set order might make it difficult for an unaided applicant to present his case properly, since the majority of those who appear before tribunals are unaccustomed to the distinction between evidence and argument which a set order of events would seem to require.' (Report paragraph 75.)

Here again is a matter in which there is uniformity in the courts and disparity in tribunals. In the courts the principle is that he who first applies to the court for relief, opens the case.

But as we noted earlier (p. 143) there are tribunals whose rules of procedure still say nothing about an order of events (e.g. tribunals dealing with national insurance, supplementary benefit, furnished rents and war service pensions). It may be thought that this is appropriate, since these are the tribunals where the claimant is usually an unrepresented member of the public, unaccustomed to court-like procedures. On the other hand informal practice may operate to his disadvantage. Most of these tribunals appear to follow the practice of the civil courts and to ask the claimant or appellant to present his case first, with the respondent following and the appellant having the right of reply; though within this framework the appellant may enjoy considerable latitude and informality – for example at a hearing before a National Insurance Commissioner claimants may call their evidence before, after or even in the middle of addressing the Commissioner. Other tribunals which normally require the appellant to open are the pensions appeal tribunals, industrial tribunals, the Immigration Appeal Tribunal and adjudicators, local valuation courts and the Special Commissioners of Income Tax.

It is, however, open to question whether this is apt in all cases, for example, cases in which government departments appear. A high proportion of appellants are unaccustomed to putting their thoughts into words in public, and indeed in the supplementary benefit appeal tribunals, whose clients mostly come from the least privileged and articulate members of the community, the presenting officer of the Supplementary Benefits Commission invariably opens, if only because the appellant would in most cases be incapable of doing so effectively.

But should *any* unrepresented appellant be asked to speak first? Many cases turn on a single point (e.g. was the form of notice to quit legally correct, does an appellant's part-time study disqualify him from unemployment benefit?). Unless the appellant is able to recognize that this point is crucial to his case and to present evidence material to the point, much of what he tells the tribunal may be irrelevant. Again it may only be when the insurance officer or departmental representative addresses the tribunal that the crux of the matter may emerge. Finally on this point, it may well be that the person speaking second has an advantage in that he can rebut statements made by the first speaker. For these reasons it may well be thought that a more appropriate order of events at this kind of tribunal would be to require the insurance officer or departmental representative to open the proceedings by setting out the facts as known to him and his reasons for refusing the claim.

Among the tribunals existing at the time of Franks the local valuation courts provide an example of sensible compromise. Regulation 6 of the Rating Appeals (Local Valuation Courts) Regulations 1956 provides that the appellant shall begin, but that if the appellant agrees the court can direct any other party to begin. The sort of occasion when a valuation court will make such a direction is when an appellant looks like being over-awed by the occasion and likely to have difficulty in explaining his case clearly; the court will then ask if he would mind the valuation officer opening, so that he can succinctly describe the property and thus save the court a lot of time. The ratepayer usually gratefully agrees.

The Lands Tribunal, which is among other things the appellate tribunal for these courts, is somewhat more formal. Rule 35 provides that the appellant 'shall begin and the other parties shall be heard in such order as the tribunal may determine'.

The only comment which the Franks Committee had to make on the subject, following the statement that we have already quoted, was that 'the point can be met by giving tribunals a discretion to vary the procedure if it appears to them desirable in the interests of justice', and this advice has been followed in varying degrees in the principal tribunals which have been created since the time of their Report.

Most flexible are the Rent Assessment Committee Rules, which merely provide that 'the parties shall be heard in such order and, subject to the provisions of these regulations, the procedure shall be such as the committee shall determine'. The rules of the industrial tribunals also provide (Rule 11(2)) that 'Subject to the provisions of these Rules, the Tribunal may regulate its own procedure', but a previous rule specifies that the parties, and the Minister if he is not a party and he elects to appear, shall be entitled to make opening statements, to call witnesses, to cross-examine a witness called by any other party, or by the Minister if he is not a party, and to address the Tribunal. It specifically provides that a party can give evidence on his own behalf.

Immigration Rules follow the same general principle. Rule 25 governs the conduct of proceedings at a hearing before an adjudicator. It leaves the order of events to his discretion, save that under Rule 7(3) the respondent must, at the beginning of an appeal, be given an opportunity to amplify orally the written explanatory statement, or to make an oral statement if there is no written one and under Rule 25(b) each party to the appeal must be given an opportunity, after any evidence has been taken, of making representations on the evidence and on the subject matter of the appeal generally. In practice, adjudicators normally invite the appellant to open, after the Home Office representative has been asked whether he wishes to amplify the Home Office statement.[16]

*Representation*

There is now no difference between the courts and tribunals as regards

[16] Rule 25 also applies to proceedings before the Appeal Tribunal, where the appellant is normally asked to open, the respondent to reply, and the appellant is given the last word. Immigration Appeals (Procedure) Rules 1970.

the *right* to legal representation;[17] the differences are of practice and necessity, matters which we discussed on pp. 176–181. All that need be added to what we have already said is that it is important to avoid undue 'polarization' between those who advocate and those who oppose legal representation. For it is sometimes said by those who feel strongly on the matter that if parties at tribunal hearings are normally to be represented by lawyers tribunals might as well cease to exist and their jurisdictions transferred to the county courts; or alternatively that if judicial proceedings can be conducted equally well without lawyers the legal profession is itself redundant. A reasonable position seems to be that because of their specialized knowledge and their informality, including the ability of lay specialists to question the parties on technical matters and of a lawyer-chairman to uphold the law, legal representation is only necessary in exceptional cases; and that because the sums of money are for the most part small the cost of universal legal representation would be disproportionate; in any case, as matters stand, there is no incentive for the legal profession to specialize in tribunal law and practice. Incentive is further diminished by the fact that only exceptionally do tribunal rules of procedure allow them to award costs.

Naturally cases occur when a tribunal's decision may turn upon a legal point, or where a claimant would greatly improve his chances of success if he were to produce certain evidence or marshal his facts in a particular way. What is most urgently needed is some mechanism whereby the exceptional case can be identified and legal advice or representation provided. The various community law centres to which we referred on p. 179, supported by a gradual extension of the £25 scheme from legal advice to legal aid, seem to be a fruitful development towards this end.

These are of course general statements which apply to the central 'bloc' of tribunals where individual claims are being made against employers, landlords or government departments. Naturally there are tribunals of another kind where skilled advocacy is as important as in the courts – notably in the patents, revenue and taxation tribunals and at the Lands Tribunal, where specialist lawyers do in fact practice and where large investments may be at stake. Equally there are others where legal representation would be superfluous – for example those where the issue turns upon a medical examination and where the

[17] With the sole exception of national health service committees. This is a considerable change from the days of the Franks Committee, when legal representation was not permitted at, for example, tribunals concerned with national insurance, national assistance (as it then was) and family allowances.

most that is needed is that a trade union or an ex-service organization should hold a watching brief.

*Privilege for Witnesses*

This is a matter which has so far had no practical significance, but it must be mentioned here because it exemplifies a specific difference between courts and tribunals, and one moreover to which the Franks Report drew particular attention in these words (paragraph 82):

> '... a witness who gives evidence in a court of law cannot be sued in respect of something he has said in his evidence. He enjoys absolute privilege. A witness before a tribunal does not enjoy the same degree of protection. If he is sued he can rely on the defence of qualified privilege, which will probably succeed in most cases, but he may be put to considerable expense in establishing the defence. Absolute privilege has long been considered necessary to the administration of justice in the courts, and there is a strong case for saying that it is equally necessary for tribunals – at any rate in those cases where evidence is given on oath.'

Qualified privilege protects a witness against an action for defamation if it can be shown that the words were spoken without malice.

The Council on Tribunals discussed the question in 1960 at the request of the Lord Chancellor, but their deliberations were inconclusive and the matter has rested there since that time.

The Council took the view that it was unnecessary to make statutory provision, and that in any case it might be unwise to do so for fear of encouraging malicious statements. The common law was admittedly not clear as to which tribunals already enjoyed absolute privilege,[18] but it was probably best to leave the courts to decide particular cases as they arose. This attitude has so far been justified since the question has never arisen; on the other hand *should* it arise some unfortunate witness would presumably be put to the expense of High Court litigation in order to ascertain whether qualified or absolute privilege applied in his own case.

*The Burden and Standard of Proof*

In general the burden of proof at tribunals follows the practice of civil

[18] At common law the defence of absolute privilege extends to an 'authorized inquiry which, though not before a court of justice, is before a tribunal which has similar attributes' – this general rule was laid down as long ago as 1892 (in *Royal Aquarium Society* v. *Parkinson*, [1892] 1 Q.B. 431) when tribunals, as we know them today hardly existed. Moreover, it gives very little guidance as to which tribunals would be considered to have 'the attributes of a court'.

litigation in the courts, namely that he who makes an assertion must prove it, but one of the things which distinguish tribunals from the courts is that the rules of some tribunals state this specifically (or specifically modify it), others do not mention it but leave it to be assumed, while there are a number in which the concept of proof would hardly arise.

A statement of the normal requirement may be instanced from the Immigration Appeals (Procedure) Rules, in which the effect of Rule 28 is that it is for the appellant to prove that he is, for example, exempt from immigration control or that he is of a certain age, but it would be for the Home Office to prove that, for example, the date stamped on a passport was forged. Similarly in an appeal to the National Insurance Commissioners a claimant for unemployment benefit must prove his entitlement, but if he has been disqualified on account of misconduct those who allege the misconduct must prove it. Sometimes the burden of proof may shift; for example it would be for the insurance officer to prove that a claimant was following an occupation, but once he has done so it is for the claimant to prove matters relating to earnings, availability, consistency and usual main occupation.[19]

There are, however, modifications of the principle. For example, the Redundancy Payments Act (s. 9(2)) provides that unless the contrary is proved a person's employment shall be presumed to have been continuous and that an employee who has been dismissed shall be presumed to have been so dismissed by reason of redundancy; thus the applicant makes the assertion but it rests with the employer to prove that it is untrue, i.e. that the dismissal was for a reason other than redundancy.[20]

The rules governing *entitlement* appeals at the Pensions Appeal Tribunal have to take into account the fact that the alleged origins of disability or illness may lie in the distant past and frequently the point in issue is whether a particular condition can be attributed to former service or to some extraneous cause, including the normal process of growing old; accordingly the rules contain an unusual provision that after a lapse of time the burden of proof shifts (and incidentally the standard of proof alters). Thus if a disability is noted on enlistment and/or the appellant makes his claim within seven years of the termination of his service the onus is laid on the Department to prove its case beyond reasonable doubt. If it is made after seven years the onus is on

[19] Regulation 7(1)(i) of S.I. 1967 No. 330.

[20] In *O'Brien* v. *Associated Fire Alarms*, [1968] 3 I.T.R. 182 the Court of Appeal held that the burden of showing the terms of the contract of employment is on the employers. In *Kitching* v. *Ward*, [1967] 2 I.T.R. 464 the Divisional Court held that it was for the employer to show that an offer of alternative employment was made.

the appellant to prove his case on the preponderance of probability.[21]

An anomalous position arises in the local valuation courts, where the burden of proof rests, in accordance with the normal principle, on the party who makes a proposal to change a rating assessment. But when a new list comes into force the valuation officer does not have to justify a single assessment. Thus if a ratepayer disagrees with the assessment of his property in a new list *he* has to make a proposal for a reduction and if the valuation officer objects the ratepayer has to prove that the new assessment is too high. In short the ratepayer has to prove that the assessment is wrong but the valuation officer never has to prove that it is right.

In the wide range of tribunals that are given no statutory guidance about the burden (or indeed the standard) of proof the nature of the proceedings will generally make the intention apparent. For example, hearings before the 'copyright' group of tribunals (e.g. Plant Varieties, Performing Rights, Patents and Trade Marks) are so closely analogous to civil litigation in the ordinary courts as to leave no doubt. In the social security group, on the other hand, the burden of proof will usually lie on the claimant for an insurance or supplementary benefit, depending on the particular situation or statutory provision to which the appeal relates;[22] while in the traffic licensing group the applicant must obviously satisfy the tribunal about the need for a service and his own competence to provide it.

Finally there are tribunals which for a variety of reasons are not concerned with the burden of proof at all, notably the group whose jurisdiction is one of valuation rather than the establishment of a right or claim. Here it is for a tribunal to inquire and decide as it thinks best, rather than for either party to prove. The most obvious examples are rent assessment committees and tribunals, but for slightly different reasons agricultural land tribunals could be included, as indeed in some of its varied jurisdictions could the Lands Tribunal; the common feature being that the tribunal finally makes up its mind after a site inspection when it employs the evidence of its own eyes.

The *standard* of proof may in general be assumed to be that prevailing

[21] Article 4(2) and 4(3) of the Royal Warrant.

[22] Thus as to supplementary benefit a claimant is required by regulation to furnish information and documents in support of his claim (regulations 4 and 10 of S.I. 1966 No. 1067) whereas the onus will be on the Supplementary Benefits Commission if, say, the issue is cohabitation (see below) or the reduction of an allowance under discretionary powers. But since most of the proceedings are not adversarial in their nature the question where the burden of proof lies has little importance, and indeed many supplementary benefit appeals have much in common with 'valuation' hearings.

in civil cases, i.e. the 'balance of probabilities', rather than that which is associated with criminal jurisdiction, i.e. 'beyond reasonable doubt'.[23]

There have, however, been some cases of difficulty. For example, we have already noted that the Pensions Appeal Tribunal requires one standard when the onus is on the appellant and another when it is on the Department. This arose from a judgment by Edmund Davies J. in 1966.[24] The point in issue was whether severe cervical spondylosis resulted from a fall in 1943 or whether it was a constitutional and degenerative condition. The Tribunal had found that the Minister had discharged his responsibility by establishing the latter on the balance of probability. The Court held that it had been wrong, and that since the relevant regulation (Article 4(2) of the Royal Warrant) provided that the benefit of any reasonable doubt should be given to the claimant the Minister must establish his case beyond reasonable doubt and not on the balance of probabilities:

> 'I therefore hold that the standard of proof applicable to pensions claims is identical with that required in criminal trials.'

Secondly, there has been difficulty in supplementary benefit appeals over the disallowance of benefit to a woman who is cohabiting. This is a matter of some controversy at the time of writing, so much so that the Supplementary Benefits Commission has published a report which explains and attempts to justify the Commission's administration of the relevant provisions of the Social Security Act 1966.[25] The report acknowledges that there has been criticism that evidence obtained by the Commission has been acted upon even though it would not stand up in a court of law. The problem which the Commission faces stems from the very definition of 'cohabitation' – how does one assess whether the parties are living together in a common law marriage? As the report points out, this will depend for example on 'whether the couple are publicly regarded as living together as man and wife; whether they are really sharing the same accommodation; and if so how the household expenses are shared and what the sleeping arrangements are. It is not enough to show that a man is sharing the same house – he may be a bona fide lodger. Nor is it enough that a man may visit the house from time to time and sleep with the woman'. Clearly these are matters on

[23] For example, the Court of Appeal, the Divisional Court and the Industrial Court have all ruled that in respect of redundancy cases the standard of proof is the balance of probability. *Hindle* v. *Percival Boats Ltd*, [1969] 4 I.T.R. 86 at 92, *W. Gimber & Sons Ltd* v. *Spurrett*, [1967] 2 I.T.R. 308 and *Parkes* v. *B. and M. (Bodyworks) Ltd* [1972] 7 I.T.R. 48 at 50.

[24] *Judd* v. *Minister of Pensions and National Insurance*, [1966] 2 Q.B. 580.

[25] HMSO 1971.

which it is difficult to obtain hard and fast evidence; indeed very often the Commission's officers will have to rely on hearsay, such as talking to neighbours. Given this problem of investigation, the Commission's report states that the inquiries of their investigating officers 'are intended to discover facts on which to make a judgment about the case as a whole. This will include a decision as to whether on the balance of probabilities cohabitation is shown – a judgment which can be challenged forthwith in an informal appeal tribunal.' This language could be taken to imply that the Commission envisage a higher standard of proof when a case goes to appeal. But the report has no legal force and there is no assurance that all tribunals will apply a higher standard than is required in the civil courts and will insist that the Commission show beyond reasonable doubt that there was cohabitation before rejecting the appeal.

Finally, there must naturally be a higher standard of proof than the balance of probabilities if there is any suggestion of criminal conduct, for example if an insurance officer were to allege before the National Insurance Commissioner that someone had been fraudulently in receipt of benefit. Similarly in tax cases the Commissioners would normally look for the balance of probabilities but in Penalty proceedings, although there is no firm judicial guidance as to this, they tend to weight the balance in favour of the defendant.

In some kinds of proceedings the concept of a standard of proof is as irrelevant as that of the burden of proof in others. In the valuation group of tribunals, for example, the corresponding concept would be consistency or uniformity. Or to take an extreme example from another sphere, a mental health review tribunal may be largely guided by intuition or subjective judgment. The nature of an applicant's illness and the state of his progress may be defined with as much precision as medical science allows, but the ultimate issue before the tribunal is how a man is likely to behave if restrictions on his liberty are eased. This is a matter of prophecy rather than of proof.

These shifting patterns of requirement in both the burden and the standard of proof illustrate once more how tribunals differ not only from the courts but from each other.

### *The Rules of Evidence*

We have said earlier that tribunals may seek their own evidence in addition to hearing that which is put before them; that they may take account of their own expert knowledge; and that they are not so strictly bound as are the courts by the actual rules of evidence.

Examples of the first of these powers (the summoning of further witnesses, the commissioning of reports from independent experts, medical examination, site inspection, etc.) have already been given (pp. 146–7). Evidence may also be sought from a department in the form of a report submitted to a tribunal before a hearing. For example, in the immigration appeal procedure, as soon as practicable after a rejected immigrant gives notice that he intends to appeal the respondent (usually an immigration officer or the Home Secretary) is required to prepare:

> 'a written statement of the facts relating to the decision or action in question and the reasons therefor and [to] take such steps as are necessary to ensure that the statement is referred to an adjudicator or the Tribunal, as appropriate, and that a copy thereof is given to the appellant.'[26]

A similar procedure exists for applications to agricultural land tribunals under the Land Drainage Act 1961 (e.g. for an order that a ditch be cleared). On receipt of the application the tribunal is required to call for a report from the Ministry of Agriculture, Fisheries and Food.[27] The officer making the report is entitled to make a recommendation as to whether or not the order should be made and copies of his report are required to be served on the parties. The applicant has then one month to give notice to the tribunal as to whether or not he agrees with the report.

A somewhat more questionable instance concerns the road haulage licensing authority, to whom the police, local authorities and other specified bodies have a statutory right to lodge an objection to a licence application. In such cases the onus of proof is on the objector, and the applicant knows the case against him. However, when a licence holder applies to renew his licence the licensing authority also receives reports from the staff of the Traffic Area, which normally consist of his standard of vehicle maintenance and a record of any successful prosecutions or prohibition notices served on his vehicles. Before refusing a licence the authority will give the applicant an opportunity of appearing at a public hearing, at which he will detail the case against the applicant and give him an opportunity of replying and of cross-examining the Area staff who have prepared the report. However, the reports themselves are not made available to him, and in that sense he is not fully appraised of the case against him.

[26] Rule 7(1). If there is insufficient time before the hearing to prepare a written statement, it may be given orally at the start of the hearing (Rules 7(2) and (3)).

[27] Rule 18A, Agricultural Land Tribunals and Notices to Quit Order 1959.

Clearly the inquisitorial nature of the way in which evidence may be gathered could run counter to the *audi alteram partem* rule, which after all has been formulated by judges accustomed to the adversarial procedures of the courts. This rule does not prevent a tribunal from obtaining its own evidence (whether by report or inspection) but it does require reports or evidence received either *ex parte* or of its own motion to be made available to all parties, and further requires that all parties be given the opportunity of accompanying the tribunal on any inspection. Thus if a tribunal receives an undisclosed report,[28] or receives evidence or makes an inspection in the presence of one party only,[29] or has a private interview with a witness,[30] or being an appellate tribunal communicates privately with the tribunal of first instance about a case,[31] there is every likelihood that the decision will be quashed.

An interesting case in this regard is *R* v. *Deputy Industrial Injuries Commissioner ex parte Jones*[32] in which the Commissioner, after an oral hearing decided that he needed the assistance of a rheumatology specialist. The Commissioner had statutory power[33] to obtain the assistance of an assessor and to refer any question to a medical practitioner for examination and report. The Commissioner was entitled to regulate his own procedure in this regard. In this instance he sent the case papers to a specialist and read his notes of evidence to him. The specialist then advised him, giving as his opinion that the appellant had not, in medical terms, received an injury arising out of and in the course of his employment. On the basis of this advice the Commissioner dismissed the claim. In the Divisional Court Lord Justice Parker C.J. after pointing out that

> 'such a tribunal is not entitled, apart from express provision, to continue privately to obtain evidence between the end of the oral hearing and its decision without notifying the parties thereafter of the advice and information received, so as to give the parties an opportunity of having a further hearing if need be, or at any rate commenting on the information and making their final submissions thereon.'[34]

then went on to discuss the position of an assessor

[28] *R.* v. *Architects Registration Tribunal*, [1945] 2 All E.R. 131 (tribunal used undisclosed letters to reach its decision) and *R.* v. *Deputy Industrial Injuries Commissioner ex p. Jones*, [1962] 2 Q.B. 677 (discussed below).

[29] *R.* v. *Deputy Industrial Injuries Commissioner ex p. Jones*, [1962] 2 Q.B. 677.

[30] *Palmer* v. *Inverness Hospitals Committee* 1963 S.C. 311.

[31] *R.* v. *Huntingdon Confirming Authority*, [1929] 1 K.B. 698.

[32] [1962] 2 Q.B. 677.

[33] Now contained in National Insurance (Industrial Injuries) (Determination of Claims and Questions) Regulations.

[34] At p. 685. Cf. dicta by Parq L.J. in *R.* v. *Westminster Assessment Com-*

'When there is an oral hearing, it seems to me that the assessor must sit with the Commissioner, not necessarily through the whole hearing but throughout that part of the hearing which is dealing with the evidence on the point as to which the Commissioner desires assistance.'

and

'. . . the assessor advising the Commissioner as to the weight to be given to medical evidence must have the medical evidence before him. It is quite a different thing to have before him such notes of the oral evidence as the Commissioner has taken.'

In other cases it has been said that an assessor's function is not to supply evidence but to help the judge or tribunal to understand the evidence, and that he is to be treated in the sense of a specialist dictionary, i.e. someone who will help the tribunal to understand specialist evidence.

As regards a *report* from a specialist Lord Parker stated: '. . . it would be only proper and right that the commissioner could notify the parties of the report he has obtained and give them at any rate an opportunity to comment on it'.[35]

The courts therefore place considerable emphasis on the rule of disclosure, but two reservations need to be added. Firstly the rule only requires disclosure of reports and the opportunity to comment or produce evidence in rebuttal – it is not necessary that the author be subjected to cross-examination.[36] Secondly if the statute or regulations provide for the report to be received in confidence (e.g. on the grounds of damage to the appellant's health or to national security) then the rule does not apply.

The other main problem which tribunals face in connection with the *audi alteram partem* rule is the use of members' expertise. Judges are not permitted to take into account facts or considerations that are within their private knowledge[37] but this is precisely one of the reasons for establishing special tribunals; and yet the undisclosed use of expertise by a tribunal may be contrary to the *audi alteram partem* rule. Faced

*mittee* (see below) that an expert witness or adviser 'must not be substituted for the tribunal. Those whose claim is being considered have a right to question and to test every statement he makes and any opinion he expresses'.

[35] At p. 688.

[36] See *Ex p. Jones* (above) and *Miller* v. *Minister of Housing*, [1968] 2 All E.R. 633 per Lord Denning M.R. at 634.

[37] The very restricted doctrine of 'judicial notice' permits only matters of common knowledge (i.e. which everyone is presumed to know) to be considered by a judge without first being proved in evidence.

with this conflict the courts have yet to lay down hard and fast rules. On the one hand where a tribunal is obliged to observe the rules of evidence it seems clear that it cannot use its expertise as a substitute for evidence;[38] in this situation (as in the case of the expert report) expertise can only be used to interpret and supplement evidence. On the other hand, where a tribunal is not under any such duty the position is not so clear, and rent assessment committees in particular have been encouraged by the courts to attach as much weight to their own knowledge as to evidence, or even to let it override the evidence. In an early case it was held[39] that

> 'the experience of an expert tribunal . . . is part of its equipment for determining the case. Litigants must take that experience as they find it, and, because the tribunal is assumed to be impartial, they have no grievance if they cannot test it by cross-examination.'

In 1967 the Lord Chief Justice said:[40]

> 'It is idle in my view to think of gentlemen manning this committee and sitting maybe day after day without acquiring experience and knowledge of conditions in the locality, and to say that they should shut their eyes to what they know of their own knowledge, and act only on such evidence as may or may not be put before them, seems to me to reduce the matter to absurdity.'

Later in the same year the then Mr Justice Widgery said:[41]

> '. . . the rent assessment committee is entitled, and indeed in many circumstances bound . . . to hear any evidence that is tendered, but it is not bound by expert opinion, and if in the last analysis it finds expert opinion unsatisfactory, then it must use its own knowledge and impression.'

This use of their own expert knowledge does not, however, absolve the committee from a duty to point out to the parties matters of which they might be unaware.[42]

[38] *Moxon* v. *Minister of Pensions*, [1945] K.B. 490. (Pensions Appeal Tribunal dismissed an appeal on the basis of the medical member's opinion. Held that a dismissal of the appeal would be invalid.)

[39] *R.* v. *Westminster Assessment Committee*, [1940] 4 All E.R. 132 at 143.

[40] *Crofton Investment Trust* v. *Greater London Rent Assessment Committee*, [1967] 2 Q.B. 955.

[41] *Metropolitan Properties Co. Ltd* v. *Lannon*, [1968] 1 All E.R. 354.

[42] See *Crofton Investment Trust* (op. cit.) at 968, and *R.* v. *Paddington etc. Rent Tribunal ex parte Bell London and Provincial Properties*, [1949] 1 K.B. 666 at 682, and *Metropolitan Properties Co. Ltd.* v. *Lannon* (on appeal) [1968] 3 All E.R. 304 at 309.

*Precedent*

All tribunals are of course bound to follow precedents set by decisions of the High Court and the courts above, and where there is an appellate tribunal system the lower tribunal is bound by the decisions of the higher and must take account of them in making its own future decisions.

The principal appellate tribunals are the National Insurance Commissioners, the Lands Tribunal, the Transport Tribunal and the Immigration Appeal Tribunal, and in the case of the first two, because of the great number of local tribunals and decisions, a large number of chairmen and officials have to become familiar with a large body of case law.

The National Insurance Commissioners attach particular importance to the observance of precedent, since consistency has to be maintained throughout Great Britain by hundreds of insurance officers deciding many millions of claims each year, and by two hundred local tribunals deciding appeals running into tens of thousands. With this in mind the Chief Commissioner selects decisions, known as 'reported' decisions, for the guidance of insurance officers and others, and these are published by Her Majesty's Stationery Office. A further selection, known as 'numbered' decisions, are available to inquirers at the Commissioners' offices, although they are not printed.

Local valuation courts also take a great deal of notice of precedent, and it is one of the duties of their Clerks (chairmen and members being part-time and unpaid) to keep abreast of Lands Tribunal appeal decisions, as well of course as decisions in the Court of Appeal and the House of Lords. When it is known that a particular appeal to the Tribunal or the courts is likely to be a test case the information is circulated throughout the valuation panel service, and similar appeals which may be pending will be held up until the case is decided.

The Transport Tribunal (the appellate tribunal for the licensing of goods traffic by road) currently deals with few cases, but one of great interest arose in the Court of Appeal in 1962.[43] Over the years the Tribunal and its predecessors had built up a very large body of case law, and in this particular case it had been careful to follow the precedent set by a closely comparable one. The Court of Appeal held that it was not bound to follow its own precedents, and indeed that if it habitually did so it would be restricting the proper use of its discretion:

> 'No doubt it is right that the tribunal should have regard to consistent practice in dealing with applications for licences. But in the exercise of a discretionary power of this kind an applicant is entitled to have his

[43] *Merchandise Transport Ltd* v. *British Transport Commission*, [1962] 2 Q.B. 173.

application considered on its merits and in the circumstances of his particular case. If the tribunal makes a practice of relying on previous decisions in respect of other applications that have come before it there is in my opinion danger that the discretion of the tribunal may not be applied in an unfettered and proper manner.'

In immigration appeals adjudicators are bound by the Appeal Tribunal's decisions in matters of law and the interpretation and application of the Immigration Rules, and they also have regard to the decisions of their fellow adjudicators, though they are not bound by them. The Appeal Tribunal itself is not bound by its own previous decisions, each individual appeal being treated on its merits, but it nevertheless takes note of them where there are points of similarity to an appeal determined previously.

Turning to 'single-tier' tribunals, industrial tribunals are not bound by each others' decisions, though they have regard to them for guidance. However, the Tribunal publishes its own Industrial Tribunal Reports, which contain all decisions of the courts on appeal and a few selected decisions of tribunals at first instance. These Reports were originally a broad-based anthology of tribunal decisions for the general guidance of the early tribunals, but as the work developed and a reasonable flow of High Court decisions was established they came to resemble a genuine Law Report, and became largely restricted to decisions binding on tribunals. Members of tribunals also receive from the Tribunal President a quarterly loose-leaf indexed supplement of decisions on appeal, which is of practical value in the day-to-day work of hearings.

In the valuation group of tribunals precedent is an elusive concept, as has been shown by a series of judgments of differing emphases in the Divisional Court.

In 1968 the Court held[44] that

'. . . there can in no circumstances be any question of a rent assessment committee being required to treat a particular comparable as being a determining factor in the absence of evidence to the contrary.'

But in 1970 the same judge gave committees some encouragement to observe precedent to the extent of taking as a yardstick earlier decisions on comparable properties (provided they had been taken in the fairly recent past) even though in this particular case it only gave the landlords a return of less than 4 per cent, in contrast to their own figure which would have given them 8 per cent. The Court accepted

[44] *Metropolitan Properties Co. Ltd* v. *Lannon*, [1968] 1 All E.R. 354; on appeal, [1968] 3 All E.R. 304.

that 8 per cent was not an unreasonable return, but that a landlord's return on capital investment, while providing a check or guide on rental values, was by no means conclusive, and that recent registered fair rents were a perfectly proper yardstick. This judgment was of course given at a time when the inflation of property values was less rapid that it was soon to become, and it is also relevant that the 'comparable' in question was as nearly identical as it could well be, i.e. a flat of the same area in the same set of buildings.[45]

The logic of this judgment could have confined the decisions of committees within a somewhat rigid framework, but later in the same year the Court held in another case[46] that the relative importance of the various criteria could not be precisely assessed, but that 'it must be a case of stirring up the lot, taking them all into consideration and arriving at an estimate of fair rents as a result'.

These differing emphases suggest that in the shifting sands of property values the attempt to be guided by precedent is legitimate but may well be difficult, and that in any case it is only one of a number of factors.

We turn now to two ways in which tribunals may differ from the courts in matters which can be more fundamental in that they touch on civil liberties – public hearings and the power to exclude parties.

*Public Hearings*

The hearing of judicial proceedings in public seems to have acquired the status of a basic principle of civil liberties. A leading authority on administrative law contends that this is not so, however: 'Courts are not obliged to sit in public; there is no rule of natural justice requiring other adjudicating bodies to sit in public'.[47] Indeed there are convincing arguments why certain kinds of tribunal should not do so. In terms of general principle there are two conflicting influences on tribunals – that of the courts (which lean heavily towards working in public) and that of the Administration (which leans towards privacy). As the authors of a study of the British legal system ask 'Exactly why is it so important that anyone should be able to walk into any court hearing a civil case? The general public is excluded from hospital operating rooms; it is not invited to see the Civil Service at work.'[48]

[45] *Tormes Property Co. Ltd.* v. *Landau*, [1970] 3 All E.R. 653.

[46] *Mountview Court Properties Ltd* v. *Charles Devlin*, [1970] 21 P. & C. R. 689.

[47] S. A. de Smith, *Judicial Review of Administrative Action* (2nd ed. Stevens & Sons, 1968), p. 179.

[48] Abel-Smith and R. Stevens, *Lawyers and the Courts* (Heinemann, 1970), p. 207.

One can extend this line of argument: 98 per cent of national insurance cases are settled by an insurance officer or by an internal administrative review of his decision. If this body of claimants have the benefit of their claims being decided in private, why should the 2 per cent who wish to take their appeal further have to have their private affairs aired in public? Again, Commissioners of Income Tax hear cases in private, since financial affairs are normally so regarded, or possibly because taxpayers may be prepared to divulge their earnings more readily in private, and yet if there is an appeal against their decision to the High Court the case is heard in public.

The Franks Report itself reflects this ambivalence between the public working of the Courts and the private working of the Administration. The Report[49] was in no doubt as to the general principle which should prevail in tribunal procedure:

> 'We have already said that we regard openness as one of the three essential features of the satisfactory working of tribunals. Openness includes the promulgation of reasoned decisions, but its most important constituent is that the proceedings should be in public.'

It goes on to say:

> 'We are in no doubt that if adjudicating bodies, whether courts or tribunals, are to inspire that confidence in the administration of justice which is a condition of civil liberty they should, in general, sit in public.'

But if this is the general rule the Report recognized that a very good case could be made in favour of exceptions, and went on to propose three such exceptions, namely cases where considerations of public security are involved, where intimate personal or financial circumstances have to be disclosed, or where the hearing is a preliminary investigation of a case involving professional capacity or reputation.

Current practice is less simple, and a full classification of the rules governing the admission of the public is extraordinarily complicated.[50] Its salient points, leaving out a mass of minor variation, are that a few tribunals always sit in public and a few always in private, leaving the majority in a middle area where they usually sit in public but where there is a certain amount of discretion to go into private session – either at the request of one of the parties or on their own determination.

Only seven tribunals are required *always* to sit in public – the Traffic

[49] Report, paras. 76 and 77.

[50] The remarkable number of drafting nuances in these rules, often saying the same thing in different words, was noted on p. 54.

Commissioners,[51] road haulage licensing authorities, and the Transport Tribunal, which have an obvious affinity; and four which have no affinity at all – the Commons Commissioners, milk and dairies tribunals, mines and quarries tribunals and the Performing Rights Tribunal.

Those which always sit in private are the supplementary benefit tribunals, the General and Special Commissioners of Income Tax,[52] the Betting Levy Appeal Tribunal,[53] and the Service Committees of the National Health Service Executive Councils; to which may be added for practical purposes the mental health review tribunals.[54] These clearly conform to two of Franks' three criteria; the third – public security – arises principally in connection with certain immigration cases and is dealt with later (p. 281).

In the 'middle ground' the great majority usually sit in public, the Lands Tribunal invariably so unless it is acting as arbitrator under a reference by consent. It is impossible to generalize or summarize, and perhaps the most satisfactory thing will be to say a word about those which meet most often:

*National insurance local tribunals* meet in public 'except in so far as the Chairman may otherwise direct if he is of the opinion that intimate personal or financial circumstances may have to be disclosed . . .'. This is a somewhat curious provision because such circumstances have nearly always to be disclosed, and it is not clear how they differ in kind, though doubtless they differ in degree, from supplementary benefit cases which are always heard in private. As a matter of observation, it is as often the appellant as the chairman who asks for privacy, and it is possible that more would do so if they understood their right and knew that members of the public were present.

[51] Except for unopposed applications for variations of road service licences.

[52] To which may be added the two rarely used revenue tribunals which deal with capital allowances and tax avoidance devices.

[53] A point of minor interest about this tribunal is that the procedural rules are in conflict with the statute. Section 28(10) of the Betting, Gaming and Lotteries Act 1963 makes it a criminal offence to disclose 'any information which identifies a bookmaker concerned in the proceedings before the tribunal, without that bookmaker's consent'. Rule 7(2) of the procedural rules (S.I. 1963 No. 748) allows a member of the Council on Tribunals to attend in his capacity as such. On one occasion the tribunals' chairman properly refused admittance to a member of the Council, pointing out that his only legal means of obtaining admittance would be to ask his bookmaker to request his attendance.

[54] Privacy applies to all 'informal determinations'. A patient can request a 'formal hearing', but the tribunal has discretion to decide whether the hearing shall be formal or informal. If a formal hearing is held the applicant can request that it be in public but the tribunal still has a discretion to grant or refuse such a request. Mental Health Review Tribunal Rules (1960) Rules 20 and 24.

*Local valuation courts* sit in public 'unless the court otherwise order on the application of any party to the appeal and upon being satisfied that the interests of one or more parties to the appeal would be prejudicially affected'.

The position at the *Pensions Appeal Tribunal* is complicated, at any rate on paper. Cases arising from the First World War may be public or private at the Tribunal's discretion; those relating to the Second World War are normally in public (under later procedural rules), exceptions being made if official documents or information have to be disclosed or if the appellant requests privacy for reasons which the Tribunal find acceptable.

The practice of the *industrial tribunals* varies with the nature of the jurisdiction. In dealing with taxation (the training levy and selective employment payments) they follow the normal revenue rule of sitting in private (unless the appellant requests otherwise); the others in public (unless the tribunal determines at the request of a party that it shall be private).

*Rent assessment committees* meet in public 'unless for special reasons the committee decide otherwise', but the intended emphasis in the *rent tribunals* appears to be towards privacy, though their hearings are normally thought of as being open. Their regulations prescribe that '... the Tribunal may if they think fit, and at the request of either party shall unless for some special reason they consider it undesirable, allow the hearing to be in public'.

To see these matters in perspective, it must be pointed out that most national insurance, pension and rent tribunal hearings are in effect private since they are not advertised and members of the public are hardly ever present. Local valuation courts and industrial tribunals customarily notify the press of their schedule of hearings, and the former are often well publicized in the local press.

In comparing tribunals with the courts in this particular context it is worth pointing out that no tribunal has the power to order the suppression from publication of names or evidence. In the courts this has been found to be an excellent method of preserving the principle of public hearings while ensuring some degree of privacy to witnesses, and it is possible that the rather large area of privacy in tribunal hearings could be diminished, should this be thought desirable, if a similar practice were adopted.

Meanwhile the principle of 'openness' is to some extent safeguarded in the tribunals which sit *in camera* by the fact that recent practice has been to include a provision in regulations to the effect that where privacy is observed 'a member of the Council on Tribunals shall nevertheless be entitled to attend any hearing in his capacity as such', and only in the Betting Levy Appeal Tribunal does this appear to conflict with statute law.

*The Withholding of Evidence and the Exclusion of Parties*

One of the problems of openness in tribunals is the need in certain circumstances to withhold evidence from a party to the proceedings, a power which is given to some tribunals where disclosure might be harmful to an appellant's health, or where the tribunal has received confidential information, or where the public interest or national security is involved.

The first of these circumstances is largely an aspect of medical ethics or medical judgment, and may arise in national insurance, medical appeal, mental health review or pensions appeal tribunals. In the case of the first two only *medical* advice or evidence may be withheld[55] but there is no provision for notifying the appellant or any other person that it *has* been withheld. In the case of mental health review tribunals the discretion is wider – *any* information which the tribunal consider to be 'undesirable . . . in the interests of the patient or for other special reasons' or which appears 'not to be relevant' may be withheld,[56] but this very wide discretion is balanced by the fact that it may be disclosed in confidence to some other person, e.g. a relative or legal representative. The rules of the Pensions Appeal Tribunal are interesting and explicit. The Department is entitled to omit from the Statement of Case sent to the appellant any medical information which the Secretary of State considers 'would be undesirable in the interests of the appellant to disclose to him,' but in such a case the President of the Tribunal is required to 'use his best endeavours to assist the appellant to obtain a suitable person or organization to represent him', and if a representative is obtained the Department is required to send the omitted information to him.[57]

The second reason for withholding information is confidentiality, which tends to be characteristic of licensing tribunals, and which may arise either from trade or commercial secrecy or from the investigation of personal records.

For example, the Air Transport Licensing Board was not required to disclose information that it had received from the Minister in regard

[55] Reg. 13 National Insurance (Determination of Claims and Questions) (No. 2) Regulations 1967; Reg. 11(5) National Insurance (Industrial Injuries) (Determination of Claims and Questions) (No. 2) Regulations 1967.

[56] Rule 13, Mental Health Review Tribunal Rules 1960.

[57] Rule 22, Pensions Appeal Tribunal (England and Wales) Rules 1971.

to negotiations with other Governments,[58] or to furnish information or documents (which it had the power to require) to other parties without their consent – in particular having regard to 'whether the information is of a confidential character'.[59] In the case of its successor, however, the onus is changed. The Civil Aviation Authority *is* required to furnish such information provided the person or body who provided it is first 'consulted' and provided also that

> 'the Authority shall not furnish any information which in its opinion relates to the commercial or financial affairs of the person or body who has provided it and cannot be disclosed to the prospective recipient without disadvantage to the person or body which has provided it, which, by comparison with the advantage to the public and the prospective recipient of his disclosure to him, is unwarranted.'[60]

Another licensing authority, the road haulage licensing authority, has to take different considerations into account, such as the character and record of applicants (especially in regard to previous driving or safety convictions). It may acquire information from the Department, the police or the local authorities; the applicant is apprised of any adverse information, though he does not see the actual reports.[61]

Finally there are questions of public interest and national security, which may occasionally arise in such unexpected places as agricultural land and national insurance local tribunals. It is, however, in the sensitive area of immigration that national security is most likely to arise, as was evident in the case of Mr Rudi Dutschke which was described on p. 241.

## THE ATMOSPHERE OF COURTS AND TRIBUNALS

In comparing tribunals with the courts we have discussed procedures and principles, but general atmosphere is also an important standard of comparison, especially if one is trying to approach the subject from the viewpoint of the ordinary man in the street, who is more fearful of the courts than many lawyers suppose.

Recent trends suggested that the courts and tribunals are drawing closer together in atmosphere and outward appearance. On the one hand certain tribunals, notably the Transport Tribunal and the Lands Tribunal, proceed with much of the formality and procedure of the

[58] S. 2(3), Civil Aviation (Licensing) Act 1960.
[59] Reg. 9, Civil Aviation (Licensing) Regulations 1964.
[60] Reg. 12, Civil Aviation Authority Regulations 1972 (S.I. 1972 No. 178).
[61] See above, p. 270.

High Court. On the other hand the county courts, which are the true standard of comparison for most tribunals (in that it is they rather than the High Court which would have to resolve disputes in the field of national insurance, redundancy payments, rent and rates and various personal rights and entitlements if there were no special tribunals established for the purpose) are now relatively informal. For example, the judge will usually adopt a conversational tone and will try to make an unrepresented defendant feel at home, and even, within limits, to assist him. To the average man, however, the word 'relatively' is important, for few people feel at ease in the atmosphere of a court.

It is here – as we remarked on p. 130 – that tribunals have perhaps made their most important contribution to the judicial system, though it consists in an accumulation of small matters and is difficult to define. But on entering a tribunal hearing, for example, an appellant is normally greeted by name, invited to sit down opposite the tribunal members, and an explanation given of how the tribunal will proceed. It is made clear that the tribunal wishes to help him if it can; he is asked if he understands what has been said and whether he wishes to ask any questions. It is no denigration of the county courts to say that they are by contrast somewhat aloof and formal – no doubt rightly so, as the dignity and formality of the Queen's Courts ought to be upheld; perhaps this merely confirms the supposition that the business of most tribunals is unsuited to the Queen's Courts, and that the growth of tribunals to supplement them is meeting a manifest need.

The success of tribunals in making themselves acceptable to the average man was explicitly acknowledged by the President of the Industrial Court as its opening sitting.[62] He remarked that although the new institution was properly called a court it would 'seek to function more in the manner and with the speed which is associated with the word "tribunal" than that of "court".' The Court has indeed been meticulous in abolishing what the President called the 'traditional court attitudes and procedures' – for example, members of the Court wear ordinary clothes, sit almost on a level with the parties, invite anyone addressing them to sit or stand as they prefer, and to dispense with titles which are so confusing and embarrassing to the layman, preferring a straightforward and simple 'Sir'. As to the Court Rules,[63] these are not our proper concern, but we may remark that the statutory forms are of the simplest and that the President said that 'any attempt by professional advisers to turn them into complex legal documents will be resisted'. It would in fact be misleading to compare the procedures of this Court

[62] 1 December 1971, reported in *New Law Journal*, 9 December.
[63] Industrial Court Rules (S.I. 1971 No. 1777).

with those of any other, since it may have to deal with matters of very great urgency and to improvise in a way which no other court would contemplate. Nevertheless its flexibility is remarkable.

At the time of writing the Court is the centre of political controversy, an incidental aspect of which is that the Court's informality has been called into question on the ground that abandonment of 'pomp and ceremony' has caused it to be less respected than it would otherwise have been. It seems therefore that informality is a subject on which one should hesitate to be dogmatic; nevertheless, the Court's experiment is bold and interesting, and it remains to be seen whether the President was misguided or far-sighted.

There has been a corresponding move towards simplicity and economy in the county courts, occasioned by the County Court (New Procedure) Rules 1971,[64] which became operative in March 1972. Of particular importance is Rule 13, which provides for a 'pre-trial review' by the Registrar, who has the duty to 'consider giving directions for securing the just, expeditious and economical disposal of the action'. This is hardly a development which can be said to have been influenced by tribunals, as pressures for the reform had been building up from many quarters – from the advocates of small claims courts, notably the Consumer Council, from the recommendations of the Committee on the Enforcement of Judgment Debts (Cmnd. 3909) and from dissatisfaction among the informed public and the legal profession at the disparity between the elaborate processes of the courts and the modest nature of many claims – especially of claims so modest that court action is effectively ruled out. Nevertheless the pre-trial review is nearer both in spirit and in practice to a tribunal than to a court.

At the time of writing the experience of pre-trial reviews has been too brief to allow conclusions to be drawn. They appear to have been successful not so much in preventing cases from coming to court but in greatly shortening the court proceedings by clearing the ground, and in this way they are of course instrumental in effecting economies. The Rule does not in fact represent a fundamental new departure, since County Court Registrars have frequently called the parties together informally in the more complex disputed cases, but it now makes the practice mandatory and universal.

A similar practice has more recently been adopted by a tribunal at the administrative end of the spectrum, namely the Civil Aviation Authority. Regulation 13[65] gives the authority the power to hold preliminary meetings, which are in practice of an informal kind, with the

[64] S.I. 1971 No. 2152.
[65] The Civil Aviation Authority Regulations (S.I. 1972 No. 178).

parties to a case, the object being to clarify the issues before the arguments are deployed at the subsequent public hearing. The very brief experience gained at the time of writing has been similar to that in the county courts.

## CONCILIATION

The pre-trial or pre-hearing review has some affinity with conciliation, and it may be appropriate to end with some discussion of this subject. Neither courts nor tribunals are concerned with it to any large extent, but neither is it wholly excluded from their competence.

Traditionally it has only been a function of the courts in matrimonial matters, until the creation of the National Industrial Relations Court in 1971. Its predecessor, the Industrial Court of the 1919 Act, was in effect an arbitration body, since although it adjudicated in disputes and made awards it had no power to enforce them, and the ultimate sanction of enforcement is inherent in a court of law. Judges may always have used their position to promote conciliation, in the sense of suggesting that the parties should go away and think things over, but it has not been their recognized function.

For the most part tribunals also hear opposing cases and judge between them, and neither their procedural rules nor their common practice allow for conciliation. There are, however, a few partial exceptions.

The word cannot be precisely defined, and the few examples that can be quoted illustrate different emphases of meaning. It is often used to mean no more than bridging the gap between disputants by persuading them to meet each other half way; as a refinement of this, it may be attempted when parties have failed to agree during proceedings, but instead of merely trying to find a compromise acceptable to them both the decision will be reached by a third party in the light of settled criteria to which they must both subscribe. Either of these processes, however, could perhaps more accurately be described as arbitration than conciliation. Conciliation as a precursor of tribunal proceedings may involve deciding what is right in the light of standard criteria, irrespective of whether the parties agree with the decision, or indeed whether they would have agreed with some different decision; but in the course of deciding what was right the parties would have been allowed to bring evidence and arguments at informal proceedings, at which the deciding authority could have indicated his own views and tried to get the parties to understand and accept them. This somewhat complicated definition – it is difficult to put simply – is well illustrated by the kind of decision that a rent officer has to make in the ordinary course of his duties.

This official, who has to decide what is a 'fair rent', may appear to play a conciliator's role, since he usually has to contend with a landlord and tenant who are in dispute. Indeed, when the Rent Bill was introduced into Parliament in 1965 the Minister likened him to a conciliation officer of the then Ministry of Labour. The comparison was not strictly accurate, however, because his object must be to reach a solution satisfactory not only to the parties but to himself. A fair rent is objectively defined in the Act and the rent officer must decide what it is. If he can carry the parties with him so much the better, but he must determine a proper rent irrespective of whether the parties would have agreed to something higher or lower. There would be danger in simply seeking an acceptable compromise, since the tenant might feel under pressure to agree with the landlord for quite extraneous reasons.

There are in fact many examples of fair rents determined at a level higher than either party was asking for, or different from the rent which both parties had agreed on and had jointly applied for. A count in London in 1971 indicated that in some 20–30 per cent of joint applications to the rent officer he determined a rent different from the one applied for. And if the parties agree on a fair rent during the proceedings, but the application for the registration of a fair rent is not withdrawn, the rent officer has to go ahead and determine a fair rent in accordance with the statutory criteria, which may well differ from the rent agreed by the parties.

It is not possible to clothe such concepts in legislative form, but the intention is well understood by rent officers, and translated into practice.

*'Concurrent' Conciliation*

Industrial relations have always been the classic field for conciliation, but until the passing of the 1971 Industrial Relations Act industrial tribunals were not involved in the process, either directly or indirectly. This Act, however, extended the scope of their jurisdiction to include 'unfair industrial practice', relating either to trade union membership or unfair dismissal, and in such cases, under section 146, the Department's conciliation officer is notified when a complaint is presented to a tribunal and it is then his duty to try to promote a settlement, and thus make it unnecessary for the complaint to be determined by a tribunal. In other words the process of conciliation and the preparation of the case for hearing by a tribunal proceed simultaneously.

This section of the Act goes some way to implement an interesting recommendation in the Donovan Report.[66] This might well have application to other tribunals where the contending parties are of equal strength and resources, though as we have just been saying it would be dangerous to apply it as between landlord and tenant:

> 'In all proceedings between employers and employees it should be a primary duty of the tribunal to bring about an amicable settlement, and the procedure should be designed so as to make this as easy as possible. Each hearing should be preceded by a "round table" meeting in private between the parties and the tribunal, or one or two of its members, in order to settle the case. If this fails, further attempts at a settlement should be made in the course of the further proceedings, Experience abroad has shown that labour tribunals can settle a very large proportion of all cases before them. There is no reason to believe that a similar result would not follow here.'

As with the pre-trial reviews in the county court, there has been insufficient experience at the time of writing to say with confidence how effective section 146 of the Industrial Relations Act has been. However, the experience of the first few months[67] was remarkably encouraging, since very nearly 50 per cent of the cases were satisfactorily conciliated, the respondents often agreeing to comparatively substantial figures in settlement of redundancy claims.

*A Chance to Talk Things Over First*

Conciliation in the form of trying to reach informal agreement before going to formal adjudication is practised in one area of national insurance. By what is colloquially known as the 'dissatisfaction procedure',[68] when a contributions question (i.e. a question reserved for the Minister's determination) arises on a claim before an insurance officer, he is not obliged to notify the claimant of his right to appeal (as is normally required in the case of adverse decisions) but shall inform the claimant that if he is dissatisfied with the decision he should give the reasons for his dissatisfaction. Subsection 3 makes clear that after any appropriate investigations and explanations have been made the claimant, if he is still dissatisfied, must be notified of his right to appeal to a local tribunal. The Department were at one time considering

[66] Royal Commission on Trade Unions and Employers' Associations 1965–8, Cmnd. 3632, para. 584. The proposal was based on German Labour Court practice.

[67] The section became operative on 28 February 1972.

[68] National Insurance (Determination of Claims and Questions) (No. 2) Regulations 1967 (S.I. 1967 No. 1570), Regulation 5(1) and (3).

whether this principle could not be extended to adverse decisions on the actual substance of a claim, where the contribution record is not in question.

National Health Service Executive Councils are encouraged but not compelled to make arrangements for conciliation in two different aspects of the work of their service committees. First, the mundane human problem of badly fitting false teeth has given rise to the little known mechanism of Denture Conciliation Committees, which consider complaints relating solely to the fit and efficiency of dentures; their constitution and functions are set out in Regulation 10 of the Service Committees and Tribunal Amendment Regulations 1953. Second, in 1968 Executive Councils were encouraged by administrative memorandum (E.C.N. 662) to appoint a lay member, assisted by a practitioner member, to conciliate informally in complaints about the general medical service. Such complaints may of course be serious and specific, but in a large number of cases ill-feeling or nervous strain may have clouded an issue which is intrinsically trivial. In the official words:

> 'The Government consider that in a proportion of cases an informal stage would help to clear up complaints made by patients and would have the advantage of doing so without causing such distress or inconvenience to doctors and patients as may sometimes arise under the present procedure. If the patient and the doctor can be brought together and reconciled so that both are content that the matter need not be further pursued, this would be to the benefit of the Service.'

Fifty-seven of the 134 Executive Councils have established Dental Conciliation Committees, and 69 have appointed general conciliators.

*A Chance to 'Settle Out of Court'*

Lastly, some tribunals, while taking no active part in the process of conciliation, customarily do all they can to encourage it. For example, the Lands Tribunal frequently grants extensions of time or stay of proceedings to enable a settlement to be reached, and even during a hearing an adjournment is often granted, at the request of the parties or even on the Tribunal's own initiative, if it appears that this could resolve the dispute, or even narrow its area.

The Special Commissioners of Income Tax also are always willing to adjourn a hearing for the parties to discuss a compromise.

CHAPTER 11

# POSSIBLE FUTURE DEVELOPMENTS

It has been a recurring theme of this book that since tribunals have been created departmentally and *ad hoc*, to meet new situations arising from particular policies, the picture that they present as a whole is untidy; a fact that has led many observers to advocate some measure of rationalization. What has usually been meant by rationalization has been the amalgamation of jurisdictions, so that there would be fewer and larger tribunals; so that – for example – the distinctions between furnished and unfurnished rents, or between 'insurance' benefits and 'supplementary' benefits, would disappear. In general terms this has indeed been the policy advocated for many years by the Council on Tribunals.

This kind of amalgamation, however, is only one aspect of rationalization, and possibly the most controversial. Other aspects are a common staffing service to replace the multiplicity of secondments from departments; common purpose-built accommodation to replace the multiplicity of leased or hired premises; a common type of structure, with national presidents and co-terminous administrative areas; more logical scales of remuneration for presidents, chairmen and members; a code governing the award of costs and the payment of expenses; a reduction in the multiplicity of procedural rules based on common procedural principles; and a consistent method of appointing those who preside over tribunals. Moreover the fact that most tribunals originated departmentally, and that the Lord Chancellor's responsibility for them has never been more than partial, has created patterns of ministerial accountability which do not necessarily correspond to function. For example, the Lord Chancellor is himself responsible for the Lands Tribunal, but its subject matter comes wholly within the province of other Ministers; while the Secretary of State for Employment would be responsible to Parliament for the Industrial Tribunal, whose jurisdiction however extends to revenue matters. In this chapter we examine these variations on the theme of rationalization.

It must be said at the outset that rationalization in terms of jurisdictions, staff, premises or structure would only make sense in the context of the small central 'bloc' of tribunals, and that it would merely confuse discussion to suggest that comprehensive rationalization would be possible or necessary. Expert adjudicators in the copyright of plays or gramophone records have nothing in common with those considering plant genetics; independent schools tribunals which meet two or three times a year have no need of permanent supporting services; there would be no advantage in applying the same machinery to licensing an airline and a dairy. In amalgamating jurisdictions, therefore, what we are considering are the tribunals which deal with industrial relations, social security, rent, rates, valuation and taxation, though in contemplating a common tribunal service, common premises or a common staff it would be possible to go a little further afield than this.

## THE AMALGAMATION OF JURISDICTIONS

Many people closely concerned with tribunals are sceptical of the value of this particular kind of rationalization. They argue that since each tribunal was fashioned to meet a unique set of circumstances it is almost a contradiction in terms of talk of rationalizing them, and that rationalization would be the beginning of the road back to the kind of 'all-purpose' jurisdiction from which the original object of tribunals was to break away. This view is to some extent contradicted by the success of the Lands Tribunal, which replaced a plethora of panels of arbitrators and referees, and its heads of jurisdiction have been greatly enlarged since its inception in January 1950; they may now be set out in ten main categories and they derive from a score of statutes.[1] Equally, the versatile industrial tribunals have been praised rather than criticized for the fact that their jurisdiction embraces all aspects of conflict and dispute in industry, even though an industrial background is the only thing they have in common.

### *Starting Point – the Franks Report*

The possibilities of amalgamation were first discussed in the Franks Report (Part III) in the light of proposals put forward by Professor W. A. Robson and the Society of Labour Lawyers. The Committee

[1] There is a very interesting section in the Lands Tribunal Act 1949 which is relevant to this chapter at a number of later points. Section 4(1) deals with the power to add to the Tribunal's jurisdiction by Order in Council. This may be done where the questions are appropriate for the Lands Tribunal and where 'it is desirable to transfer a jurisdiction:

(i) to promote uniformity of decision
(ii) to use economically the services of those having experience in the valuation of land and other special qualifications
(iii) to make possible the winding up of a statutory tribunal having little work to do.

considered three possible groupings – tribunals adjudicating on money claims in the social services, those concerned with land in its widest sense and (a question which has since become redundant) those concerned with the various aspects of national service. However, they made no positive recommendations, partly because they did not think the functions 'sufficiently cognate', and partly because they thought that amalgamation, with the need for tribunal members to acquire large new areas of knowledge – including case law – would be incompatible with a tribunal membership which they thought ought in the main to continue to be part-time and 'amateur'. As we shall see, a good deal turns on this latter assumption; if it is valid, at least so far as chairmen are concerned, the possibilities of amalgamation would certainly be restricted.

But thirteen years later the Council on Tribunals speaks with a different voice:

> 'We are increasingly impressed by the need to avoid undue proliferation of tribunals by, wherever possible, organizing them into fewer and stronger units and to ensure that each group has a proper structure and, where necessary, adequate arrangements for appeal.'[2]

If we look at the Franks Committee's first group there has in fact been a certain amount of rationalization since their day, in that the work of the Family Allowance Referees *has* been absorbed into that of the national insurance tribunals, and that of the old compensation appeal tribunals, which heard disputes about compensation for loss of employment or pension in nationalized industries and local government, has gone to the industrial tribunals. There remain – of the group the Committee were considering – the pensions appeal tribunals and the supplementary benefit appeal tribunals. But the fact that they both adjudicate on claims for money does not necessarily mean that they have any natural affinity with national insurance or with each other.

The pensions appeal tribunals are discharging an obligation on the part of the state to those who have given military or comparable service, whether in the regular or conscripted forces; their assessment work is wholly medical and their entitlement work partly so; they were originally established (by the War Pensions (Administrative Provisions) Act 1919) after the first world war; and they are a presidential tribunal with independent premises and a direct link with the Lord Chancellor's Department.

The possibility of amalgamating them with medical appeal tribunals has in fact been mooted, on the grounds that the nature of the two jurisdictions is broadly similar and that amalgamation would result

[2] Annual Report, 1969–70, para. 44.

in the more economical use of medical adjudicators. But what would otherwise seem to be a clear case for rationalization is complicated by a consideration which is perhaps irrational, namely that in tradition if not in specialized experience arising from war service conditions the Pensions Appeal Tribunal is somewhat remote from national insurance. In any event fusing a presidential and a departmental organization would not be a simple operation, and the Pensions Appeal Tribunal was the pioneer presidential system which later tribunals took as their model.

As to supplementary benefit appeal tribunals, it may appear at first sight that being serviced by the same Department as the national insurance tribunals they might as well be merged with them. They are of course different in that insurance benefit is a contractual right and that supplementary benefit contains strong elements of discretion. On the other hand 'insurance' is something of a fiction (and family allowances do not depend on contributions at all), while the scales of supplementary benefit are in given circumstances a statutory right. Both are increasingly thought of as different kinds of claims on the state under the wide umbrella of social security. But there is a more fundamental difference between them than appears on the surface. In much of their work the SBATs are not so much tribunals as an extension of social case work – opportunities for having a second look at difficult problems. And the administration is far more elastic: although financial entitlement starts from the base of a set of rates and conditions applying to the normal case, there is much scope for judgment in settling what is 'appropriate' or 'reasonable', and the diversity of human situations gives the tribunals unrivalled opportunities of exercising the discretion that the statute allows for taking account of 'exceptional circumstances'. They are adept at finding special grounds for special treatment.

This is not to say that national insurance tribunals would be incapable of adjudicating on supplementary benefit cases. A judge has to apply his mind to matters much further apart than insurance benefit and supplementary benefit, and if chairmen were to become full-time professionals even wider amalgamations might be justified.[3] But if tribunal service is to be part-time (whether fee-paid or voluntary), and if only natural affinities are to be grouped together, there is no real affinity between the two: all they have in common is that both are to do with the payment of money. Members of a combined tribunal would

[3] It must, of course, be remembered that a tribunal chairman is normally only one of a triumvirate, and that his colleagues would change from one hearing, and probably from one jurisdiction, to another. Also that they can outvote him – even legally qualified chairmen have from time to time been outvoted by their lay colleagues.

have to enlarge their knowledge and expertness and be ready to make a quick switch of their methods and cast of thought whenever they passed from one branch of legislation to the other.

Whatever keeps the two sets of tribunals distinct, it cannot be laid at the door of separate departmental boundaries. It is only since 1966, it is true, that the matters going to the tribunals have been the business of the same government department, but for nearly forty years the SBATs and their predecessors for unemployment assistance and national assistance have, each in their day, been set up in legislation promoted by the same Ministers, and answered for in Parliament by the same Ministers, as those responsible for their insurance counterparts, from the Courts of Referees onwards.

*Rent Jurisdictions*

Two jurisdictions which apparently ought to be amalgamated without question are those of the rent tribunals and the rent assessment committees. Indeed, as we have seen, the Council on Tribunals pressed hard for this when fair rents were introduced by the Rent Act 1965, on the grounds that it would avoid dispute as to where jurisdiction might lie, and would also avoid competition for staff. The Government agreed in principle but were compelled to differ in practice because of the urgency of getting the Rent Act on the Statute Book without delay. Moreover everywhere except in London the organization of the rent tribunals has been brought within the areas of the rent assessment panels, and although the tribunals continue to have an independent existence they work under the general oversight of a common president and are served by the same staff.

Yet when one examines the facts there is, once again, less in common between the two jurisdictions than might be supposed. The fact that they are both determining a rent is unimportant compared with the fact that they are doing so for different reasons and in different circumstances. Rent assessment committees perform an economic function; although in most cases under legal chairmanship they are essentially a valuers' tribunal, determining a rent in accordance with given criteria and taking no cognizance of scarcity value or of human need. Applications to fix a rent, on appeal from the rent officer's figure, are often made by large property companies, and solicitors and counsel frequently appear. Rent tribunals are wholly different in atmosphere and purpose. In a sense they have no business to exist, as they were designed to meet the supposedly short-term emergency in post-war housing, and at the time it was confidently expected that they would become redundant within a decade. Unfortunately this did not happen, but what they are doing has more natural affinity with a supplementary benefit appeal tribunal than with a rent assessment committee. Furnished rented accommodation is still supposed to be a staging post on the way to a permanent home, but in fact thousands of people cannot escape from it, and their most urgent need is to retain their foothold in it. Accordingly the exact amount of rent, though nominally the cause of an appeal or application, is usually subsidiary to the need for a few more months' security, which is what most cases before rent tribunals are about. There pass before these tribunals either the poorest and least secure in our society or those who may be neither particularly poor nor insecure but who cannot get to the top of a housing list. Among the criteria which concern rent tribunals is human behaviour as well as human need, for they must often balance one against the other and consider such questions as whether arrears of rent, ill-treatment of property, all-night noise or unsavoury reputation justify eviction. This is a very different matter from valuing an unfurnished flat.

Again, it is not suggested that members of a tribunal, assisted by a valuer's expertise, could not determine a 'fair' rent for an unfurnished house and a 'reasonable' rent for an unfurnished one, and indeed the two jurisdictions have it in common that in many cases they both operate in a hypothetical world of balanced, or better balanced, supply and demand. To some extent this distinguishes them from local valuation courts, which are required to operate in a more realistic world by determining the rent at which a hereditament 'might reasonably be expected to let' in the existing market[4] – a fact which does not prevent us from suggesting below that all *three* jurisdictions could well be exercised by one tribunal or court if amalgamation were dealt with rationally. Our point in developing the differences between them, and in pointing out that rent tribunals have to deal with the same kind of human and domestic problems as supplementary benefit appeal tribunals, was simply that if the two rent jurisdictions were joined, as we think they ought to be joined, a corollary would be that members would need wider experience and more flexible approaches and that chairmen at least might have to cease being part-time amateurs.

In both social security and rents a strictly practical argument for some kind of amalgamation is the under-employment of many members of the various panels. Those who are called upon to sit two or three times a year may not only lose interest but may lack the necessary experience to be effective when they *do* sit. This is a common experience, which the supplementary benefit tribunals have recently done something

[4] Though an element of unrealism is supplied by the fact that they must disregard disrepair, and also tenancy covenants.

to mitigate by reducing the number of tribunals, but which it is difficult to eliminate altogether, either because tribunals rarely meet on a particular subject or in a particular locality, or because, as with the industrial tribunals, it is difficult to predict the volume of applications or appeals which may arise from hitherto untried legislation.

A recurrent difficulty about amalgamation is that of 'putting new wine into old bottles'. On the face of it, it would seem simpler to use an existing body than to set up a new one. But when a new tribunal is proposed it usually incorporates modern ideas, and to graft it on to an existing tribunal in the same field, but fashioned according to the ideas of a previous generation, would involve delay, in order that earlier legislation could be repealed or amended; almost always there is great urgency in getting new tribunals established, so that there has perforce to be fragmentation. This is precisely what happened over rents, the Minister admitting that he would have liked to integrate furnished and unfurnished jurisdictions, but insisting that there was no time to do so; so that again (as with the tribunals in the field of social security) fragmentation could not in this instance be blamed upon departmental separatism, for the two tribunals fell within the same division of the same Department.

*Revenue Tribunals*

At the time of writing a comparable situation has just arisen over the Value Added Tax tribunals.[5] If the argument of this chapter is accepted the first question to be asked is 'why not merge this jurisdiction with that of the existing tax tribunals?', namely the General Commisioners of Income Tax. But within the terms of the Government's proposals about VAT this would be manifestly impossible. The VAT tribunals, in line with current thinking, are to have a full-time national President and a number of full-time chairmen[6] appointed by the Lord Chancellor, and panels of qualified members appointed by the Treasury, and it is expected that 80 or 90 tribunals will be needed to cover the country. But the General Commissioners are the least professional of tribunals, with no designated chairmen, an unpaid membership and part-time Clerks, and although the intention is to reduce their divisions to about 450 there were actually 571 in 1971. No doubt the VAT tribunals would be fully competent to deal with the business of the General Commissioners, but, once again, the fact that the subject of taxation is common to them both is less important than that the kinds of appellant and the kinds of issue are dissimilar. Most of the cases dealt with by the General

[5] Government White Paper on Value Added Tax, Cmnd. 4929 of 1972.
[6] Probably one for each of five or six 'regions'.

Commissioners concern delay in the submission of business accounts or other information required for tax purposes, and they also hear appeals on disputed points of tax liability. Their clientele are for the most part self-employed or small businessmen. The VAT tribunals will be applying a novel law whose provisions may affect – and give rise to appeal from – any supplier, manufacturer, wholesaler or retailer.

But leaving aside the General Commissioners – who may be likened to a special kind of lay magistrates – the number of separate jurisdictions in the taxation field is considerable, and it is arguable that at least a limited degree of amalgamation would lead to a more economical use of expert manpower.

The Special Commissioners, as we have seen, have concurrent jurisdiction with the General Commissioners over a wide area in which an appellant may choose to appeal to either, though in practice the Special Commissioners are usually preferred where difficult points of law arise; and they have additional and exclusive jurisdiction in more complex matters arising from the Taxes Management Act and the Income and Corporation Taxes Act, both of 1970. But under the latter Act (s. 463), and under the Capital Allowances Act 1968 (s. 26), two further *ad hoc* tribunals have been established to deal with specific issues. They share the same Chairman, a leading counsel, and the same Registrar, a barrister who combines his duties with that of a Law Reporter at the House of Lords; their membership, however, is different, the former comprising two chartered accountants and two eminent businessmen, the latter being drawn from a large panel representative of industrial and professional interests. The one, which has no distinctive name, is concerned with tax avoidance, the other, known as the Board of Referees for the purposes of this section of the Act, with the depreciation of plant and machinery for capital allowance purposes. And now the VAT tribunals are making heavy demands on legal, accountancy and industrial expertise.[7]

Admittedly the annual case loads of these various tribunals vary from several thousands to a mere handful, and special knowledge is

[7] The industrial tribunals also have two revenue jurisdictions. They are of a somewhat different order, since one of them has to decide whether particular employers qualify, in terms of the Selective Employment Payments Act 1966, for a refund of SET, and the other hears appeals by employers against assessment to training levy in terms of the Industrial Training Act 1964. Nevertheless they require much the same kind of expertise as the other revenue tribunals. The supplementary benefit appeal tribunals also have a SET jurisdiction, though a minor one: appeals against decisions of the Supplementary Benefits Commission as to refund where the employee gives nursing or domestic assistance in certain circumstances (only fifteen appeals in 1971).

required for some matters, notably the depreciation of machinery, which would be irrelevant for others. Nevertheless the amalgamation of the Special Commissioners, the VAT tribunals and the two little used tribunals would have the advantage of economizing in the use of knowledge and experience. Moreover a multi-purpose tax tribunal of high standing, with a national president, would remove one of the few remaining anomalies of tribunal membership, namely that the Special Commissioners, though completely independent of the Board of Inland Revenue in their judicial capacity, are none the less established civil servants, and thus do not accord with the principle of manifest independence from the executive.

*Land and Property Valuation Tribunals*

It is, however, in the valuation of land and property (whether including or excluding furnished rents) that some degree of rationalization seems most needed, for the fragmentation of jurisdictions between the two types of rent tribunal, local valuation panels and the Lands Tribunal is not easy to explain, or at any rate to justify. The jurisdictions that we have in mind are shown in the Table:

| | |
|---|---|
| Rent tribunals (1946) | 'Reasonable' rents for furnished property. |
| Rent assessment committees (1965) | 'Fair' rents for unfurnished private property.[8] |
| Local valuation courts (1948) | Valuation for rating, the economic rent for all property: domestic, commercial, industrial and agricultural<br>Valuation for drainage rating.[a] |
| Lands Tribunal (1949) | Appeals from local valuation courts<br>Compensation for compulsory purchase<br>Compensation arising out of planning decisions. |

[a] This provides a minor example of rationalization. Drainage rate appeals under Part IV of the Agriculture (Miscellaneous Provisions) Act 1968 were added to the jurisdiction of the local valuation courts instead of a new tribunal being created.

The local valuation courts are of particular interest, not only in this immediate context but in a much wider one, and we must digress in order to recall a few facts about them.[9] Taking one year with another

[8] Members of the rent assessment panels are also required to serve on rent scrutiny boards to review council house rents, though in this capacity they are acting administratively and not judicially.

[9] The Society of Clerks of Local Valuation Panels, having learnt of the preparation of this book, appointed a Committee to review the situation from their own point of view, and were good enough to submit a comprehensive memorandum to the authors. This chapter draws on the memorandum at a number of points.

they hear more cases than any other tribunal. They are unique in that neither chairmen nor members are appointed either by the Lord Chancellor or by the Secretary of State for the Environment, but by quasi-independent Appointing Authorities – the councils of counties and county boroughs, acting within the provisions of a statutory Scheme governing the constitution and composition of each Panel. After initial approval of a Scheme by the Minister, the function of each Appointing Authority is limited to the appointment of the members of the Panel for six-year terms, though Appointing Authorities are given no guidance as to the desirable qualities of, or qualifications to be held by, panel members, except that not too many of them should be members of the rating authorities themselves. They have in common with the General Commissioners of Income tax that they appoint their own Clerk and that they are themselves unpaid; their Clerks, however, are full-time officers, and although neither civil servants nor local government officers their status is higher than that of the civil servants who serve most other tribunals, as is perhaps to be expected, since they are expert Clerks advising as well as servicing a lay tribunal. There are 95 panels in England and Wales, but no regional or national (or of course presidential) organization; each panel is a separate entity. Members are expert only in the general sense that they are widely experienced in property values, but not in the more precise sense of having a lawyer-chairman flanked by two people representing specific interests or having specific qualifications; indeed, panel members are simply invited to serve on courts in rotation, being selected in whatever manner is prescribed in their particular Scheme. A curious feature about the courts is that, unlike the rent assessment panels and the Lands Tribunal, they have no statutory power to inspect the properties under discussion, though they customarily do so if both parties agree.

Because in this country rents and rates are indissolubly linked, and the valuation of property is an expertise of immensely wide application, even the advocates of individuality in tribunals might well agree that the local valuation courts are a strange anomaly. They have an unusually successful record. The Franks Committee reported that they had 'received no important criticism' of them,[10] and the few complaints about them to the Council on Tribunals can be numbered on the fingers of one hand, and have been of a minor character, even though the Council have in recent years paid special attention to their working and have visited them in action.[11] The only contentious matter of any importance has been that the panels have included too many local

[10] Report, para. 155.
[11] Annual Report for 1968, para. 23.

councillors and retired local government officers, so that the beneficiaries of the rates, i.e. the local authorities, might appear to have too much say in their determination. Such members are not in fact appointed to sit as judges in their own cause, and there is no evidence of complaint that they have done so, but this is one of the many instances in the composition of tribunals where care needs to be taken to avoid any outward appearance of partiality. The former Ministry of Housing and Local Government urged the Appointing Authorities to limit the local authority element to about 50 per cent and to recruit independent business and professional members in their place, but this has not been done to the extent to which the Ministry and the Council on Tribunals would have wished.

Not only, then, are comparable jurisdictions divided between three (or four) different tribunals, but these are far apart in structure and organization. The Lands Tribunal is a central national Court which goes on circuit; the local valuation courts are drawn from 95 panels which have no connection with each other; the rent assessment committees and rent tribunals are drawn from 16 panels, each under the surveillance of a president, with a *primus inter pares* national President in London.

As to the Lands Tribunal, the settlement of disputes about compensation for compulsory purchase, which could well be achieved locally since the purchasers are usually local authorities, is second in numerical importance only to appeals from the decisions of local valuation courts. Between 350 and 400 compensation proceedings are instituted in an average year and although, as with most of this Tribunal's business, a substantial proportion are settled without recourse to a formal hearing,[12] a great deal of the Tribunal's time is nevertheless taken up with these cases.

In this situation the 'rationalist' could be said to have two objectives – the short-term objective of bringing the local valuation courts into the main stream of tribunals, instead of leaving them in a limbo between central and local government; and the long-term objective of bringing together eight separate jurisdictions affecting the valuation of land and property which would be suitable for settlement by some kind of local tribunal.

The short-term objective could involve – ideally – the appointment of chairmen by the Lord Chancellor and of members by the Secretary of State on the recommendation of appropriate professional bodies; a more precise definition of the qualifications for membership and the

[12] A decision is arrived at on the strength of the written evidence, the Tribunal's own inquiries and an inspection of the site.

constitution of an individual court; the placing of staff on the same footing as those in the central tribunal bloc; the grouping of the 95 panels into some kind of regional framework comparable to that of the 16 rent assessment panels; and the adjustment of procedural rules to formalize site inspection, though this has never been a contentious matter in practice.

Often it is a cynical triusm that the time is never ripe for changes of this nature, but in this particular case it is possible to forecast an opportune date with some confidence, since changes in the constitution of the panels must follow the restructuring of the local authorities in April 1974. The changes will not operate concurrently with those in local government, since this would coincide with the peak load of rating appeals after the 1973 revaluation. But it seems likely that April 1976 will be chosen, mid-way between local government reorganization in 1974 and the following revaluation in 1978.

The longer-term objective of combining a number of jurisdictions in what could best be called 'local land tribunals' is admittedly handicapped by the fact that no time could be *less* opportune, for in the years immediately ahead both local valuation and rent assessment panels will be fully stretched in discharging new responsibilities – the 1973 general rating revaluation on the one hand and on the other the extension of the 'fair rents' principle to council tenants.[13] The case for local land tribunals is none the less strong, and is worth examining in terms of four or five years ahead.

We have already recorded[14] that in considering how to implement the fair rent provisions in 1965 the Minister gave no more than a passing glance at local valuation courts. Their value as an instrument for his purpose had been urged upon him by the County Councils Association, and at the same time the Rating and Valuation Association made the suggestion that clerks of local valuation panels should be appointed clerks of the new rent assessment committees. These suggestions were rejected on the ground, among others, that the pattern of local valuation panels did not accord with the areas in mind for the projected rent assessment panels. This was true, but as we have seen the valuation panels are about to be enlarged.

In the light of hindsight it should not have been beyond the wit of the same adjudicators to deal with the precise and individual circumstances of particular tenancies in assessing a fair rent and the somewhat broader, 'tone of the list', criteria in assessing rateable value; especially

[13] As we have already said, this is not a judicial function, but it is one which will make heavy demands on the time of members of rent assessment panels.

[14] Ch. 9, p. 243.

as the volume of the rent assessment committees' work has been much less than was expected.[15]

As to the Lands Tribunal in this context, its jurisdiction in assessing planning and compulsory purchase compensation has several times been called into question so far as *small* claims are concerned. In 1969 *Justice* proposed the creation of inferior courts to deal with claims not exceeding £5,000, with the proviso that if both parties wanted it the dispute could still be determined by the Tribunal – for instance where there was a point of principle or law.[16] They recommended 'small claims compensation courts' in which the claimant would be free from court fees and from the possibility of having to pay the other side's costs, and in which there would be a minimum of formality. More recently a similar suggestion was put forward in an article in a professional journal,[17] in which the author suggested the establishment of:

> 'unified professional courts to sit as courts of first instance in all matters at present within the jurisdiction of local valuation courts, rent tribunals [sic] and the Lands Tribunal . . . organized on a regional basis . . . and with members selected from panels of professionally qualified people.'

He went on to adduce a number of advantages which would flow from his proposal – relief of the Lands Tribunal, financial economy to the parties, many of whom are currently deterred from going direct to the Lands Tribunal by the prospect of having to meet costs out of all proportion to the sum at issue, increased professionalism on the part of the adjudicators and the saving of administrative overheads by amalgamating officers and staff.

## A COMMON TRIBUNAL STAFF

The staffing of tribunals was described in Chapter 5. The salient points for the purposes of this discussion were that most of the tribunals which require full-time staff[18] are served by officers seconded, or lent, by the

[15] 2,957, 2,336 and 3,240 hearings in 1968, 1969 and 1970 respectively, compared with the local valuation courts' 35,000, 27,816 and 25,513.

[16] *Compensation for Compulsory Acquisition and Remedies for Planning Restrictions* (Stevens & Sons, 1969), paras. 91–8.

[17] In the *Chartered Surveyor*, October 1971 issue, Mr Michael Beaman, FRICS. Three years earlier the Society of Clerks of Local Valuation Panels had submitted a comprehensive memorandum to the Minister of Housing and Local Government on comparable lines.

[18] Many of course meet on comparatively few occasions and their servicing is incidental to the normal work of a Department.

relevant department, the exceptions being the national insurance and supplementary benefit tribunals, which are served by officers of the DHSS who usually also perform other duties within the Department, and the local valuation courts, which appoint their own staff.

*Seconded Staff*

The secondment of staff by a department seems a simple and natural arrangement, and it is in any case an inevitable one unless one is to postulate a tribunal service comparable to, or part of, the Court Service of the country. For it would be undesirable, and probably impracticable, for each tribunal to employ its own independent staff; the local valuation courts, which are the only tribunal employing full-time staff to do so, suffer seriously from the frustrations of a narrow field for promotion and of limited career prospects for their staff.

On closer examination secondment is open to a number of criticisms.

Primarily, it does not accord with the essential independence of tribunals. A seconded officer may give loyal service to his President or Chairman, but nothing can alter the fact that his future lies with the parent department, service with the tribunal being no more than an episode in his career. The head of the tribunal has no part in his selection or in his eventual transfer. Staff may leave either as a result of a visiting promotion board, a civil service 'trawl' or open advertisement. The more senior staff, who were originally lent by a department as distinct from being recruited directly and locally, seem to experience a common dilemma: on the one hand their work is more than usually interesting and they do not wish to give it up; on the other hand it does not lead to anything beyond itself in the tribunal world, with the result that they are 'looking over their shoulder' to the department from which they came. In general, staff are uncertain about their future, and a not uncommon attitude is to regard a tribunal posting as a dead end.

As for the departments, they act, on the whole, correctly, respecting the independence of the tribunals with which they are associated and not seeking to bring departmental influence to bear. On the other hand their reasons for seconding staff to tribunal work are not necessarily that they are the most able or appropriate officers available; nor do they invariably remember that a tribunal is not 'their' tribunal, or that the officers serving it are not their own officers. There is no reason to apprehend deliberate impropriety; there is, on the other hand, the occasional 'slip-up', and even if these are innocent the possibility of their occurring at all ought not to exist in an institution in which judicial decisions are being made concerning the rights or property of individuals.

Presidents and chairmen are not (so far as may be judged from a brief pilot study) by any means agreed upon these matters. In general, as might be expected, those who hold part-time appointments are satisfied with the current arrangement and believe themselves well served by the officers seconded to them. Those who are full-time, and who themselves hold some administrative responsibility, are less impressed, and find it frustrating that they have no part in recruitment or transfer; they are frustrated also by the fact that in so far as they do control their staff there is little scope within the area of any one tribunal to offer wider experience by internal transfer or the stimulus of a promotion prospect.

These various shortcomings, which in our view outweigh the advantages of secondment, have given rise to the question whether a common tribunal service might not be the proper aim. Before attempting to answer this we must glance briefly at those tribunals which require full-time staff but are differently circumstanced.

*Social Security Tribunal Staff*

In the field of national insurance and supplementary benefit it is possible to identify a few officers who may be said to be employed full-time on tribunal work, though in national insurance the work of a Clerk is not of a responsible kind and the actual individuals are changed from time to time without difficulty. Supplementary benefit appeal tribunals tend to rely more on the departmental experience of their Clerks, who are of Executive Officer grading and are usually attached to a small group of tribunals for two years at a time – a period which gives them long enough to become familiar with tribunal procedure but is not so long as to make them become remote from their field work in the administration of benefit.[19] Medical appeal tribunals are more demanding of staff, because of the large amount of preparatory

[19] Until 1971 these posts carried a higher status and were filled by Higher Executive Officers. The Department does not see the clerks as in essence including advice among their duties, but some at least of the chairmen undoubtedly look to them for a contribution derived from earlier supplementary benefits work. If the tribunal wants to know about the view of the law taken by the Supplementary Benefits Commission it will of course turn to the Commission's representative at the hearing, but sometimes the tribunal can have recourse only to its Clerk – that is, after the appellant and the officer have left the tribunal to reach its conclusion. The tribunal is empowered either to confirm a decision or to substitute one of its own, the latter being 'any determination which the Commission could have made' (Ministry of Social Social Security Act 1966, s. 18(3)). The tribunal therefore needs the same expertness as those assessing benefit for the purpose of the decision of first instance and may seek the clerk's help, not of course as to the amount to be awarded but on the technicalities of getting benefit into payment (effective dates, pay weeks etc.);

medical evidence and other paper work, and officers of up to Senior Executive Officer grade are employed in the work. In all these cases, however, the officers are ordinary members of the Department's staff and in most cases they are also employed on other duties.

There is here the familiar situation that while no-one would suggest that departmental staff are other than impartial in their tribunal duties, nevertheless from the viewpoint of justice being 'seen to be done' their status is ambivalent.

*Local Valuation Court Staff*

Local valuation courts are in this, as in other respects, the 'odd man out', and their position again requires special consideration. Their staff problem is cogently described in the memorandum to which reference has already been made:

> 'The urgent need is to create more progressive career opportunities for advancement both within and beyond the bounds of the Service itself, and to put an end to the anomalous non-status position in which officers find themselves vis-à-vis personnel undertaking duties of a similar nature under comparable tribunals, e.g. Rent Assessment Panels. At present each panel is nominally the employing authority for its own handful of staff, but in practice merely makes appointments within salary and establishment scales authorised by the Department of the Environment. Such scales are perforce relatively static, being related to broad bands of hereditaments or rateable value within the panel area. Consequently there is a total absence of any prospect of advancement worth dignifying with the name of career structure within the Service, because although theoretically it is open to a clerk to secure promotion by applying for a vacant post in an area larger than his own, no compensation for disturbance is payable on transfer, so that the costs of household removal so outweigh any marginal increase in salary that movement on these lines is virtually non-existent.'

These comments are important, having regard to the prominent place which LVCs occupy in the total picture.

In the light of these facts, which suggest that a unified tribunal service might possibly be desirable, we must consider whether it would be practicable. This would turn to some extent on whether the staff of

or it may be a case of checking that the new decision is framed and explained by the tribunal in a way that, as well as being understandable for the appellant, makes sense to the officers who, later on, may have to take consequential decisions – for example on a change of personal circumstances or in the rates of benefit.

tribunals need to have greater expert knowledge of their subject matter than would normally be acquired in the transfer from one executive or administrative job to another. This ought to be necessary only in those tribunals where the Clerk is expected to *advise* a tribunal in reaching its decision, as do the clerks of valuation panels, or perhaps where the tribunal draws on the clerk's experience of the technicalities of departmental procedure, as with supplementary benefit appeal tribunals. The former have no required qualification, and in fact their experience has variously been in local government or in professional valuation; it is nevertheless a relatively expert field and the necessary experience would take time to acquire. The knowledge required to service a supplementary benefit appeal tribunal is not inconsiderable and, for the reasons explained earlier, the tribunals find it useful – especially when a chairman has not been long in office – to have a Clerk with departmental experience of the subject matter of the appeals. Too much must not be made of this, but if the Clerks were simply people of general executive or administrative ability supplied by a unified service there would probably be for the tribunal some loss of performance to be set against the advantages of the change.

The other aspect of practicability is more dubious, i.e. whether there could be a satisfying career in a Tribunal Service. The probability is that there could not, as the staff 'pyramid' would be too broad and shallow, a position which could be rectified only if tribunal staff were part of the court service, doing spells of secondment from courts to tribunals.

### *Tribunal Staff and Court Staff*

This assertion is supported by figures. In a pilot study of Birmingham and the West Midlands the numbers and grades of staff employed in tribunals and courts were seen to be in striking contrast as is shown by the first table.[20]

[20] Unfortunately Departmental Regions do not coincide with Court Circuit Areas, and this comparison is perforce between the West Midland Region and the larger Midland and Oxford Circuit; a true comparison might involve scaling down the Court Service figures by some 10 per cent; even so the figures adequately support the point we are making. The figures contain one other deficiency, namely that it is impossible to strike exact equivalents in grade and salary between civil servants and the staffs of local valuation panels, who are themselves on 'hybrid' local government scales. Moreover, the Society of Clerks of Valuation Panels have long been in dispute with the Department over salary scales and the whole position is fluid. The equivalence which has been adopted slightly over-states the grading of local valuation panel staff, but to have equated them with the civil service grade below would have under-stated it to a greater extent.

| | *Tribunals (Civil Service)* | *Local Valuation Panels* | *County Courts* | *Circuit H.Q. Staff* | *Crown Courts* |
|---|---|---|---|---|---|
| Under Secretary | — | — | — | 1 | — |
| Assistant Secretary | — | — | — | 1 | — |
| Senior Principal | — | — | — | 4 | — |
| Principal | — | — | 1 | 1 | 3 |
| Senior Executive Officer | 3 | 5[a] | 17 | 2 | 15 |
| Higher Executive Officer | 4 | 5[a] | 59 | 7 | 27 |
| Executive Officer | 20 | — | 208 | 4 | 16 |
| Clerical Officer | 25 | 6 | 415 | 14 | 39 |
| Clerical Assistant | 15 | 6 | 30 | 2 | 2 |

[a] Approximate equivalence.

The foregoing figures relate to one region, but the national picture is not a great deal more than a regional picture multiplied by the number of regions, as there are elsewhere very few posts above SEO. The approximate figures at the time of writing, including the Lands, Mental Health Review and Pensions Appeal Tribunals, the Special Commissioners and the non-legal staff of the National Insurance Commissioners, are shown in the table below.

| | *Principal* | *SEO* | *HEO* | *EO* | *CO* | *CA* |
|---|---|---|---|---|---|---|
| Immigration | — | 1 | 1 | 2 | 10 | 14 |
| Industrial | 1 | 1 | 13 | 87 | 84 | 79 |
| Lands | 1 | — | 2 | 4 | 12 | — |
| Mental Health | 1 | — | 3 | 4 | 4 | 3 |
| National Insurance (Local)[a] | — | — | — | 38 | 97 | — |
| Medical Appeal[a] | — | 2 | 4 | 24 | 36 | 20 |
| National Insurance Commissioner | — | 1 | 6 | 2 | 8 | 4 |
| Pensions | — | 1 | — | 1 | 7 | — |
| Rent Assessment Panels | 1 | 2 | 16 | 62 | 79 | 11 |
| Revenue—Special Commissioners | 1 | — | 6 | 3 | 5 | 5 |
| Supplementary Benefit[a] | — | — | — | 28 | 14 | 21 |
| TOTAL | 5 | 8 | 51 | 255 | 356 | 157 |
| Rating—Local Valuation | — | 60 | 34 | — | 10 | 100 |
| TOTAL | 5 | 68 | 85 | 254 | 367 | 257 |

[a] These figures have been estimated by the DHSS as the full-time equivalent of work which is in fact done as part of more general duties.

The corresponding figures for the unified Court Service are: (as at 1 July 1972).

| | *Principal* | *SEO* | *HEO* | *EO* | *CO* | *CA* |
|---|---|---|---|---|---|---|
| Crown/High and County Courts | 46 | 266 | 616 | 1,321 | 2,320 | 262 |

Circuit and Courts Administrators' Offices

| *Under-Secretary* | *Assistant Secretary* | *Senior Principal* | *Principal* | *SEO* | *HEO* | *EO* | *CO* | *CA* |
|---|---|---|---|---|---|---|---|---|
| 6 | 8 | 20 | 8 | 14 | 45 | 24 | 74 | 10 |

To replace the existing network of departmental secondments by a 'Tribunal Service', and to integrate this with the Court Service, would of course present immense practical difficulties, and would doubtless be impossible unless – as we later suggest – the existing responsibility for tribunals vested in departmental ministers were to be assumed by the Lord Chancellor. Even so, it is only recently, i.e. since the establishment of the unified Court Service, that there has been opportunity for interchange or promotion within the various Lord Chancellor's Departments themselves. The point of interest here is that the staff of the two tribunals for which he is directly responsible – the Pensions Appeal and Lands Tribunals – receive the benefit of these new opportunities, so that there appears to be no objection in principle to the advancement of tribunal staff as such within the Court Service. The difficulty in practice might be that while the experience gained in some tribunals might qualify for service in a County Court or Crown Court centre – and *vice versa* – the level of responsibility of other tribunal staffs, for example in the social security field, certainly would not.

## COMMON TRIBUNAL PREMISES

An observer who sets out to attend every kind of tribunal which is open to the public will have little idea whether he will find himself in a town hall, an office block, a hotel, a magistrates' court, a departmental annexe or even a building for religious worship. A passer-by from whom he enquired the way would probably have been able to direct him to the local court but not to the tribunal he is asking for, for tribunals have no home, but meet wherever they conveniently can.

In the City of Birmingham, for example, they meet at one time or another in sixteen different premises, only one of which is Crown property. The industrial tribunal, the rent assessment panel, the rent tribunal and the local valuation panel are in four different sets of rented office accommodation which provide both their office and hearing facilities. The social security tribunals and the visiting Pensions Appeal Tribunals rent commercial office accommodation for their hearings only, their preparatory work being done in their own offices. The General Commissioners of Income Tax have a floor in the building used by the District Offices of the Revenue, an arrangement which departs from the usual one that appeals against the Revenue are not heard on Revenue premises; while the Special Commissioners and the Lands Tribunal, visiting on circuit, use premises which are hired for a wide variety of purposes. The Regional Estate Office of the Department of the Environment, which is responsible for finding accommodation for tribunals, also manage to fit in to the same leased or hired premises some of the less frequent tribunals as well as a number of other adjudicatory bodies such as the Criminal Injuries Compensation Board, the Official Referee's Court, the Industrial Assurance Commissioners and a number of Wages Councils.

These arrangements work, in the sense that the Department of the Environment manages to prevent them from breaking down, but they are hand-to-mouth, and seem to be unworthy of the institution which tribunals have now become.

The alternative would be to provide tribunals with a recognized home comparable to the Crown Courts, with adequate office accommodation, flexibly designed hearing and waiting rooms and common ancillary services. This proposal, however, encounters both practical difficulties and objections in principle, which we must now examine.

The practical difficulty is that tribunals are relatively unpredictable in their incidence. Some may meet several times in a week; some once a week; some twice a month; some, including the principal circuit tribunals, at irregular intervals or when sufficient cases have accumulated to justify a hearing. They are not always able to give long notice of their requirements and it is of course a matter of chance whether their demands on accommodation conflict or are evenly spread. In Birmingham the Department of the Environment have contemplated the possibility of tribunals being under one roof, but their provisional conclusion is that a single building which tried to meet the average demand would be in danger of being under-used for some of the time, while being unable to meet the occasional peak demand, thus requiring a reversion to commercial hire. The present arrangements, while open to criticism, are at least flexible.

On the other hand it may be pointed out that some of the present leased accommodation, notably that which is provided for hearing purposes only and does not accommodate office staff, also stands empty for a good deal of the time.

The objection in principle which is often advanced is that 'grandiose' premises would be out of harmony with the spirit and intention of tribunals, whose physical setting ought to be as modest and unpretentious as possible since they mostly deal with the private affairs of people in some sort of difficulty. Such people, it is held, prefer to go to some relatively anonymous address than to a well-known public building analogous to a court.

While taking the point, we believe that the balance of advantage lies in the other direction. From the point of view of service to the public, it is known[21] that some tribunal premises are shabby and inadequate, often lacking waiting rooms, so that the parties wait in corridors, sometimes even with inadequate lavatory facilities. Moreover the addresses at which inquiries about tribunals ought to be made are not well publicized, and members of the public, some of whom incidentally are applicants to more than one tribunal, are known to make unnecessary journeys to the wrong office.[22] It would be a great convenience to the 'customer' to be able to consult one person at one address about his various statutory entitlements. There is no reason why the major tribunals should not to this extent act as their own 'citizens' information bureaux'; it is not of course a proper function of tribunal staffs to give personal advice, which could however be sought if needed from the local citizens' advice bureau.

From the point of view of the efficiency of the tribunals themselves and quite apart from any long-term financial economy in commercial rents in city centres, it would seem to be an advantage to make use of certain common facilities. For example, several tribunals need an X-ray and medical examination room, and not all of those in current use are of a high standard. Again, it is common to all tribunals that their work involves a burdensome amount of copying and circulating documents,[23] and while each tribunal tends to need its own distinctive works of

[21] Visits by members of the Council on Tribunals and personal observation.

[22] Evidence of the citizens' advice bureaux.

[23] The DHSS estimate that nationally over seventy copy-typists are fully employed in the social security tribunals.

reference a common library of legal and other reference books would be an asset. A comprehensive centre could also offer refreshment facilities, a small advantage but one greatly appreciated by applicants waiting under strain.

It is in any case unnecessary for purpose-built premises to be grandiose, for they can be designed to forestall this very criticism, as are some of the modern Crown Courts; indeed, but for the fact that it might be unwise to associate an appeal to a tribunal too closely with litigation in a court of law some of the modern court buildings could well accommodate tribunals.

These suggestions naturally apply to regional centres and other large cities where there is a concentration of tribunals which meet regularly. In smaller places arrangements for accommodation must obviously continue to be made *ad hoc*, and they are in fact usually provided either in the local council offices or the magistrates' court. The use of the latter is questionable; it may be quite suitable for an agricultural lands tribunal, let us say, but people claiming some kind of benefit, particularly supplementary benefit, would find the thought of having to go to the magistrates' court disagreeable, and it could well make the poor attendances at social security tribunals even worse. The Council on Tribunals have deprecated their use.

## A COMMON TRIBUNAL STRUCTURE

For a network of tribunals 'structure' has two connotations – the *form* of administration (self-administering – whether by individual tribunals or under a president – or departmental) and the *area* of administration (regional or unitary, the unit being the individual tribunal). The presidential form tends to go with a regional administration, but otherwise there is not much correlation between the two.

### *Presidential Administration*

Of the more heavily engaged tribunals, slightly more than half have now adopted a presidential system, viz. the pensions appeal, industrial, rent assessment, immigration and (shortly) value added tax tribunals; but those dealing with rates, national insurance and supplementary benefit remain outside it, as do the General Commissioners of Income Tax – and these, incidentally, are the tribunals which carry the heaviest case loads. The two great advantages of the system are first its manifest independence, which gives tribunals a *persona* in the public mind comparable to that of the courts, and removes the suspicion that they are part of the departmental mechanism; and second the ease of communication which enhances both efficiency and morale – thus Ministry can communicate with President without suspicion that they are seeking to influence tribunals as such, and two-way communication between President, chairmen and members results in guidance, consistency, the spread of information, the promotion of discussion and a sense of team purpose.

The presidential system does not lack critics, however. One criticism is that it is unnecessarily costly, in comparison with the system under which tribunals are serviced by departments, or with the pre-1965 rent tribunals, which existed in a sort of limbo of their own. This is not self-evident, and a considerable costing exercise would be necessary to establish how far it was true. However, if it is to be accepted that tribunals are part of the judicial system and not an appendage of the Administration, the presidential system is clearly to be preferred, and any additional cost would have to be reckoned as the cost of a system of justice; they are certainly not costly to the appellant; and certainly the old rent tribunals were criticized as being deplorable examples of judicial bodies.[24] Theoretical considerations apart, presidential systems are in vogue.

The other criticism is that men appointed for their judicial capacity, many of whom have held high judicial office, are too greatly diverted to administration, including administrative chores. There has been some truth in this criticism, but it cannot be accepted as valid since it would not arise if the supporting administration were better organized. The kind of rationalization of staff and premises that we have been discussing would go far to nullify it.

In the use of judicial manpower, if not in financial cost, presidential tribunals could well prove economical in years to come, for there are signs that the supply of qualified – or at least of legally qualified – adjudicators is beginning to dry up. Whether or not the rationalization of the *system* is to be desired the rationalization of this man-power may become essential; though it is possible that the first might be a condition of the second, and that the amalgamation of tribunals under a limited number of Presidents of what would in effect be specialized Courts – valuation, revenue, social services, industrial – would make the best use of the talent available.

We said earlier (p. 115) that there had been no difficulty in recruiting members, except perhaps doctors in industrial areas, and that even the expanding industrial tribunals had been able to fill their vacancies,

[24] The position is now wholly changed, and they were unanimously commended in the Report of the Francis Committee on the Rent Acts (Cmnd. 4609, p. 145).

though they had also been the first to sound a warning note. But several things are happening simultaneously and the position is far from static. Tribunals continue to expand in number; an important source of supply to senior and full-time posts is virtually exhausted – the former Overseas Legal Service on which the growing tribunals of the 1960s drew very heavily indeed; the newest tribunals are among the most demanding, both as to time and skill, and are likely to require a higher proportion of full-time chairmen if not of members; the amalgamation of jurisdictions (if it happens) could mean that lay, i.e. non-legal, membership would be more demanding and could become full-time; and it is increasingly evident that the present system is wasteful, in that some busy people give more time than they can spare, while in the lesser used tribunals, and in the rural areas of some other tribunals, members are frustrated by the few calls that are made upon them.[25]

These considerations taken together tend to favour not only the amalgamation of jurisdictions, but a presidential system and an increased professionalism.

*Unitary Administration*

A word must be said about those tribunals which we described as 'unitary', i.e. which have no regional or presidential organization. Among these, the Clerks of Valuation Panels seek to make good the deficiency to some extent by means of a national association, the Society of Clerks of Valuation Panels. Although working only with an honorary secretary, himself the Clerk of a Panel, the Society is able to speak with a corporate voice to the Department of the Environment, and to call occasional regional conferences which include chairmen and members of panels as well as their chief officers. The work of the tribunals in the field of social security is already organized (departmentally) on a regional basis, but in the ordinary course of business there is no contact between one chairman in a region and another. As we have said elsewhere, individual chairmen have taken the initiative in summoning conferences of their colleagues, and the Department of Health and Social Security are more disposed than they used to be to facilitate this. There is, however, no permanent arrangement of any kind, and it could be that an association of chairmen, with a paid secretary and a simple organization, would be an acceptable half-way house to a presidential system.

25 We have recorded this as a general impression derived from conversations, but it is being confirmed by the statistical results of the research now in progress in the Universities of Birmingham and Newcastle-upon-Tyne.

## AREAS OF ADMINISTRATION

The integration of staff and premises would be facilitated if areas of administration could be brought more into accord. This could never be done completely – indeed the post-war 'standard' regions proposed for government departments have only ever been approximately co-terminous – but the present discrepancies are very great. Thus of the tribunals for which it would be possible to think in terms of a common staff, the industrial tribunals have 14 administrative areas, the local valuation courts 95, and the rent assessment panels 16, while the various social security tribunals are grouped for administrative purposes in the 11 regions of the Department of Health and Social Security. The immigration adjudicators, who are currently creating an embryo regional organization, have simply chosen the four main centres of industrial employment and will presumably work *ad hoc* from that beginning. Outside what would normally be considered the statutory tribunals, the Legal Aid Committees of the Law Society are grouped in 15 'areas'.

To suggest a standard regional framework closely comparable to the government regions would be a counsel of perfection, since tribunals must vary according to the load and location of their work, but as matters stand there are some confusing situations. For example, in the Eastern Region – admittedly a difficult one to administer[26] – the headquarters of the rent assessment panel for East Anglia are at Ipswich, but for Cambridgeshire and the neighbouring counties, which are normally associated with East Anglia, they are at Luton; while the industrial tribunals are located at Bury St Edmunds for work which arises both in East Anglia proper and in Bedfordshire and Northamptonshire.

The remaining areas of the subject where there could with advantage be some measure of rationalization may be mentioned very much more briefly, partly because they are less controversial and partly because we have already given an account of the facts in earlier chapters. They are the remuneration of members, the award of costs and payment of expenses, the establishment of a common code of procedure, and a consistent method of appointing those who preside over tribunals. It is interesting to note in passing that the first three of these matters remain very much where Franks left them in 1957. In each case the Franks Committee discussed the subject somewhat cursorily but concluded by recommending that the Council on Tribunals should

[26] Even government departments are centred about equally in Cambridge and Nottingham.

review them more thoroughly and should formulate proposals. In the event the Council have been unable to make very much impression on any of them, either because they lacked the necessary power of initiative or because the investigations that would have been necessary were beyond their resources, the whole of their staff being almost immediately occupied with day-to-day work from which there was no escape – a point to which we return in a moment.

### REMUNERATION (pp. 105–7)

The unpaid, part-time volunteer, whom some hold to be the glory of British public life and others its curse, survives in the General Commissioners, the National Health Service Executive Councils and Service Committees, the local valuation courts, the members (other than chairmen) of the social security tribunals, and of course the magistrates. Of these the members of local valuation courts have, at their regional conferences, expressed dissatisfaction with their voluntary status, and it is probable that it will not survive the reorganization of local government and the payment of elected councillors; we have ourselves suggested that they ought in any case to be merged into more expert local land tribunals, which would imply the payment of professional fees.

We do not suggest that there is necessarily any point in paying people who are content to serve voluntarily, or that the voluntary principle is not worth preserving in the diminishing areas where it is possible to preserve it. It would, however, be preferable if when salaries or fees are paid they were informed by some discernible principle, and anomalous distinctions avoided. A rational, and also a realistic, scheme of payments may become increasingly important, in view of the expected difficulty in recruiting adjudicators, to which we referred above.

### COSTS AND EXPENSES (pp. 181–5)

We have recorded the anomalies, and drawn attention to the facts that the Franks Committee commended certain principles and proposed that the Council on Tribunals should review the position 'as part of its review of tribunal procedures'. The Council seem to have held back, pending a formal reference by the Government, but as yet no such reference has been made. This is an area where standardization would seem to be equitable; the existing arrangements certainly are not.

### A CODE OR CODES OF PROCEDURE (p. 154 ff.)

This is a question of degree, since no-one has ever suggested that universal rules of procedure would be possible. The Franks Report (paragraphs 62–3) could not even envisage 'a small number of codes'. It did, however, go on to enunciate principles, and suggested that in the light of these 'the Council on Tribunals could formulate detailed rules of procedure for the various tribunals'. In practice, as we have seen, they have not formulated them, but have merely commented on them after they have been formulated by others, and in view of the way in which their work and organization have developed it is by no means certain that they would now be the appropriate body to have an originating as well as a consultative role. A more natural location for a central drafting body would be the Lord Chancellor's Office.

Two things would seem to be advantageous – first, that the extremes of simplicity (e.g. rent tribunals) and sophistication (e.g. the Performing Rights Tribunal) should be diminished; second, that there should be a consistent framework, which stipulated the points which every set of rules ought to cover, supplemented by such other rules as were appropriate to particular tribunals.

Such supplementary rules might well be left to departments, subject to consultation with the Council, to whom they would best be submitted through the Lord Chancellor's Office. This procedure has in fact already been followed with advantage, for example, in connection with the rules of the Mental Health Review Tribunals, and also with planning appeals and compulsory purchase inquiries – though these of course were submitted as complete sets of rules, and were not supplementary to a basic code.

The justification for a framework is not only that tribunals are untidy in this regard, but that they must observe the rules of natural justice as assiduously as the courts, that there may be further amalgamations, and that neither members of tribunals nor professional representatives are confined to a particular tribunal but move quite freely from one to another.

## THE APPOINTMENT OF CHAIRMEN (pp. 96–8)

The Franks Committee (Report paragraph 46) recommended without qualification that in the interest of manifest impartiality all chairmen should be appointed by the Lord Chancellor. This is now the rule rather than the exception, but the exceptions are important. They include, for example, the immigration adjudicators, whose jurisdiction is one of the most sensitive of all; and the chairmen of local valuation courts, which hear more cases than any other chain of tribunals. Although none of these posts requires a legal qualification, it nevertheless appears to us that the only justifiable exceptions to the rule which Franks wished to follow might possibly be the few cases mentioned on p. 103, of whom the Traffic Commissioners are typical, where the 'chairman' is a civil servant whose function is primarily administrative, and whose incidental adjudicatory function is a licensing one.

To sum up, our conclusions on the general subject of rationalization are as follow:

1. On *jurisdiction*, there is a strong case for establishing local land and property valuation tribunals which would combine the existing functions of the local valuation panels, rent assessment panels[27] and the smaller planning and compensation cases of the Lands Tribunal. There is a case on jurisdictional grounds for amalgamating some of the tax tribunals, though the organizational problem would be formidable. There might also be a case on organizational grounds, especially if there proved to be a shortage of chairmen, or if today's non-legal chairmen should ever be required to be lawyers, for amalgamating national insurance and supplementary benefit appeal tribunals, but on jurisdictional grounds the case would be difficult to support.

2. On *staffing*, there is a case to be argued for and against a common tribunal service linked to, or part of, the national court service. We believe that the case in favour is the stronger.

3. On *premises and accommodation*, we believe that the balance of argument supports a central tribunal building in the major centres of population.

4. On *structure*, we believe that the presidential system has advantages that qualify it to be the universal pattern for those tribunals which are continuously engaged. In particular local valuation courts, either as they now exist or as part of the local valuation tribunals adumbrated in (1) above, should be brought into the main stream of tribunals; and the tribunals concerned with social security could with advantage be brought into the presidential pattern. We believe also that the administrative boundaries within which tribunals operate should as far as possible be made co-terminous.

5. On *remuneration*, we believe that the pattern of full-time salaries, part-time fees and voluntary service is necessary, but that the anomalies within each of the first two categories, described on pp. 105–7 should be abolished.

[27] We have said that in practice rent tribunals tend to be as much concerned with personal social problems as with valuation, but for practical purposes we must include them in this group, especially in view of their already close integration with the rent assessment panels.

6. On the *award of costs and the payment of expenses*, we do not apprehend any injustice in the existing situation, but there are anomalies that would be better removed.

7. On *procedural rules*, we do not believe that uniformity is possible, but there ought to be a 'minimal' code stipulating the matters which ought to be covered in *any* set of procedural rules, irrespective of any additional rules to suit the circumstances of any particular tribunal.

8. On the *appointment of chairmen*, we believe that all who preside at tribunals, or who sit as sole adjudicators, should be appointed by the Lord Chancellor.

There remains the larger question, to which we referred at the beginning of this chapter, of ministerial responsibility and accountability. The recommendations that we have just made, especially those relating to the appointment of chairmen and staff, would in themselves tend to shift some responsibility from executive departments to the Lord Chancellor. We believe, however, that consideration should be given to taking the process further.

The present position may be summed up as follows. The Lord Chancellor is fully responsible for the Pensions Appeal Tribunals and the Lands Tribunal, and shares responsibility with the Treasury for the General (but not the Special) Commissioners of Income Tax. Moreover he has a greater degree of direct responsibility than he has elsewhere for agricultural land tribunals and mental health review tribunals, in that he appoints both chairmen and members, and in the case of the former even determines their administrative areas. For the rest he appoints Presidents, where they exist, and most chairmen, or alternatively he appoints panels of chairmen from which a Minister makes selections for particular posts. But even this is by no means universal – he does not do so for tribunals concerned with licensing or standards, or for immigration adjudicators or local valuation courts. With these he has no concern at all, doubtless (as we have said) for the reason that no legal qualification is required of their chairmen; on the other hand a number of immigration adjudicators are men of considerable legal experience and in practice if not by statutory requirement legal expertise is recruited to tribunals dealing with licensing, standards and copyright. Furthermore the Lord Chancellor directly appoints lay *members* of some tribunals, as well as chairmen of supplementary benefit appeal tribunals, so that the exclusion of certain tribunals from his cognizance does not appear to be governed by principle.

As to ministerial accountability, if a matter concerning tribunals is raised in Parliament it is not the Lord Chancellor (except for the

Pensions Appeal Tribunals and the Lands Tribunal) who deals with it, but the appropriate departmental minister.

These somewhat irrational arrangements derive largely from historical accidents or from decisions made *ad hoc* under the pressures of the moment, and some account of them can be found in earlier chapters. Their most consistent feature is the persistence of departmental boundaries in an area which since the time of the Franks Report has been increasingly regarded as judicial – much of which could indeed be regarded theoretically as lying within the province of the ordinary courts. And although these departmental boundaries were at one time able to provide the necessary framework within which the early development of tribunals could take place they now present an obstacle to the achievement of a more coherent system.

The transfer of fuller responsibility to the Lord Chancellor would both underline the independence of tribunals and also unite them with a Department which has special experience in dealing with the administrative problems of judicial bodies; and which, incidentally, is now better equipped than it was some years ago to undertake a task of this kind.[28] With the reorganization of the courts the Lord Chancellor's Departments (of which the 'Lord Chancellor's Office' is nominally one) now includes the Headquarters of the Courts Service, which in turn includes a Courts Business Branch, and it would seem logical that a Tribunals Branch could take its place alongside these.[29]

Accordingly we add to our eight more specific recommendations a ninth – namely that consideration should be given to transferring overall responsibility and accountability for tribunals to the Lord Chancellor, to be administered by one of his Departments.

This is in fact to say little more than was said by the Franks Committee,[30] and in view of the heterogeneous nature of tribunals the phrase 'fuller' or 'overall' responsibility clearly needs precise definition. We hesitate to be dogmatic, as it is a matter which would clearly need the expert examination of a body such as we suggest on the following page. *Prima facie*, however, it appears to us that the Lord Chancellor should be responsible for the appointment of presidents, chairmen and sole

[28] As an example of the recent rapid growth of the administrative side of the Lord Chancellor's Departments, 600 local authority employees (the Quarter Sessions staff) were absorbed, on equivalent Civil Service gradings, at the beginning of 1972.

[29] The strangeness of the present position is illustrated by the fact that in the Imperial Calendar and Civil Service List the Pensions Appeal Tribunal and the Lands Tribunal are recorded as 'Lord Chancellor's Departments', as is the Council on Tribunals.

[30] Report, para. 131.

adjudicators for *all* tribunals and for the procedural rules under which they operate; that in the case of tribunals dealing with licensing or standards – those near the administrative pole of the spectrum – his responsibility should cease at that point; but that in what we have called the central bloc of tribunals he should additionally be responsible for the appointment of tribunal members and staff, and for the organization of a Tribunal Service comparable to, or part of, the Courts Service.

Such a course would have far-reaching implications. Over most of the field it would mean the end of the principle embodied in the phrase 'ministerial tribunals' so widely used by the Donoughmore Committee, and as we ourselves have pointed out some tribunals are so intimately connected with day-to-day administration that it is not unnatural that they should have come to be regarded as part of it. To cut the cord of ministerial accountability would indeed represent the final abandonment of the administrative for the judicial concept. It is, however, the logical development of all that has flowed from Franks, and more recently from the presidential system, and we believe that the time has come for it to be seriously examined.

In the course of reaching these conclusions we have been strongly reminded that the virtues of 'rationalization' are not self-evident; that it is possible to become obsessed by mere tidiness as an end in itself; and that the onus lies on those who advocate rationalization to prove that specific advantages would flow from it. We venture to think that the opposite proposition could equally well be advanced, namely that the fragmentation of tribunals has not always had a justification in reason, but that accident and expediency also have contributed to the present pattern; and that the onus may be on the advocate of the existing pattern to prove that it is sensible. Nevertheless the main point of the criticism is taken, and it is our belief that the proposals we have made would carry specific advantages, either of economy in expertise, efficiency of operation, the convenience of the public or the status of the institution.

If the tentative conclusions at which we have arrived merit serious consideration, it would seem desirable that an independent review of them should be put in hand so that their practical implications can be assessed and opinion about their desirability ascertained and weighed. The natural body to undertake such a review would be the Council on Tribunals, which exists primarily to 'keep under review the constitution and working of tribunals . . . and to report'. It would, however, be unrealistic to suppose that the Council as it is now constituted could contemplate a task of this order. As we have seen, the Franks Committee suggested in 1957 that they should review less onerous matters than some of those we have discussed, but their resources have never permitted them to do so. This leads naturally to the question why this should be so, and whether their own position is not in need of reappraisal.

The Council's difficulty has been that a body of spare-time advisers, with a part-time Chairman and an exiguous staff, have had to give an inordinate amount of their time to day-to-day matters, and have been unable to pay adequate attention to those which the Franks Committee thought they should deliberate, or those which we have been discussing in this chapter. From the outset they became involved in dealing with complaints from the public (a possibility that had not been adequately appreciated) and much of the time that they could devote to larger matters was (again unexpectedly) absorbed by problems relating to public inquiries rather than to tribunals.

We briefly mention these facts, which can be inferred from the longer account given in Chapter 8, in order to emphasize the point that as now constituted they could not undertake an investigation into matters as large as those we have raised. Given the necessary resources they could of course investigate those which lie within the ambit of the existing system, some of which were indeed commended to their attention by the Franks Committee. But what most urgently needs attention is the place of tribunals in the machinery of government, and indeed the constitution and role of the Council themselves. Questions of this order could only be satisfactorily examined by a separate body appointed for the purpose, which would, so to speak, extend the work of the Beeching Royal Commission on Quarter Sessions and Assizes into the allied subject of tribunals. We believe we have established a sufficiently strong case for this to be done.

But however this matter is arranged, our work has convinced us that there is a need to ensure that the Council on Tribunals plays a more positive part in future both in the consideration of proposals for new tribunals and in the continuous review of the work and organization of existing ones. The Council have always had to rely on influence rather than authority to achieve the ends which Parliament had in mind for them, for the Act which created them did not give them the kind of powers that the Franks Committee had recommended. In some ways their rather ambivalent position has had advantages, since they are sufficiently independent to be regarded as guardians of the public interest and sufficiently part of the machinery of government to enjoy informal and confidential discussions with departments. Indeed, were they to have had executive powers, or powers of the kind exercised by the Parliamentary Commissioner for Administration, they would probably have been worse off, since departments would have treated them more formally.

On the other hand they have undoubtedly been at a disadvantage in some important ways.[31] Perhaps their greatest handicap has been that Parliament did not give them the statutory right to be consulted on proposed legislation involving the creation of new tribunals or the altering of the structure of the system. A Treasury circular enjoins such consultation upon departments, but this has not proved wholly satisfactory, as consultation has often been at too late a stage, when a new proposal that the Council might well have wished to modify has been taken too far to be reversed, or even greatly modified. This is a particularly vital point, since one of the clearest needs is for new tribunals to be assessed from some central vantage point instead of being determined from time to time at the 'circumference', i.e. as a more or less incidental consequence of departmental legislation on some aspect of social policy. It is to be hoped, therefore, that directions may some time be given to departments to bring the Council into consultation at the very earliest stage.

The Council have also been hampered by an acute shortage of staff;[32] alternatively it could be said that a staff which might have been adequate for the Council's true purpose of keeping tribunals under review has been grossly inadequate for the additional task of dealing with complaints from the general public; for these, many of which are not even within the competence of the Council to consider, continue to absorb a great deal of time.

A reappraisal of their constitution, functions and staff could well be a complementary task for the review body that we have suggested for our own proposals. It would be beyond our own competence, and outside the purpose of this study, to attempt to discuss the Council's affairs in more detail, but we are persuaded that an enlargement of their functions would be advantageous, and that their resources are capable of being adjusted to the requirements of a body with a more positive role to play in the supervision of the tribunal system. Such a role might well be temporary, since one ought not simultaneously to propose that the

[31] The Council's own dissatisfaction with their position is expressed in a letter from their Chairman to the Lord Chancellor dated July 1970, printed as Appendix A to their Annual Report for 1970–1.

[32] The Council's vote for 1971–2 was £53,000 for salaries and travelling and other expenses, but excluding accommodation. Its senior staff comprised the Secretary and three senior legal assistants. Below them the entire administration consisted of two Higher Executive Officers, two Executive Officers, one personal assistant, one shorthand-typist, one clerical officer, one clerical assistant and one messenger.

Lord Chancellor should assume larger responsibilities in the tribunal field and that the Council should play a more positive role. In the longer term, as the Lord Chancellor's Department developed, the Council's role would in some ways actually diminish, its emphasis shifting to advice and consultation on the one hand and to continued guardianship of the public interest on the other. In the short term, however, and for the purposes of any transitional period, their resources do not match their responsibilities.

Immediately, the need for them to play a more positive role shows no signs of diminishing, for new tribunals continue to be established or foreshadowed. By the time this book is printed the VAT tribunals will have assumed a prominent place. At the time of writing the Crowther Report on Consumer Credit is before Parliament and proposes a new legal framework for the granting of credit, including an independent body headed by a Consumer Credit Commissioner to license those entitled to make consumer loans. From the Commissioner's decisions there would be an appeal not to the courts but to an appeal tribunal of lawyers and businessmen.[33] The Younger Committee on Privacy[34] would accept comparable arrangements for 'credit-rating' agencies, and a Private Member's Bill was tabled in February 1972 whose purpose *inter alia* was to establish a data bank tribunal and inspectorate. In a totally different sphere, it is not impossible that the success of the children's hearings in Scotland could foreshadow their adoption in England and Wales.

It is interesting that in the course of their Second Annual Report in 1960, after they had first taken the measure of their task, the Council on Tribunals were saying almost exactly the same thing. 'There is no sign', they said, 'of any slackening of the rate of growth of tribunals, or in the multiplication of the occasions when public and private interests come into conflict'.[35] The same paragraph went on, in a few lucid sentences, to summarize the situation which has been the main subject of this study:

'. . . these conflicts are in general unsuitable for determination by the ordinary courts of law, yet are equally unsuitable for determination by

[33] Cmnd. 4596, March 1971. Para. 7.2.1. of the Report, which states the Committee's preference for a tribunal over the ordinary courts, is of interest. It speaks of tribunals as 'bodies of expert knowledge far greater than the courts could command, which would enable it to seize on the reality behind any pleadings, and to pursue a consistent policy in its findings.'

[34] Cmnd. 5012 July 1972. Report of a Committee under the chairmanship of Sir Kenneth Younger.

[35] Para. 11.

Government Departments in the ordinary run of business. Tribunals represent a compromise between the needs of good administration and the demands of justice. They have grown into a supplementary legal system of enormous extent. The danger that this system would get out of hand, having been developed piecemeal in many different statutes, was one of the primary reasons for our appointment.'

It is the more regrettable that exactly ten years later their Chairman should have had occasion to write to the Lord Chancellor saying that 'The Council's principal difficulty is that they have no effective means of securing attention for the tribunal system as a whole'.[36]

This would seem to suggest that during these ten years the Council had been ineffective in discharging the task which was 'one of the primary reasons for their appointment'. A study of their Annual Reports suggests that this is only partially true. They did a great deal towards seeing that the system did *not* get out of hand, and exercised a restraining influence on its tendency to fragment and to dissipate its resources still further; but they were never provided with the tools which would have enabled them to influence its reshaping.

Possibly in the perspective of history their principal achievement will come to be seen as having mapped an area of public activity, outside the courts, in which lawyers and administrators were working in exceptionally close collaboration. The credit for first identifying this area should perhaps be given to the academic lawyers, and notably to the creative mind of Professor Robson, author of the seminal *Justice and Administrative Law*, who wrote in another place:

'What is now wanted in our governmental system is a co-operative effort between the legal mind and the administrative mind; the administrator pushing the law into uncharted provinces where new standards are required, the lawyer insisting that those standards shall be of judicial application.'

The legal profession as a whole were slower to appreciate what was happening, and tended to think of tribunals, in so far as they thought of them at all, as unwelcome intruders into the domain of the established courts. If the Council on Tribunals had done nothing else their influence in changing the climate of opinion on these matters would have justified their appointment. Given the larger opportunities we have advocated they could yet play a role as significant as (if somewhat different from) that which the Franks Committee had in mind for them.

[36] Letter quoted in footnote 31 to p. 320.

APPENDIX I

# JUDICIAL REVIEW

BY P. G. HUTCHESSON

---

*The following was originally drafted as a chapter for the book, but is now printed as an appendix (see Introduction, p. 15). It is primarily concerned with judicial review, that is with the supervisory jurisdiction of the High Court in its particular relation to tribunals. There is, however, a note at the end on the provision which exists in some instances for an administrative review of decisions within the tribunal system itself (pp. 352–3).*

## The Supervisory Jurisdiction of the High Court

We propose to give only a general outline of the nature of the supervisory jurisdiction of the High Court as this has been very fully described elsewhere.[1] In fact lawyers in this country when they speak of 'administrative law' very largely mean the nature and extent to which the High Court may review the adjudicatory processes of other bodies.

The first point to note in regard to this supervisory jurisdiction is that it is *general* in nature, i.e. the High Court may review *any* decision made by a body which has legal authority to determine questions affecting the rights of subjects if that body acts in excess of its legal authority. There is thus no special supervisory jurisdiction applicable to special tribunals alone.

For the purposes of describing the review of tribunal decisions therefore we are concerned to set out the principles governing the review by the High Court of the decisions of inferior bodies insofar as those principles affect the decisions of special tribunals. For the sake of clarity we have divided this into three parts:

1. The nature of the remedies available;
2. The grounds on which review may be sought;
3. Defects and proposals for reform.

[1] See, e.g. S. A. de Smith, *Judicial Review of Administrative Action* (2nd Ed. Stevens & Sons, 1968); H. W. R. Wade, *Administrative Law* (3rd Ed. Oxford University Press, 1971); J. F. Garner, *Administrative Law* (3rd Ed. Butterworth, 1970).

## THE REMEDIES AVAILABLE

The remedies available for the review of the decisions of inferior tribunals consist of the three prerogative orders of certiorari, prohibition and mandamus, the equitable, private law remedy of injunction, and the relatively modern remedy of declaration.

### *Certiorari*

Certiorari is an order which allows the High Court to investigate a decision of an inferior tribunal or authority – in literal terms the Court, having received a complaint of injustice and wishing to be certified (i.e. certiorari) of the matter, orders that it be transmitted to the High Court for review. It is the prerogative remedy most appropriate for the review of tribunal decisions, because if the High Court is satisfied that there is a fault in the decision (an error of law or an excess of jurisdiction) or the proceedings leading up to it (such as a breach of the rules of natural justice) the decision can then be 'quashed', i.e. it becomes invalid and of no effect whatsoever.

### *Prohibition*

Where certiorari lies to review a decision or action that has already been taken, prohibition lies to review future action by prohibiting any continued excess in jurisdiction and preventing a proposed abuse of jurisdiction or breach of the rules of natural justice. In other respects the two orders are very similar and they are often (but not necessarily) awarded together, certiorari to quash an existing decision and prohibition to prevent any further irregularity.

### *Mandamus*

Mandamus issues to compel an authority to perform a public duty which the applicant has a legal interest in being performed. Thus if a tribunal mistakenly forms the view that an application made to it is outside its jurisdiction and refuses to entertain that application, mandamus will lie to order the tribunal to consider the case. Or if a tribunal hears a case but considers the wrong matters in reaching its decisions, certiorari will quash the decision, and mandamus will require the correct matters to be considered in reaching a new decision.

### *Injunction*

An injunction is a private law remedy issued to stop a person from breaking his legal obligations (on pain of contempt of court). It is comparatively rare for an injunction to be issued against a tribunal (mainly because prohibition is thought to be more appropriate) but it might issue for instance against a body (such as the Civil Aviation Authority) which combines both executive and judicial functions, e.g. if the Authority proceeded to withdraw a licence without first having a hearing as it is required to do, an injunction might be issued against it.[2]

*Declaration*

Declaratory orders are a relatively modern remedy (it was not until 1885 that they became firmly embedded as a 'remedy') and have one unique feature – they do not carry the threat of judicial sanctions or coercion inherent in the other remedies described. This arises out of the nature of declaration: as the name implies, it is an order made by the court declaring the rights of the parties in a situation where there is a legal dispute but neither party has yet committed a wrongful act which would give rise to coercive relief such as damages or an injunction. Thus if a party proposes an action which is disputed by the other, a declaration enables them to find out the legal position before the act is committed and any damage done – all the other remedies we have discussed can only come into play once a wrongful or irregular act has been committed.

*Exclusion of Review*

One important aspect of the High Court's supervisory jurisdiction is that it must be exercised in the context of legislative provisions empowering statutory authorities to make decisions. The most obvious way in which the court's powers may thus be affected is if there is a clause in the statute which specifically excludes or limits the power of review.

'Exclusion clauses' have taken a variety of forms over the years – e.g. the decision of a tribunal or deciding authority may be expressed to be 'final', or 'final and not to be questioned in any legal proceedings whatsoever'. The courts have generally sought to restrict the application of such provisions and a considerable body of case-law now records the attempts of Whitehall to stay one step ahead of the courts.

Exclusion clauses are not now the problem they once were, because of the effect of s. 11(1) Tribunals and Inquiries Act 1958:[3]

[2] See *Broadbent* v. *Rotherham Corporation*, [1917] 2 Ch. 31 (where an injunction was granted restraining the Corporation from carrying out a demolition order without a proper hearing of the owner's appeal). The position in regard to tribunals and 'judicial' functions is by no means clear – see de Smith, *Judicial Review*, p. 488.

[3] Continued in s. 14(1) of the 1971 Act.

'14. (1) As respects England and Wales or Northern Ireland, any provision in an Act passed before 1st August 1958 that any order or determination shall not be called into question in any court, or any provision in such an Act which by similar words excludes any of the powers of the High Court, shall not have effect so as to prevent the removal of the proceedings into the High Court by order of certiorari or to prejudice the powers of the High Court to make orders of mandamus.'[4]

Nevertheless there may still be circumstances where they are important in restricting the supervision of the courts, namely if they are enacted *after* the 1st August 1958, or if declaration is the remedy being sought. No instances are known after 1958, though it is believed that one was proposed.

### THE GROUNDS FOR REVIEW

The grounds for reviewing the actions or decisions of an inferior tribunal vary according to the particular remedy claimed. However as any tribunal is liable to have its decisions or proceedings impugned on any of the grounds for which a remedy will issue, we propose to discuss the grounds for review together rather than under the heading of the particular remedies to which they relate.

When one speaks of 'special' tribunals one does so for a purpose – they are 'special' in the sense that they are created (almost always by statute[5]) to perform a particular, specified function. They must perform that function and no other unless empowered to do so by Parliament. This is the key to the High Court's supervision of inferior tribunals (and, it must be added, any administrative body).

At the outset then any review of the actions or decisions of an inferior tribunal must start with an examination of the relevant empowering legislation. As well the courts have developed certain implied conditions attendant upon the use of any statutory power, be it 'executive', legislative, or 'judicial' in character. The presumption applied by the courts is that unless the legislation specifically states otherwise Parliament is presumed to intend powers granted by it to be exercised according to these implied conditions. These implied conditions may be discussed under the headings of:

[4] S. 14(2) contains a similar provision for Scotland.

[5] The only modern example of a tribunal being set up otherwise than by statute is the Criminal Injuries Compensation Board which was set up under the Royal Prerogative. It is nevertheless still subject to the same supervision by the High Court as statutory tribunals. See *R.* v. *Criminal Injuries Compensation Board ex. p. Lain*, [1967] 2 Q.B. 864.

Jurisdictional Error and Ultra Vires
Error on the Face of the Record
Natural Justice

*Jurisdictional Error and Ultra Vires*[6]

For the sake of clarity and convenience it is preferable to describe a number of different categories of ultra vires, arbitrary though this may be, but while this may be useful for the purposes of description, the reader is warned that the courts prefer to approach jurisdictional error and ultra vires as a single amorphous concept capable of embracing such matters as wrongful refusal of jurisdiction, 'unreasonableness', the wrongful delegation of the power of decision and so on.

(a) *Want of Jurisdiction.* A tribunal will lack jurisdiction and therefore be acting ultra vires if it *exceeds its jurisdiction* (the right body doing the wrong thing) or is *improperly constituted* (the wrong body doing the right thing).

As to the former the tribunal will be deciding a matter it is not empowered to decide. The *Anisminic Case*[7] provides a good example: the Foreign Compensation Commission refused to entertain an application for compensation by a British mining firm whose Egyptian assets had been seized by the Egyptian Government, on the ground that the firm had later managed to come to an agreement with the Egyptian authorities to sell the assets to an Egyptian concern (but at a price well short of their real value). The Commission held that this 'sale' barred the firm from any right to compensation. The House of Lords held that on the construction of the relevant legislation the 'sale' was immaterial to the right to compensation. Lord Reid in his judgment explained that the issue was not whether the Commission had made a wrong decision but whether they had enquired into and decided a matter which they had no right to consider.

In another case[8] an agricultural land tribunal consented to a notice to

[6] Jurisdictional error and ultra vires, although very similar, are technically not the same thing. The antecedents of each concept are different and while it is now often possible to describe the same irregularity as either jurisdictional error or ultra vires there is the problem that the former is normally a ground for the issue of certiorari and prohibition while the remedies usually appropriate for the latter are mandamus, injunction and declarations.

[7] *Anisminic Ltd* v. *Foreign Compensation Commission*, [1969] 2 A.C. 147.

[8] *R.* v. *Agricultural Land Tribunal for Wales ex p. Davies*, [1953] 1 All E.R. 1182. The 1948 Act as it relates to this case was amended by the Agriculture Act 1958. See Muir Watt's *Agricultural Holdings* (12th Ed. Sweet & Maxwell, 1971), p. 282.

quit on the grounds that a tenant's land was required to make other land owned by the landlord efficient. It was held that the tribunal's inquiry into efficient farming could only relate to the tenanted land and they were exceeding their jurisdiction in considering the landlord's other land. Put another way, the tribunal had discretion to withhold their consent even though the tenant was inefficient but they had no discretion the other way, i.e. to decide in favour of the landlord if the tenant was *not* inefficient, and it was this latter discretion which they had purported to exercise.

Rent tribunals have sometimes been held to exceed their jurisdiction for example in construing payments by tenants to landlords as a 'premium' (which entitles the tenant to have the rent reduced). Thus rent reductions made on the basis of a payment made to a builder rather than a landlord[9] or made in respect of repairs and decorations,[10] or made in consideration of the goodwill of a business and a restrictive trade covenant[11] have all been quashed on the grounds that the tribunal had no jurisdiction to entertain an application to reduce the rent in such cases.

An *improperly constituted tribunal* on the other hand will lack jurisdiction for the simple reason that it is not a 'tribunal' at all. This point arose in a case concerning the appointment of members of an agricultural land tribunal[12] where the member's appointment had not been made by the Minister as required by the Agriculture Act 1947[13] but by the secretary of the tribunal simply asking the two members on the telephone if they would serve. In fact the claim that the tribunal was improperly constituted did not succeed,[14] and while illustrating the principle that a tribunal must be properly constituted, it also shows that the courts may be loath to impugn a tribunal's decisions on this account especially if it means voiding past decisions by the tribunal.[15]

(b) *Refusal of Jurisdiction* (i.e. a tribunal wrongly refusing to do the right thing). Just as a tribunal cannot decide that which it is not

[9] *R.* v. *Birmingham Rent Tribunal*, [1951] 1 All E.R. 198, but cp. *Elmdene Estates Ltd* v. *White*, [1960] 1 All E.R. 306.

[10] *R.* v. *Fulham etc. Rent Tribunal ex p. Phillippe*, [1950] 2 All E.R. 211.

[11] *R.* v. *Barnet etc. Rent Tribunal ex p. Hillman*, [1950] 2 K.B. 506.

[12] *Woollett* v. *Minister of Agriculture*, [1954] 3 All E.R. 529.

[13] See p. 99 as to the composition and appointment of agricultural land tribunals.

[14] Jenkins and Morris L.JJ. holding that the secretary had implied authority from the Minister to appoint the members and Denning L.J. holding that the defects in appointment were cured by a saving clause.

[15] See the remarks of Denning L.J. at p. 536. The tribunal had been appointed informally for a number of years and had decided 'a great many disputes' all of which would have been put at risk by an adverse decision in the instant case.

empowered to decide, so a tribunal which refuses to decide that which it is required by law to decide is also acting ultra vires. The most obvious instance of this occurs where a tribunal mistakenly refuses to entertain an application or appeal which it ought to hear.[16]

However, the tribunal must be *obliged* to hear the case before it can be said to have wrongfully refused jurisdiction. Thus where it was held that the industrial court was acting as a voluntary arbitrator in an industrial dispute referred to it by the Minister of Labour rather than in performance of its statutory duties, the High Court refused to compel the industrial court to accept jurisdiction if it declined to do so.[17]

Refusing to entertain an application is not the only example of a refusal of jurisdiction. Deciding a different question to the one before it, rejecting relevant evidence in the wrong belief that it pertains to a matter outside jurisdiction, or refusing to take into account relevant factors because these are thought to be outside jurisdiction are all shortcomings which may be held to show that a tribunal has wrongfully declined jurisdiction.[18]

### *Jurisdictional Facts and 'Collateral' Questions*

This is one of the most difficult areas of administrative law. The general rule is easy to state: the courts will review errors *going* to jurisdiction but not errors *within* jurisdiction. The problem is to decide which side of the line a particular error falls, or sometimes whether a tribunal has the prerogative or jurisdiction to determine the nature and extent of its own jurisdiction.

Where a tribunal is held to have jurisdiction it will not be held to have exceeded or abused that jurisdiction if it misconstrues a statute, or admits illegal evidence, or rejects legal evidence, or misdirects itself as to the weight of evidence, or convicts without evidence.[19] As was said in one case, 'if a tribunal has jurisdiction to go right it has jurisdiction to go wrong',[20] meaning that if the tribunal is entitled to enter on the

[16] See *R.* v. *Paddington Rent Tribunal ex p. Millard*, [1955] 1 All E. 691, where a rent tribunal mistakenly refused to proceed with an application for security of tenure which had been adjourned pending the outcome of county court proceedings. The tribunal considered that by the time the case came to be considered the period of security of tenure had now expired and they had no jurisdiction. The High Court held that time did not run during the adjournment and therefore the tribunal did have jurisdiction.

[17] *R.* v. *Industrial Court*, [1965] 1 Q.B. 377.

[18] See de Smith, *Judicial Review*, pp. 108–9.

[19] *R.* v. *Minister of Health*, [1939] 1 K.B. 232. But, some of these matters may give rise to an error of law on the face of the record.

[20] *R.* v. *Governor of Brixton Prison ex p. Armah*, [1968] A.C. 192 at 234,

enquiry and thereafter does not commit a reviewable error (like breaching the rules of natural justice, or acting in bad faith, or taking into account extraneous considerations, etc.) its decision is equally valid whether it is 'right' or 'wrong'.[21] Moreover, by the doctrine of res judicata that decision then becomes binding in all other judicial proceedings whether right or wrong – it can only be impeached on appeal, if there is a right of appeal.

How is it possible to tell whether an error goes to jurisdiction or is within jurisdiction? The difficulties may be illustrated by a few examples. Rent tribunals have jurisdiction over furnished lettings. In one case the landlord contended that the tenancy was furnished and produced a signed agreement to this effect. Was the tribunal required to accept this at face value or could it make its own inquiry to establish whether the tenancy was furnished or not? It was held that the tribunal was entitled to make its own inquiry to establish its jurisdiction, but if it had come to the wrong decision on this preliminary question, that decision would be reviewable.[22] And yet, just before this decision, virtually the same Divisional Court had said of such an inquiry into the bona fides of a written agreement as 'A more dangerous usurpation of power by one of these tribunals it is impossible to imagine.[23] The Special Commissioners have been held to have power to establish the limits of their own jurisdiction: 'The legislature may entrust the tribunal or body with a jurisdiction which includes the jurisdiction to determine whether the preliminary state of facts exists as well as the jurisdiction, on finding that it does exist to proceed further or do something more.'[24] By contrast the decisions of the Land Tribunal as to its jurisdiction have been held not to be conclusive – they may be questioned on appeal where the statute so provides, or by certiorari.[25]

An even more difficult jurisdictional problem sometimes confronting tribunals, and because of their statutory origin one which is more likely to concern tribunals than the courts, is whether a tribunal has jurisdiction to question whether a Minister's Order conferring jurisdiction on the tribunal is ultra vires the Minister. In principle there seems to be no reason why a tribunal should not have jurisdiction to question its own jurisdiction, but there appears to be no authority on the point.

explained in *Anisminic* v. *Foreign Compensation Commission*, [1969] 2 A.C. 147 at 171.

[21] Subject to any impeachment for error of law on the face of the record.

[22] *R.* v. *Fulham etc. Rent Tribunal ex p. Zerek*, [1951] 2 K.B. 1 at 6.

[23] *R.* v. *Hackney etc. Rent Tribunal ex p. Keats*, [1951] 2 K.B. 15.

[24] *R.* v. *Special Commissioners of Income Tax* (1888), 21 Q.B.D. 313 per Lord Esher M.R. at 319.

[25] Re *Purkiss' Application*, [1962] 1 W.L.R. 902.

(c) *Procedural Ultra Vires* (doing the right thing in the wrong manner). One authority considers that this area of the law 'resembles an inextricable tangle of loose ends'.[26] This arises out of the fact that almost always the courts must decide whether the procedural requirements which have been disregarded are 'mandatory' (and therefore binding on the tribunal) or merely 'directory'. The absence of clear principles regarding this distinction has allowed the courts on many occasions to decide cases *ab inconveniente.*

To give two illustrations: where a decision of a rent tribunal was challenged on the ground that the tenant had given the name of the wrong landlord in his application (which was contrary to the regulations made by the Minister) it was held that the regulations were directory only, because Parliament itself in omitting any such requirement must be presumed to have done so for a purpose (namely that cases would often be brought by tenants without the benefit of 'lawyers to advise them and no regulations by their side'.[27]) By contrast a rent tribunal is acting ultra vires if it *decides* a case without knowing who the parties are.[28]

In another case, where a local authority was required to give reasons for the grant or refusal of planning permission it was held that failure to state reasons did not invalidate the authority's decision.[29]

What sort of procedural irregularities will be held to vitiate the proceedings? There are surprisingly few cases on this point but it has been held that failure to give notice that a right of appeal exists, as required by statute, will render proceedings ulta vires;[30] again in a case where notice of proceedings was sent not to a company's registered office but merely to an address given by the other party from which it was returned 'Gone away. No address', it was held that this did not amount to service of the notice at all and all subsequent proceedings were vitiated.[31] It has also been held that on the construction of the

[26] De Smith, *Judicial Review*, p. 126. 'When Parliament prescribes the manner or form in which a duty is to be performed or a power exercised, it seldom lays down what will be the legal consequences of failure to observe its prescriptions.'

[27] *Francis Jackson Developments Ltd* v. *Hall*, [1951] 2 K.B. 488.

[28] *R.* v. *Paddington etc. Rent Tribunal ex p. Haines*, [1962] 1 Q.B. 388.

[29] *Brayhead (Ascot) Ltd* v. *Berkshire C.C.*, [1964] 2 Q.B. 303. As regards many tribunals, the position is now covered by s. 12 Tribunals and Inquiries Act 1958 (see above, p. 150). Failure to give reasons as required by s. 12 will amount to an error of law – see *Re. Poyser and Mills Arbitration*, [1963] 2 W.L.R. 1309.

[30] *Rayner* v. *Stepney Corporation*, [1911] 2 Ch. 312. (A case concerning an invalid slum clearance notice served by a local authority.) See also *Agricultural Training Bd.* v. *Kent*, [1970] 2 Q.B. 19.

[31] *R.* v. *Industrial Tribunal ex p. Green & Thompson Ltd*, [1967] 2 K.I.R. 259.

Rent Act 1965 it is mandatory for the applicant to set out the 'rent proposed to be registered' in his application to a rent officer – the words 'rent officer to determine fair rent' do not fulfil this condition;[32] on the other hand it is sufficient simply to insert '4s 9d per square foot'.[33] Again, although the Rent Act states that an application 'may be made to the rent officer by the landlord or the tenant or jointly by the landlord and the tenant' it has been held that this is not exclusive – there is nothing that requires the tenant to put in the application himself or that it cannot be signed by his agent.[34]

There are two reasons why there are so few instances of procedural ultra vires. Firstly the courts have shown some reluctance to set aside tribunal decisions on technical grounds alone,[35] and secondly tribunals are very often the arbiters of their own procedure (see p. 142).

Two rather special instances of procedural ultra vires should also be mentioned. These are the *improper delegation* and the *improper surrender* or abdication of judicial power. Both are examples of the importance of statutory construction in this field. The courts take the view that if a statute states that a particular type of issue should be decided by Tribunal X, then Tribunal X should indeed decide the issue and not pass it over to someone else to decide. Moreover if there is in fact power to delegate, the delegation must be exercised strictly in accordance with the terms of the statute. Thus where there was power for the National Dock Labour Board to delegate its disciplinary functions to local dock labour boards, it was held that a decision made by a 'disciplinary committee' of a local board was ultra vires, because the power of delegation was limited to local boards, not their committees.[36] Similarly where a Minister delegated certain powers to war agricultural executive committees, it was held to be ultra vires for the Bedfordshire Committee to sub-delegate those powers to its executive officer.[37] Again where a board in a situation in which it was required to act judicially, appointed a sub-committee to 'investigate' the question it was required to determine, the decision of the board based solely on the sub-committee's report was held to be ultra vires.[38] It would have been

[32] *Chapman* v. *Earl,* [1968] 2 All E.R. 1214.

[33] *R.* v. *London Rent Assessment Panel ex p. Braq Investments Ltd,* [1969] 2 All E.R. 1012.

[34] *Ex p. Braq Investments Ltd,* above.

[35] See for instance the remarks by Parker L.J. in *Ex Braq Investments Ltd* (above), and also *R.* v. *Deputy Industrial Injuries Comr. ex p. Moore,* [1965] 1 Q.B. 456.

[36] *Vine* v. *National Dock Labour Board,* [1957] A.C. 488.

[37] *Allingham* v. *Min. of Agriculture,* [1948] 1 All E.R. 780.

[38] *Jeffs* v. *New Zealand Dairy Board,* [1966] 3 All E.R. 863.

otherwise if the sub-committee had been appointed to hear evidence on behalf of the board and had in turn presented that evidence (or an accurate summary) to the board,[39] but the procedure actually adopted did not ensure that the body making the decision was able to consider the evidence and submissions of the parties to the dispute.

Regarding the improper surrender or abdication of judicial power, the most obvious example is where the decision-making body arrives at a particular decision at the behest or direction of someone else. Thus unless he has express statutory authority to do so, it is wrong for a Minister to issue instructions to statutory officials (such as insurance officers) as to how they are to decide cases and wrong for such officials to abdicate their discretion by deciding cases simply according to Ministerial or departmental instruction.[40] A more subtle form of abdication is an unduly rigid adherence to policy or precedent. A tribunal is entitled to formulate a general policy for deciding cases (just as judges from time to time formulate sentencing policies) but when it becomes evident that cases are being decided according to the policy rather than the merits, the courts may well hold that the decisions are ultra vires. Thus if a tribunal has discretion to award costs and sets fixed costs to be applied in all cases before it, it is then failing to exercise its discretion. The general rule seems to be that it is in order (and in some cases desirable) for a tribunal to formulate a policy or lay down general principles for future cases *provided* allowance is made for exceptional cases or circumstances.[41]

Similar considerations apply in regard to precedent. On an appeal from the Transport Tribunal, Devlin L.J. in the Court of Appeal pointed out certain distinctions in this regard between tribunals and the ordinary courts. A tribunal, unlike the High Court, may not make rules in the form of binding precedents which prevent it or any lower tribunal from examining each case on its merits, because to do so would be contrary to the empowering statute.[42]

[39] See *R.* v. *Local Government Board ex p. Arlidge*, [1914] 1 K.B. 160.

[40] See *Simms Motor Units* v. *Minister of Labour*, [1946] 2 All E.R. 201.

[41] *R.* v. *Port of London Authority*, [1919] 1 K.B. 176 at 184, and see de Smith, *Judicial Review*, pp. 294–297, especially in regard to the policies of licensing tribunals.

[42] *Merchandise Transport Ltd* v. *British Transport Commission*, [1962] 2 Q.B. 173 at 192. (Held, that the Transport Tribunal is not bound by its previous decisions: 'A tribunal must not pursue consistency at the expense of the merits of individual cases. If the discretion is to be narrowed, that must be done by statute'. Ibid. p. 193.)

(d) *Unreasonableness, Extraneous or Irrelevant Considerations, Ulterior Motives, Bad Faith.* These are grounds on which tribunal decisions[43] may sometimes be impugned especially in regard to the use of judicial discretion. Apart from their mandatory functions, most tribunals have certain discretionary powers. These may be central to the issues that come before the tribunal (e.g. licensing tribunals and rent assessment committees are entitled to reject all the evidence before them when deciding whether to issue or refuse a licence, or to assess what in their view is a 'fair' rent) or they may be peripheral (e.g. admitting the public to hearing, withholding evidence, awarding costs, adjourning hearings and so on).

The question arises: can the exercise of such discretionary powers, whether central or peripheral, be challenged in the courts and if so, on what basis? One problem is that full-scale control and review of the exercise of discretionary powers would run counter to the accepted principle of jurisdictional control that 'if a tribunal has jurisdiction to go right it has jurisdictionto go wrong'. Put another way, if a court pronounces on whether a decision or action is reasonable or unreasonable or enunciates on those considerations which a tribunal ought to take into account and those which it ought to ignore is it not then reviewing errors made *within* jurisdiction and in part doing the job which the tribunal was set up to do?

Perhaps mindful of this, the courts have adopted a cautious approach: in the final analysis interference by the courts on the grounds listed above rests on the premiss that any discretionary power must be exercised 'according to law,'[44] – reasonableness, disregard of extraneous or irrelevant considerations, avoidance of ulterior motives or bad faith describe the ambit of what is 'according to law'. If one were to rationalize this further it might be suggested that the courts while not prepared to tell a tribunal how to do its job, are prepared to tell it how to behave. Nevertheless the distinction is a fine one and at times the boundary between errors in excess of jurisdiction and errors within jurisdiction has become a little blurred.

(i) *Extraneous or irrelevant considerations.* A tribunal is not entitled to reach a decision or exercise a discretion by considering matters which are irrelevant, or extraneous to its jurisdiction. The *Anisminic* case, the case of the agricultural land tribunal which considered other land

[43] The principles in regard to unreasonableness etc., were established in nineteenth century cases concerning the decisions of inferior courts (particularly justices of the peace) but most modern cases concern the irregular exercise of discretionary powers by Ministers, local authorities and other administrative bodies.

[44] *R.* v. *Bowman*, [1898] 1 Q.B. 663 per Wills J. at 666.

owned by a landlord, and the rent tribunal cases on 'premiums' are examples which have already been quoted (see p. 327). In another case where a rent tribunal assessed a rent de novo on a second application it was held that in doing so it had taken into account irrelevant considerations – on a second application the only relevant consideration is whether there has been any change in circumstances since the previous application.[45]

(ii) *Wrong or ulterior motives.* 'If a power granted for one purpose is exercised for a different purpose, that power has not been validly exercised.'[46] This is not a matter which has often troubled the courts in regard to tribunals (in contrast to numerous cases concerning planning powers) but one instance is to be found in a case concerning the pre-hearing procedure before a rent tribunal. A local authority which had power to refer private tenancies to a rent tribunal for consideration, referred nearly all the tenancies in a large block of flats without first considering in each case whether the rent was unfair. It was held that this was not a legitimate exercise of the statutory power of reference. In the court's view the authority had set out to use its powers to make the tribunal a 'general rent-fixing tribunal' throughout its district in disregard of Parliament's intention that they deal with individual cases of hardship.[47]

Other cases, which although not arising out of tribunal proceedings are nevertheless relevant, have decided that it is wrong to use licensing powers for discriminatory purposes, on religious or political grounds,[48] or as an indirect method of taxation to supplement public funds.[49] Likewise it is wrong to use a power to award costs to impose what is in effect a fine.[50]

It is not without significance that there are so few tribunal cases under this heading. Apart from a long established tradition of judicial integrity which has fortunately been carried over into the tribunal field, it is especially difficult to indict a tribunal's decision on this account if seemingly plausible reasons have been advanced for the decision.[51] Moreover, it seems that a tribunal or its individual members

[45] *R.* v. *Fulham etc. Rent Tribunal ex p. Hierowski*, [1953] 2 Q.B. 147.

[46] De Smith, *Judicial Review*, p. 304.

[47] *R.* v. *Paddington etc. Rent Tribunal ex p. Bell. London & Provincial Properties Ltd*, [1949] 1 K.B. 666. This was also an instance of procedural ultra vires.

[48] *Roncarelli* v. *Duplessis*, [1952] 1 D.L.R. 680; [1959] S.C.R. 121.

[49] *R.* v. *Bowman*, [1898] 1 Q.B. 663.

[50] *R.* v. *Highgate Justices*, [1954] 1 W.L.R. 485.

[51] For a case illustrating the difficulties of an appellant who wishes to con-

cannot be called on to give evidence to explain its decision or reasons.[52]

(iii) *Bad faith*. Mala fides 'may be said to comprise dishonesty (or fraud) and malice'.[53] Again, it is difficult to find specific examples and one has to fall back on weighty dicta to the effect that 'fraud unravels everything'[54] or that fraud 'vitiates all transactions known to the law of however high a degree of solemnity,'[55] pronounced in cases in which bad faith was not proved.[56]

(iv) *Unreasonableness*. The courts have been noticeably chary of interfering on this ground. The test most commonly applied is that 'if a decision on a competent matter is so unreasonable that no reasonable authority could ever have come to it, then the courts can interfere . . .',[57] which, of course, is a far cry from the court deciding whether or not it would have come to the same decision. Lord Greene himself went on to say that 'to prove a case of that kind would require something overwhelming',[58] and one authority contends that this test 'whittled down the requirement of unreasonableness till it had all but disappeared'.[59] On this basis, 'unreasonableness' is restricted to the preposterous or patently absurd decision and there is usually more chance of success in attacking the reasonableness of a decision indirectly by suggesting that extraneous matters have been considered or relevant matters disregarded.

*Error of Law*

The second ground on which tribunal proceedings may be vitiated is error of law on the face of the record. This doctrine was resuscitated by the Divisional Court in 1951[60] when considering a decision by a tribunal

vince the court that official reasons hide an ulterior motive, see *R.* v. *Governor of Brixton Prison ex p. Soblen*, [1963] 2 Q.B. 243.

52 See de Smith, *Judicial Review*, pp. 314–15 and *R.* v. *Metropolitan Goods Vehicle Licensing Authority ex p. Barrett*, [1949] 2 K.B. 17.

53 De Smith, *Judicial Review*, p. 315.

54 *Lazarus Estates* v. *Beasley*, [1956] 1 Q.B. 702 per Denning L.J. at 712.

55 Ibid., per Parker L.J. at 722.

56 The only recent Commonwealth case in which the plaintiff came close to proving bad faith is *Roncarelli* v. *Duplessis*, [1959] S.C.R. 121.

57 Per Lord Greene M.R. in *Associate Picture Houses* v. *Wednesbury Corporation*, [1948] 1 K.B. 223 at 230, and see *Luby* v. *Newcastle-under-Lyme Corporation*, [1964] 2 Q.B. 64 where this test was applied to the assessment of 'reasonable' rents by a local authority.

58 Ibid., note 5 above at p. 230.

59 De Smith, *Judicial Review*, p. 335.

60 *R.* v. *Northumberland Compensation Appeal Tribunal*, [1951] 1 K.B. 711; affmd. [1952] 1 K.B. 338 (C.A.)

to award compensation to a local government employee for loss of office on the basis of only part of his service in local government. Contrary to previous authority, the court held that it was entitled to call up the record of any inferior court or tribunal to examine whether there was any error of law in that record and if so, to quash it.

This doctrine can only operate if the record is a 'speaking order', that is if it gives the facts of the case, or the evidence, or the reasons for the decision – if it merely recites the decision itself and no more the record becomes, in Lord Sumner's graphic phrase, 'the inscrutable face of a sphinx'.[61]

Clearly the two issues most likely to arise in cases under this head are: what is the 'record'? and what is an 'error of law'?

Lord Denning has suggested that the record includes 'at least the document which initiates the proceedings; the pleadings, if any; and the adjudication; but not the evidence, nor the reasons, unless the tribunal chooses to incorporate them'[62] and went on to state that if necessary the court could order the tribunal to complete the record if relevant documents have been omitted.[63] In a later case[64] his Lordship suggested that the decision of first instance constitutes part of an appellate tribunal's record, even where the decision at first instance is given by a civil servant acting in a judicial capacity (on this basis the initial determination of insurance officers, rent officers, valuation officers and possibly immigration officers, in fact any official decision from which there is a right of appeal to a tribunal, would automatically form part of the tribunal's record). The remainder of the House of Lords preferred to reserve their views on the point,[65] and Lord Tucker expressed considerable reservations about the views expressed in the Northumberland case.

It has also been held that a schedule giving the reasons for a decision

[61] *R.* v. *Nat Bell Liquors Ltd*, [1922] 2 A.C. 128 at 159.

[62] *The Northumberland case* (above), [1952] 1 K.B. 338 at 352. (The judgment continues: 'If the tribunal does state its reasons, and those reasons are wrong in law, certiorari lies to quash the decision.')

[63] Ibid., at p. 354. In a later case (*R.* v. *Medical Appeal Tribunal ex p. Gilmore*, [1957] 1 Q.B. 575) Lord Denning suggested that the court had power to order the tribunal to complete the record by making a finding on the material facts because the tribunal could not defeat certiorari by sending up an imperfect record. (Moreover, under the jurisdiction doctrine (see p. 13) the court would be the final arbiter as to what are 'material' facts.)

[64] *Baldwin & Francis Ltd* v. *Patents Appeal Tribunal*, [1959] A.C. 663 at 687–690.

[65] The majority decided the case on the basis that assuming (but not deciding) that the decision at first instance was part of the record, no error of law was in fact disclosed.

and attached to the decision itself is part of the record,[66] and more surprisingly, a report referred to in a tribunal's decision has been held to form part of the record.[67]

In the absence of an authoritative statement of the law by the House of Lords some doubt must remain as to the extent of the 'record'. However the Tribunals and Inquiries Act 1958 had clarified the position to some extent. Firstly the Act requires most tribunals when giving a decision 'to furnish a statement, either written or oral, of the reasons for the decision, if requested' (to do so).[68] Secondly any statement of reasons, (this including oral reasons) given by such a tribunal 'shall be taken to form part of the decision and accordingly to be incorporated in the record'.[69]

The other major issue likely to arise under this head concerns what is, or is not, properly to be deemed an 'error of law'. Clearly a wrong interpretation of a statute[70] or a misapplication of a legal doctrine will be an error of law. However the courts have thrown the net considerably wider than this, holding for instance that failure to adjourn a hearing to give a party an opportunity to be heard,[71] wrongly back-dating a pay award,[72] making a finding which the facts could not reasonably sustain,[73] and taking into account irrelevant considerations,[74] are errors of law

[66] *R.* v. *Paddington etc. Rent Tribunal ex p. Perry*, [1956] 1 Q.B. 229.

[67] *R.* v. *Medical Appeal Tribunal ex p. Gilmore*, [1957] 1 Q.B. 575 (an extract from a specialist's report indicated in tribunal's decision – held that this made the *whole* report part of the record).

[68] S. 12(1). (As also of the 1971 Act, which reproduced the provision). There are exceptions to this requirement, viz:

(i) tribunals not covered by the Act at all (e.g. Criminal Injuries Compensation Board, Foreign Compensation Commission, etc., see p. 59), although such tribunals may have their own statutory requirements as to reasons.

(ii) tribunals expressly excluded by order of the Lord Chancellor and Secretary of State (on the ground that it is unnecessary or impractical to give reasons) – s. 12(6). So far this power has not been exercised.

(iii) where national security precludes the giving of reasons – s. 12(2).

(iv) a statement of reasons need not be given to a 'person not primarily concerned with the decision' if the tribunal is of the 'opinion that to furnish it would be contrary to the interest of any person primarily concerned' – s. 12(2).

[69] S. 12(5) of the 1971 Act.

[70] As in the *Northumberland case* (above); *R.* v. *Medical Appeal Tribunal ex p. Griffiths*, [1958] 1 W.L.R. 517 (tribunal wrongly construed the 'paired organs' provisions in the Nat. Ins. (Ind. Inj.) (Benefit) Regs. 1948); *R.* v. *Westminster Compensation Appeal Tribunal*, [1953] 1 All E.R. 687 (tribunal wrongly construed the term 'compensation' to include damages for wrongful dismissal).

[71] *Priddle* v. *Fisher*, [1968] 3 All E.R. 506.

[72] *R.* v. *Industrial Disputes Tribunal*, [1953] 1 All E.R. 593.

[73] *Edwards* v. *Bairstow*, [1956] A.C. 14, *Griffiths* v. *Harrison*, [1963] A.C. 1.

[74] *Wootten* v. *Central Land Board*, [1957] 1 W.L.R. 424.

and it is said by one authority that the improper admission or rejection of evidence by a tribunal which is obliged to observe the rules of evidence will amount to an error of law.[75] Furthermore if there is a duty to give reasons (as in the case of most tribunals) the giving of inadequate or inconsistent reasons will amount to an error of law.[76]

*Breach of the Rules of Natural Justice*

These are the third set of implied conditions on which any statutory power is to be exercised. Despite their high-sounding connotations they are not now a universal ethic which those deciding disputes or using special powers must attain, but simply a convenient shorthand for the minimum procedural standards required of tribunals (or any other authority deciding a judicial type question) by the High Court in the absence of any statutory guidance. They are not as important as they once were in the field of tribunals because most tribunals of course now work to a prescribed code of procedure. The exhortations of the Franks Report in favour of 'openness, fairness and impartiality' and the subsequent efforts of the Council on Tribunals when vetting new rules of procedure[77] have been instrumental in the flavour of natural justice being imparted to new rules of procedure.[78]

The rules of natural justice are based on two principles, firstly that no man shall be condemned unheard, and secondly that no man shall be a judge in his own cause, but whether and how the courts apply those principles depends on the circumstances of particular cases.

(a) *The Circumstances in which Natural Justice must be observed.* For many years the duty to observe the rules of natural justice was confused with a duty to act judicially (i.e. the exercise of 'judicial' or 'quasi-judicial' functions).[79]

At the heart of the matter is the question of whether it is correct to draw a distinction between the procedural and substantive aspects of the rules of natural justice, that is, is it correct to decide first and without any reference to any alleged breach of natural justice whether a tribunal or authority is amenable to the jurisdiction of the prerogative writs and

[75] De Smith, *Judicial Review*, pp. 114 and 120.

[76] De Smith, *Judicial Review*, p. 120 and see *Re Poyser and Mills Arbitration*, [1963] 2 W.L.R. 1309 in which it was held that reasons given according to section 12 must 'not only be intelligible, but (also) deal with the substantial points that have been raised'.

[77] See J. F. Garner 'The Council on Tribunals', *Public Law* (1965), p. 321.

[78] There are exceptions – see s. 9, Immigration Appeals Act 1969.

[79] As opposed to 'executive' or 'administrative' functions.

only then to consider whether there has been such a breach, or should the amenability to jurisdiction be inferred from the fact that there has been a breach of natural justice?

In the early cases[80] the judges looked purely at the substantive law involved, i.e. had there been a breach of the rules of natural justice? If so one of the prerogative writs would lie. However, towards the end of the eighteenth century (or perhaps even earlier) the notion crept in that the authority whose action is compained of must have been acting in a judicial capacity at the time.[81]

In *R.* v. *Electricity Commissioners*,[82] Atkin L.J. enunciated in terms of general principle a test of the circumstances in which the writs of certiorari and prohibition would lie to review a decision of an inferior body:

> 'Whenever any body of persons having legal authority to determine questions affecting the rights of subjects and having a duty to act judicially, act in excess of that authority they are subject to review by these writs.'[83]

This remains the classic statement on the subject, but rather than clarify the law it produced confusion, largely because of the differing interpretations and glosses put on this statement by later judges.

Firstly, it was said[84] that there must be superadded to the characteristic of rights being affected the further characteristic that the authority was at the time under a duty to act judicially, i.e. these were considered to be two separate conditions that had to be shown independently of each other before the High Court could accept jurisdiction.

This resulted in the profitless circular argument that 'natural justice must be observed where the function is judicial; and the function is judicial where natural justice is required to be observed.'[85]

Secondly it was said a 'judicial' function was not involved when the issue or withdrawal of a licence was being considered (a licence being a 'privilege' and not a 'right').[86]

[80] E.g. James Bagg's Case (1615) 11 Co. Rep. 93b; Dr Bentley's Case (1723) (1723) 1 Str. 557.

[81] E.g. *Re Hammersmith Rent Charge* (1849) 4 Ex. 87 ('no-one is to be punished in any *judicial* proceeding unless he has had an opportunity of being heard').

[82] [1924] 1 K.B. 171.

[83] Ibid., at p. 204.

[84] In *R.* v. *Legislative Committee of the Church Assembly*, [1928] 1 K.B. 411, and *R.* v. *Manchester Legal Aid Committee*, [1952] 2 Q.B. 413.

[85] Wade, *Administrative Law*, p. 172.

[86] *Nakkuda Ali* v. *Jayaratne*, [1951] A.C. 66, *R.* v. *Metropolitan Police Commissioner ex p. Parker*, [1953] 1 W.L.R. 1150.

Thirdly it was considered that there was a distinction between those situations where the decision is determined accordingly to policy or executive discretion and those in which there is a duty to act judicially.[87] Such a distinction does exist but the way it was drawn overlooked the fact that a Minister or other administrative body may well be under a duty to observe the rules of natural justice before he is free to exercise the unfettered discretion that may have been conferred on him.[88]

In *Ridge* v. *Baldwin*[89] the position was greatly clarified: the distinction between 'rights' and 'privileges' was disapproved, and it was held that the observance of the rules of natural justice depends not on the function of the person exercising the power but was to be implied from the nature and effect of the powers exercised on the complainant of the injustice.

(b) *The Right to a Fair Hearing.* This is usually expressed by the maxim *audi alterem partem* ('hear the other side'), the principle being that a person who is likely to be adversely affected by a decision on his rights ought to be given a fair hearing and the opportunity to state his side of the case before the decision is made.

The leading case is now *Ridge* v. *Baldwin*[90] which concerned a Chief Constable who was dismissed by a Watch Committee without being informed of the charges against him and without being given an opportunity of being heard in his own defence. The chief constable's solicitor had been allowed to appear and make representations to a meeting of the Watch Committee (*after* the dismissal) but this was held to be insufficient to discharge the audi alterem partem requirement because he had not been given the opportunity of being heard in his own defence before the dismissal, nor had he been informed of the charge against him and the Committee's reasons for wishing to dismiss him. *The content of the rule*: Some general guidance as to what does and does not come within the scope of the rule is afforded by the judgment of Lord Loreburn in *Board of Education* v. *Rice*.[91]

> 'In such cases the Board of Education will have to ascertain the law and also to ascertain the facts. I need not add that in doing either they must act in good faith and fairly listen to both sides, for that is a duty lying upon everyone who decides anything. But I do not think

[87] See *Franklin* v. *Minister of Town and Country Planning*, [1948] A.C. 87.
[88] See H. W. R. Wade (1949), 10 *Cambridge Law Journal*, p. 216.
[89] [1964] A.C. 40.
[90] Above.
[91] [1911] A.C. 179.

they are bound to treat such a question as though it were a trial. They have no power to administer an oath, and need not examine witnesses. They can obtain information in any way they think best, always giving a fair opportunity to those who are parties in the controversy for correcting or contradicting any relevant statement prejudicial to their view.'[92]

One authority has pointed out that the minimum standards of fairness in adjudication imposed by the courts cannot be higher than those prescribed by the courts for themselves and for this reason the rule does not encompass public hearings, the giving of reasons, or the keeping of a transcript of proceedings.[93] Nor does it require any right to cross-examine,[94] or (possibly) any right to legal representation.[95]

On the positive side the rule does require:

(i) *Adequate notice of the hearing* – but what is 'adequate' in terms of time, the content of the notice and the persons to be notified will vary according to the circumstances of the case.[96]

(ii) *An opportunity to be heard* – as to the *right* to be heard, if a person's rights (whether personal or property rights) are likely to be affected by the decision they are entitled to be heard.[97]

As to what constitutes a '*hearing*', it is normal for this to be statutorily defined as an oral hearing but we have already pointed out two instances (National Insurance Commissioners and Mental Health Review Tribunals) where tribunals have a discretion to decide a case 'on the papers'. However this means that the tribunal must give the parties an opportunity to make written representations and to rebut those made by the other side. In a case where a tribunal with power to determine cases 'without a hearing' had dismissed an appeal after simply considering the notice of appeal and statement in reply, it was held that the tribunal was not permitted to dispense with a hearing of any kind: they were bound to give the appellants a hearing in the sense of an opportunity to make out their case and to correct or rebut the statement in reply.

[93] De Smith, *Judicial Review*, p. 179.

[94] *Miller* v. *Minister of Housing*, [1968] 2 All E.R. 633.

[95] *Pett* v. *Greyhound Racing Association* (No. 2), [1969] 2 All E.R. 221, but cp. *Enderley Town Football Club Ltd* v. *Football Association Ltd*, [1971] 1 All E.R. 215.

[96] These are matters usually covered in the rules of procedure of tribunals: see, e.g. *R.* v. *Industrial Tribunal ex p. Green and Thompson Ltd*, [1967] 2 K.I.R. 259, noted at p. 331n above.

[97] *Ridge* v. *Baldwin* (above). The chief constable's pension rights were affected by the decision to dismiss him.

Without this the appellants had not been given a 'hearing' at all.[98]

If there is an oral hearing then all the parties must be allowed to participate – one party cannot be allowed to give oral evidence if the others are restricted to written representations.[99]

(iii) *Knowledge of the case to be answered* – not only has a person whose rights are effected the right to be heard, he also has the right to know the case he has to meet.[100] There is no general duty of disclosure before the hearing (although the procedure before the Lands Tribunal requiring, in certain cases, an exchange of valuations and comparables is a statutory case in point – see p. 139). Nor is it necessary that *full* details of the case to be met must be made available. It is sufficient that the general line of argument to be presented at the hearing is made available and that a party taken by surprise at the hearing is given adequate time (if necessary by an adjournment) to consider his reply.

The audi alteram partem rule has been formulated by judges accustomed to the adversarial procedure of the courts but it can at times run counter to the inquisitorial methods adopted by some tribunals. Two problems in particular arise – the duty of disclosure to be placed on a tribunal which gathers evidence for itself (e.g. by medical or property inspections or by obtaining an independent report from a consultant or assessor employed by the tribunal) and the use of the tribunal's own expertise. We discuss these aspects of the audi alteram partem rule in Chapter 10.[101]

*The Rule Against Bias*

The second of the two rules of natural justice is usually expressed by the maxim *nemo judex in causa sua* ('no man shall be a judge in his own case') but that expresses rather literally the principle that a tribunal ought to be impartial and unbiased in its proceedings. In one of the early leading cases[102] a decree made by a Lord Chancellor in favour of a canal company in which he held shares was set aside by the House of Lords on the grounds that justice must not only be done but be seen to be done.

The most obvious disqualifying interest on the grounds of bias is financial interest. At common law the rule is that any direct pecuniary

[98] *R.* v. *Housing Appeal Tribunal*, [1920] 3 K.B. 334, but there may be circumstances in which natural justice does not require an opportunity to rebut the other party's case, cf. *Wiseman* v. *Borneman*, [1969] 3 All E.R. 275 discussed below at p. 345.

[99] *R.* v. *Kingston-upon-Hull Rent Tribunal ex p. Black* (1949), 65 T.L.R. 209.

[100] *Ridge* v. *Baldwin* (above).

[101] See p. 271.

[102] *Dimes* v. *Grand Junction Canal*, [1852] 3 H.L.C. 759.

interest no matter how small disqualifies a man from judging a case.[103]

On the other hand if it is suggested that a personal interest of a non-financial nature may give rise to bias it must be shown that there is a 'real likelihood' of bias before the courts will interfere. Thus where it was shown that the chairman of a rent tribunal was a solicitor living with his father who was the tenant of a flat owned by a company which was connected with the landlord company in a case before him, and furthermore that the chairman's firm had acted for tenants against the same landlords, it was held that he was not entitled to sit.[104] In another case a solicitor acting as clerk to the local justices retired with them when they considered a dangerous driving charge: the solicitor's firm were at the same time acting for the accused in a civil claim arising out of the same accident. It was held that even though the clerk had not been consulted by the justices their decision should be set aside.[105]

Others cases involving justices (there have in fact been very few tribunal cases on bias) show that the courts will be ready to infer a real likelihood of bias if an adjudicating body shows strong personal hostility or animosity towards a party, or the converse, namely personal friendship, or if there is a family or professional or business relationship.

*A New Approach to Natural Justice?*

The courts in recent cases have shown not only a desire to broaden the application of the rules of natural justice,[106] but also a willingness to reappraise the content of the doctrine. This view that natural justice is a flexible concept varying in its requirements from one situation to another has led to what Professor Garner terms 'a kind of "mini" natural justice'.[107] Thus in Re H(K) (an infant)[108] an immigration officer had refused admission to a Pakistani immigrant on the grounds that the immigrant was over 16 and therefore not entitled to be admitted as a dependant. It was alleged that the immigration officer reached his decision before contrary evidence could be given. It was held that the immigration officer was indeed under a duty to observe natural justice; but he was under no duty to act 'judicially' in the sense of holding a full-scale inquiry and adopting judicial process and pro-

[103] *Dimes case* (above).

[104] *Metropolitan Properties* v. *Lannon*, [1969] 1 Q.B. 577.

[105] *R.* v. *Sussex Justices*, [1924] 1 K.B. 256.

[106] Recent decisions which have expanded the area of operation of the doctrine include *Ridge* v. *Baldwin* (above), *Durayappah* v. *Fernando*, [1967] 2 All E.R. 152, *Anisminic* v. *Foreign Compensation Commission* (above), Re H(K) (an infant), [1967] 1 All E.R. 226 (see below).

[107] Garner, *Administrative Law*, p. 117.

[108] [1967] 1 All E.R. 226.

cedure; moreover regard must be had to the legislative framework under which the administrator is working; in this context natural justice simply required the immigration officer to be impartial, to bring his mind to bear on the problem and *to act fairly* – this he had done.

In a case regarding a tribunal under s. 28 Finance Act 1960[109] (which determines whether certain dealings in securities have been entered into to avoid tax, there being a right of appeal to the general or special commissioners – in a sense therefore the tribunal's decision is only provisional, or, as Lord Reid put it, the tribunal determines whether or not there is a prima facie case of tax avoidance) it was again held that the tribunal was simply required to act fairly and that this did not preclude the tribunal from withholding from the taxpayer the counter-statement made to it by the Inland Revenue Commissioners.[110] And in a case concerning the Gaming Board[111] (a body which issues licences to gaming clubs) it was held that the Board in refusing to issue a licence in respect of Crockford's was bound to observe natural justice which in this context meant acting fairly. More specifically, this meant giving the applicant sufficient indication of the objections against him to enable to refute them but this did not extend to the Board being required to disclose the source of its information, or to disclose every detail,[112] or to give reasons for its refusal. Another example of the new approach to natural justice is to be found in a case concerning the duties of a Justice of the Peace when acting in an administrative or executive capacity under the Food and Drugs Act 1955.[113] Before making his decision on an application under the Act the justice, after hearing the case for the application, had retired to consult official experts in private and had then returned to announce that he was not prepared to issue the certificate applied for. It was held by the Divisional Court that even though the justice was acting in an administrative or executive capacity, he was bound to observe a limited form of natural justice which in this case amounted to the observance of the Franks principles of 'openness, impartiality and fairness' and these had not been observed when the justice took private advice from experts.

109 *Wiseman* v. *Borneman*, [1969] 3 All E.R. 275.

110 Lord Wilberforce added the necessary corollary that the counter-statement should be made available in any appeal from the tribunal's findings, and if the tribunal considered the counter-statement to be so exceptional that to decide without disclosure would be unfair, it ought to be disclosed before the tribunal itself reached a decision (at pp. 287–8).

111 *R.* v. *Gaming Board ex p. Benaim*, [1970] 2 All E.R. 528.

112 'Chapter and verse' may well be required if the case concerns dismissal from office or deprivation of property – per Lord Denning M.R. at p. 534.

113 *R.* v. *Birmingham Justice*, [1970] 1 W.L.R. 1428.

## DEFECTS AND PROPOSALS FOR REFORM

Lord Denning has, in a well-known passage,[114] aptly described the prerogative writs as 'pick and shovel' methods for providing relief against irregular administrative actions, for each of these remedies has serious shortcomings. *Certiorari* and *prohibition* cannot be sought to control the actions of domestic tribunals[115] and, as we have seen (p. 340) are bedevilled by the concept of the 'duty to act judicially'. There are also very considerable procedural defects: there is no proper interlocutory process[116] (e.g. no provision for the discovery of documents if there is a conflict of evidence), the time limit for applying for an order is very short (normally only six months from the date of the proceedings),[117] and the two orders cannot be married up with other actions[118] (i.e. one cannot ask for an injunction or damages as well as certiorari in the same action). The main defect in regard to *mandamus* is that it will not issue against the Crown 'or any servant of the Crown acting in his capacity as servant'.[119] This same defect is even more pronounced in regard to *injunctions*.[120] There is also the problem that if the plaintiff cannot show either that his private rights are being infringed or that as a member of the public he is suffering special damage peculiar to himself as the result of interference with the public right, he must ask the Attorney General to institute the proceedings for

114 *Freedom Under the Law*, p. 126.

115 *R.* v. *National Joint Council of Dental Technicians ex p. Neate*, [1953] 1 Q.B. 704.

116 See *Barnard* v. *National Dock Labour Board*, [1953] 2 Q.B. 18 per Denning L.J. at 43, and de Smith (*Judicial Review*, p. 441) who points out that there has probably been only one case this century in which cross-examination has been permitted on an application for certiorari.

117 R.S.C. Order 53, rule 2(2). Leave to apply out of time may be granted if the delay is satisfactorily explained.

118 This arises out of the public nature of the origin of the writs, i.e. they were the prerogative of the Crown and a subject had to request the court that they be used on his behalf.

119 *R.* v. *Secretary of State for War*, [1888] 21 Q.B.D. 313, per Charles J. at 334. A working paper of the Law Commission (see p. 347 below) describes this as a 'most troublesome area of the law' (para. 38). It seems that if a Crown servant is performing a designated duty rather than acting as adviser to the Crown mandamus will lie. Thus mandamus will be granted against the Special Commissioners of Income Tax (see *E.* v. *Special Commissioners* (1899), 21 Q.B.D. 461) but not against the Inland Revue Commissioners (see *R.* v. *Inland Revenue Commissioners re Nathan* (1884), 12 Q.B.D. 461.

120 An injunction cannot even be issued against a Crown servant performing a designated duty – s. 21(1)(a) and s. 21(2) Crown Proceedings Act 1947 and see *Merricks* v. *Heathcote-Amery*, [1955] Ch. 567.

an injunction (by a 'relator action').[121] There is also some doubt as to whether an injunction is an appropriate remedy in regard to 'judicial' acts as opposed to 'administrative' or 'executive' acts.[122] *Declaration* is now probably the most popular remedy because it does not suffer from many of the defects described above; it may be sought against domestic tribunals, the time limit is six years not six months, there is provision for interlocutory procedures and it will lie against the Crown. However declaration also has certain limitations. The requirements in regard to locus standi are considerably stricter, and, unlike certiorari, it is not available for error on the face of the record. The latter point is illustrated by *Punton* v. *Minister of Pensions (No. 2)*,[123] where it was alleged that the National Insurance Commissioner had wrongly interpreted the relevant provisions of the National Insurance Act. If this were the case, the plaintiffs could have obtained certiorari to quash the Commissioner's decision, but instead they elected to apply for a declaration that the decision was invalid because of the error. The Court of Appeal held that even if there had been an error they could not issue a declaration because that would not expunge the Commissioner's decision. All that would happen would be that there would then be two inconsistent decisions, one of which declared that the other was wrong, *but not invalid.* Furthermore, under the terms of the Act, it was a favourable decision by the Commissioner rather than the Court of Appeal (or any other court for that matter) which was a condition precedent to the payment of the benefit and therefore a declaration issued by the Court of Appeal would not help the plaintiffs at all.

Because of these defects the Law Commission has published a working paper[124] which suggests the reform of the remedies available in administrative law by replacing the present remedies with a single remedy to be known as an 'application for review' which would enable the court

> 'to *quash* the particular administrative decision or order, to *enjoin* the administrative authority from exceeding its jurisdiction or powers, to *command* the authority to act where it is under a duty to do so, or to *declare* the action or order invalid and of no effect.'[125]

as appropriate. Furthermore it is envisaged that in future the High

[121] *Boyce* v. *Paddington B.C.*, [1903] 1 Ch. 109 per Buckley J. at 114; de Smith, *Judicial Review*, pp. 464–6.

[122] One problem is that an injunction is normally an *inter partes* remedy and there may be the practical difficulty of finding a defendant if an injunction is sought against a tribunal: see de Smith, *Judicial Review*, pp. 489–90.

[123] [1964] 1 W.L.R. 226.

[124] Law Commission Published Working Paper No. 40, 11th October 1971.

[125] Ibid., para. 75.

Court should have discretion under the new remedy not merely to review the proceedings before an inferior tribunal but to go further and consider the merits of the case by way of declaring what the applicant's legal rights or entitlement are[126] (which is what the court in *Punton's Case* could not do because its decision on the plaintiff's rights would have had no effect.)[127] This amounts to 'review' in the full sense of the word, but there are some limitations. A significant feature of the proposals is that the new remedy would only be available on the same grounds as exist at present (namely ultra vires, breach of the rules of natural justice, error on the face of the record). Thus the proposed powers of review on the merits would only come into operation if the court had first discovered some irregularity or illegality in the tribunal proceedings. This means that it would not be open to a national insurance claimant simply to use the High Court as a 'court of appeal' on the merits from a decision of the National Insurance Commissioner. Nor presumably could an intending claimant apply to the court for a declaration as to his entitlement *before* lodging a claim for benefit (thus using the court as the arbiter of his claim rather than the insurance officer/local tribunal/Commissioner machinery).

This suggested innovation is proposed more out of convenience than anything else (to save claimants from having to go back and forth between the tribunal and the court) but it does remove one of the biggest defects of the present remedies for plaintiffs, namely, that even if they are successful in obtaining certiorari or mandamus they may in the long run be no better off and greatly out of pocket. Thus a plaintiff who is aggrieved at the decision of a tribunal may discover some procedural irregularity and obtain certiorari to quash the decision. But then he will have to make a new application and when his case is heard a second time by the tribunal[128] it may well take the same view on the merits as it did on the first occasion and arrive at the same decision as before, but this time without the irregularity which attended the first proceedings, all of which is little consolation to the plaintiff who would naturally prefer to see the merits of the case reviewed as well as the tribunal's procedure when he applies to the High Court.

Other proposals included in the working paper are that all forms of relief under the new remedy should be available against the Crown, and the position in regard to locus standi should be clarified and made

[126] It is envisaged that the courts would not exercise this discretion in all cases but would on occasion refer the matter back to the tribunal.

[127] A further problem is that the tribunal itself may have no power to correct its errors even if these were to be pointed out by the High Court.

[128] It should be pointed out that in most cases the tribunal is differently constituted for the second hearing but this is not always possible.

uniform on the basis that any person who is adversely affected by administrative action should have locus standi.

These are important proposals which would do much to alleviate the present inconsistencies caused by the overlapping roles of the present remedies, each of which has certain advantages over the others and certain disadvantages. Not the least of the problems facing an applicant for review at present is that he must often choose between one remedy and another (especially in the case of certiorari and declaration). As Professor Wade points out: 'The litigant is forced to make a choice at his peril. This is so obviously unreasonable that there is an urgent need for reform.'[129] It is to be hoped that the Law Commission's working paper foreshadows that reform.

## PROPOSALS FOR REFORM OF THE APPELLATE AND REVIEW STRUCTURE

The Law Commission's proposals are, at the time of writing, under active consideration by a group of government lawyers, and may have had some practical result by the time this book is in print.

Of more academic interest, but worthy of mention at this point for the sake of putting the whole subject of this chapter in a wider perspective, are proposals that have been made from time to time for altering, and rationalizing, the entire structure of appeal and review. They have taken various forms.

Professor W. A. Robson argued in evidence before both the Donoughmore and Franks Committees that there should be a general administrative appeal tribunal; since he was concerned with alleged maladministration as much as with tribunal decisions his proposals have been met in part by the subsequent creation of the Parliamentary Commissioner for Administration, but even in relation to tribunal decisions the Franks Committee could not support him, on the grounds that an appeal would lie from an expert to an inexpert body, that the unifying control of the superior courts would be breached, and that the way would open to two parallel systems of law (Report paras. 120–3).

Another proposal has been for an Administrative Division of the High Court, which would have avoided the last two objections but would still have been open to the first. The proposal was made in evidence to the Franks Committee by the Inns of Court Conservative and Unionist Association (Report paras. 124–6) but has most recently been advanced in a different form by *Justice*.[130] Their Report advocates a Division

[129] Wade, *Administrative Law*, p. 142.

[130] *Administration under Law* (Stevens & Sons, 1971). Chairman: Kenneth Goodfellow, QC.

in which judges could sit with assessors when necessary. It would have both original jurisdiction (exercised by a single judge, as in the other divisions of the High Court) and an appellate jurisdiction (exercised by its Divisional Court, consisting of three judges) from decisions of inferior courts and tribunals.

In 1970 the Society of Conservative Lawyers published a 'Proposal for an Administrative Court',[131] the President of which would have the status of a High Court Judge and would sit with lay members experienced in administration, commerce and industry. The Society likened it to the Restrictive Practices Court, though one would have thought that the National Industrial Relations Court might have been a happier analogy. The Court would deal with 'miscarriages of administration', which the Report was at some pains to distinguish from the 'maladministration' which was the preserve of the Parliamentary Commissioner. It would have two Divisions, an Enquiry Division presided over by the Registrar and sitting in private, and a Judicial Division, presided over by a judge and sitting in public. Appeal would lie in appropriate cases to the Court of Appeal.

Clearly there is a school of thought running right through the legal/political spectrum that the appellate and review structure is in need of overhaul.

## REVIEW BY THE SCOTTISH COURTS[132]

Scots law has been more successful than English law in adapting 'ordinary' (i.e. private law) remedies for the review of administrative action and the decisions of inferior jurisdictions. There are broad similarities between many of the remedies available in Scotland and their English counterparts but in essence Scots law is more simple, more comprehensive and less prone to the procedural limitations of the prerogative orders.[133]

The prerogative orders do not exist in Scots law – hence the adaptation of private law remedies as a means of judicial control. This means that a far greater variety of remedies are available to the Scottish litigant, and in most cases remedies can be pursued in tandem, unlike the prerogative

[131] Society of Conservative Lawyers: Trilogy of Committee Reports 1970.

[132] This is no more than a cursory description of the Scottish position: for a fuller account, readers are referred to Published Memorandum No. 14 of the Scottish Law Commission, 'Remedies in Administrative Law' and especially the excellent paper by Professor A. W. Bradley attached thereto, from which the material in this section was taken.

[133] One difference is that a reliance on ordinary remedies has not led to any distinction being drawn between 'administrative' and 'judicial' functions.

orders. Moreover many of the ordinary remedies available in Scotland are unique to Scots law, which makes any comparison with English law on the point difficult.

The essential difference between English and Scots law then is that whereas in England it is usually necessary to tailor an action to fit the technical and procedural aspects of a particular prerogative order (in terms of rights being affected, locus standi, the particular limitation period, the breach of jurisdiction involved, etc.), Scots law allows far greater flexibility in the way an action is presented. Among the many remedies available in Scots law, we have chosen three to illustrate the point.

*Reduction* is a remedy of considerable importance in the private law sphere where it may be used to impugn any written instrument (e.g. a deed, a will, or a contract) – the same principle applies in its application in the public law sphere: the Court of Session may impugn the decrees of inferior courts (and moreover its own decrees) and those of officials. As regards inferior courts and tribunals reduction roughly corresponds to the English remedy of certiorari enabling the Court of Session to quash decisions on the grounds that they are 'unlawful, incompetent, ultra vires, or in excess of jurisdiction',[134] including taking into account irrelevant considerations, serious procedural defects, bias and other breaches of natural justice, abuse of discretion, breach of a statute or regulations. These are matters which relate to jurisdiction or competence; it seems that reduction may not be available in respect of error of law within jurisdiction (cf. *R.* v. *Northumberland Compensation Appeal Tribunal*, discussed at p. 336).[135] Because reduction is an 'ordinary' remedy it may only be sought by the ordinary full procedure of civil litigation.[136]

*Declarator* as its name implies, is the Scottish equivalent of the English remedy of declaration, although much older in origin and better established in the legal system. Like its English counterpart declarator exists to establish the legal rights of the parties where no wrongful act has been committed which would give rise to coercive relief.

*Interdict* is a remedy which combines the functions of the English remedies of prohibition and injunction. It is available to restrain any statutory authority from acting ultra vires where the action would infringe an individual's rights – this includes the review of a tribunal

[134] Bradley, p. 13.

[135] The point is evidently not free from doubt – see Bradley, p. 55 ff.

[136] One oddity of this is that the limitation period is apparently twenty years (in contrast to the six months for certiorari).

decision which is directly enforceable against a citizen, but unlike prohibition, interdict is not restricted to the review of 'judicial' bodies and may be sought in respect of executive and legislative powers.

Scots law may have considerable advantages over the prerogative orders but it is not without its own drawbacks, and Professor Bradley, for one, has suggested that Scots law might well benefit from the introduction of the new petition for review proposed in the English Law Commission's study paper.[137]

## Review within the System

In addition to judicial review by the courts there is provision in the case of some tribunals (mostly those concerned with individual claims to a statutory right or benefit) for review within the system itself, by way of a re-hearing on fact or law, either on application by one of the parties or on the adjudicating authority's own motion. The usual grounds for such review are fresh evidence or changed circumstances.

Thus the Pensions Appeal Tribunals Act 1943 (section 5), as amended by the Chronically Sick and Disabled Persons Act 1970 (section 23), says that a decision by the Tribunal may be

> 'set aside and the appeal from the Minister's decision heard again by the Tribunal . . . by reason of the availability of additional evidence'.

The National Insurance (Industrial Injuries) Act 1965 (section 40) uses the phrase

> '. . . fresh evidence in consequence of non-disclosure or misrepresentation of material fact'

or (in relation to a medical condition) 'unforeseen aggravation'.

The National Insurance Act 1965 (section 72) prescribes that an insurance officer, a local tribunal or the Commissioner may at any time review a decision

> 'if satisfied by fresh evidence that the decision was given in ignorance of, or was based on a mistake as to, some material fact'
> or, 'that there has been a relevant change of circumstances since the decision was given'.

The Rent Act 1968 (section 75(1)) also uses the expression 'change of circumstances', and supplementary benefit differs from the rest only

[137] Bradley, pp. 7 and 52.

in that the review of a decision is provided for by Regulation and not in the principal Statute.[138]

## ADMINISTRATIVE REVIEW

It is perhaps open to argument whether these provisions for a fresh hearing are correctly described as 'judicial' or 'administrative' review, but whichever expression is used they must not be confused with the strictly administrative review of decisions which may take place within a department, thus making it unnecessary for an appellant to bring his case to a tribunal in the first place.

Internal review of this kind is most common in claims for supplementary benefit, where about a quarter of all appeals are resolved to the satisfaction of the appellant by review either in the area office or at regional headquarters, and another ten per cent are withdrawn after discussion. Moreover the remaining two-thirds which were eventually determined by a tribunal represented only 0·26 per cent of the total number of *claims* processed during a recent year.[139]

It is natural that internal review should be a characteristic of claims for supplementary benefit, since as we say elsewhere the task of adjudication in this field is as much to review difficult 'case-work' decisions and to establish facts as to make strictly judicial determinations. More controversial was the practice in the Department of Health and Social Security of offering to review cases if the appellant agreed to defer his appeal to the Pensions Appeal Tribunal, a matter which was discussed on p. 167.

[138] Ministry of Social Security Act 1966 s. 17(1)(d) and Supplementary Benefit (General) Regulations 1966.

[139] These facts are taken from a pamphlet by R. J. Coleman, *Supplementary benefits and the administrative review of administrative action* (Child Poverty Action Group, July 1971). The pamphlet is an analysis of relevant information made available to Mr Coleman by the Department over a period of one year.

APPENDIX II

# FORM OF APPLICATION FOR A DETERMINATION BY AN INDUSTRIAL TRIBUNAL

*(Extract)*

4. I HEREBY APPLY for a decision of a tribunal under the (delete whichever is inapplicable) CONTRACTS OF EMPLOYMENT ACT 1963/REDUNDANCY PAYMENTS ACT 1965/INDUSTRIAL RELATIONS ACT 1971.
5. State briefly what complaint is being made or what the tribunal is being asked to decide.

6. Date of birth
7. Place of employment
8. Occupation or position in company/organization
9. Employment began on and (if appropriate) ended on
10. Basic wages/salary
11. Other pay or remuneration
12. Normal basic weekly hours of work
13. Relation to the organization (tick as appropriate)
Member Former member Applicant for membership
14. Date on which action complained of took place or first came to my knowledge
15. Has complaint been made to the Registrar of Trade Unions and Employers' Associations? YES/NO
16. If the answer to 15 is YES, give the date on which the Registrar gave his decision. If he has not yet given it, you should defer submitting your application until you receive notice of his decision.
17. The grounds of this application are as follows:

18. If you were dismissed, what in your opinion was the real reason for your dismissal?

APPENDIX III

# TRIBUNALS AND THE EUROPEAN ECONOMIC COMMUNITY

Now Britain has joined the European Economic Communities, tribunals will have a power to refer questions of Community Law to the European Court of Justice in Luxemburg for a preliminary ruling which the tribunal can then apply to the case before it. Article 177 of the EEC Treaty[1] provides:

'The Court of Justice shall have jurisdiction to give preliminary rulings concerning:

(a) the interpretation of this Treaty;
(b) the validity and interpretation of acts of the institutions of the Community;
(c) the interpretation of the statutes of bodies established by an act of the Council, where those statutes so provide.

Where such a question is raised before any court or tribunal of a Member State, that court or tribunal may, if it considers that a decision on the question is necessary to enable it to give judgment, request the Court of Justice to give a ruling thereon.

Where any such question is raised in a case pending before a court or tribunal of a Member State, against whose decisions there is no judicial remedy under national law, that court or tribunal shall bring the matter before the Court of Justice.'

At the time of writing the effect of Article 177 on British courts and tribunals must necessarily be somewhat speculative. The following comments are made tentatively.

Firstly it will be noted that the European Court's jurisdiction is limited, broadly speaking, to questions arising out of the Treaties and the legislation made under them. In practice most of this legislation is economic in character and it seems therefore that only tribunals likely to be affected by such legislation are those in the fields of social security (supplementary benefits, national insurance and pensions), transport

[1] The other treaties contain kindred provisions.

charges and licensing, restrictive practices, plant and seed varieties and immigration.[2]

Secondly, although on the face of it it seems that this offers a wide field for a considerable number of references to the European Court it is felt that there will in practice be very few cases arising before British tribunals with the necessary 'conflict of laws' element to necessitate a reference.[3]

Thirdly, it is important to understand the nature of a reference to the Court. It is not a right of appeal which can be invoked by a party. Cases are referred to the Court by the courts and tribunals of member nations for rulings as to the interpretation of EEC legislation – having received this ruling the court or tribunal then proceeds to determine the case before it having regard to the facts and the European Court's ruling.[4]

Fourthly, there is the problem of when reference ought to be made to the European Court, in which connection it should be noted that *any* national tribunal or court *may* make a reference to the court.[5]

Lastly, there is the question of which tribunals *must* refer cases to the European Court (see footnote 5). It is not yet settled which these are, as the Court has yet to decide what constitutes a 'judicial remedy', and until this is resolved it is not possible to say with certainty which tribunals are mandatorily bound by the provision. It seems likely that there are few, if any. It also seems probable that very few would feel it appropriate to exercise their *power* to do so; they are more likely to leave it to a higher English court up the ladder of appeal to take this initiative.

[2] Taxation might be thought to be a fruitful field, but the EEC legislation on this subject is mostly concerned with customs and excise duties and import tariffs for which there are no tribunals in this country.

[3] Cases brought by British applicants before British tribunals will not normally involve questions of EEC legislation. Migrant workers on the other hand are a more likely source of references.

[4] The EEC's court's ruling is technically binding but it has no power to intervene if that ruling is then perversely applied to the facts by the national court or tribunal.

[5] Only in those cases where there is no further judicial remedy *must* there be a reference.

# BIBLIOGRAPHY

## ADMINISTRATIVE LAW

The subject of tribunals is dealt with in all text-books on Administrative Law, and notably in J. F. Garner, *Administrative Law* (1970, 3rd ed., Butterworth), J. A. G. Griffith and H. Street, *Principles of Administrative Law* (1967, Pitman), and H. W. R. Wade, *Administrative Law* (1967, Clarendon Press). More briefly, and very readably, in David Foulkes, *Introduction to Administrative Law* (1972, 3rd ed., Butterworth). There are also particularly stimulating discussions in R. M. Jackson, *The Machinery of Justice in England* (1972, 6th ed., Cambridge University Press).

The major official document is the Donoughmore Report, Report of the Committee on Ministers' Powers, Cmd. 4060, 1932, with Memoranda and Minutes of Evidence. The Report was reprinted in 1954.

### TRIBUNALS IN GENERAL

The standard work is W. A. Robson, *Justice and Administrative Law*, (1951, 3rd ed., Stevens). In its discussion of principles it is unequalled; its defect for the contemporary reader is that the last edition was published before the Franks Committee was appointed. Slighter works, which span several tribunals but by no means the whole conspectus, are Kathleen Bell, *Tribunals in the Social Services* (1969, Routledge & Kegan Paul), and H. J. Elcock, *Administrative Justice* (1969, Longmans Green). N. D. Vandyk, *Tribunals and Inquiries* (1965, Oyez Publications), is useful for reference.

The major official document is the Franks Report, Report of the Committee of Administrative Tribunals and Enquiries, Cmnd. 218, 1957; the Memoranda and Minutes of Evidence are a mine of information and interest, much of the contents being as fresh and relevant today as in 1956.

The unofficial pamphlet published by *Justice*, *The Citizen and the Administration* (the Whyatt Report), 1961, examines the question of discretionary decisions by administrators and the criteria by which they might be considered 'justiciable'.

Among innumerable articles are two which, although written many years ago, have a lasting interest:

W. A. Robson: 'Administrative Justice and Injustice: A Commentary on the Franks Report', *Public Law*, Spring 1958.

J. A. G. Griffith: 'Tribunals and Inquiries': 22 *Modern Law Review* 1959 (in effect a commentary on the Council on Tribunals).

## TRIBUNALS IN PARTICULAR

*The Social Services Group*

The most prolific writing has predictably been on national insurance. Background books are Geoffrey S. King, *The Ministry of Pensions and National Insurance* (esp. Ch. VIII; Adjudication) (1958, Allen & Unwin), and Bentley B. Gilbert, *The Evolution of National Insurance in Great Britain* (1966, Michael Joseph). See also Kathleen Bell and H. J. Elcock, op. cit.; Chapters 1 and 2 of *the Hamlyn Lectures*, Harry Street (1968, Stevens) and Chapter 11 of A. H. Hanson and Malcolm Walles, *Governing Britain* (1970, Collins).

There is no up-to-date comprehensive book on the work of the National Insurance Commissioners, or on national insurance law in general, but the standard reference books are *The Law relating to Family Allowances and National Insurance* and *The Law relating to National Insurance (Industrial Injuries)*, edited by J. St L. Brockman of the office of the Solicitor of the DHSS. In the more restricted field of the National Insurance Adjudicators – Gordon A. Hoskings, *Pensions Schemes and Retirement Benefits* (1968, Sweet & Maxwell).

There is no standard work on supplementary benefit appeal tribunals in public circulation (the Handbook being restricted). A brief but authoritative study is Melvin Herman, *Administrative Justice and Supplementary Benefits*, Occasional Papers on Social Administration (1972, G. Bell & Sons).

*Official Publications:*

Reported Decisions of the Commissioners
Index and Digest of Decisions with Supplements 1–16,

Appeals Procedure in Social Security: Report II (International Social Security Association, Geneva, 1965),

Annual Reports of the Department of Health and Social Security,

Annual Reports of the Registrar of Non-Participating Employments.

Nothing of substance has been written about the specifically judicial functions of the NHS Executive Councils and Service Committees or about the Pensions Appeal Tribunals, though for the last named there is a booklet 'Legal Information in connection with Pensions Appeal Tribunals'.

*The Land and Valuation Group*

A good deal has been written about the Lands Tribunal, notably R. F. C. Roach, *Lands Tribunal Practice and Procedure and Guide to Costs* (1961, Sweet & Maxwell); and M. Roberts and R. Emeny, *Lands Tribunal Index* (1968, Royal Institute of Chartered Surveyors); and there are in addition a number of legal works on specific jurisdictions, e.g. G. H. Newsom, *Restrictive Covenants affecting Freehold Land* (1967, 4th ed., Sweet & Maxwell), and D. M. W. Barnes, *The Leasehold Reform Act 1967* (1968, Butterworth).

The principal jurisdiction of the Scottish Lands Tribunal is dealt with in J. M. Halliday, *The Conveyancing and Feudal Reform (Scotland) Act 1970* (W. Green & Son). The Tribunal itself is described in an article in the *Scots Law Times* 26 February 1971.

There are no published works on rent tribunals, rent assessment committees or local valuation courts, but the first two are usually given generous treatment in the general works referred to earlier and have been the subject of fairly frequent articles in legal and professional journals. It is only possible to refer to the standard legal texts on the subject matter of their jurisdictions, such as Megarry on Rents and Ryde on Rating. The same is true for agricultural land tribunals, for which the standard legal work is T. C. Jackson and J. Muir Watt, *Agricultural Holdings* (1959, 11th ed., Sweet & Maxwell).

*The Revenue Group*

One book and one Royal Commission Report provide the best background to the work of the General and Special Commissioners of Income Tax:

J. A. Johnstone, *Comparative Conflict Resolution Procedures in Taxation*, (1968, University of Michigan).

Report of the Royal Commission on Taxation of Profits and Income, Final Report, June, 1955, Cmd. 9474.

The work of the Betting Levy Appeal Tribunal is explained on pp. 117–19 of J. T. Chenery, *The Law and Practices of Bookmaking, Betting, Gaming and Lotteries* (1963, 2nd ed., Sweet & Maxwell).

*The Industrial Tribunals*

The fullest treatment of the subject is to be found in K. W. Wedderburn and P. L. Davies, *Employment Grievances and Disputes Procedures in Britain* (1970, University of California Press), but see also any standard text-book on industrial or labour law. Articles:

'What is the Verdict?', *Personnel Training Management*, January 1968,
'Industrial Tribunals', R. Rideout, *Current Legal Problems*, No. 21,
'Industrial Tribunals', Spenser Weisband, *New Law Journal*, 9 October 1969,
'Tribunals and the Courts'. An interview with the President of the Industrial Tribunals. *New Law Journal*, 19 November 1970,
'The Redundancy Payments Act in the Practice of Industrial Relations', *British Journal of Industrial Relations*, November 1970.

*The Traffic Licensing Group*
The literature of road and air transport licensing is so far confined to official reports:

Report of the Committee on the Licensing of Road Passenger Services (the Thesiger Report) (1953 HMSO),
Annual Reports of the Traffic Commissioners,
Annual Reports of the Road Licensing Authorities,
British Air Transport in the Seventies – Report of the Committee of Inquiry into Civil Air Transport, Cmd. 4018, 1969,
Annual Reports of the Air Transport Licensing Board 1961.

*The Copyright Group*
There is a copious legal literature surrounding the subjects of Patents, Designs, Trademarks and Performing Rights, but it is not one that has lent itself to other writings.

*The 'Personal Rights' Group*
The official reports to which the Mental Health Review Tribunals and Immigration appeals system owe their origin are respectively:

Report of the Royal Commission on the Law relating to Mental Health and Mental Deficiency, Cmnd. 169/1957, and
Report of the Committee on Immigration Appeals, Cmnd. 3387/1967.

A study of the mental health review tribunals in England and Wales was published by the Social Administration Research Trust – Cyril Greenland, *Mental Illness and Civil Liberty, 1970.*

There is as yet no published study of the immigration appeals system.

*Children's Hearings* (Scotland)
The official reports which provide the background are:

Report by a Committee appointed by the Secretary of State for Scotland (the Kilbrandon Committee) Cmnd. 2306/1964,
Social Work and the Community – Proposals for reorganizing local authority services in Scotland, Cmnd. 3056/1966.

Three leaflets or booklets have subsequently been published by HMSO for the Social Work Services Group, Scottish Education Department:

The Social Work (Scotland) Act 1968: Children's Panels and Hearings,
'Children's Hearings', 1970,
'Children's Hearings – Questions and Answers', 1971.

Since this book went to press the First Volume of the Fourth Revision of Halsbury has been published and contains what is possibly the best short exposition of Administrative Law now available, by Professor de Smith.

# INDEX